THE RIDE'S BACK ON
Wrongly Accused

Dave Courtney

First published in Great Britain in 2002 by
Virgin Books Ltd
Thames Wharf Studios
Rainville Road
London
W6 9HA

A catalogue record for this book is available from the British
Library.

ISBN 1 85227 9788

Typeset by TW Typesetting, Plymouth, Devon
Printed and bound in Great Britain by
Mackays of Chatham PLC

CONTENTS

INTRO: MAN BITES DOG   1
 1. BAD SEED   4
 2. THE KINKY HOUSE   13
 3. HOW A CORRUPT POLICEMAN CAN SEND
    YOU TO JAIL FOR A CRIME YOU DIDN'T
    COMMIT   17
 4. BELMARSH   25
 5. KEEP YOUR FRIENDS CLOSE, YOUR
    ENEMIES CLOSER   32
 6. TIGHTROPE WALKING – BE COOL   37
 7. THE MEET   42
 8. A VERY NAUGHTY NICKING   46
 9. HANGMAN   52
10. 'ANYTHING YOU SAY . . .'   61
11. WHEN THE LIGHT AT THE END OF THE
    TUNNEL IS A BLOODY BIG TRAIN   73
12. INNOCENT AS CHARGED: WITH BELLS ON   78
13. TWO FUNERALS: PART TWO   87
14. FORTY BLACK SUITS IN SHADES: GANG
    WARS   93
15. PORN IN THE USA   107
16. DEATH BY PAPERWORK   117
17. 'THERE GOES THE KNIGHTHOOD!'   120
18. THE TRIAL – BRING 'EM ON!   125
19. THE TRUTH, THE WHOLE TRUTH & THE
    BITS THEY DON'T TELL YOU ABOUT   133
20. JUDGEMENT DAY   151
21. THE LENS IS MIGHTIER THAN THE
    SWORD   160
22. WHO POLICES THE POLICE WHO POLICE
    THE POLICE?   174
23. ROLLING, ROLLING, ROLLING   186

24. PREPARE FOR LANDING!   196
25. 'FUUPIIFINNGLY-*FRRUUFFF!!*'   210
26. A DIFFERENT WICKED   217
27. LOCK, STOCK AND TWO SMOKY BACON,
    PLEASE   224
28. KISS KISS BANG BANG   239
29. GET COURTNEY   253
30. BRIGHT LIGHTS, BIG TITTIES   264
31. EXTRA MEDIUM   274
THANKS   278
INDEX   280

INTRO: MAN BITES DOG

Just to say 'ello and give you a low-down on the showdown, and taster of what's to come. You can't get off now – we're moving!

I made a New Year's resolution to stop swearing, masturbating and smoking. But I couldn't be fucked so I banged one off and then lit a cigar. Fuck me I felt better.

Oh but *stone* me, so much has happened since I last saw you! Listen: attempted murders, shootings, me knocking out a copper in court, gang warfare, wedding day bomb scares, Reggie Kray and Charlie Kray's funerals, mayhem in Spain, New York clubbing, TV documentaries, porn films in LA and *Playboy* models, twin Russian lap dancers, my and Joey Pyle's weddings in Las Vegas, me going Big In Japan and large in Italy, my new film *Hell To Pay!* in the can and showing in Cannes *and* I got my cycling proficiency badge and learned to bake. *Shut* up.

And last but by no means least we've got a starring appearance by bent Old Bill in the Old Bailey. Yeah, that's right, this features my six-week appearance at the Bailey, charged with perverting the course of justice. I wouldn't mind but I don't even *know* a bird called Justice. (I do know her sister Charity, though, and I do give regularly.)

So just when you thought it was safe to go back into a bookshop – here I am. With what I like to think of as the official follow-up to *Stop the Ride I Want to Get Off*.

One thing I did learn was that as well as being a big-selling book *Stop The Ride . . .* was also a big-nicked book. It was top of the 'Most Stolen' books list. What kind of characters am I attracting into bookshops, for fuck's sake? 'People that are obviously fucking good shoplifters' is the answer. I took it as a big compliment actually, but then again I could do with the money so go easy! My mum used to be a store detective at Woolworth's, so I'm thinking of sending her on a nationwide 'Bookwatch' tour, to keep an eye on mine. So if a grey-haired Irish lady karate-chops you to the ground, ties your legs in a knot and tells you to pray for forgiveness . . . just say 'hello' to my mum, will you?

When it comes to right-handers she taught me all I know.

Have you heard the one about the bent copper? Well you're gonna. Shocking reading it makes too. And just you wait till you hear the punchline, and I mean *punch* (and you will have to wait 'cos that bit don't happen until a later chapter).

Ever since I organised Ronnie Kray's funeral, and especially since *Stop The Ride . . .'* I've been properly targeted by the Old Bill for a big dose of comeuppance. That's how they see it. As a result I got dragged into this whole 'perverting the course of justice' trial. Mostly because in my former days I made fucking good use of one particular corrupt police officer I'd met.

That's what they don't tell you on *Crimewatch* – just how many bent Old Bill there are. You don't even have to find a straight one and try to corrupt him – loads of them come already done, ready assembled: 'and here's one that was made earlier . . .'

So part of all this is about this bent copper that tried to set me up and dirty my name and get me shot in the process. I know, I know; I thought I'd left all that behind as well. But sometimes that light at the end of the tunnel is a train. And that light ain't no help, it's a fucking big hindrance. Well, my eyes are open wider than most to what goes on in the shadowy bits of law enforcement in this country. More truth comes out day by day, but the authorities do really try and keep you in the dark. So consider this book you're holding a great big floodlight. Don't worry, I'll pay the electric bill.

I do hope you've got your 'Oh Wow Fuck Me!' head on because what happened to me recently is a proper 'Oh wow, fuck me!' story. Even more so for it all being God's honest truth. In fact, if you saw it in a film you wouldn't believe it. Even if the hero was played by Bruce Willis instead of me (we share the same hairdresser though – Mother Nature).

Talking of films, I didn't let all what was happening in Britain – not to mention the gang wars I got caught up in in Spain – put me off my usual lifestyle one fucking iota, mate. Did I let it stop me from making my own gangster film, taking it to Cannes and meeting Russell Crowe and Quentin Tarantino on the way? I most certain did not.

Anyway, halfway through all the usual madness I had to decide to carry out the old MAN BITES DOG routine. What the fuck is that, I hear you ask? Right, let your Uncle Davey explain . . .

Life is a series of habits (or if you're a nun with diarrhoea, a series of filthy habits). What I mean is this: if you wake up at five in the morning to go for a three-mile run, and you do that enough times, then you will automatically wake up at five in the morning. Like when some geezer's released from prison he'll still wake up at six, get hungry at twelve and feel like bed at ten, 'cos that's how he's lived for the last few years. Habit.

And that's how they train police dogs.

They're trained to chase a moving target from behind, take the target's arm and drag it down. You've all seen those police training films where there's some poor prick dressed up as the Michelin Man running for his life. Alsatian chases him, grabs the arm and pulls him down. Job well done. The dog gets a biscuit, a pat on the head and one up the arse from his handler back at the kennels.

Now, if you were being chased by one of those German Shepherds that's how it would go . . . but (and I ain't saying it's not a big 'but'), if you are brave enough, and if you do this – stop running, turn around, run at that dog and ATTACK it – there is no way in the fucking world that that dog will kill you. Trust me on this 'cos I've done it, mate. If it's a fight to the death there's no way any dog in the world is going to kill me. Something that's only three foot tall and can't punch, can't kick and can't head-butt is never gonna kill me. The only way it can beat me is if I give in to the fear and lie down and let it kill me. Once you've got over the fear there's no way that something three foot tall is gonna beat you. That'd be like losing a fight to 'Prince' Naseem Hamed.

But because you're taught that every time a dog goes *Arrrggh!* you're supposed to be scared then you *will* be scared, and you will run. That dog's got its own propaganda going on – the teeth and the snarl and the dog snot flying everywhere is *supposed* to scare you.

Truth is this though: if you turn, run at it, and kick it in the head, punch it, stab its eyes, even bite the cunt, then all of a sudden that dog gets *proper* fucking sensible, mate! It sees something four times bigger than itself having a go back at it and it will *fuck* off: and that will fuck that dog up for the rest of its life. I know 'cos I've done it.

You break the habit of the way the dog attacks, and you break the habit of your own fear.

Another example. When you skid the car, if you actually turn towards the lamppost then you get back control and you can turn away. It's the hardest thing to do, though. I know people who've had a dozen skids and always crashed 'cos they've never once done it right. But to learn it you've got to have at least once done it!

Now what the fuck has all this got to do with the price of eggs? Well, during this court case I was involved in I had to turn towards the biggest lamppost I've ever faced in the biggest skid of my life; and run at the biggest police dog there is – the London Metropolitan Police Force.

Before we get down to the juicy details, the long and the short of it is that this bent copper from Bexley Heath, DC Austin Warnes, got himself in some shit and tried to drag me down into it with him. Now, I don't mind paying the price for my own mistakes, but I'll be fucked if I'll pay for someone else's. So this whole case became a pretty fucking big battle for me, for reasons that'll become clear later on.

It also led to an awful lot of people who don't know me, and a few who should know me well enough to know better, to look at me and go, 'What the fuck is he doing?'

You're now about to find out exactly what I was doing . . .

Read on.

1. BAD SEED

Back to my earlier days of villainy and how to try and turn bad to good.

This thing kicked off about eighteen months ago, but before that it really started about fifteen years ago when this geezer, Austin Warnes, was introduced to me by a third party as a bent policeman. And he was. Bent enough to double up as a corkscrew.

You could tell straight off that he was a bit of a villain groupie type, this fella, one of those who loved being around the criminal fraternity. He couldn't wait to throw favours at me to show he was 'alright'. As if. Villains are supposed to do dodgy stuff, ain't they? – it's part of the job description – but coppers are supposed to be straight, so how could you trust one of them that betrays his own.

But that don't mean that if you come across a bent one you ain't gonna use him for your own ends. Know what I mean? So that's what I did, used him for all he was worth. As I later said in court, 'It is my duty as a criminal that if I find a prick like that to help me and my mates get out of trouble, I should use him to his full capacity, pass him round to everyone who needs him, and then when his sell-by date is up, I'll drop the cunt and get a new one!'

Ain't that the truth. There's plenty out there. I got my own bent copper when I was in my early twenties (I always was advanced for my years) when I first met Warnes. I was living in East Dulwich at this time and I had an interest in a number of nightclubs in the Old Kent Road, Peckham, Woolwich, Abbey Wood and the West End. Not long after I first met Warnes he saw me at a nightclub.

On that same night, funnily enough, there was a geezer there called Tony Thompson, who was working on a book he was writing called *Gangland Britain* (cracking good book by the way). Anyway, Thompson was stood next to me when Warnes approached me, said he'd heard about me, and made it clear that he was a bent copper and that he had information that some of my friends were being looked at. Now that's got to be worth a second listen in anyone's book. Especially to someone like me, who is pretty old school about being big on the loyalty to friends front. I weren't gonna turn down an opportunity to help them, basically.

Now, Tony Thompson, who is now chief crime reporter for the *Observer* newspaper, witnessed and heard all this from Warnes. Which was a bit of a touch for me, considering that years later me just knowing Warnes would come back and bite me on the bum. (Another peach of a suggestion Warnes came out with that night was that he wanted to keep all the class A drugs that my doormen confiscated on the doors.)

We had loads of little scams going on. He'd leave doors open for us on certain premises and we'd go in and clear them out of stuff to sell. I was living with a good friend of mine at the time and Warnes tipped us off about this place that had hi-fi, recording equipment and suits in it. So we did the gaff and then later he came round and asked us for some money for the gear. Cheeky cunt! So I told him to fuck off.

You have to establish early on that the balance of power lies with you. Not massively, 'cos then they do feel like they're being played, but just enough to establish who's in charge. I ain't a fisherman – I like my fish to know its plaice (boom boom), which is on a plate, battered and in the company of chips – but I imagine it is very much like coaxing in a big fish. If you show too much of your hand and tug the fucker then the line will snap. So drop the bait, tease it in, let it swim back out a bit to restore its pride, then jerk it back again. Anyway, enough of this fish crap, I sound like Captain fucking Bird's Eye. But you get the idea.

A big reason for me recruiting and developing Warnes as a tool was so I could pass him around among my mates so they could make use of him themselves. Which they most definitely did, as my mates later testified in court.

One time a friend of mine, who was living on a houseboat at the time, suspected he was under surveillance (I think it was the scuba divers in police helmets that tipped him off). So I got Warnes to check it out and he told us which houseboat the Old Bill had their cameras set up in. Their next roll of film must have caused a bit of embarrassment when they picked it up from Boots, 'cos the next night we all went out on deck, dropped our pants and mooned them for all we were worth. Gold medal synchronised mooners we were that night.

Come to think of it, it's a shame we never got nicked on suspicion of doing that 'cos the identity parade would've been fucking funny – 'No, not that one, officer. It wasn't that hairy!'

Another time friends of mine were doing business with some Irish geezers. We got the tip from Warnes that these Irish were also IRA people and were being looked at by the anti-terrorist squad. So my friends backed off to avoid getting dragged into what could've turned into a proper little nasty one.

Of course, you could use Warnes for silly little stuff as well, right down to if you got pulled for speeding and had to produce licence, insurance, V5, MOT, note from your mum, all that shit. He'd make sure that it was falsely recorded that you'd shown them – 'cos I always did have trouble getting that note from my mum.

And because of the 'word on the street', so to speak, that he would get from other coppers, he'd find out things like when there were units after me, or one of my lot, or surveillance units on us, or an investigation under way. Valuable stuff.

That's how it was then. I used him and my mates used him but we never felt we owed him anything. Like you use your vacuum cleaner, but you don't give it a fucking cigarette afterwards and say 'How was it for you?' It's there for a purpose: and to villains who have the ability to play them along, bent coppers are there for a purpose. You don't make all that plain to them, of course, 'cos then they'll take their bat and ball – and their ability to access the police computer – and go home crying.

So along the way you have to do a bit of flattery here – 'Yeah, all the chaps think you're blinding, mate!' a bit of bribery there – 'So-and-so will pay you five grand to help him get off his charge'; and a little ego-massaging as well by throwing a few birds at him (usually prostitutes) who owe you a favour, and help keep him coming back for more.

That's one of the major baits, actually. Women. For some men as much if not more than money. Coppers ain't short of money, especially once they've got out of fancy dress and into civvies, and especially if they're bent. But that don't mean you're gonna get laid as much as you want with as many women as you want to, especially if you're a tubby little geezer.

Warnes liked a bird as much as the next bloke and him moving on the edges of my world meant he got access to the more willing ones that I nudged his way. That keeps most coming back for more. I never paid him a farthing – I offered money to other bent coppers later on – but with him I didn't need to, and something about him made me fucking loath to as well.

I never needed him a massive amount myself so passing him on to be used by mates was a pleasure; I certainly ain't gonna take any money off my mates to help get them out of trouble. But because I put him into so many different people – people from a different circle to me and more financially well off – he ended up being paid fucking fortunes, mate.

He'd also already got a taste for the old nose candy, so we kept him sweet with that too. I know, it ain't exactly *Inspector Morse*, is it? In the real world Inspector Morse would've probably got his Jag from some geezer called something like Big Teddy for turning a blind eye to his car-ringing operation.

So Warnes liked to hang around with us and play the big man of the world. He did like the birds and the charlie. There is, as well, something about the old villainy world that attracts a certain kind of person, both men and women. Whatever else they get out of it, sex or money, is a bonus to the thrill they feel being part of it.

As I've already said, Warnes was a good one to know to get me and mine out of trouble. He helped a mate of mine, Stormin' Norman – you might remember him from *Stop The Ride* . . . – when Norm got nicked (and that little episode was resurrected at the trial, just by coincidence). Ray Bridges was another one that we got help for from Warnes; as did Danny, Mark and Ron, Mark 2, Wolfie, Ian Tucker, Marcus and loads more.

His reward was to get to hang around in circles that he obviously got off on, along with the money he made from selling information and from the 'false informant' scam thing he had going.

Yeah, the false informant scam. Listen to this . . .

Warnes told me about this scam he had going – well, not just him but every other bent copper – where he'd put in false informant logs saying that such-and-such information had been received, and then get clearance from his bosses to pay this supposed 'informer' some money. In fact it was all crap and he'd take the money for himself and split it with the pretend informer. But he couldn't do this alone, obviously; he needed real people who could make an appearance at the station, or wherever, to physically pick up the cash. Afterwards Warnes would get his cut.

Where I came in was in throwing people at him that would go up for the cash. They got a tidy little earner out of it, and I got Warnes more dependent on me than ever, so if ever I got nicked for anything in future – 'cos I was still very active at this point – then I knew I had my own little bent Old Bill I could call upon.

And this practice, the whole false informant money con, is fucking widespread, mate. I'm talking about over the whole country! Sometimes it's just for a few hundred quid and sometimes it's twenty, thirty, forty grand involved. But because of the 'secrecy' thing that's supposed to surround where the police get their info it just makes it easier and allows corrupt coppers to get away with murder.

Newspaper reporters do the same scam all the time. They might get a call from someone saying there's a woman lives across the road with two heads and three arses and the geezer supplying the information wants two grand for it. Well if the tip-off is just telephoned in then no one gets paid, so the reporter arranges for someone to go in and pick up the cash. Then they split it. It don't fucking matter if the story turns out to be a load of bollocks. It's all fake anyway, it's all about as real as Elton John's dandruff.

It's the same kind of trick. Dodgy Old Bill do it with pretend informants.

Think about it – these officers are in a position to give, say, £40,000 in cash of taxpayers' money to moody, non-existent informants who give false names; and then meet them afterwards and get a fucking big chunk of it! No wonder so many of the fuckers are bent. I'm telling you, they've got brothers, dads, mums, next-door neighbours all queuing up to get great lumps of this untaxed, unreported, unlimited cash. And all they need is a body to go up and pick it up. I know it sounds too easy, but believe me it's true. It's 'cos it is so easy that it happens.

It's been going on up and down the country, week in week out, for absolutely fucking years. Everyone involved obviously knows about it but has fucking good reason to keep quiet. As you will see, the only reason I had to blow the lid on it (years later) was when the police nicked me for something they knew I was fuck-all to do with.

Anyway, I had Warnes on a string and we were using him for whatever the fuck we could get from him to fuck up any police investigations.

There was one downside to all this, ain't there always, and that was this – that any copper can't just look at police files and reports and computer records without a fucking good reason. The best reason a copper can give is that an informant of his has told him something and he needs to check it against what's already on the files. What that means is that someone has to put themselves up to be in that position.

Now if any man views himself as leader material, which I most fucking certainly do, then he has to lead from the front and not ask any other poor cunt to do something he wouldn't do himself. So I practised what I preached and stepped forward into the breach! It weren't no secret 'cos everyone knew what I'd done, and exactly why. And they soon saw the benefits when I used this position to get Warnes to find out information to help out me and my people.

It's like when a copper goes undercover and pretends to be a drug dealer to try to get information on what drug dealers are up to. The Old Bill go undercover to infiltrate the criminal world, and we do the same thing, use the same coup – by pretending to give information so we could use bent coppers to find out what the other police were up to. It's like in football – you do a dummy to make him go one way so you can go the other. Same in real life.

We were using their own fucking tactics against them. And it worked. Perfect! Take *that!*

Well, it weren't exactly perfect 'cos years later when the police found out what I'd been doing to fuck up their investigations they tried to get their revenge – during this trial I'm going to tell you about – and get their revenge by making out that I really had been an informer. Cunts.

Now this method that we were using to get information was an almost foolproof method. I say almost 'cos there was just one thing about it that could lead to some . . . shall we say . . . embarrassment; or even, it turns out, something worse. What it was was this: most of the time the fake informant scam worked like a dream and we were fucking loving it that we were getting people off charges. What could be better than watching your mate walk free? Wicked. Proper spontaneous orgasm time. Sometimes, though, despite my best efforts I couldn't stop someone getting sent down if, for example, there was just too much evidence. The bad thing there was that, when that happened, the person that had put themselves up as the pretend informant would actually have their name put down on a case that had resulted in a conviction. You see what I mean? So to people not in the know, it could look like one person had given information and the other geezer had got sent down. When actually they'd been trying to get him off!

A good example of that is when we tried to get information out of police files to help my mate Ray, who was up on a charge. It worked in that we managed to give him enough help to justify getting him a retrial, which is a result in itself, 'cos that's a fucking difficult thing to pull off, ain't it, getting a retrial? So that gave Ray another bite at the cherry to get a not guilty. Unfortunately that didn't happen and Ray went down, and that would've been one of the cases where a name had to be put down as the informant.

What I meant when I said it could lead to embarrassment '. . . or worse' was that at the time we was fairly young, so we didn't really see into the future about how the police might try and turn this around. I had big ideas about what I wanted to do but didn't really foresee how much the Old Bill would really, really come to want me put away. Nearly twenty years down the line the stakes had got much higher and the police had got much cleverer about how to portray criminals in a certain light. And about how the media could be used to create a false image of someone.

Anyway, that was to come. That was The Big One coming up to deal with.

Oh *listen* to this, fuck me you'll love this one! Just as the police can plant people in criminal organisations, well it can also work the other way round. I actually put my own plants into the police.

I had people as Special Constables, and I know a load of people who pay people to join the Specials just so they've got someone in the police force, learning, listening, seeing stuff. The girls especially are worth the money. Girls have only got to do a few hours to be kept on so if you get some young bird going in there wanting to be a Special the proper coppers are all over them! In reality the bird's only a working girl but she goes in there, has a flirt, trying to pull the highest ranking officer, and she'll probably be the sexiest thing around. Nothing makes a man blab and brag more than when all the blood drops into his dick head. (And that's when he'll behave like one.)

Traffic wardens! That's another good one. Yeah, they do have their uses sometimes, I mean apart from using them as bollards, speed bumps or target practice. I'd get some sexy little lap dancer bird to get a job as a traffic warden. Now her job at night is stripping naked and being a bloody good actress, 'cos she makes geezers fall in love with her every five minutes at a tenner a go. She knows the moves to make and the faces to fake. Get her in a traffic warden's uniform, though, and she is now a civilian inside a police station – but underneath she's a sexy dancer who works for me trying to look ordinary, and the fact she ain't got a criminal record allows her to move into those jobs. (Some of these birds even ended up stopping dancing 'cos they were getting more money making a normal wage, PLUS a big fucking healthy backhander on top from whoever was paying her to milk information.)

These 'traffic wardens' go into the police station two or three mornings to have breakfast; and she will get her hooks in a copper, and most probably the one she went in there to get. Everyone's human, even some ginger copper, and if a sexy little bird comes into your canteen every morning you would fancy your chances, no doubt about it. And it don't matter if this 'new' traffic warden leaves the job after a couple of weeks, the copper would still carry on seeing her and she'd carry on pumping him. And there's nothing like a bit of pillow talk.

Or you just get a prostitute to start an affair with a copper. She works him like a punter and he's an easy mark and easy money for her; and the silly fucking policeman . . . most of them are married so he only wants to see her once a week, but she'll be such a good shag he will fall in love with her. It's well worth the wages you pay to those little inside-job birds, believe me. Women can be as much a man's weakness as his strength. Sex is always a good pull, and if you get a geezer just thinking about cunt then he'll eventually end up behaving like one.

Another good one was civilian blokes that had contracts to work in police stations. The fact that a lot of the general public work in police stations is a godsend for anyone who has the idea of using insiders. Even I can't believe the amount of info I've got over years from some cleaning lady on the take! They don't miss a fucking trick. Also, private security firms are now doing the prisoner runs and the blokes who work for these firms are just normal, everyday geezers. If I didn't have a prison record I could apply to be one! I could plant myself in a position like that – but I'd still be me, still naughty – and I'd have access to inside prisons and transporting prisoners. And I do know naughty geezers that haven't yet got criminal records and can be placed in those jobs. They are genuine diamond-finds, actually, to find a proper naughty fella who ain't got no record. They can boldly go where no naughty geezer has gone before.

One funny story that came out of this was told to me by someone who was in a police canteen and overheard a conversation. He came round my house still wetting himself thinking about what he'd heard. He didn't hear the beginning but dropped into it in the middle, and they were obviously talking about my house: I'd just made it into my castle – big and theatrical. But one of these coppers was saying. 'Course we've got problems if Courtney's *fortifying* his home, we could have another Waco situation on our hands!' *Ha*. They thought I was barricading the thing up so we could hole up there! Fucking hell. Top compliment. And this was before the drawbridge went on.

Another one we'd do: we'd single out Customs officers in the same way that the police single out someone that *they're* after. So you can go up somewhere and single out the Customs fella we needed in our pocket, go to his local, befriend him, get him pissed, let him pull a bird that was with us . . . and before long we'd be into him for favours.

Fucking hell, at one time I had more plants on the go than Alan Titchmarsh and the Chelsea Flower Show. I even had a floral knuckleduster.

See, *they* do it. The Old Bill do it all the time – the plant thing. They send some cunt into you to pretend they're this and that so they can do you harm. But they think everyone else is too thick to do the same to them. Wrong. They try and tell the public that none of us on this side are intelligent enough to do that. Another big 'wrong'. How intelligent you are decides how high you go in a business (except in window cleaning – you just get a taller ladder) so if you're only a burglar or a car thief you never have that problem of working out people's motives. I eventually had so many people working for me that I wouldn't have got to that stage if I hadn't got good at reading people. I think I got good at it 'cos it came natural to me, which is lucky for me, and because I don't like the consequences of not knowing what is going on.

For example, when someone comes up to me now because they've read the book I know what they're going to say. You can only say so many things. And if I didn't have an answer for them by now I'd be a fucking idiot. Similarly, when someone's caught climbing out of a house window the copper who nicks him has heard all the lines in the book, all the excuses. In addition, 'cos the copper's had some slippery cunts in front of him that have actually talked themselves out of trouble, he remembers them for pulling a clever move and tries to close that door – so no one will ever get it past him again.

You have to *learn* your enemy if you intend to beat him. You must do that. If you know what they are thinking you can beat them, or at least stop them getting you. Learn their strengths and then you can see their weaknesses. You can't distance yourself from whatever it is that's trying to stop you. Don't hide – confront. Or to put it another way: Confucius say, man with one chopstick go hungry. Clever geezer that old Chinese philosopher, Confucius, and he still had time to make all those bloody fortune cookies.

Good villains should know how to think like a copper (to get one step ahead) and coppers also sometimes end up thinking like villains; but sometimes those coppers end up thinking like villains full-time. Like if I was paid to do a twenty-mile cross country run every day but then someone showed me a short cut that meant I could shave ten miles off the distance, I could either use the short cut or decide not to. Either way I get paid the same, but if I go one way I'll only be half as knackered. What the police do is *learn criminal short cuts and use them in the name of the law.*

If they come round and raid your house it ain't all twelve of them that drop the little packet of gear in one of your trainers when you're not looking. It's only one of them. Eleven of them don't know. So one will drop the gear and another one will genuinely find it and later on he'll get up in court and swear on the Bible and all that. He thinks he's done a good day's work. Well done, Sherlock! And the other one who planted the stuff thinks that he's done a good day's work as well 'cos he's successfully fitted you up!

Anyway, more likely than not the copper that found the gear would, deep down, know that there really hadn't been three ounces in that Nike trainer, and he'd know that just from seeing the geezer's reaction. The copper's seen a thousand people get nicked with gear and try to fake surprise (and not quite do it), or just sigh at being caught or get angry they've been caught or try to make a run for it when they've been caught: so the copper *knows* a genuine shocked geezer when he sees one. But what's he gonna do? When he gets back to the station to write up his report with his policeman pals is he going to say that as a trained police officer he had doubts about the genuineness of the find?

Is. He. *Fuck*.

He ignores the truth of that. It's a done thing. And he ain't even broken the law because all he's doing is pretending in his mind about something. Like when a firing squad line up to shoot someone they always make sure there's one blank in one of the guns so you can go to bed that night thinking it weren't your fault.

Another major thing was that later on I got charged with something miles out of London in Oxfordshire which meant I was under the jurisdiction of another police force. Now, coppers can't just access the files of other police forces willy-nilly unless it's something to do with some information: so this turned into another one of those times where me pulling a scam with Warnes allowed him to get access to some info on what the Old Bill had on me on this case. In fact, this is a perfect example of how the con works. Listen . . .

I was in trouble, allegedly, for something out in Oxfordshire that could've led to me getting big bird. Now with that being another county, miles out of London, how's my bent copper gonna help me out? Simple, we made up a fake informant report saying that I was some geezer called 'Tommy Mack' (fake name) who might have information on what Dave Courtney's been up to out in Oxfordshire. Then Warnes uses that as an excuse to ring the outside police force and find out what evidence, if any, they think they already have on me. If you know what they've got – you know how to fight it. Right?

So think about that a second – in this case I actually *grassed myself up*! Technically. But not really 'cos it's all fake. And the info got me off it, which is the exact idea, funnily enough! Result. And this Oxford thing is the most perfect, *perfect* example of *exactly* what I've been talking about. Now that's ingenious!

When I ran into problems it was with people who didn't know the full details of the trick or were too simple to understand it.

So these were all the little acts and tricks and ploys that were used to beat the Old Bill at their own game. Sometimes in the old villainy game, especially when up against modern policing methods, you need all kinds of help. And sometimes that means using the police's own bent coppers *for* you and against them.

As you do.

The funny thing is, though, that although it's the bad coppers you've got to watch out for, it's also the bad coppers that you can bribe! *Ain't* life funny.

2. THE KINKY HOUSE

Bent coppers, straight sex, and machetes. What more do you want!

Just as crabs can only walk straight when they're drunk, some people only show their true colours under stress. Like this geezer I know who backed my Rolls Royce out of my driveway to make way for another car. Unfortunately, he ended up flying backwards down the road in two tons of out-of-control metal, smashing into every parked car on the way and severely battering the arse of the Rolls. He ran back up into my house a gibbering wreck and broke down in front of me.

That immediately showed me exactly what he'd do if he ever ended up in a police station being questioned. Jelly on a plate. Some other people, though, accidentally let their colours shine through when they're relaxed. Or as relaxed as you can be when you've got a hard-on.

Which brings me to the sex parties. You ain't never been to one? Listen, you've got to try it at least once. Or twice. Oh fuck it, go for the hat-trick.

We used to go to this naughty little place in Forest Gate that we called The Kinky House. It was a house that held these horny get-togethers every month. And it was a proper saucy little gaff, mate, believe me. All the women were there for one thing as much as the men. And I don't mean the cheesy nibbles. You could live out your fantasies or satisfy your fetishes there. They even had dungeons and whips if you were into that. Warnes liked a bird as well, so he started coming to The House with us.

Listen, what really fucks it for a copper is this: no matter how matey they try to get with people no one ever really forgets they're still a copper, right? You know that. On paper they're supposed to be the Good Guys, but a lot of the general public don't see them that way and so if they're out at a party, or in a pub or whatever, a lot of them don't broadcast what they do. 'Cos everyone tenses up a bit don't they, around Old Bill? Even straight 9 to 5ers. Everyone starts thinking, Is he always on duty? Can I risk smoking some puff? What if I drink and drive? Has he noticed the sawn-off shotgun down my sleeve?

So they almost have to hide the fact that they're coppers 'cos people act a certain way around them. I understand that, because when people found out what I did – post offices, mostly – they'd act a certain way around me. When you think about it, we – that's me and mine – were supposedly the Bad Guys, but we seemed to get all the birds, the showing off, the flashing-it-about and the get-a-load-of-me bit. That must be a hard one for the Old Bill to swallow, don't you think? Must be. Trying to get your head around that if you're a copper must be a tough one. But oh dear, how sad, never fucking mind!

Anyway, Warnes started coming along to these sex parties and I introduced him as 'Austin Warnes, the bent copper', and he just could never get his head around why I did that! It was fucking funny, actually.

But what I knew deep down was that because we were using him for the fake informant scam – for the reasons I've already explained – then he could use that bit of paper to try to get me in trouble in the future if he decided to. To counteract that I made sure that all my mates knew exactly what the score was with him, and then we all used him for all he was worth!

We didn't hide him. I actually introduced him as a dodgy Old Bill and he just could not get his fucking head round it how we were so blatant about him. But we were already preparing for the day when he might try to fuck me by pretending I was a real grass. (As if a corrupt policeman would even think of doing that! I hear you cry. Well, I wouldn't even trust a rabbi with a fucking ham sandwich, mate.)

At these sex parties then I introduced him as an iffy one. He didn't really want to be known as a copper at all, but I said I wouldn't introduce him as something else 'cos if people found out it'd only look bad. I only ever took him into company that wouldn't do him or them no harm. Which is why Warnes never got to meet my mate Mad Pete.

Mad Pete's got a heart as big as a bull's, but instead of charging red flags he charges blue uniforms. And if they're wise they get out the way sharpish. Because Mad Pete in full-on, nostril-flaring, teeth-bearing, cop-crushing mode is not a pretty sight, mate. Fuck me, no. He once told us this story about being attacked by three geezers, and one of them had a machete. He ended the story by saying, 'Anyway, after I was hit by the machete . . .' Fucking 'ell. Listen, even for the people I know that is one fucking casual way of putting it.

Anyway, back at the sex parties I introduced Warnes as exactly what he was, and you could see him go into Bent Cop Mode straightaway. In normal company to be known as a bent copper would be a bad thing, but in this company and in the company of villains you'd actually be better thought of for being dodgy! So, like I say, I watched him click into Bent Cop Mode and start doing to them what he did to me when he first introduced himself – meaning, he went out of his way to show how bent he was.

So then he'd start throwing favours and gifts at people, trying to buy friendship. Oh, and get this – all the policemen's and policewomen's uniforms that they had at Kinky House, for people to dress up and fuck each other in, were all real uniforms that Warnes had nicked! He was that eager to please. You cannot fucking make that stuff up, can you? God's honest truth. The Metropolitan Police were half a dozen uniforms light 'cos they'd been nicked by a bent copper for some shag palace in East London. (And don't even ask what happened to the truncheons he nicked.) Sometimes life is so sweet.

Tell you what, though, after all the times the Old Bill had tried to fuck me it was a real pleasure to dress some bird up as a WPC and get my own back. And there's nothing quite like a revenge-fuck. Good fun debriefing an 'undercover' woman as well.

Warnes also used to get hold of stuff like pepper sprays, nightsticks, stun guns, night scopes, handcuffs, coshes, body armour, all that kind of gear. Most of my mates got their bulletproof vests through Austin Warnes. He was like the Littlewoods fucking catalogue of the Metropolitan Police – 'Yeah, I'll have two sawn-offs and a truncheon on the 40-week repayment plan, please.'

It's at places like the Kinky House that people get to live out their fantasies. It was a members-only club, people were vetted, everyone knew each other so people relaxed; and that's when true colours do shine through. So when people got swopping their little dirty stories Warnes pitched in with his and revealed what an iffy little fucker he was. Much more than even I'd thought.

He started talking about how if he was having an affair with someone's wife and he thought her geezer was in danger of finding out (and especially if the bloke was the kind who'd batter Warnes for it), then he'd set the bloke up for something and get him nicked. Then he'd carry on banging his wife whilst her old man was inside. He said he also fucked around with women of blokes that were in prison. He'd let them believe that if they fucked him he'd help with their old man's court case or prison sentence. The woman ain't gonna tell her old man that's she'd doing it 'cos she thinks she's sacrificing herself for him. But what Warnes was really doing was gaining evidence on her that could destroy her marriage – 'cos if she'd fucked a copper once then he could blackmail her into gang-banging all his mates, and videoing it as well, stuff like that.

Those were his 'sexy' stories, but he told too much of the nasty bit before he got to the sex bit, and everyone disliked him for it. And because, in time, he forgot that he'd told these stories, later on when he tried the same tactics on my missus Jennifer, when I was inside, I could see it. Like I've told you before in *Stop the Ride . . .*, if the police can nick a year of your life off you by putting you on remand, they will do. Then they've got twelve months to set about fucking up your missus, your kids and your home life.

Anyway, one night at The House something happened that properly pinned his true colours to the mast for all to see.

It was early one morning and the party was in full swing. Me and Jennifer were getting it on with a lap dancer girlfriend of hers, in another room a little orgy was on the go, people were fucking in the shower and the local vicar was swinging from a light fitting, having Marmite spat on his bollocks by a young bird in a rubber nurse's outfit – you get the idea. You know what they say, sex is only dirty if you're doing it right.

Anyway, suddenly there was a banging on the door, but as there was banging going on everywhere in that place we could've easily ignored it. Except you could tell it was a copper's knock. What is it about that? Do they go on some special fucking course called 'Knock Like A Copper'? Warnes especially knew that sound and he must have jumped off whatever bird he was on quicker than if her fanny had grown teeth.

I went downstairs to deal with it and passed Warnes on the stairs. He was having a real big panic attack 'cos he could already see the headlines in his mind, 'CORRUPT OFFICER CAUGHT IN HOUSE OF SIN!' or 'TOP COP NICKED WITH PANTS DOWN!!'

That's when you tell what someone's made of, when they're under deep duress. He was practically begging me to do something to get him out. I told him to calm down and see what it was all about first. And all it was was that the geezer who lived in the house over the road had found his driveway blocked by one of our cars and called the local police. It weren't a raid at all, just some young copper asking us to move the car! Panic over.

Too late then though for Warnes to change how he'd behaved, and 'cos he knew everyone had seen it he started kicking off about the bloke over the road who'd complained. He went over to the doorman I had working there, Frank, and a mate of mine, Phil, and asked them if they could get something off the bloke across the road; something like a cig butt from his car ashtray. They were like, what the fuck for? Warnes explained to Frank that he could use it to set the guy up for something and get him out the way; like drop the cig butt at the scene of the crime so it's found with his DNA on it.

Frank and Phil were like, fuck off!

So you can see why people turned against him. The other House members just thought, Fuck me, what a dirty little cunt. And they didn't want him there any more. I hadn't heard most of those 'shagging stories' off him before, so I was more than happy to ban him from the house. But, because he was still useful to me on the old Fuck The Police front, I handled it in a certain way. I told him that he weren't wanted there any more by the other members, which was true, but that I'd see what I could do to get him back in, which was a lie.

By this stage it was a proper smile-through-gritted-teeth routine between him and me. It fucking burned him to get banned from The House, because it was a real touch to get invited there with all these dead-cert, up-for-it birds; and he got really, really addicted to the whole group sex and coke scene.

Deep down he knew I'd banned him, he knew it was me. He had to pretend to still like me, though, to get the other benefits – the charlie, the other birds he met, the people I was putting his way to do the false informant con, and the whole fucking buzz of it that he got off on.

Next thing I did was put this bird onto him that was actually a prostitute. He started shagging her on a regular basis and she'd tell me about any little bits of info he let slip during pillow talk that I could use. She was a fucking good actress that girl as well, 'cos he actually fell for her. So we got a big gold dildo and gave it to her as an Oscar.

When you think about it, what I was doing in using him to get help for the criminal world was a bit like the 'Neighbourhood Watch' scheme in reverse. 'Cop Watch'! And you won't find Nick Ross presenting that one on telly.

3. HOW A CORRUPT POLICEMAN CAN SEND YOU TO JAIL FOR A CRIME YOU DIDN'T COMMIT

Prepare your 'not guilty' plea now. But don't fucking bank on it.

If you see something that's a challenge, take it on and relish it. Because it will make you better. Win or lose, it will make you better. One of my little challenges along the way – in the middle of every-fucking-thing else I was doing at the time, promoting, running clubs, running London's biggest firm of doormen, etc. – was to keep DC Austin Warnes bubbling away on a ring. Careful not to let him go cold or boil over.

But you can see how me playing him along, and trying to get all the benefits any naughty geezer would want to get from a bent copper, also meant that I was sailing a bit close to the wind in terms of what I might have left myself exposed to. And by that I mean the thing that did eventually happen when the Old Bill tried to portray me as a grass.

What happened over time was that Warnes gradually let us in on the dirty tricks of the trade that corrupt policemen used to fit people up. It came out bit by bit, and although sometimes it weren't intentional, and sometimes it was just bragging, I could see that some of it was there for another reason. He was talking about all this shit he'd done and *could* do and then letting it sink in.

Could only be for one reason, and that was as a threat. A sly one, and not one you could pull him on 'cos the story was always about some other poor cunt. I thought, why is he doing this? It can only be a sort of unspoken threat. Trying to get the power balance back and tip it his way by showing me what he can do and how easily he can set people up.

This ain't conspiracy theory stuff either. This is where your straight living, 9 to 5ing, law-abiding, council tax paying, *Inspector Morse* watching person might start to doubt a little. But these are real things that go on, and have been doing so for years. Just because you ain't heard them told before and might find them difficult to believe does NOT mean that they don't happen. Men have walked on the fucking moon remember! Actually landed on another *planet*, got a parking ticket, had a shit in the spacesuit and got back home safely. So, next to that, how unlikely is it that there's some corrupt policing down here on earth?

You don't have to be a rocket scientist to realise that it does go on. These are some of the things that he got up to.

He told me that when the DNA testing first came in it meant that when they got someone they definitely got them, if you know what I mean, no arguments from anyone. But it also ruled out suspects that might have been convicted on just suspicion alone in the old days. So the way they got around that was by falsifying the DNA evidence! That gives you a definite, watertight, 24-carat, 'Go Directly To Jail' fit-up.

How it's done is this – a bent copper would follow certain people around nightclubs and wait until they stubbed out a cig in an ashtray on the bar or dropped it on the floor, and then when they moved away he'd go and pick it up. Or if they had some geezer under surveillance they'd break into his car and take a dog end out of the ashtray. Now, keep that cig butt safe and then drop it at a crime scene three months later, and they've got an item with saliva with DNA in it.

When that geezer gets into court and when the prosecutor asks him how a dog end with his DNA on it was found at the crime scene, what the fuck can he say? He don't even know how it got there. All he can say is, 'I don't know'. Oh, really? The jury thinks, we *do* know. GUILTY!

Another one, similar thing: pick up an empty fag packet left behind by someone which has their fingerprints all over the box and use that to drop at a crime scene in the same way. How did that get there Mr Smith? 'No idea, your honour'. Judge says, 'Really, Mr Smith?' Jury thinks, GUILTY!

And all you non-smokers sat there reading this thinking you're safe – you're not! Another one was to buy a magazine and tear off a corner of one of the pages, and plant that at a crime scene. Then, when the police search your car, what do they find? The rest of the magazine in the door pocket. Wonder how that got there then? And the torn page matches exactly the torn piece they find. How do you plead Mr Smith? 'Not guilty, your honour' Really? Well, Fuck *OFF!* PACK YOUR BAGS FOR PRISON AND DON'T FORGET YOUR TOOTHBRUSH!

That would even fuck up the Pope's chances of getting off, mate, I'm telling you! Faced with that kind of 'evidence' Prince Charles would have to get used to porridge and a bunk bed, serving time At His Mother's Pleasure.

Warnes said that if a defendant stands in court and says that he's been fitted-up and had drugs planted in his house, the judge will say this, 'Please tell me how a police officer earning eighteen thousand pounds a year would get the money to buy the 64 thousand pounds' worth of drugs found on your premises?' And the geezer can't answer that because he don't fucking know how.

This is how.

When a bent copper nicks someone with, say, fifteen ounces of cocaine, by the time that geezer gets down the station he suddenly finds that he's only charged with five ounces. He thinks to himself, fucking funny that! But he ain't likely to jump up and go, 'No! There's been a mistake, it was actually fifteen.' No one would be dumb enough to do that. Those other ten ounces that went missing on the way to the station end up in stash for future use. That's how they get drugs to plant. They don't have to fucking buy the stuff.

Another one was if a dealer gets caught in a car with 500 Es, they just take them out the car and tell the geezer to fuck off. Which he would do pretty sharpish, thanking his lucky stars. Now Warnes has that bag of Es to use to fuck up someone he wants to stitch up, rather than just catch another fucking E dealer that he couldn't give two tosses about.

The other way of using the cache of 500 Es was to not let the geezer go but say to him, 'Listen, you're gonna get fifteen years for this lot of class As unless you do me a favour.' And then he'd ask the geezer to pick a Mr Smith out of an ID parade and say he saw him getting out of, say, a blue Escort outside of Barclays bank last Wednesday. So they've now got a 'witness' that didn't exist before, until they created him.

Fuck me, I've just realised that this 'Mr Smith' of ours gets about a bit though, don't he? What is he, a one man bleedin' crime wave, or what? Anyone out there called 'Smith', change it now!

A fella might be too smart to talk on his phone so what they do is this: get someone to ring up a geezer's home phone when they know he's out and leave a message on saying 'that last batch was top, I'll have some more next week' – beep. All recorded on surveillance tape. Next week, same call, another message left like 'okay I'll have another two every week for the next year'. The geezer coming home don't know what the fuck these are. But the police might have a two-year surveillance on the bloke, so 24 months down the line they've got a proper collection of loads of these little 'messages' on his phone. Add that to a bag of heroin 'found' in the boot of his car, and later on in court that starts to look pretty fucking convincing to a jury. While the geezer's just stood in the dock not knowing what's hit him. He can't get his head round it. Even he ends up thinking he's a big-time drug dealer!

Or they might do the false number plate scam. Buy a couple of plates for a tenner made up to match the car of the geezer they want; stick them on a same car type and deliberately get caught on speed cameras up the road from a crime scene. For good measure they might throw in a dog end with his DNA on it found at the crime scene. Present that to a jury and that poor fucker ain't coming home until his wife's tits are on her hips and his sons are both shaving. *Job well done!* – in their eyes.

See it how they see it and then you see it for what it is. Just another bunch of ordinary coppers justifying the means by the end. And fancy being fucked over and fitted up by a bunch of everyday ordinary bastards! It's not even like you've been got by Sherlock Holmes!

Now that the police know that we can handle the hard-nut prison side of things they go for another line of attack, which is against your home life. I've always said that if I'm happy at home I can take on the world. Any man with his missus fully behind him is twice as strong. Or three times as strong in the case of my Jen. I've seen geezers in prison who'd have a go at half a dozen screws but when they got the Dear John letter from the missus they fell to bits.

The police have a fear of the bond between a man and wife, that's the one partnership that is 99 per cent of the time the best partnership you can get as a man. The police think that a bloke's partner in crime is the best partnership, but if you and your wife are strong then that's the best. And because my Jennifer knows it is one of the Old Bill's tactics to destroy that bond, she holds strong against that; but she's probably left more vulnerable than me because she is being punished just for being my wife. And I hate them for that.

So a new kind of dirty tricks came in when they finally got wise to where the true bond was. Tricks like getting some tart in a short skirt to meet a geezer in a pub and flirt with him. He thinks it's his lucky night and 'cos it never really happens to him he's as flattered as fuck, and by the time they've left he's also half pissed. She asks him to give her a lift home and she just happens to live near the local red-light district – oh dear. So when he pulls over and she gets out there's a copper there waiting to pounce. Surprise so-fucking-prize. He gets done for drink/driving and soliciting a known prostitute, and the local papers are tipped off about it when it happened and who to.

Now, that geezer is proper *fucked*, mate. And he didn't even *get* fucked. His home life is totally screwed. The wife will chuck him out of the house, probably screaming that he'd better have an AIDS test before he comes back to see the kids. Not long after that would be a prime moment for the Old Bill to approach the wife and see if there's anything she might want to tell them about how her old man's been earning a living for the last ten years.

The Old Bill know that more things are likely to be said between a man and his missus during an argument. Everyone does it. Usually you can make it up with an 'I didn't mean it, babe'; but if it's all been caught on tape 'cos your house is bugged . . . So, make the couple have an argument by getting a policewoman to ring the house when the bloke's not there and ask for him by name. It don't take many of those to get the old lady on gas mark ten. By the time he gets home she's boiled right fucking over and is ready to take on Mike Tyson with the Dyson.

Another vicious one is when they raid you at home when they know only you, your missus and the kids are there. That's deliberate, 'cos they know when they 'find' something in the house and they ask if it's yours you're gonna say no; and then when they ask the wife she's gonna say no – so they nick you *both*. Here's where the vicious bit comes in. Because there's no other adults in the house, they get the kids taken into care! It's only a matter of time before the bloke ends up confessing to something that he ain't even done for the sake of getting his kids away from Social Services and back to their mum. In any other circumstance they couldn't have got that geezer to confess if they'd pulled his arms and legs off.

Basically, it's like a massive, police-sponsored wrecking ball being swung into the walls of Home Sweet Home. Don't bother knocking 'cos the front door's now in next-door's back garden.

I'll tell you one thing, women don't like those methods, those underhand attack-the-family type coups. Which is why when coppers split from their wives a lot of those ladies have insights into what really, really goes on with policemen at work. No one knows you more than someone who has lived with you for ten years and fucked you, sucked your cock, cleaned up after you, gone through your pockets, heard you on the phone, listened to you bragging with your mates, heard your drunken confessions, read your e-mails, opened your letters – all that shit and more. (Which is why the book that Jennifer's working on now about stories by coppers' ex-wives and girlfriends will be such an eye-opener.)

You've got to remember though – and this is important if you're gonna grasp how easy it is for it to happen – you've got to get over the idea that the dodgy police think they're doing anything *wrong*. What I mean is – they're just doing *what everybody else does in their own job*: corner-cutting, cheating, and trying to get away with it when no one's looking. Office workers do it, factory workers do it, bin men do it, bank workers do it. Every lorry driver goes over the speed limit. So, for example, an officer will show a witness a photograph of someone before they go to see an ID parade. That's a normal, everyday situation. Everyone does what he has to do to make his job easier. The only big difference is that the consequences of a copper doing those things is that someone might get illegally banged up for a five-stretch, based on Mickey Mouse evidence. But the copper thinks he's pulled off a good one, he ain't in turmoil over it.

You've got to realise that they are normal, everyday men who are only putting on a uniform. They have ways and means of getting things done, and they're never gonna admit it 'cos they'd have to grass up their workmates. And they know how many cases would have to be reopened.

The ordinary police ring up the Vice Squad and go, 'I need a tart for a job . . .' just like one doorman will ring up another doorman on Saturday night and say, 'we need another two more down here, mate'. The plod ring the Vice, the Vice ring the Drug Squad for some gear . . . they're members of the same gang helping each other out.

The criminal fraternity might think I'm flattering the police by considering them human, but that's the point. They're all too human. I've never thought they were anything but. Unless they want to say 'When we put our uniforms on we are not human' then they can't say they are any different. The public, though, are brainwashed into the idea that their police wouldn't do any harm, and that's given them carte blanche to do what they want.

There's many ways to get someone. I've heard a prostitute say that when she was caught with drugs for the third time she was told she was looking at a life sentence 'cos of that 'three strikes and you're out rule'. The Old Bill knows she's HIV positive so he offers her a 'no arrest' if she'll fuck this geezer that he points out to her. She was there, large as life, talking about giving some poor cunt a blowjob first so she could try to cut his skin with her teeth. And that's a copper trying to set that up. You don't know the fucking half of it, mate.

They fuck up your home life 'cos they know it hurts you more than prison. Even if you are banged up at least you've got the thought of going home to look forward to, but if you're out and you've got no home life you've got fuck all.

Don't make the mistake of thinking that it's only people involved in villainy who get fitted up. Good example was at the party at The House I told you about when Warnes wanted to fuck up the bloke across the road for complaining his driveway was blocked. See, when these bent Old Bill properly get their snouts stuck into the old trough of corruption it just becomes second nature to them, mate: rule bending and breaking; their instant little fix for curing any problem they have. Big or small.

Is all this making some kind of sense to you? Or sounding even half likely? I'm so used to knowing that it's true that I sometimes forget just how mental it can sound to ordinary people. No, actually, I don't really ever forget how mental it sounds 'cos I only have to think back to when I first found out to remember how fucked-up it sounds. So I do understand whatever difficulties you might be having coming to terms with this.

I know that if you tried to tell this to someone else they'd say, 'Oh that ain't true just 'cos you've read that in a book. Just 'cos Dave Courtney says so.' Well I ain't the only one who says it, but the trouble is that a lot of the other people who are saying it are trying to be heard through a two-by-two prison cell window with bars across it. See how much attention you get then. The police have already fucked your credibility by stitching you up for a crime you didn't do, who's gonna want to believe you. Especially if they fit you up for child pornography or drugs or being an informer – anything to just make sure you get zero fucking sympathy!

The follow-up to corrupt policemen getting hold of drugs in the way they do goes like this – a copper on his way to work in the morning phones in an 'anonymous' tip-off to his own police station about some geezer they are already investigating. By the time the copper gets to the station a search warrant is already being sorted out. Then he goes on the bust and when he's 'searching' this geezer's house he drops the drugs in a shoe. One of the other officers (and one who's straight and don't even know this is going on – yeah they do exist) finds the stuff and hey fucking presto, they've got a bust! And just for good measure they might find a torn bit of a magazine there as well. Oh dear, I think I feel another GUILTY verdict coming on . . .

Now all this leaking of information by Warnes happened over years. Bit by bit. Most of it said directly to me and to others. Some of it came from pillow talk with the prostitute that he fell for; some came from when he was bragging, or drunk, or when he was deliberately using it as a threat of what he could do.

See, a bent copper feels like he's getting the best of both worlds. On the one hand he's a copper, with all the perks that brings, and on the other hand he's doing criminal stuff and getting all the perks that brings. But it don't work. Not for them anyway. When villains use bent coppers it's just to get information, no other reason. But when bent Old Bill start hanging around with the naughty fraternity it's usually because they get off on it, and they're half jealous of that life. But you can't have a foot in both camps. Like Confucius say, *Man who scratch arse should not bite fingernails.*

So, yeah, there were two main reasons he talked about this stuff. One – he was a naturally lairy cunt who just liked to brag about his power. To him, mouthing off about this scam or that con was like a bent copper's version of a boxer telling you his best fight stories, or a football player reliving that thirty-yard free kick into the top corner. And two (and this is the one that crept up on you slowly) – it was his way of slyly showing you what kind of tricks he could pull to fit you up for something but without directly threatening you.

Years later, when he got himself in bother and asked me to tell a little lie for him, he knew that I knew about what he could do. Which also is why I tape-recorded him admitting that I weren't actually giving him information at all, but just giving him a lie to use. Another big, big thing on my mind at the time was this – now that I knew I had him on my tape admitting to being bent, I could use that to not only protect myself and my mates from him, but also to get more out of him. (But we'll get into the full details of that later on when it actually happens.)

So why did I carry on seeing this geezer? I'm a very firm believer in the old saying, 'Keep your friends close but your enemies closer.' If you don't do that then you don't know what they're up to, and that's worse. Not everyone can do that, though, 'cos they cannot disguise their dislike of their enemies. They have a pop at them, and their enemies slip back into the shadows. Then the first thing they know of an attack is when it comes out of the dark. It also put me in an important position to learn about all these tactics. 'Power is knowledge' – ain't that the fucking truth. Or 'Forewarned is forearmed', as my nan used to say. And my nan always got 'not guilty', bless her. (Fucking unlucky of her to get caught on her last bank job though: I blame the getaway driver – he just couldn't get the best out of that electric shop-hopper.)

Not forgetting, of course, that he was a good one for a naughty person to have on the books, so to speak. I knew chippies for if I wanted a door putting on, sparkies for electrical work, car thieves for getaway drivers, handy geezers for debt collecting and door work, DJs for clubbing etc., etc. And bent coppers for getting info from the police computer. A place for everyone and everyone in Peckham!

Another thing entered the equation when people became wary of telling him to 'fuck off' like they wanted to, because he'd made it so plain that he was a past master at fitting people up. As I found out personally.

My house started to get raided constantly. Door kicked in, kids dragged out of bed, furniture turned upside down. All the fucking time. Nothing was ever found. And I thought this campaign of harassment was spearheaded by Warnes – the old 'anonymous' tip-off to the station from a phone box routine. Even if the Old Bill do suspect that the calls are just malicious or part of a vendetta – which they must do after the twenty-seventh call! – they are still more than happy to follow them up if it's about someone like me. And if, after all the unsuccessful raids, something happens to be 'found' one time, in a shoe, then all the better.

After years of being 'Up for rent', as Warnes was, and people using him that way, if you then started to distance yourself from him, as I was, then he right got the hump.

You see that's what happens when you try and throw something away that's as bent as a boomerang; it just spins back and whacks you. Unless you duck. Soon enough I got given enough reasons to do more ducking than Daffy and Donald put together. But ducking ain't really my style, as you probably know. I'm more of a 'stand up and be counted' geezer.

Sometimes, though, if you do stand up to be counted, and you're the only one who does, you can end up a bit of a sitting duck, funnily enough. But you know what they say: 'A quack is the best form of defence.'

Fuck me, y'know I never got all this grief when I was a dustman.

So things were simmering along. Not yet boiling point, but I had a feeling it wouldn't be that long.

Sure enough . . .

4. BELMARSH

While I'm banged up in Belmarsh Prison pawing over the porn some more bad seeds are sown.

It's a known fact that in 1996 I was banged up on remand in the A-Cat Unit at Belmarsh on an importation charge, but even less of a known fact that I was found innocent of all charges brought against me. Not that many people, in the general public, would have known I was found innocent because the police slapped a press reporting ban on the trial. That gutted me 'cos it was the biggest win I'd had. Not that I jumped for joy when the verdict came through. Which, at the time, made me realise the truth in something that a wise lawyer once said to me – that guilty people who are found innocent punch the air, but innocent people found innocent just feel massive relief.

You're not even winning anything, are you? Y'know what I mean? You're just being given your life back instead of being robbed of it – which is a different thing than coming back from the dead.

However, it would have been a very, very unknown fact that I got 'not guilty' if I hadn't made sure every fucker knew when I wrote about it in *Stop the Ride I Want to Get Off* (now out in paperback, £6.99. Thank you!).

One thing you can't imagine unless you've been through it is how easy it is for the authorities to dirty your name, and how little they fucking care about helping to clean it once they've been proved wrong! I know 'cos I've been there. They really do play the old 'No smoke without fire' game for all it's worth. What they don't point out is who actually started the fucking fire in the first place. And it often isn't the geezer who ends up getting his fingers burned.

While I was on remand that time in Belmarsh a solicitor visited me. I thought it was still worth a crack at trying to use Warnes, so I gave my brief a letter to give to Jennifer, and in it I asked her to get in touch with Warnes to find out what the Old Bill thought they had on me. I was genuinely innocent of the charge, so I was even more interested to know what made them think they could rope me in on it.

Because the double A-Cat wing is all camera-ed up to high heaven – you can't even have a crap without it steaming up a camera lens somewhere – I knew that me passing the letter would be caught on film but correspondence between a defendant and his counsel is protected by law. Now this geezer weren't my usual brief but just a young fella sent down at the last minute. When he left the visiting room the guards demanded the letter from him and, not knowing any better, he handed it over! Cheers, mate.

In the end it didn't matter 'cos Warnes couldn't find out anything anyway, he said. Whether that was true or he just wanted me to go down, I don't know.

The police had already had suspicions about Warnes being bent and this letter of mine, which was passed on to them, dropped him right slap-bang in it. They couldn't use the letter later because they had obtained it unlawfully. But anyway, now they knew. They were onto him from that minute.

It must've caused a bit of a stir at police HQ because a couple of coppers came to question me in Belmarsh about the letter. I didn't say anything about it to them. That letter weren't meant for their eyes and Warnes hadn't done anything to me. Yet. That came later when he tried to set me up.

One of these coppers was a geezer from CID called Paul Barran. He was the one who originally said to me that it don't matter if I get a not guilty verdict, because they'll nick a year of my life off me anyway by putting me on remand until the trial. Nice fella.

Anyway, when they questioned me in Belmarsh he tried to convince me that one of my friends was responsible for me being roped in on the charge. I weren't buying it 'cos another police tactic is Divide And Conquer; cause chaos in the enemy camp and exploit it. They try to play one off against the other. He didn't name names, but what I picked up from what he was saying was that in another situation, like not having other people around, he would tell me who it was. That's how I read it anyway.

So that was that and they fucked off.

In prison you ain't really got anything but too much fucking time to think, so I mulled over what he'd said. And I decided if the little signals I'd picked up on were really there then Barran might be another bent copper on the make that I could use when I got out. So I made a note of that: 'Dear diary, things to do – (1) Pick up shopping, (2) Wash car, (3) Shag missus, (4) Try to cultivate another potentially bent British police officer.'

The Metropolitan Police didn't immediately nick Warnes, because the police now handle things in a different way. They handle it in a way that ain't widely known to the public, so do you think I should tell you? Oh, go on then, seeing as it's you.

What they do now is this – they let them run. Forget the arrest. Let them run. This means that they put a two-year observation on you and bug your house, your phone, your car; and they get enough evidence to crucify you in the first three or four months. But they let you run for another eighteen months in the hope they'll get all your mates as well.

And now the 'Profits Of Crime Act' makes it legal for them to seize houses and cars and whatever they think has been bought with illegally gotten gains. So they might carry on the surveillance for another year until they find the villa, the bank account, the houses, and your wife's jewellery.

So they let Warnes run.

Meanwhile I was still locked up in my cell in the high security unit inside Belmarsh prison. I was kept there for a year for something I knew I never did. Oh, how I laughed! Well I did actually, 'cos I knew I'd be going home. Unlike most of the geezers in there who were looking at fucking big stretches. It ain't the happiest atmosphere in there 'cos everyone is in line for big chunks of time. So because of that I took it upon myself to try and entertain everyone else in there, which I like to think I did.

It was in Belmarsh that I first became friends with Charles Bronson, or Britain's Most Dangerous Prisoner, as he's known. Charlie's the only one that's had more books out than me and all while he's still inside! That's a fucking big achievement if you ask me. At one time Charlie had a habit of taking hostages and doing rooftop protests. He's been on more roofs than Father Christmas.

On the outside, though, Austin Warnes decided to try to get his own back for lots of little things that had built up over the years.

As I've said, I used to go to lots of fetish dos and parties. I'm lucky 'cos I've got a beautiful missus in Jennifer who likes a bird as much as I do. Wicked that. So we'd both have a good time with each other and other birds. Warnes used to go out on the fetish scene, and he got into that in a big way. But in the wrong way. The fetish scene ain't actually about just anybody perving over anybody else. It's more controlled than people imagine. Women get much, much more hassle at a normal club than they ever would at a fetish one. So a dirty old man still stands out as a dirty old man even in those clubs. Warnes stood out like Hitler selling bacon butties at a Bar Mitzvah.

Later when I was doing interviews for *Stop the Ride . . .* a full-page feature appeared in the *Daily Sport* on 7 March 1999, and in parts of it I talk about the whole fetish thing. The headline said: 'I've seen cops at fetish parties. They recognise me, but it still doesn't stop them.' In their usual restrained manner the article said 'Gangland killer Dave Courtney has revealed how he regularly comes face-to-face with the law . . . at SWINGERS PARTIES! Dave sensationally says he often sees top-ranking cops joining in the wild ORGIES.'

Warnes always had the hots for Jen. So while I was in Belmarsh he called around to see Jen at the flat in Woolwich. He thought he was grassing me up by telling her loads of birds were writing to me in prison. What he didn't know was that through the page I write in Terry Turbo's magazine *The Scene*, Jennifer had actually arranged for me to judge a readers' birds competition! That's my Jen!

I got letters and photographs from women all over London. I could've put together my own 'A to Z of Filth'. I got Polaroids of everything from big black babes from Barking to skinny tarts from Tottenham, and more Arsenal than you could shake a stick at. By the way, whoever sent me that picture of a sheep wearing suspenders – thanks.

I ended up with so much wanking material that I got into a backlog situation, a build up of unwanked-over pictures, and had to start doing overtime. Nearly fucking killed me. Now Britain's part of Europe every man has to meet the minimum European quota of weekly wanks. Or they send the police around to jerk you off. Bit like they've been doing to me for the last ten years, as it happens.

You can imagine how pissed off Warnes was as his little bombshell blew up in his own face, when Jenny told him that she'd arranged for the letters to be sent to me! He thought he'd have to offer her a shoulder to cry on but the only shoulder he got was the cold one. Jen's about as far away from a pushover as you could get, mate.

He didn't let that stop him from trying though. Which was about par for the course. In the past we'd heard him say that he'd got geezers sent down so he could have a go at their wives. Like the time he said he was having an affair with this geezer's missus and got this bloke sent down in case he found out.

Anyway Jen told him to fuck off. She told him she would tell me, so he knew I would know.

So, after nearly a year on remand, I got my 'not guilty' verdict, left all the dirty pictures behind and walked out of Belmarsh with one arm bigger than the other. Me and Jen celebrated in a five-star hotel where I made a year of fantasies come true. And if you think it was easy getting a goat past reception, you're wrong.

Now this is where things started to get a bit strange with Warnes. After I came out I made sure that he was more at arm's length. And he kept his distance, which suited me down to the ground 'cos that's what I'd been after for some time. But I knew he was double-active with everyone else that I knew. Still, I knew exactly how he felt about me over things like stopping him coming to the shagging parties. I knew how much he hated me, but had to carry on smiling.

I'm much more forgiving with wankers than most geezers I know. I'll tolerate them for the good they can do. In the past I'd introduced Warnes to a lot of geezers so he could help them out of situations. I knew the kinds of things he could do as a corrupt copper – find out if someone's being watched or investigated, and what evidence there is against them; check car registration numbers and find out identities; get unlisted phone numbers; get evidence doctored in forensics; pull or 'lose' files and evidence; find out what some geezer's previous is; sign forms saying you'd produced your forms of ID; get in police computers for information; get bulletproof vests and other gear. Hundreds of things.

I never knew what he did for a lot of the people I put him in touch with because I didn't want to know. Sometimes it's better that way. He'd started out as an avenue for people to get information but he was an avenue that turned into a cul-de-sac.

Every villain would like their own bent copper, but not everyone can develop and cultivate the geezer into what they want him to be. Especially if you want to be the one in the driving seat. If you want it that way round and don't want to pay fortunes for it (which is my forte – getting stuff for nothing!), then it needs some skill to pull it off.

One score I had left to settle with Warnes was for when he tried to cause trouble between me and Jen while I was banged up. I couldn't immediately batter him for that because over the years he had deliberately let slip all the little tricks at his disposal to stitch people up. That was his little insurance policy against anyone having a go at him.

So I tried to keep Warnes at a distance but he'd pop up occasionally like the old bad penny, and that 'smile and be nice' thing that 99 per cent of the population do with policemen I did with him. He knew he deserved a smack and he knew why he wasn't getting one.

See, early on I'd cottoned on to his little game. I'm an analyser, I read people well. I saw why he gradually let it be known what the dirty tricks of his trade were. His motive was definitely to make me wary of him. Now in among all the people I know there are a few loose cannons, to say the least, and they are friends of mine only because I don't want them being enemies. So I bring the loose cannons into my fold but keep them distant.

I played that game with Warnes.

Still, I was trying to work out in my head why he'd chance his arm telling me about the cons and the stitching-people-up tricks. Then I realised that it must be something that he already knows works for him – something tried and tested. So the veiled threats that he'd made . . . he must have made good on them before. Then I knew he was letting me know what he could do if he had to. And I just thought, Woh! Fuck me.

Same thing as him thinking that I've given the nod for people to get topped; people not done in because I said so, but it was run past me first and I could've stopped it if I'd wanted to, but I didn't, so it happened. Knowing that must have frightened him a good bit as well.

I logged all this information, and life carried on.

I got pulled over one day driving down the road, something to do with it being illegal to break the sound barrier. When they ran my details they found that there was a warrant out for my arrest 'cos I hadn't paid some traffic fines months ago. So they took me in. When I was down the station who should walk in but Paul Barran, the copper that questioned me in Belmarsh about Warnes.

We had a chat and I arranged to meet him later to talk about what he'd mentioned before about him knowing someone trying to grass me up.

I told everyone in my circle what I was doing. If Warnes was approaching his sell-by date as a bent one, then maybe I could get Barran as a replacement.

He met me at Stringfellows, a favourite little haunt of mine, and fuck me if he didn't bring a one-legged copper with him! That's what it looked like anyway, with this other geezer hobbling beside him with a straight leg. I know the police had got rid of the 'minimum height' rule they used to have, but you would've thought two legs were pretty fucking essential.

Barran asked me what I wanted. I said if it was true that someone I knew had tried to set me up for the importation charge, then I'd give him ten grand for the name. He wouldn't tell me. Then he turned it around and asked me if I'd be his informant. And I said in no uncertain terms absolutely fucking no way.

After him and Peg Leg Pete left I wondered that if he'd got pissed off by me turning him down he might try and get me nicked for attempting to bribe him.

What I now know he did was go back to the office and make out a report that he'd gone to meet me; that he'd asked me to be a grass and I'd said no; and that I'd offered him ten grand to work for *me*. And I'm fucking glad he did make out an official report because it did prove two things: that I used coppers, or tried to, when I could find a bent one, and also that I refused all offers to turn grass.

(In his Witness Statement he says 'I made several attempts to cultivate Courtney and those attempts were all unsuccessful' and also 'Courtney offered £10,000 to myself if it could be ascertained who the male was whom he suspected had set him up').

His report cropped up later in the conspiracy trial where the Met tried to paint me as a grass, and I'm glad it did crop up 'cos, like I said, it proved I didn't grass and that given half a chance I'd buy a bent copper for information and use *them* as informants. But because Barran's report helped prove my case and show that I was using them rather than the other way around, guess what? Go on, guess . . . Yeah, during the court case *they wouldn't let the report be used as evidence*. That would've been like letting one of their own officers damage their case! Strange, almost like they were trying to smear my name, wouldn't you say?

Now we can all see that that ain't fair, but by now how many of us are expecting the law to be fair? Just the village idiot at the back, then.

And by the way, that night when Barran turned up to see me – I tape-recorded the whole fucking conversation. Now that's a blinding bit of proof on my side, is it not? So blinding that when the Old Bill searched my house they took the tape with them. Then when I asked for it back I was told that . . . wait for it . . . that they couldn't find it! Was I surprised? Ever so fucking slightly NOT. Me and my solicitor are still in contact with them even now, trying to find out what happened to it.

As I'm sat here now doing this book I'm picturing you people reading it. And I'm no fool, I know it's not just loads of naughty geezers that buy my books, in fact it's mostly straight-as-a-die people who've never had a run in with the law. So I keep throwing these examples at you – provable, documented examples – in the hope that at least a few of them stick and open your eyes to what does actually go on.

Another thing I'd like to say while I'm at it, 'cos I don't think I've made this point yet, is that even though I'm banging on about bent copper this and bent copper that, I do not believe for one second that they are all like that, or even the majority. There's an awful lot of good ones. But there's enough of the bent kind to make sure an awful lot of innocent people go to prison.

Speaking of which . . .

Months later I was sat at home at about three o'clock in the morning, doing my accounts and tax returns whilst eating muesli, drinking carrot juice and watching Jobfinder on the Teletext. Or was I sat feet up smoking a cigar, eating a bag of pick'n'mix, drinking brandy and watching *Gladiator*? (I bet you don't need 'phone a friend' on that one.)

Actually, what I was doing was having a game of pool with my good mate Big Marcus.

Now, you know what my house looks like, don't you? Well, for those of you who didn't see it in '*Hello!*' magazine, it's been turned into a white castle with lances and flags and renamed Camelot. That's after King Arthur's gaff, not the National Lottery company! Although, it does look a million dollars. One side of the house, all three floors high, has been painted with a mural of me as King Arthur on horseback with Jenny as my Guinevere. It was done by my mates Kevin and Steve and it looks the absolute fucking bollocks, mate. And it's floodlit at night. There's at least one car crash a week in the street outside, when someone catches sight of it for the first time.

Anyway, so there I am, 3 a.m., playing one-handed pool like the flash bastard I am, when we heard a noise outside and when I looked at the security camera monitor who the fuck should I see creeping about but Austin Warnes! Fucking hell, I couldn't believe it. I went to the window and before I could do anything he looked up, saw me and then suddenly started pointing at the wall and saying something.

I went outside, duster in one hand behind my back, and he started coming out with this crap about how he was just passing and stopped for a look at the mural! I said, 'What, at three in the fucking morning! What the fuck are you on?'

He carried on with this 'just having a look' crap. I let on that I believed him 'cos the minute I actually showed him what I thought of him then that fragile 'being nice on the surface' pretence would crumble; and then he'd be more dangerous. And I knew what he was fucking capable of.

I also made sure he knew I'd clocked him on the security cameras. He didn't know they'd been set up at the house. He tried to make a bit more chat, which wasn't easy in the circumstances – me in my boxer shorts and Marcus stood next to me looking like 'a one-man-monument to menace', as he was described by Piers in *Front* magazine. Warnes left. We made sure he drove right off down the road.

That was a bit of an eye-opener, let me tell you, finding him doing something so fucking obvious as creeping around my house. That's when I realised I really needed something that I'd been thinking about for a long time – some kind of insurance policy against him going out to set me up.

Little did I know then that the opportunity to get that insurance policy would happen soon. And that Warnes would actually be the one who'd give me the chance to get it.

5. KEEP YOUR FRIENDS CLOSE, YOUR ENEMIES CLOSER

Right here, right now, things start to get serious. Plots and plans are hatched behind my back.

OK, this is where things get interesting and a bit fucking heavy. So go to the bog now, put the kettle on (suits you), turn the cat off, put the TV out and settle down because it's gonna be a bumpy ride.

Three years after I came out of Belmarsh I started getting more publicity and appearing in papers and magazines. Even on television. What, shy little me? I'd always had bits of press on me, right back to the Chinese waiter swordfight incident in 1980. It blew up big in '95 after I organised the security on the day of Ronnie Kray's funeral. The police took one long hard look at the army of geezers that I produced that day, and then set about going after me with a vengeance. Even my legitimate businesses were closed down.

I used to have a pub called the Albion. The barman who ran it was called Sarski, from New Zealand. Warnes went in one day and offered Sarsh money if he'd put a package in my safe in the pub. Sarsh refused to do it and afterwards got really concerned about Warnes' motives – obviously this 'package' was something incriminating that Warnes wanted 'found' in my pub. Sarski got frightened of being roped into it all. He knew Warnes was bent Old Bill and dangerous with it.

He actually went right back to New fucking Zealand because of it! Get that. Which I don't blame him for one second, but before he left he of course told me what had happened. He also let me videotape him saying it all to camera so there was evidence of it happening. He said if I ever needed him to stand up and testify to it he'd come back to the UK.

Anyway, Ronnie dying and Reggie still being in the papers about his appeals for parole, seemed to kick-start a new interest in the British crime scene. Everyone seemed to be sick of American gangsters and interested in British villainy all of a sudden. Me, I've been doing press for fucking years, before it became fashionable, because I always knew the power of the media.

Most people that 'advised' me always said not to go public, run away from cameras, cover your face and all that. But I saw people do that and I thought it looked really bad. So you all know what I did when Roger Cook came banging on my door one morning with his *Cook Report* camera crew. I said, 'Hold on, Rog. Let me put my pants on, pick up my duster, plait my nose hair, and I'll meet you outside for a chat.' And I did. No one had done that before. I came out of the programme smelling of roses 'cos I gave myself the opportunity to justify the things Cook was accusing me of.

In fact a lot of what I said for that programme ended up on the cutting room floor 'cos if they'd shown too much it would have undermined their 'Let's-hiss-the-bad-guy' routine that they like to encourage. They don't like to admit that all baddies aren't always bad and the guys who are supposed to be the good guys aren't always good. They like to keep it black and white in certain sections of the media. You know, God forbid that they give you both sides of the story and you start thinking for yourself! People thinking about things too much would fuck it right up!

One thing I did learn is just how they can change your image by what they leave out. As much as by what they show. That's one thing you can't really know until you've someone come to interview you – and might have even been as sweet as pie about it – and then you pick up the paper the next day or turn on the TV and see how things have been edited to try and make you look a certain way.

Anyway, when the cameras turned on the 'British crime scene thing', I was fucking ready and waiting for it, matey. I've been on stage performing all my life, one way or another, even if it's just entertaining a houseful of mates. So the media thing didn't faze me one little bit.

Then after a TV discussion programme we'd both been on I started talking to this geezer (who later became a friend of mine) Piers Hernu. He was the editor of a new magazine that was starting called *Front*. They did an interview/feature on me in the first edition. In the same issue they did an article on my mate Ian Tucker who was on the run and one of Britain's Most Wanted at the time. What we did was take Tucker out into Leicester Square and got two coppers to pose for a picture beside us, with us wearing toy policemen's helmets, like we were tourists. Tucker's photo had been on *Crimewatch* and then there he is – appearing in this new magazine as bold as brass with two coppers who didn't recognise him! It was fucking wicked.

From then on I got my own page in *Front* to write about whatever the fuck I wanted. Touch! It was the absolute bollocks, mate. Much later it became invaluable as well, when the press started believing and printing some things about me that the police were telling them. *Front* gave me a platform to tell the truth about it all.

Then *Lock, Stock and Two Smoking Barrels* came out and other people started writing about how Vinnie Jones' character Big Chris was based on me. Public interest in me went mental. Most people were pleased for me, but some weren't. You can't please everyone and even if you could the effort would most probably give you a heart attack.

Jealousy is a powerful emotion though, ain't it? One of those people stood in the wings getting sick with jealousy was Austin Warnes. One thing he was good at was being a bent copper, and over the years it had earned him fortunes – more than I'd earned from my chosen field 'cos I didn't get into the drugs business like some.

Warnes was one of those who looked down on people he thought he earned more than, so when things started properly cooking for me on the media front – I started popping up on telly and in the papers – and you can imagine just how big a bee Warnes got in his bonnet over that. It was the size of a fucking eagle.

But, as always, nothing was said directly to me. We were still both OK with each other on the odd occasion that we met, but we had both figured out long ago that we hated each other's guts. As I've said before, keep your friends close and your enemies closer. So when I saw him I did the smiley bit and gave him no excuse to think he had a reason to stitch me up. He was earning too much money from people I knew and he was taking money off to help them out. We later found out that he hadn't touched his wages for years! Just banked it, never drew on it, and lived off the other money.

(On top of that, what he was also doing was going back to the station and writing down the names of these people he was helping out, but putting their names down as informers and sources! So he's winning both ways – looking like the blue-eyed boy back at the nick, and also taking pay-offs from the blokes he's helping.)

So when I got a call from him asking me if I'd help him out I was a bit fucking surprised and a lot fucking suspicious.

Now, before we go any further I'm gonna backtrack and tell you what had happened to lead to that phone call from Warnes. One important thing first – at the time I got the call I didn't know any of what I'm about to tell you, but I'm going to fill you in so you're not as confused as I fucking was! You are my readers and I do look after you! (Basically, it's about a husband and wife fighting for custody of their kid. The husband uses a bent copper, guess who, to set up his ex for drugs so he gets the kid.)

Here we go. Hold on tight, room for one more at the back . . .

A few months before all this, in March, a young lady called Kim James started divorce proceedings against her old man, Simon James. This Simon James geezer is sure that his wife will get custody of their son, Daniel, so he goes to see a private investigator called Jonathan Rees. They decide to put his missus under surveillance to get evidence on her about something they can use to blacken her name during the custody battle.

By the following Monday the surveillance don't reveal anything about the wife so there's nothing they can use. Friday of that week, the investigator, Rees, tells the husband that for a price some drugs can be planted on Kim James, the wife, and then when the gear is found she'll get sent down and lose the kid. OK? So far, so bad.

The week after, Rees contacts a mate of his called James Cook. Rees then tells Simon James he's got a 'planter' and they talk about paying him and paying whichever police officer they use.

Later Rees gets paid £5,000 by the husband – with more dough to come afterwards – to get the job done.

On the Saturday a few days later the whole plot comes together. The private investigator, Rees, gets in touch with his mate, James Cook, who's going to plant the gear. CIB3 officers already have Kim James' Fiat Punto under observation. Cook breaks into the car and plants the stuff.

A few days later the CIB3 boys secretly take her car in the early hours of the morning and search it. They find the gear, fifteen wraps of charlie, that Cook's planted there (he thought it was surveillance gear). So CIB3 replace it with seven wraps of baking powder and take her car back. Later there was a conversation recorded by surveillance tape of Warnes and Rees saying that the missing eight wraps must have been nicked by a bent copper! Warnes contacts another copper and tells him that that night would be a good time to search Kim James's car. He says his 'source' said so. The police know Warnes ain't got no source 'cos they've been listening in to him arrange things, but they play along.

That same day the Old Bill raid Kim James's flat and car and find the gear in the Fiat. She's fucking upset, obviously, and straight away realises it's her old man that's trying to set her up so he can get the kid. The police know she's right but don't tell her.

Next day Rees, the private eye, rings Cook and tells him it's all gone to plan.

The day after is also a day when plenty happens. Warnes fucks off on holiday. Obviously the fact that he's just set up an innocent woman to try to nick her kid off her ain't worrying him enough to stop him getting a suntan. Which can only mean he's done it so many times before that he don't give a fuck. As Warnes flies off into the sun Rees tells Simon James to inform Social Services about his wife Kim's arrest; and James agrees the rest of the money for the scam with Rees. Rees also makes up a false version of a conversation he'd had with Kim James: he puts down that she admitted to holding drugs in the house before.

The husband finds out that his wife ain't been charged and the police want to talk to him 'cos she's been telling them it's a set-up. So he gets hold of his son and runs off to Wales. Fuck me, like that kid hadn't suffered enough . . . and then he got took to bleedin' Wales!

The wife is saying it's a stitch-up but Warnes' boss DI Latham already knows that's true because of the surveillance on Warnes. Latham also knows that the police bugging of Warnes and his mates has shown there's *no* informant (they didn't need one as the info came from the husband); the police have them all bang to rights. So – and this is the big, big bit – the police already *know* about me using Warnes and realise that this is their big chance to drag me into this. So the day after the Old Bill found the husband and the kid in Wales Latham told Warnes to arrange a meeting with this 'informant' of his that was supposed to have given him the information. They knew full well that I was the only criminal that was making full use of Warnes as a bent officer, so they knew he would come to me for help. And they were right, he did.

OK. End Of Part One. Take a breather. Go have a piss and put the kettle back on. And to think that just a few years ago I was thinking of giving it all up to become a priest. (That noise you hear is the Catholic Church breathing a sigh of relief.)

Part Two. So now you know the basic ins and outs of the whole thing; the husband, the private investigator and Warnes all trying to stitch up the mother to get the kid. Hardly a Walt fucking Disney movie, is it? More like The Bad, The Bad and The Ugly.

And knowing what you now know, not just about this drugs plot thing, but the whole scenario of what's been going on for years with corrupt police in general and Warnes in particular, then you must be able to imagine the millions of different things zipping through my head when I got that call from Warnes asking me if I'd meet him. I thought it can't do any harm just to see the geezer and see what he has to say so I said yeah, I would meet him.

I mean what could possibly go wrong. Ha!

6. TIGHTROPE WALKING – BE COOL

Here I walk out on the tightrope but it ain't as dangerous as it looks 'cos I know what I've got beneath me.

Oh fucking hell, I haven't told you this bit yet! Listen to *this*.

I found out later that a unit had been set up to investigate me when the Old Bill got hold of my letter in Belmarsh and found out that Warnes was on the take and I was using him. So they set up an incident room down in Putney to sort out stuff on me. From the minute I left Belmarsh they were out to get me for corrupting a police officer. Not that he needed any help on that score. He did a very good job of corrupting himself, thank you very much!

This was the unit that bugged my house, set up cameras over the road, had the helicopter swoop overhead every so often (which is why I had my eyes and 'FUCK YOU' painted on the roof of my house). There was also a CIB3 unit investigating bent coppers in general, and Austin Warnes in particular.

Somewhere along the way those two units must have put two and two together. They were just about to arrest Warnes; they've got the whole scene – the estranged husband, the iffy private investigator that arranged the set up, the geezer who stuffed the stash under the car's dash, and the bent copper – all that, *the lot*: enough to wrap it all up, tie a bow on it and give it to the Crown Prosecution Service.

But then my name must have cropped up as someone that Warnes was working for. Cat among the pigeons time for the police. Fucking hell, I bet they fell on the floor when 'Dave Courtney' came up as a name. So they put a hold on arresting everyone involved in the other case. They must have thought, 'Hold it! If we delay wrapping up the case with Warnes we're working on maybe we can get him to get Courtney involved.'

Warnes had already fucked off on holiday so they rang him and told him that the wife, Kim James, was saying that the drugs discovery was a fit-up. They asked him what made him search the car in the first place, knowing he'd have to say someone had told him. So they asked him to prove that, knowing that he could only come and ask me for help.

Bingo! They get two for the price of one, or so they think.

Warnes gets back from holiday even more hot and bothered than when he was sun-bathing. He'd had a bit of time to think about things. He knows something's not right but he's not sure how much his neck's on the line; but he don't know that the police know all about the set-up he's been involved in.

Right, back to where we left off before – me getting the phone call. Remember I knew nothing about the custody battle for the kid, the husband contacting the PI, the whole drugs planting plot – I only learned that later

THE RIDE'S BACK ON

— but now you can see why he called me. The fact that his boss DI Latham had asked him to produce a source for the info tipped off Warnes that something might be wrong, 'cos coppers like him don't usually get asked to do that. So he got twitchy.

The police know he never had an informant telling him that Kim James was dealing drugs; (1) Because she wasn't, and (2) Because they had Warnes under surveillance and they had tapes of the other geezer ringing him and asking to set her up. But they also know by now about his moody informant scam and my name being connected to it, so they're hoping to rope me in at the end as a bonus.

Warnes realises he's got to drag someone in to help get him off the hook. That's when he called me. I agreed to meet him to see what it was all about. He doesn't know at this point that CIB3 were gonna nick him anyway, whatever, 'cos they already had him on tape. He just thinks he's got the 24 hours they've given him to try and come up with an explanation. He don't know that they've delayed his arrest just so they can use him to try to fuck me over. And I didn't know they were doing that either.

So on the day I went up to Plumstead Common at the top of my road and met him. He seemed a bit panicky.

His pitch to me was this: he thought he was under suspicion for knowing me and he needed an excuse for being seen with me while he'd been helping out me and my mates.

He made it sound like he was a fucking charity, which I thought was bang out of order and he needed reminding of something. 'You seem to forget the fortunes you've made along the way, and all the other fucking perks as well.'

He kept going on about how he was in trouble upstairs with his bosses, but that's all he said it was, a bit of bother that could be sorted out.

I started to think that maybe they had just found out about the moody informant scam and that he'd been using some of my people to do it. It was feasible that he'd just got into trouble for being seen with me or having my number in his phone book, or whatever.

I thought, I don't really want to get involved in this and he could see that and he got all nervous and trembling. Him being like that made me the opposite. He looked vulnerable and anyone vulnerable makes mistakes. Then you can find their weakness and exploit it.

Anyway, he kept banging on about it and also throwing in other things along the way. I thought, wait a minute, this is a threat. What he's saying here is that there will be repercussions if I don't help him out. Don't forget that I know about all his fitting-up techniques and planting evidence tricks: and he knows that I know 'cos that's exactly why he used to tell people, so it was always there in the background. And me being in the press a lot had got his goat as well.

It was one of them moments when things suddenly come together. Things that might have been brewing for years. Like the fact that he'd been bent for years, so that meant there was always a chance he'd get caught. And I'd been using him as a bent copper for years so the longer that went on there was a chance I'd get pulled for that. Well, this was that moment.

He went into more detail and said that recently he'd made up some information that he pretended he'd got from a source about two birds who were dealing drugs in a club somewhere. He thought that's what had made his boss suspicious, so he just needed me to confirm it. Once that was done, he said, he'd be in the clear.

I was stalling him a bit as I was talking to him, thinking to myself, Fucking hell! He's putting me in a proper position here. If he is in a bit of bother and this would mend it then . . . why not – it would mean he was still free for me to make use of. But if he gets done for it he might try and take me and some of my mates down with him 'cos it's his association with us that's landed him in trouble; and knowing what he can do maybe it's better if I do help him get out of it.

On top of all that was the other thing to consider – that this was all a big fucking pack of lies and he was trying to set me up. That wouldn't exactly have been out of character for him.

So you can see that there was a million things to think of, and weigh up, and figure out. One thing I was thinking was I wished I wasn't bald then I could use the excuse that I had to stay in to wash my fucking hair!

Another thing. Apart from the fact that if I helped him it would keep him on the scene for future use, I thought there must be something else, something more that I could get out of this . . . and then it hit me! I had one of those lightbulb moments. Y'know, like in a cartoon where they get an idea and – pop! – a lightbulb appears. Well let me tell you, I got a whole fucking football stadium floodlight popping up above my head, mate. Lordy, I had seen the light! I suddenly realised how I could kill all birds with one big stone: (1) Help mend this thing for him and keep him active and useful; (2) Make a safety net for myself in case it all went belly up; (3) Take away this little power thing he thought he had over people with his sly threats of fitting people up; and (4) Get something on Warnes to use on him and keep him in line. I could mend all that in one fell swoop. But – and it is a big but – it meant me doing some proper high wire tightrope walking.

Now you know me, I fucking love a challenge, I do. Every man should. What a lot of people don't realise about me, though, is this. That more often than they know, when they see me do certain things which to them look risky – have a row, defend myself in court, go up against the police, go public with things that I've done, etc. – well more often than not it ain't actually as risky as it looks, because I have got one thing on my side. A SAFETY NET.

A bloke can tightrope-walk a hundred feet in the air dressed as a Mars Bar over a pit of bulimic crocodiles ready for a binge and he'll look really brave. But if he knows there's a safety net below him he can do backflips all fucking day long without giving a toss. And he'll probably land every one of them for the same reason.

So, I said to Warnes that I'd do it but only under one condition. That, just in case it all went belly up, he would let me tape record him admitting that I was only doing this to mend his little problem with his boss, that I didn't know anything about whatever the fuck else this might be about, and that I am not one of his informers. I thought that just about covered everything. (I stopped short of asking him to say that I wasn't driving Diana and Dodi's Mercedes and that the Millennium Dome weren't my idea!)

I was figuring that if he agrees to be taped then I've got evidence of my own which stops him from turning around later on and trying to threaten me. I could produce my tape of him admitting the truth. 'Safety net', remember? Not only that but – and this is the absolute BEST bit – once I've got a tape of Warnes admitting that he's fucked up a police investigation, I can use *that* against him! That then becomes my insurance policy against Warnes trying to stitch up me or any of my mates; and I could use it to get him to help us out in future.

All this is coming to me and running through my head in a few seconds while he's still blabbing on about the rest of it. I'm sat there thinking, Risk, Reward and Safety Net: (1) What am I risking? (2) What will I gain? (3) How do I safety net the whole fucking thing?

I figured that taping him admitting the truth would cover it all. It got me the rewards and safety-netted the risk.

The only thing that would blow it out the water is if he refused to do the tape. So I had to be fucking adamant about it. So I told him I'd do it but only if I could record him saying I was making it all up to try to mend his little 'boss' problem. He agreed. Which, to be honest, fucking surprised me.

That got the old brain cogs whizzing double-speed, thinking about what it might mean, given that he's agreed to do it! Like, either he's only agreed to let me safeguard the whole thing because he is actually setting me up; or that he genuinely is in trouble and isn't looking beyond solving his immediate problem.

I said I'd have to think about it and told him to wait there until I called him.

On the way back down to my house I had another lightbulb moment and saw why he'd said yes to it. I could see it was because he was so focused on fixing the immediate problem of convincing his boss he had a source, he didn't really look beyond that. Me giving him a quick fix was too tempting for him to say no to. He wasn't looking beyond that to how I might use the tape afterwards.

I call it my 'Ball Over The Pocket' theory. I've described this kind of thing before in the chapter 'Going Dutch With Dougie' in *Stop the Ride . . .*, when this deal I was involved with in Holland went wrong and a geezer shot my partner dead. Really he should have shot me first, but Dougie was nearer and took one in the chest. That gave me the chance I needed and I shot this Dutch fucker in the head. However, him giving in to the temptation of the 'easier' shot at Dougie saved my life.

So here's the 'ball over the pocket' theory. In a game of pool you might have a couple of balls over the pockets and you know you should leave them there as blockers, but sometimes you wanna hear that ker-plonk! potting noise too much. So you pot them. That makes you feel good. Two less to pot. Then you miss the next shot, stand back, see that he's got six pockets to shoot at instead of four, and it causes you to lose. Short-term fix, long-term fuckover!

Well Warnes had his 'ball over the pocket moment'. I offered it to him to see if he'd take it. And he did. Ker-fucking-plonk, mate! I had both of his balls over the pocket!

See, I was standing back and looking at the big picture. He was up close, seeing a bit of it. Having said that, there was all the stuff in the background that at this time I didn't know about – the whole drugs-planting plot that he'd been involved in which even Warnes wasn't sure that his boss knew about. But, in case they did know, Warnes thought he was tricking me into helping him get out of it. Which in a way he was. He was tricking me into that. Still, because CIB3 had had him under surveillance they knew I weren't involved. Didn't stop them from letting Warnes rope me in on it though, did it?

FUCK ME! Ain't this getting complicated!? Oh what a tangled web we weave, in-fucking-deed! See, I'm even quoting Shakespeare now I'm an author. I do hope you're all keeping up at the back there, 'cos I'll be asking questions later and any stragglers over sixteen and in the netball team are gonna get spanked.

Seriously, though, how do you think I felt being in the middle of all this? You've got time to read it, re-read it, and think about all the possibilities. I had to fucking live it – and come up with explanations about what I thought was happening and why it was happening all in the space of a few minutes.

I'll tell you something now, though. When this was going on, and Warnes agreed to let me tape him, I couldn't help but think, YES! What a fucking good chapter this'll make for the next book!

What I didn't know then was that it would make a book on its own.

7. THE MEET

Ever been to Plumstead Common? You ain't missing much. Although, one day up there you did . . .

Now I know I was gonna be sailing close to the wind doing what I was gonna do but I couldn't see how I could lose, y'know what I mean? I've had to tell you to what extremes Warnes would go to understand why I did what I was about to do. Yeah, I knew it had risks of being misread – just like all those years ago, letting him use my name as one of his fake 'informants' so he could get access to police information – but if it came off, if it worked (like I thought it would), then what a fucking good one to win!

So I went back down home before I went back to meet him and ran the whole plan past Jennifer and Brendan. There were some other people at the house but Jen and Bren heard the details and it was them that I wanted to go over it. As I later said to the police, everyone who knows me knows at least two things about me – I am no grass and I am no fool; and if I was guilty of what I was later accused of I'd have to be both those things. 'Cos if you were genuinely grassing someone up – especially a nasty little one like fitting-up a mother for drugs to get her kid – then I am fucking 100 per cent positive you would not do it at the top of the road where you lived, and also take your missus and mate along to witness the proud event! Common sense should kick in here big-time.

Anyway, I didn't think I'd missed anything, but you can't be too sure. Jennifer, as I've said before, is 51 per cent of me. My arms and legs. Brendan has a genius brain of his own and would see all the angles. He's also one of the mates that I've used Warnes to help over the years.

We went through exactly what I could get out of this. If it all went to plan then I'd get to tape him admitting I weren't involved, and also that he was screwing up a police investigation. I hadn't really made my mind up what I was going to do with the tape afterwards; just keep him in his place with it or use it like the ace up the sleeve to get me out of trouble in future. Whatever, I just knew I'd have him on his back foot. And with Jennifer and Brendan as witnesses.

We went over it to check it through. And, y'know, to be honest . . . I couldn't resist it. I just could not fucking resist trying it! Because he'd already agreed to be taped. I thought, if he is genuinely in trouble then he's just thinking about healing that. He ain't actually thinking beyond getting over the first hurdle.

I thought we may as well do this in style. So we went out and caught a No 67 bus. Oh shut up! Silly bollocks. I threw my leg over the Harley, didn't I? Jen threw her legs round ME, and we set off for Plumstead Common with Brendan following on. We rode up there like the three musketeers – apart from the fact that none of us were French, one of us was a woman, we didn't have any swords, and everything else about us was wrong.

So . . . not like the three musketeers AT ALL, in fact. But we felt like them! Fuck me, give me a bit of slack, I'm trying to paint a picture here!

Brendan dropped back and positioned himself where he could see from the car, and me and Jen went into the park and saw Warnes sat on the bench.

He looked as twitchy as fuck, and trying to figure out exactly what he was twitchy about was one of the problems. Anyway, he laid out what the problem was again – trouble with his boss 'cos he had to produce a name for someone who'd given him some bullshit information, some made-up stuff that he'd been doing the old pretend informant scam with, blah-blah-blah. My brain's going ten to the dozen, replaying everything again. Thinking, OK, if he's trying to set me up then the tape I'm about to make of him will protect me from that one; and if he is properly in bother about this then I'll do this little favour for him, and then have the tape on him for future use. Bingo. Win-Win situation.

He said he needed some confirmation of these birds that'd supposedly been dealing. We agreed that I'd make up some stuff for the record to make it look convincing. He threw in a few bits and I made some bits up, but it was crap. The stuff I was throwing in was anyway (later on I found out his stuff weren't). I got the tape recorder out and recorded him saying that I was just pretending to be his source and that I wasn't really involved. Jen took a photo of us, showing the tape recorder. After it had been done and I saw the relief in his face that's when I really thought he was in some bother.

At one point he got a bit cocky and I had to give him a bit of a talking to. He said something that was very carefully worded so I could take it either way – as a threat or as a joke. Something like, 'This could go well for you, or it could not . . .', that kinda phrase.

I pulled him up on that pretty fucking sharpish and made it plain I was in the driving seat now. I wanted to stamp my authority on it from that second I had the tape in my hand, because I knew then that he couldn't screw me (if only I'd known then that it was the Met trying to screw me).

Because he was panicking his mouth was going into gear before his head. I thought I am definitely the one behind the wheel now. (What we didn't know then was that we weren't the only ones on the common. Behind some big recycling bins on the edge of the common were some officers from CIB3 videoing the meet.)

OK, bit of a change of gear here. Put on your Star Wars clobber because we're going to do a little time travelling. We're going to do a flash-forward. You've seen flashbacks in films; well I've just invented the flash-forward. It'll catch on, don't you worry. Steven Spielberg will be doing it next year.

I really should wait but I just can't resist telling you this right now. Sorry. But when this whole time-bomb blew up big style a few months later on down the line, the police took a statement off Warnes. It said:

Page 11: Austin Warnes statement

Mr Warnes: Okay my main motive for it (*setting up the wife*) would have been the reward but I never received it and partially because of all the problems around it afterwards DAVE COURTNEY never had anything to do with it in relation to the initial facilitating. He was never consulted, I never phoned him, I never said 'Dave, will you help me out on this? (*the stitch-up*) Well you know about it so you can lie later.' I never said that to him. Dave had absolutely no involvement whatsoever. When DAVID COURTNEY did become involved was when my DI needed to see the source of my information. Then I had to approach Dave and say 'would you do this for me?' and he declined. He wouldn't do it. I then had to try and persuade him because I realised I was in a hole and a bit of a mess. I then had to try and persuade him to help me, which wasn't easy. I didn't say 'Dave, you do this for me and I will protect you from everything.' I never said I'll give you money. He didn't offer me any favours. He never put me on the spot by saying, 'You're gonna owe me big time.' I don't know why he eventually agreed to do it. I think probably 'cos something to do with an audio tape you're gonna play me later had something to do with swaying him into helping.

And that's straight from the police horse's mouth. You bet your little cotton fucking socks it was 'something to do with an audio tape'. I just wish I could've put it out on CD, DVD and widescreen video!

Warnes was deliberately playing it a bit dumb there when he said he don't know why I eventually agreed to do it. By that time he must've knew I did it so I had the audio tape over him, but he can't exactly say that without looking like a prick.

Anyway, I just had to get that bit out. I ain't really spoiled the story 'cos you knew that anyway. There is still a twist in the tale coming up – I grow a beard, wear false goofy teeth, talk like a cunt, and appear on *Stars In Their Eyes* saying, 'Tonight, Matthew. I'm going to be . . . you.'

So, after the meet I knew I had taped evidence, photographic evidence and two witnesses. Despite what he later said in that statement he knew he was gonna owe me because I'd got him out of trouble, so I had that on him. The bottom line was this: if I'd asked him to do anything he'd have had to do it and – important one this – it took the threat out of him for fitting me up with some dodgy charge in future. I had him by the bollocks. Result.

Despite the safety net I'd made I was still dicing with something big. I knew that. All you've got in the criminal world is your reputation. Your life depends on your handshake and what people think of you. So taking a risk with that meant I made fucking sure I had proof that I was using him and not the other way round.

Funny thing is that we both sort of tricked each other into getting what we wanted. I got what I wanted from him by helping him with what I thought was his little bit of trouble. And he got something that he thought he could use as an alibi for trying to stitch up Kim James on the drugs charge.

Anyway, the follow-up to this was that I had to play this little act out for Warnes' boss Latham as well, just to try to make it look convincing. We met at a pub called the Black Prince and for some reason I didn't really feel right. I still wasn't 100 per cent sure that Warnes wasn't trying to trick me and stitch me up somehow, so I had to safeguard myself as to what he might be up to.

So we met in a car at Crayford golf course and I gave Warnes' boss, this geezer DC Latham, this made up information. I named a club that don't even exist, that I couldn't have worked at 'cos it's never been there. To be honest, I couldn't properly remember what lies we'd agreed I should tell, so I just made up some more! I made the end of this story as not right as I thought the fucking beginning was. I remember thinking I might be fucking it up by coming out with the wrong lies.

Then Latham started going on about some on-going case, and it might go to court – and I was thinking What?! Maybe there is more to this. Then I saw some bikes go past and I said, 'I'm not a fool. That looks like a copper.' And Warnes went, 'It is, it's SO19.'

I was thinking, Fuck – is even Latham on the level here, or is it all part of some whole plot to get me seen to be doing this? But I kept thinking, I've got the tape of him, I've got the photo of him, I've got the witnesses to prove it.

I left thinking I'd done the bit for Warnes, and we all got back down home and me and Jen and Brendan listened to the tape and were well chuffed with it. I might've been out on the tightrope but I had the net below me. So, like the flash bastard I am, I started doing a bit of juggling as well. Little did I know that now that they had got all the 'evidence' they wanted, the police were doing a bit of juggling of their own.

Only thing to do now was wait and see if any balls were dropped.

8. A VERY NAUGHTY NICKING

This chapter I get tailed, I travel the country and I get nicked half-naked (or half-cocked). Back in London – back in the cells.

Months went by and nothing more happened on the old bent copper front. I didn't see hide nor hair of Warnes. I thought, well maybe it was all true then, and that bit of bother he had with his boss had been smoothed out. Good. But I still had the tape I made of him for future protection against a fit-up.

Or maybe the silence was just the quiet before the storm and black clouds were gathering on the horizon.

See how poetic I've got since I've become an author. My autobiography, *Stop the Ride I Want to Get Off*, was published by Virgin. Up until then I'd never even met a virgin, let alone worked for one. The book really kicked off big-time. We even got 'Book of the Week' in the *Mail on Sunday*, and without sending the boys round! Wicked.

We had a top book launch party at my mate George's place the Tardis Studios. All the chaps turned up to show their support. I didn't even know they wore one.

All the time, though, when these things are happening I'm aware of the fact that my past is either frightening people or prejudicing people against me, or threatening to creep up and bite me on the bum, so to speak. I ain't saying that I'd change a thing about what I've done or for one second try to hide it. That much is obvious by the fact that I've written about it and gone public. Doing that was good for me, in many ways, but it also got up the nose of the police in a big, big way, mate, believe me.

Like when I did the security for Ronnie Kray's funeral in '95. The Old Bill saw me hitting the streets of London with hundreds of six-foot-wide naughty geezers and viewed it as an act of defiance. They then set about systematically undermining and destroying my legitimate businesses. But no use crying over spilt blood.

So a few years later when the papers were writing about me as one of the inspirations for Big Chris in *Lock, Stock . . .*, *Front* magazine had me writing for them every month and then *Stop the Ride . . .* came out and put me back in the news again . . . do you think the London Metropolitan Police Force were queuing up to slap me on the back, or stab me in it?

No wonder they were beavering away behind the scenes – and all during these quiet months when I was wondering if fuck-all was happening – to try and hook me and fuck me over by dragging me into the case they'd already built up against one of their own corrupt police officers. The police know the power of the media when they use it themselves in *Crimewatch* and *Crimestoppers* and stuff like that. They know it works or they wouldn't do it. So there must have been a crop of very high-ranking Met officers looking at me with mounting fucking horror as they thought I was undermining their whole 'crime doesn't pay' routine.

In the old Russia or East Germany the KGB or the Stazi would have shot me by now. But that don't happen over here . . . does it? (More on that later.)

So, being the windswept and interesting author that I am, I found that I had a *Stop the Ride I Want to Get Off* book-signing session to go to up in Manchester. 'Have Pen Will Travel', that's my motto, mate. Virgin, kindly laid on some transport for me. I could choose between one of their trains or Richard Branson's balloon.

So I got in a car and drove up.

Only kidding, chaps. I didn't drive at all. My pal Ebo did. I was in the back with my Jen. Little did I know then that we had someone behind us. Usually the only thing behind me is exhaust smoke and other drivers going, 'Fuck me! See the speed of that Rolls?!' But this time we had a little uninvited guest.

Anyway, we belted up the M1. I think the geezer who had the car before must've chopped up the odd line of charlie in the fuel tank and got the engine addicted 'cos it just naturally went towards the white lines. Fucking funny, but a bastard when you try and take a turn-off and you've got to fight the wheel.

While I was on the way to Manchester, Virgin and *Front* magazine, both got calls from someone who didn't want to be named. Eoin McSorely took the call at *Front*. The bloke on the phone said, 'I am a serving police officer, you must warn Mr Courtney that they are out to get him one way or another.' Now that gobsmacked me when I heard about it 'cos even though I've always got on well with the bobby on the beat, for one of their own to ring *Virgin* and *Front* and try to warn me meant that they must know their bosses have it in for me big-time.

But I was heading for Manchester with nothing more on my mind than having a fucking good time, seeing loads of mates, selling loads of books, and moving a few copies of *Stop The Ride* . . . around the Waterstones shop just to surprise a few people – I thought we'd put one in the 'Cookery' section (just to fuck up the head of a Delia Smith fan), one in 'Religious Studies' (just to make a Christian go, 'Jesus!'), one amongst the sex manuals (showing that practice makes perfect!) and one smack-bang in the middle of the Winnie the Pooh books. Actually, not many people know this but that Pooh Bear was a bit of a face. Yeah, he had the old honey market sewn right up, mate.

Manchester's a cracking little city though, ain't it? I mean now they've got electricity. And you always get the sexiest sheep in the north. Weird that. And don't you love it when you visit a new place and get trapped on their one-way system? Oh, how we laughed! By the time we got off it I had to re-shave my fucking head.

We walked into this massive Waterstones bookshop where I was doing the signing, and giving a talk as well. A proper value for money night, I'd say. Fuck me this place was big. Four floors of books. I didn't realise I had so much catching up to do. I've actually written more books than I've read – what's that about?

Before the event the Waterstones' people got me in a back room. I thought, they're ganging up on me to throw down a challenge – bookmarks at twenty paces. But they just wanted me to sign a mountain of *Stop the Ride* . . .' My pleasure. Then some geezer from the *Big Issue* came to interview me. Smartest looking homeless fucker I've ever seen in my life. Even his dreads were combed.

By the evening there was loads of people there and all my Manchester mates like Stuart, Big John, Isaacs, Kevin Suma, came along, and Scousers Robbie, John and the Liverpool boys had come across to see me. Before the signing session I had an 'Audience With . . .' for an hour with a question and answer session afterwards. You know the kind of thing: Audience – 'What are you going to do next?' Me – 'A post office!' Someone asked how I'd react at my daughter bringing her first boyfriend home. I said I'd be fucking astonished 'cos she's only two.

I knew there'd be some undercover Old Bill sat in there pretending to be punters. What the fuck do they think I'm gonna say in public that they don't already know I can't imagine. It must be one of the best surveillance gigs going, though, 'cos I tend to throw in more jokes than most. I am only here to please.

John, being a tuned-in Scouser, can sniff Old Bill out like a proper bloodhound, mate. After the talk he pointed out the people he thought were iffy. I had to say, 'No, John. That one's my MUM.'

Anyway, a good crime book was had by all and me and Jen jumped back in the car, with Ebo at the wheel, and we headed off to Liverpool with John, Robbie and the boys leading the way. We felt a little club-inspired *Raving Lunacy* (Virgin, 16.99) coming on. Yer dancin'? Yer askin'? . . .

We went club hopping around Liverpool, including John's new table dancing club, where we met the talented 'Going off Big Time' crew.

After that we headed off down the M6 back to London. We'd only just got on the motorway and me and Jen were having a back-seat bonk, as it happens, when all these cars pulled alongside and blokes started screaming at us to pull over. I thought, bit strong for autograph hunters this innit? Or maybe it was my own gang of stalkers on a club outing. Fuck me, synchronised stalking. Then a helicopter appeared and hit us with a massive light, it was like an alien landing.

(Actually, we knew they were plain clothes Old Bill. Who else shops at Man, at C&A and Ratners?)

Ebo pulled onto the hard shoulder. When I bent down to tug my pants on, the coppers outside, pointing guns at me, all went fucking mental. I think to them it looked like I was going down for a weapon, but that definitely ain't what I came back up with in my hand (although in my time I have used it as a tool).

Then I thought, Oh fuck this! And got out the car with my pants still down. I said, 'As you can see officer, all I've got "on" is a "hard"!' They just looked at me, gob-smacked. Then one of them launched into the old 'Anything you say will be taken down' routine, to which I couldn't even reply 'pants' 'cos they already were taken down. Can't win 'em all.

I did recognise one of the Old Bill from the book signing. He'd said he wanted one signed to this old geezer called Bill who drank in his pub. So I'd signed the book, like he'd asked, 'To my favourite old Bill, Dave Courtney'. And now this young copper was stood in front of me, grinning because he knew he'd got me to sign a copy of '*Stop the Ride . . .*' to my favourite Old Bill. I could see he was still buzzing off it – and to be fair I had to take my hat off to him 'cos it's the kind of trick I'd pull. So I just smiled back and gave him his little moment. Cunt.

They said they were arresting me for conspiracy to pervert the course of justice. They read me my rights, including the new bit they've added about 'Anything you fail to say now which will be later used in your defence' which is absolute bollocks and don't let them kid you with it. Since when has not saying anything been an admission of guilt? Well, since they made it so.

What I did say, though, and I say this all the time as a joke (I have done for ages) was, 'I blame the parents!' I always say that when I'm nicked or at moments when things go wrong, and it usually raises a smile. But what I didn't know at this stage was that because of what this case was about – the husband trying to get custody of the kid – it made it look like I was making a comment about the whole thing!

But the coppers nicking me don't know that I don't know. They didn't say what they were nicking me for apart from perverting the course of justice, no more details than that. I didn't even know what it was all about yet. What I did know was that those storm clouds had finally landed.

Jennifer tried to find out where I was being taken but they said she had to keep away from me 'cos I was now incommunicado (which is a lie, I was in Armani). She dealt with that one straightaway. She said, 'Hold it! I don't even know that you're police! You're all in plain clothes, pulled up the side of the car with guns, whip Dave off the streets, chuck him in a van and you ain't telling me where he's going?!'

They said, 'We'll let you know. Don't ring anybody.' She said, 'How the fuck can I not tell anyone what's happened! – a load of blokes drag my geezer out a car and I'm not allowed to tell anyone? I'm gonna ring everyone, mate. Trust me!' So they let her speak to me and I said everything would be OK.

'Babe, I'll be home,' I said. We got this pact me and Jen that if I say not to worry then she knows not to.

They took me back to Manchester first for a couple of hours, fuck knows why. Like I hadn't seen enough of their one-way system. I think it was just to show me off to the Manchester police, to be honest. Probably to make up for the last time I was nicked up north, about a year ago in Liverpool. For those of you who got my last masterpiece *Raving Lunacy* (Virgin, all good bookshops) you'll know the story already, but for those of you not up to speed (or up on it) I'll give you a run down.

I was in Liverpool filming a programme called *Jerry Sadowitz Versus The People* for Channel 5. Jerry's show can get a bit lively at the best of times. Well when the host is a big-nosed Glaswegian comedian who calls his audience 'thieving Scouse cunts!' then you've got to expect a bit of agg.

Any road, I was Jerry's on-stage minder and things were going well until I had to eject one of the audience who got on stage and started slagging me off. *Me!* I hadn't even said anything to him. The foul-mouthed Scottish-Jew in the top hat – that's Jerry – called him a 'cunt' but this punter told ME to fuck off. So I threw him through the scenery and, as it happens, threw myself through as well for good measure. I, of course, landed on top. Best bit was that it was all caught on camera so it made a wicked programme when it came out. (I'd love to have seen the late night, hard-of-hearing version of the programme, y'know the one where they have that bird in the corner doing sign language. Talk about wrist sprain trying to keep up. And how do you hand-sign 'Fuck off you cunt!'?)

The geezer I chucked off stage ran out of the studio and went off to the local nick and reported me for assault. The Liverpool police turned up, nicked me (again all on camera) for ABH and took me off. They were proper buzzing 'cos they thought they had me bang to rights and started ringing up police forces in other areas fucking bragging! I swear. They even rang the Met in London. I took it as the compliment I'm sure they didn't intend it to be.

But I got out of it in a way I won't tell you here – buy the other book, ha – and that pissed them off something chronic, let me tell you. They thought they'd had one over on all the other forces, especially Manchester and London, by nicking me, but with one mighty bound Courtney was free!

Anyway, that was then. Back to what was happening now. I thought, well I'd set off back to London in a Merc with on-tap naughtiness in the back with Jen only to end up in the back of a fucking police van with half a dozen coppers as company. I think that's what they call getting the shit end of the stick, and what George Michael calls a good night out.

But that's got to be one of the naughtiest little nicks I've had, ain't it? I mean in mid-shag. 'Did you take down Mr Courtney's particulars, officer?' 'No, Sarge. His wife had already beaten me to it.' Ha-ha.

I was still proper buzzing from my book signing, 'cos it was all new to me then and that was one of the biggest ones I'd done. So I was just cracking jokes all the way back home.

What I did learn, though, which was really funny, was that they had been coming to arrest me in London just as I left to go to Manchester, so they decided to follow instead, thinking something was going on! Something *was* going on, but they didn't know it was just a book signing! Then I'd jumped back in the Merc and shot off to Liverpool, so they tailed us there as well. They must've been on the old radios going, 'He's going to meet the Liverpool connection, Sarge!' Fuck me, we only wanted to get connected to the dance floor and the bar. Which we most certainly fucking did! I just love the idea of some undercover Old Bill trying to 'blend in' in some of the clubs we go to and look inconspicuous. It just ain't gonna happen, y'know what I mean? Some geezer stood there dancing like your dad.

I weren't worrying 'cos I didn't actually know what this 'conspiracy' charge was. I was just thinking that Austin Warnes had been caught out with whatever trouble he looked like he was in when he met me. I knew something must've been thrown out to get me, otherwise they wouldn't have had me off the street like that. I also knew that meant either Warnes or the Met had taken this chance to properly fuck me.

Long-term, once you've been in prison looking at a twenty stretch for something you've never done, like I was in Belmarsh in '96, you have to have faith in yourself and I knew I'd got a safety net. You've done the hard bit; the rest of it should follow. Already I was thinking thank Christ I made that tape recording.

When we got into London they took me to a nick just round the corner from the *Front* offices, funnily enough, in Albany Road. The whole of this police station was completely deserted. It had been re-opened by CIB3 to interview me and Warnes.

Within a few hours I'd gone from celebrating the success of my book with my mates and missus to being banged up and under guard back in London. Almost spoiled my day!

9. HANGMAN

The police move in: slippy bastards! But sometimes you just have to give 'em enough rope . . . and hope.

Funny how other things that happen can affect your life. Even when you don't know they're happening. Like me, for instance, when I was up in Manchester and Liverpool book signing and clubbing, not knowing that the Old Bill were planning on doing a swoop at exactly the same time on everyone they thought was involved in the conspiracy plot. Me included.

Apparently everyone suspected had been arrested at the same time. And every one of them I didn't know, of course (apart from Warnes), because I'd never even met them: Simon James, the husband; Rees, the private investigator, and Cook, the PI's colleague

Another thing I didn't know was that the following morning and afternoon after my arrest – when I was sat in a cell polishing my head – Austin Warnes was being interviewed by two coppers. What he said during these interviews I didn't find out till later (fuck me, typical, you're always the last to know!), but I'm gonna give you the benefit of knowing it all, as it happened. This stuff all comes from the official police interviews with Warnes done by a DS Laverick and a DC Lawrence.

First, he begins by sticking to his lies and saying that I gave him the info about the gear in the car, that I was his informant, and that he acted professionally on the information he got. Now, that is all to be expected 'cos at this early stage he don't know that the police know that what he's saying is all absolute bollocks – he still thinks he has a chance of talking his way out of it by blaming me. So he sticks to his lying guns. Put yourself in his position, he's not gonna own up to working for me for fifteen years!

He also denies that his relationship with me was corrupt – meaning he was actually giving me information from police files. Which again, at this early stage, he ain't gonna drop himself in it even more by admitting to that. He might be an idiot but he ain't a complete idiot.

So at this point in the interview DS Laverick asked Warnes to prove what he was saying was true and produce evidence that I gave him information. He answers by saying that all this 'evidence' has suspiciously 'gone missing' or been shredded. Oh, what a big surprise! Could that be because it never existed?

It goes on like this – Warnes trying to cover his tracks and talking bollocks about me supposedly being his informant, blah, blah, blah. It's obvious though that the two coppers interviewing him are getting quickly pissed off at hearing this crap 'cos they know what he was actually doing:

A. WARNES: To be honest I don't really see what relevance this has got to what I've been arrested for.

DS LAVERICK: Well, part of what we are suggesting is that part of all this, and what we've suggested remember, is that you falsely attributed information to David Courtney, and we are suggesting that your relationship with David Courtney isn't professional but it is corrupt.

I couldn't have put it better myself, 'falsely attributed information'. Fucking bang on, mate. That's one of the few times I was glad that a copper agreed with me!

Anyway, Warnes ain't having any of it. He carries on trying to blame me. I think at this stage he must've thought he could still lie his way out of it. Maybe he saw some light at the end of the tunnel but didn't realise it was just me coming at him on the Harley shouting, 'You CUNT!'

They carried on interviewing him and telling him they thought he'd made up the information reports about the wife having drugs:

DS LAVERICK: I am going to suggest to you that you didn't actually get that information at midday. And now this report is false

And then:

DS LAVERICK: Cause again, if the allegation is correct then again you did not receive this information from David Courtney.

But at this point Warnes is still at the 'no-it-wasn't-me-miss-honest' stage: y'know, like when a kid is caught red-handed by the teacher his first reflex is to go 'It wasn't me, miss, honest!' So he carried on insisting on his own innocence, which meant he had to fit me up as a grass.

A really important bit in his interview came up here, though, when the copper actually asks Warnes if he got the information about the drugs being planted from someone else. Not just anyone else but someone else in particular that Laverick actually names – another officer I'd been using. Now that to me suggests they must have a bloody good reason for naming the person they think Warnes got the info from. Not only that but – listen to this – this guy was an ex-copper *and* one that had worked around Warnes *and*, get this, the police went on to say that the only reason this geezer hadn't been arrested was because he'd left the country! Oh that's not suspicious at all is it? Fucking hell, wake up. (I can't name him for legal reasons and as far as I know he's still AWOL.)

To me, when stuff like that happened it was just the sound of another piece falling into place.

Then they got to me meeting Warnes on Plumstead Common and played him the surveillance video of it. Warnes is still banging on with his 'Me good – Dave bad' routine, but even the two coppers weren't buying it:

DS LAVERICK: Because, obviously in line with this whole allegation, we would suggest that he didn't give you the information and the reason he was nervous or didn't want to meet anyone was because he realised he could be implicated in some serious offences.

Why did he jab you in the chest?

WARNES: He didn't jab me in the chest.

DS LAVERICK: Was he upset that you basically attributed false information to him. Is that why he was gesticulating and pointed at you.

Well, it appears to me that consistently, and you've mentioned this in earlier interviews, you didn't ask Dave Courtney. He came to you when he wanted, and I would say that this video that we've just shown you illustrates the true relationship between you and David Courtney.

So even the police know that Warnes is my bent copper. Like I've always said, and like I said in my own interview, when you find a bent copper use him for all he is worth until his sell-by date expires. Then get another one. Which is exactly what me and my mates had done. And I gladly hold my hands up to that one. If a bent copper can't be used by the criminal fraternity then what is the world coming to!?

So you can see that during the interview the two coppers were sort of playing 'Hangman' with him. Remember Hangman, that game you'd play at school where you had to guess the name of something and draw out someone getting hanged? Well they were drawing out the truth from Warnes and, as it happens, letting him hang himself along the way. So with his head in the noose he weren't the long arm of the law any more, more like the long neck.

There's another funny thing here. At the end of one of the interview tapes one of the coppers asks Warnes' solicitor if it's okay to continue and she says, 'Apart from the fact that I'm dying, yes.'

When I was reading that bit back later I thought, Dying? Oh yeah, dying from embarrassment at having to try and defend the prick sat next to her.

Anyway, in the last part of the interview Warnes spares his brief any more embarrassment 'cos he decides not to say anything else! He makes a statement to the interviewing officers saying that in light of further evidence he's been shown he is not going to answer any more questions. I'd guess that must've been about the point he'd felt the rope tightening around his lying neck.

The two Old Bill carry on with their questions anyway. Warnes' not answering is written down as 'No response'. They also questioned him about the fact that on the surveillance tapes he was heard giving misinformation about undercover police vehicles:

DC LAWRENCE: When you said, 'That's another one, take that one because I swear to you he's a fucking 4-2.' Do you accept that a 4-2 is a surveillance motorcyclist?

WARNES: No response.

DC LAWRENCE: Because you know full well that David Courtney knows high-tier criminals, don't you?

WARNES: No response.

DS LAWRENCE: You've even gone so far as to giving details of registered keepers of vehicles that you believe are police vehicles.
     It just shows the type of relationship you've had with David Courtney, that it wasn't a professional relationship and I put it to you that this goes to show the corrupt relationship you've had with him.

WARNES: No response.

DS LAVERICK: When you were asked if you ever passed that information onto anyone you've said 'No, never'. This clearly shows you are lying. Have you lied about anything else in the series of interviews we've had?

WARNES: No response.

No fucking response indeed! I'll bet there wasn't. You are the weakest link – goodbye. Who was dying more at that point, do you think, him or his solicitor. And listen, at this stage we're only into the first day of interviews and already it's become apparent that, (1) I'm fuck-all to do with the conspiracy charge, and (2) Warnes has been lying about me being a grass.
     I knew all this, of course. I just didn't know that *they* knew it all as well. Not yet anyway.
     Warnes had been interviewed until about five o'clock in the afternoon – which at this stage I knew fuck-all about. It wasn't until ten at night that two officers came to interview me, a DS Walsh and a DC Tyson from the Anti-Corruption Unit at Scotland Yard. I thought, I bet you've got your work cut out with that gig. Full time job there, mate. It must be if they've got a whole bleedin' unit doing nothing but investigate corruption. It's fucking criminal.
     Okay, The Rules Of Arrest, in case you've forgotten, go something like this: from the *very second* they clamp their hand on your shoulder, you should consider yourself being tape recorded – even though you're not – but, act as if you are. Because every word you say, every action you make or attitude you show is being documented by those surrounding you. And coppers write these things down in unison sat round a table in the canteen or office while you're stewing in your cell, so don't give them fuck all to work with.

Say nothing. Well, maybe just the odd knock-knock joke. Or knob gag. If you are innocent you do not have to say anything, and if you are guilty you do not have to say anything. Even if you're innocent and they want to *make* you look guilty they could do. Unless you're sure what you're doing keep it buttoned.

The first thing they say is that you are *not* allowed to say *nothing*, which as I've said before is ABSOLUTE BOLLOCKS. And if you didn't get that I'll say it again for the hard of thinking – IT IS ABSOLUTE BOLLOCKS. We live in Britain not fucking Afghanistan. Say absolutely *fuck all* if you want. And quote me on that.

So then they hit you with the big authority buzz and say you have *got* to tell them. Or what? What are they gonna do – tickle you? Punch you in the head? Make you eat worms? Then they'll say that you not saying anything must mean you're guilty! Sorry, but that's just plain fucking silly. Even if you had the worse possible barrister in the world he could still convince a jury that a person not saying something isn't the same as a person going, 'Yes I'm guilty.' But they will try to frighten you into speaking.

Now you know me, and as I've said, generally the golden rule during questioning is to go 'no comment'. Don't give them a fucking thing. But there is the very odd occasion when if doing that is cutting off your nose to spite your face then it's best to present your side of things. I've done 'no comments' for twenty years and it took that long for the time to come round – this time, right now – when it would've been genuinely more damaging for me not to say something; but it was me that decided that, not the police. That's the important thing, *you* decide – not the cunt sat opposite you with the side-parting, the dandruff and the chewed Biro.

(Remember: if you do go 'no comment', accept their offer of a duty solicitor – but don't trust him, he's really just an extension of the police – then agree to an interview, and then say 'on the advice of my solicitor I'm going no comment'. Job done. Then get your own brief!)

But I would not advise anyone to try to do what I did when I was sat in a nick being tape-recorded. That little battle of wits and tongues is best left to those who've been there many times before. I'm not trying to sound big-headed about it, I just don't want you to get fucked. And most policemen's capabilities when it comes to this are better than 9 out of 10 of the general public's. Coppers do it every day.

The general public doesn't notice the pattern of police behaviour because their life isn't the criminal life, but if your life consists of run-ins with the police then you get to know how they operate: their patterns and tactics. Because you lot out there only sample police behaviour one or two times in your lives, you don't know what's usual and not. But because I'm surrounded by naughty geezers that have police attention all the time, and my own life of having run-ins with them, it means things are very plain to see to me.

So, on the odd occasion it's actually in their interests if you *don't* speak. And if any situation fell into that category then this one – some bent Old Bill trying to stitch me up and paint me as a grass – fell very, very heavily into that category. I certainly weren't gonna help Warnes in his plan to fuck me over. Far from it, I was going to bury the cunt. But I had to give my side.

Little did I know then that the police already knew much more about the truth of what had happened than they were letting on. But if there's one person they're not gonna make it any easier for than they have to . . . you're looking at him. (Well, you're not, but if you flick back to the cover you are; and does that look like the mug of someone on top of the police's 'Be Nice To' list? Fuck off.)

DS Walsh and DC Tyson went through the interview procedure of breaking the seal on fresh cassette tapes 'in your presence', putting them in the tape machine and asking if that's OK. I objected to blank tapes and requested a bit of drum and bass but no luck.

With me was my brief Tokumba Okonola. Now that's a name you could score a few points at Scrabble with, ain't it? Tokumba Okonola. I think when he was christened as a baby his mum accidentally cleared her throat at the wrong time, and he got called Tokumba. What really she meant to say was 'Kevin'.

I just called him 'Tokes' to be on the safe side. His law firm was called Dholakia & Cummings-John, which I always thought was a sexual offence, but there you go. Tokumba Okonola of Dholakia & Cummings-John. I thought, fucking 'ell, that's one Christmas card I'll have to hand deliver.

And what did the police call me? Here we go, as it happened:

DS WALSH: Before we commence any further, I hope you don't mind if I call you Dave?

COURTNEY: No. Actually I'd like you to call me Carol.

DS WALSH: (Laughter) I think 'David' for the purposes of the tape.

Worth a try. If my brief is called Tokumba I don't see why I should get boring old 'Dave'. This is when they hit you with the old, 'You do not have to say anything, but it may harm your defence if you do not mention something which you later rely on in court.' That naughty little rule they brought in a few years ago. That's the closest they dare get to admit that they actually fucking presume you guilty until proven innocent. Please tell me how just *not saying anything* can mean they can use it against you? Explain that to me.

That's just one of the new 'edges', as I call them, that they've created for themselves (later on, I'll tell you all about the others).

They'd already searched my home and found 'an item of property which is indeed a firearm'. Oops. I did mean to tidy up before I left. No, I did tidy up, so they must have found the gun inside the Dyson – fuck me, those things can suck. Actually it was one of the deactivated ones that I use in photos. But they said they thought it was 'a submachine gun of some kind'.

So that was the tasty little starter, and then we moved on to the main course and he laid out the whole conspiracy plot: the husband Simon James hiring the PI Jonathan Rees to plant some gear in his wife's car to fuck up her chances of getting custody of the kid, etc., etc. None of which I'd known fuck all about until I got pulled in. Talk about always being the last to know! I blame the parents.

You can see how that old 'blame the parents' joke I used when they arrested me in Manchester made it look like I knew what it was all about! But try explaining that afterwards. Another jokey one I use is 'I'm not gonna get dragged into it!'

Well, this actually was one that I definitely was not gonna get fucking dragged into! Despite the Old Bill's attempt to do just that. If there was going to be any dragging going on then there was also gonna be a lot of kicking and fucking shouting at the same time.

Anyway, then it was my turn to give my own account 'uninterrupted by us' as they put it. Well, thank fuck for that:

COURTNEY: I was introduced to Warnes by some friends of mine, he was quite well known for being a bent copper. He was used for getting people's registration numbers and all that, and I think he just enjoyed being around criminal fraternities. He was having a problem, not knowing which one he was, a policeman or a baddie. He actually took it upon himself to sort of try and befriend me. It wasn't to my liking but I didn't want to sit there and go fuck off to a copper, and my thoughts about him were right because as time went on he became a real nuisance, just turning up.

When I sort of kept him at arm's length, visibly, he took offence to that and decided to use whatever methods he could to fuck up my life. You know, whatever friends he had in whatever police station, I was getting plagued by raids. I had him approach me and ask me to buy seven kilos of puff. I knew he was setting me up for something.

On the said day he actually came down, very panicky, and asked whether I could help him out. I said I would as long as I could safeguard myself by taping the conversation. I didn't actually know it was all . . . what the end result would be. You understand what I mean, I'd made an enemy of the man – I'd actually seen him selling drugs from obviously a raid he'd done and kept, and was aware that I could wake up one day and find seven kilos of puff in the boot of my car – and this (the tape) was an extra weapon in my arsenal against him.

I kept the thing and I've never seen him or heard from him from that day to this, and here you are. And I feel very lucky that I did it (tape him) and now it's hopefully gonna be the saving grace in this case.

DS WALSH: Okay, we appreciate it's a candid account you've given there.

'Candid'? Fucking 'ell. You mean throwing a bent copper back at them and blowing a hole in their case against me? I suppose 'candid' is one description for it. 'Throwing a peach of a right-hander off the ropes' is another.

And that was that, for the night anyway. The last thing left to do was the 'seal the interview tapes and sign them' routine. My hand was still aching from signing stacks and stacks of *Stop the Rides* . . . up in Waterstones in Manchester. But, in for a penny . . .

DC TYSON: And if you'd just like to sign and seal and just print your name underneath please.

COURTNEY: I've got very good at doing signatures lately.

DC TYSON: So I understand.

One more autograph never hurt anyone. Apart from John Lennon.

And that was that. The tape was switched off and they fucked off to their warm beds and I went back down to the detention cell to a mattress that felt like it had been on hunger strike. I've actually smoked fatter joints. It was like lying on three anorexics strapped together. And fuck me, I don't think I'd been to bed before eleven before. Not since I was seven. No, tell a lie, not since I was on remand in Belmarsh. One thing about being banged up – it properly fucks up your social life.

Anyway, what I'd thought might happen had happened, hadn't it? Warnes had tried to land me in it and pull me down with him. But, 'safety net', remember? The 'extra weapon in my arsenal against him' that I'd kept for future use, I now had to pull out the bag. Thank fuck I had it.

What I'd been arrested for left me no option but to explain the extent of my involvement and, mostly, complete non-involvement. At the beginning of it, as this stage, I suppose even I was a little bit embarrassed because at the very, very beginning I didn't tell them everything. It was only later on when I found out what lies Warnes had said that I called for Brendan to come up and bring the tapes and photos. But first, at this stage, it was damage limitation and the wait-and-see game. Just as Warnes didn't want to tell all about how corrupt he was, I also didn't want to tell too much about just how many bent coppers I'd been using! It was only later when I realised what the cunts were *trying* to pin on me, and what the repercussions could be, that I knew that admitting to using corrupt police officers was the lesser of two evils.

It goes against every grain in me to confess to anything, but I'd rather be rightly accused of using bent Old Bill (any naughty geezer would be proud of that) than wrongly accused of being a fucking grass. So the decision was made.

I'd sometimes wonder if it was a curse to be able to see ahead and predict things. Y'know, the old 'ignorance is bliss' thing could seem attractive sometimes. But then that 'bliss' bit would only last until reality kicked in so, all in all, I think it's better to live with the knowledge.

So I drifted off into the land of Nod (whoever the fuck he is) still puzzling over those questions that haunt every man at night – If the police arrest a mime do they tell him he has the right to remain silent? If man evolved from monkeys and apes, why do we still have monkeys and apes? And whose cruel idea was it for the word 'lisp' to have an 's' in it? (I'd have to ask Mike Tyson that one.)

I know, little things please little minds. And little things snap little spines. If things went as they were planning then I'd be facing a fucking big thing. They were gonna try and paint me as a fucking grass. I could feel the dog was out – that big panting Alsatian called the Metropolitan Police was out of its kennel and breaking into a trot. Expecting me to run, boys? Well, too bad, 'cos I knew a little trick when it came to dogs on the attack.

So sleep on that, Fido.

10. 'ANYTHING YOU SAY . . .'

Here the Old Bill finally show their hand, but who's got the ace up their sleeve? But fuck me – they want me bad!

Next day I had to be up by nine o'clock. Nine! That's got to be an infringement of my human rights. I'd usually only be up at that time if (a) The bed was on fire, (b) I was just coming in from the night before, or (c) I was nicked. Well one out of three ain't bad.

And listen to this. While I was there in Albany nick (sleeping on a fucking Ryvita!) my mate Ebo started coming up three times a day bringing the most exotic food you could ever ever imagine being served in a prison. Quail eggs, veal, roast duck, salmon. Caviar was the least of it. The offices of *Front* magazine were near by, so they sent up loads of copies of the magazines and most of the coppers were asking me to sign them. They were lapping it up. I've always got on OK with the ordinary plod on the beat, though. It's the uniforms upstairs that don't have a sense of humour about some of the things I do, and obviously anyone that don't have a sense of humour is going to have a problem with me.

See, they try so hard to convince the public that there's no such thing as a baddie who can be good, and no such thing as goodies who can be bad. Which we all know is not the case.

All this time I had fuck-all idea what was going on, but we now know that the ones that had actually planned the conspiracy had all been nicked. Warnes had started off denying it all, until he saw what they had on him, but that happened a bit later.

Anyway, it was now about ten o'clock the next morning and I was being questioned by Walsh and Tyson again. First thing they did this time was go through the false 'contact' sheets that Warnes had filled in:

DS WALSH: The officer is alleging, he stated on this information that she deals on Fridays and Saturdays and she does it in the company of another female. He is also alleging that the information said she was due to receive a large supply for the weekend. Is any of that information correct?

COURTNEY: Absolute garbage, as the tape will show that. Y'know it's absolute rubbish.

DS WALSH: Have you ever met Kim James or the other female?

COURTNEY: Never in my life.

DS WALSH: Did Warnes explain what he was going to be placing on these contact sheets?

COURTNEY: No, no. I laid my trap to catch the bastard. You know I intended to hurt him in whatever way I could, but this just sort of brought it forward a little bit.

DS WALSH: What I hope to do is before we go through these bits, you've alleged some threats that he may have imparted on you in the past.

COURTNEY: It was a dislike from me because I decided not to have him near me, or have him in my company or introduce him to any of my friends because I suspected he was double-dealing. Y'know, pretending to be one thing, and actually do another. Which eventually proved true.

This little popularity thing that was happening with me at the moment, with the books and films; the envy in him was very, very visible and he made it a personal vendetta to bring me down in some way. And by actually putting me down as a 'grass' I should imagine he thought that would definitely stop the popularity where Dave Courtney is concerned.

I didn't really truly believe there was other people involved and all that.

At this point I could see where they were trying to go. By now even these Old Bill must be realising I'm fuck all to do with this. But they'd always known that 'cos they'd had Warnes under surveillance for years, and saw him try to drag me into it right at the death. But d'you think the police were thinking 'Oh, poor Courtney! Nearly stitched-up by one of our own'? Were they fuck. They were just thinking about some other way to nail me. Which is when they started slyly edging around to what little scams people had used Warnes for in the past.

Now this is a naughty one they were pulling here because they know I ain't a grass, but they pretend as if they think I am that so they can ask, 'Well, why did you know Warnes then? Give us a reason.' Knowing that the reason is that me and mine used Warnes to get info on investigations and surveillance. So in explaining away one thing, they're trying to get me to drop myself in it for another!

So in order to prove I weren't a grass I have to prove my relationship with him was purely, 100 per cent corrupt. But then they'll try and do me for *that*.

I could also see they were building up to asking me about friends of mine that he'd helped out. So I nipped that one in the bud straightaway:

COURTNEY: I'd like to say at this point that if at any time during this interview it actually falls upon me, through getting myself out of whatever trouble, it means me dropping somebody else in it I will have to go 'no comment'.

DS WALSH: This is a search for the truth.

COURTNEY: If I know the truth and you don't and you actually expect me to tell you something that might put somebody else in it, I really can't do that. Apart from this person here (Warnes), I would personally dig his grave.

DS WALSH: Irrespective of digging graves, it remains your right during the course of the interview to make no comment at any time.

So now we know that *they* know. If you know what I mean. They know the truth about what went on – he was as bent as a fucking corkscrew and I milked it for all it was worth. As any decent criminal would. Even the police's own surveillance tapes showed I weren't involved:

COURTNEY: I've actually got him saying it on tape it's all completely made up. I didn't actually know what the end result was to be.

DS WALSH: I think, in fairness, having listened to the tape, that's how you come across. As not knowing the full story.

COURTNEY: Like I say, I thought it was actually a trick on his part to have me actually be put down as a grass. But I mucked it up (his plan) in the beginning by doing the tape, you understand what I mean?

DS WALSH: So concerning this matter. Did you believe that Warnes was doing anything legitimately then as a police officer, that this was a proper conduct of a police officer investigating drug dealing?

COURTNEY: No. I didn't know whether it was a complete police conspiracy because, you know, you can't really like the thought of Dave Courtney being up there; and your kids going, 'Dad, Dad can I have the money to buy Dave Courtney's book or film?' I should imagine it's pissing a few police off!
So I thought it might be a conspiracy to get a piece of paper saying I was a 'grass', and then leak it to someone and then hopefully I'd be found in the Thames with another belly button. You know, 'best out of the way' sort of thing. You know what I mean?

DS WALSH: I do.

COURTNEY: I should imagine a lot of what he says, now that the truth is actually proven, can be taken as toilet paper. You know, anything he has ever said about anything, it's got to be completely dismissed.

DS WALSH: Unfortunately, as a current serving detective in the Met Police, that appears to be the case. But that's not for me to judge.

Fucking result or what. Even these two were admitting it. And after that I thought that if the Met top brass and the CPS persisted in trying to charge me with this pathetic, jumped-up charge – when even their own officers could see it was crap – then it could be down to nothing other than vindictiveness and a desire to dirty my name. But the Old Bill wouldn't do that to me, would they? Never. Not with them being so fair and uncorrupted . . .

Anyway, never one to miss an opportunity to boost the sales of *Stop the Ride* . . . I made them an offer I thought they couldn't refuse:

COURTNEY: Are you interested in buying a book?

DC TYSON: Thanks very much. We'll discuss that later.

DS WALSH: And it's Sunday tomorrow, there is only one book. And that's the Good Lord's book.

Christ, I didn't know I was being questioned by Cliff Richard. I couldn't believe he'd said that. There ain't only one Good Book though, there's two. The one by old Holy Hands upstairs, and mine. Not that I've got delusions of grandeur or anything. Jesus. No, just call me 'Dave'.

The next thing they did was produce the undercover surveillance video of the meeting on Plumstead Common. Y'know, if I ain't got Channel 4 or Channel 5 following me around with cameras it's the Old Bill. Or as this particular police video should have been called – 'You've Been Framed!' Spot on, mate.

So there was me and Jen on the video turning up on the motorbike looking as cool as fuck, me making a call on my mobile. I said I was probably just talking to the speaking clock, knowing that I look really good on the bike! Actually, I was calling Brendan to make sure he was parked up where he could witness the meeting:

COURTNEY: The whole event was actually done to get him, not to get anyone else in trouble, that was my motive for doing it.

DS WALSH: You've actually pointed at him there with your index finger above his chest. What did you say there?

COURTNEY: It was a sort of a threat he said to me, y'know, like he could make life shitty for me and I turned around and said I wasn't gonna have him threaten me when I was in the driving seat. That was the pointing of the finger. At this time his stomach must have been going in knots.

Weird seeing yourself filmed when you're not aware of it. You get to see an awful lot of the back of your head, 'cos normal telly usually prefer you actually facing the camera:

COURTNEY: Crikey, I'm bald.

I was actually playing a sticky wicket here because he was supposed to be helping an awful lot of other people in their own individual sort of problems, and some of them were known to me and I didn't actually want to ruin whatever it was he was doing for them. So I had to be very careful there and still have to be. Because I am sure in his own damage limitation bit he isn't gonna go and confess to an awful lot of things that he'd been doing; and I am also not gonna help you out by telling you what they were.

The film ends up with me and Jen back on the bike and, in my words, 'Driving without doing my crash helmet up, which is another illegal offence, and drives off into the sunset looking rather cool. Thank you.'

Then they produced the photo of the meet taken by Jennifer, which the police had taken when they raided my house. Fortunately the photo was dated. Well, not 'fortunately', it was planned that way of course.

COURTNEY: They're clever them Japanese you know, with them cameras.

DS WALSH: Is there any comment you'd like to make about that photograph at this stage?

COURTNEY: Well, no. I'm glad you've got it. It was never going in my album! Again, it seems ironic that I have actually caught this man by surveillance methods, which are being used on me. Y'know, it's very rewarding for myself to . . . erm . . . I hate to sound like I am gloating, I really hate it, but I am! Sorry (laughs).

DS WALSH: Please indulge yourself.

I couldn't help it, readers! Call me childish, but I just could not help being so fucking satisfied. Imagine being in my position and the things that had happened – a bent copper had gone double-bent on me, then tried to stitch me up to protect himself, then got caught by his own lot, who then tried to rope me into it all, until I showed that I had my own fucking proof of my innocence. Forgive me for doing a few cartwheels because I'd been smart enough not to let myself get fucked over, y'know what I mean?

Towards the end of their investigation into this case, when they had almost wrapped it up, they must have seen my name popped into the frame as someone they could go after . . . they must have fucking wet themselves with joy. They only thought they were getting one of their own, which can't be a good gig for any copper, nicking another copper; but then Warnes, having a suspicion his number's up, drags me into it.

The Old Bill must have been planning 'We've Got Dave Courtney' parties! Not knowing what aces I could pull out of my sleeve and go Da-Dah! Read 'em and weep.

I thought I'd shown massive restraint not to gloat more, to be honest. 'Cos everything they hit me with – their tape, their video, etc. – which they thought would bury me, I just said 'Great!' Glad you've got the video bit 'cos I've got the audio bit that I made myself: play that!'

So they cracked open the seal on the last cassettes for the final leg of Dave Courtney vs. the Met. The usual procedure.

DS WALSH: We are here in the interview room at Albany Street Police Station, here in London, and I am interviewing . . . could you just identify yourself please on tape.

COURTNEY: Julian Clary (laughs) . . . David Courtney.

DS WALSH: Yes. Just to re-iterate that it is, in fact, 'David John Courtney', and not Julian Clary that I am interviewing at the present moment of time. Also here is your legal representative. There is no one else present here today, apart from already mentioned.

You can't buy this stuff, can you? He had to seriously 're-iterate' that he was talking to me and not Julian fucking Clary! 'Cos me and Julian get mistaken for each other all the time, what with me being a shaven-headed, 14-stone tattooed geezer, and Julian being a camp, 7-stone stick insect with bleached hair. It's like we were separated at birth.

And as the copper said, 'There is no one else present here today.' Just me, my solicitor and the two geezers that were interviewing me. Laurel and Hardy.

Then they got to my equivalent of Beckham's thirty-yard free kick over the wall and into the net – meaning, my Dictaphone tape recording I made of Warnes admitting that I was just helping him out of a little spot of bother he'd got in with his boss for being seen in my company. At the same time I'd jumped at the opportunity to get something on him for future use, something to get him under control. Because since I'd made it clear that I didn't want him in my company it seemed like he'd been out to get me:

COURTNEY: He's been doing other activities to actually bring Dave Courtney to a downfall or to ruin the good publicity I am getting at the moment, that was, y'know, he has actually instigated people to raid my home; I've had kids dragged out of bed with guns, twice I've had the house raided for guns. I've actually caught him walking around in my back garden at three o'clock in the morning!

DS WALSH: If I could ask you, you mentioned about the fact that you were gonna use this tape as a type of insurance, I've got to ask you why you never saw fit before to bring that tape to the proper authorities.

COURTNEY: I didn't know whether to keep it as an insurance policy to make him go away, but the thoughts in my head and the constant information I was getting from everyone else that he was actually trying to spearhead the movement to bring me down publicly and humiliate me. I didn't know whether to sort of keep it as an insurance policy or actually just come out for no reason . . . and because I'd never heard from him from that day to this, everything was on the backburner, so to speak. And then when it all started actually happening . . .

Once I actually realised the sort of man he was, he was not my cup of tea – but I also realised he was well involved with an awful lot of other people that I knew as well and I didn't want to be the one to go, 'Fuck off you horrible cunt I don't want nothing to do with you', right. So I had to sort of tread water around him. But then it became, when he was trying to force himself on me as a friend and I actually had to go, 'Fuck off'. That is when he could not allow me to be out in the general public going, 'He's this, he's that' (about Warnes), so his intention was to put me inside.

They finally, at last, got to the bit they'd been building up to for a while. You see, as it became more and more obvious that I weren't involved in the conspiracy plot then their chances became less and less of convicting me. So they realised they only had two other ways left to get me: (1) Charge me with the conspiracy thing anyway, and hope the 'no smoke without fire' brigade do me damage, or (2) Try and charge me for the other thing – the actual using of Warnes in his capacity as a bent copper.

I'll go over it again just to be sure you're on the ball on this one. How it worked was this – Warnes was trying to hide the fact that he'd given information to me (because that proved he was bent), so he turned it around and said that I had given him information. So in order to prove that weren't true I had to provide examples of when I had used Warnes. Now that's a clever little one on their part, innit? 'Cos they're going for self-incrimination there, cheeky bastards. Asking me to drop myself in it. Which I'd do, if I had to to prove I weren't a grass. They also wanted me to mention the other people I knew that had used Warnes as well to help fuck up cases against them. But as for mentioning anyone else I knew that had used him, that was a 100 per cent strict fucking no-no. I could see it coming, though.

COURNTEY: I know exactly what you are gonna say here.

DC TYSON: I am merely looking to corroborate what you are saying about him (Warnes) doing that (hindering cases).

COURTNEY: But in doing that I would have to mention somebody else's name or a certain case. I am not gonna go and jeopardise another friend of mine getting in any trouble whatsoever. So I would have to have it as 'hearsay', and it can't be used. Because I cannot give you another man's name that would be arrested, even in trying to do what I want to do, I can't do that.

There are people out there that, if it meant keeping him as a friend or helping me, they will help me. If they ain't gonna get nicked for it . . . they come to me to get out of trouble and it is my duty as a criminal that if I can find a fucking sap that wants to give me information about the police for nothing, I'll fucking use him, pass him onto as many friends as I can to help them, as I am actually more of a consultant than an active member of the criminal fraternity. I never need any help: I ain't doing jack shit. But it is my duty to help as many people as I can with what information I can.

But, after they initially said that people wouldn't get nicked for talking about how they used Warnes . . . guess what? Yeah. The Old Bill decided to threaten everyone with being nicked. Just to fuck up my chance of getting these people to help me out. What was that I said earlier about having faith in the British justice system? Maybe I was being a bit optimistic.

COURTNEY: The way he was introduced to me was here is a bent copper and these other things that you can use to get what you want out of him.

DS WALSH: Would you be prepared to say who that person was that introduced Austin Warnes to you?

COURTNEY: No.

DS WALSH: Okay.

COURTNEY: And when I met him he actually knew quite a lot of people that I knew, you know, in his work, that he had met. He was actually working from both sides, which I don't think none of us really realised up until today – how he'd actually help you get out of trouble but also go back to your little lot and say, 'I've made a contact where I've met this geezer.' So we're all sitting there thinking that he's actually helping everyone when he was actually going back and spilling half of it to the police, what he was doing. And because we was getting results from him, and he actually did inform quite a lot of people on who was under surveillance and who wasn't, y'know; rumour has it he'd been able to tap into the computer as readily as he wants. That's a godsend for someone like myself. Not just myself. Like I said, *it is my duty to pass someone like that on to people in my game.*

These computers . . . he could find out what all this sort of contemporaneous notes were, or the unused evidence he could get hold of, y'know, it was a jumble sale for information for a million different people.

DS WALSH: Did he receive money for information passed on?

COURTNEY: Not from me, not a fucking tenner – which is another reason he doesn't particularly like me.

But he has received money for information . . . and acceptance into the company that he wanted to be in, you know, just to be one of the chaps.

Anyway, before the tape ran out again (and gave me a chance to re-introduce myself as Elton John!) I mentioned something that one of the arresting Old Bill had said to me in Manchester. And it ain't the first time it's been said to me, either:

COURTNEY: May I say, actually on tape, is there any truth in what the police officer said to me in Manchester: – 'No bloody magistrate's going to give you bail now you've been in the A-Cat Unit (Belmarsh), and then let's see after a year of that whether they want to buy your book!'

DS TYSON: Well.

COURTNEY: Is there any truth in there?

DS TYSON: There is no truth in that whatsoever, you have previously brought this same subject up. And it was said then and it's being repeated now in the presence of your solicitor. Erm . . . that officer had no right to say that to you. I don't know why he said that to you. It certainly hasn't originated from us.

COURTNEY: It ruined my tea.

DS TYSON: I'm sorry if it did that. I don't know why he said it, he shouldn't have said it.

'It ruined my tea'! Even though this is serious stuff I still can't resist throwing in them odd lines, y'know what I mean? 'Julian Clary'. It always makes fucking funny listening for any jury that happens to get my cases. Anyway, Walsh ended the interview by saying he weren't in a position to say whether I was gonna get bail or even be charged. That was yet to be decided, he said.

Meanwhile . . .

All the time that was going on, in another room Warnes was being interviewed again and this time he'd decided not to go for the Oscar for Best Lying Cunt, but to actually come clean about it all. Again, I didn't see the transcripts of his interviews until I'd been charged 'cos then they're presented as evidence, but we'll look at them now so we can see what was going on at the time.

First, they cleared up the fact that I had used him as a bent copper:

DS LAVERICK: I'll ask do you accept that you passed Police National Computer details to David Courtney?

WARNES: I do, but I can explain the circumstances arising. I've got no excuse for doing that obviously.

Then it got down to the truth about where he definitely *did not* get his information from (the info he used to try to fit up Kim James with) and also where it really might have come from.

DS LAVERICK: Did Dave Courtney give you that information?

WARNES: No he did not.

DS LAVERICK: Where did you get that information from?

WARNES: I don't want to answer that question.

DS LAVERICK: Did you get that information from Xxxxx Xxxxxx?

WARNES: I don't want to answer that question.

DS LAVERICK: Did you realise that that information came from the company Law & Commercial?

There's that name again (crossed out) the other copper that the police had wanted to question about the whole affair but couldn't 'cos he'd just happened to have left the country. That firm Law & Commercial was actually the private investigation company co-directed by Jonathan Rees, and Rees was the private investigator that Kim James's husband went to. That fits in well, don't it? Turns out that Rees had been using his office as a Stop-&-Shop firm for bent coppers to do their work through! Shame he didn't get away with it, he could've opened up a chain of them. One in every high street next to Poundstretcher, call it something like 'Cops R Bent'. How's that? Could catch on.

In fact, even before the Warnes case an anti-corruption task force (bet they're busy) was already bugging Rees's office, after they'd got information that officers were corruptly selling him info from the Police National Computer.

So by this stage Warnes has been given what the police call 'full disclosure' on the case, which means they tell you everything about all the evidence they've got against you. Warnes getting full disclosure meant he knew he was fucked, no point in him lying any more, so he comes out with the truth at last in the hope of making things easier for himself when he gets sentenced:

WARNES: Okay, my main motive for it would have been the reward but I never received it, and partially because of all the problems around it afterwards. Dave Courtney had nothing to do with it in relation to the initial facilitating. He was never consulted. I never phoned him, I never said, 'Dave will you help me out on this? Well you know about it so you can lie later.' I never said that to him. Dave had absolutely no involvement whatsoever.

And:

DS LAVERICK: Can we confirm then, I know you've already said, that all the documentation that you completed, all the informant reports relating to Kim James are false?

WARNES: Absolutely.

DS LAVERICK: You said, 'Oh I mean I've got a source telling us exactly when it's gonna happen.' So was that not true?

WARNES: That was a lie.

Then Warnes was questioned on why there was loads of money going into his accounts over the years but little coming out. He was on the take so much he didn't draw on his wages for two fucking years! Here Warnes slipped back into 'No response' mode for every question.

By now even the Old Bill knew I weren't involved. But between them and the CPS they must've decided they had nothing to lose by charging me with it anyway. Maybe they thought if they got the right combination of a stupid jury, a tough judge and shit-hot prosecutor they could get me sent down. *And* they wanted to use my tape as evidence to help nick Warnes. Fucking hell, though, I hadn't bargained on that one. Some bright spark must have gone, 'Hang on here! If we let Courtney off we can't use his tape as evidence against Warnes 'cos it's Courtney's evidence not ours.'

They knew I'd never turn up at court voluntarily so the only way they could get me to appear was to nick me as well. Then 'cos I'm nicked for the same charge – attempting to pervert the course of justice – they know I have to produce the tape to prove my innocence. I never expected it to actually come to something like this where I'd have to produce in court. But at the same time I was thinking, Thank fuck I taped him.

Another thing that happened here was this – their thinking would go 'If Courtney wasn't involved in the fit-up and we can't get him on that, what we can do is get him along to the court and during the case accuse him of being an informer and chuck enough mud at him that some of it sticks.' That's it in a nasty little nutshell.

That's real. That goes on. I've already explained to you how they work that one. I'd heard it first-hand from a copper that did it, remember. Like I said, they play the old 'no smoke without fire' game. So I had an idea that that was the next big battle I had to fight.

Here is where the police would have made a deal with Warnes, that if he continues to plead 'not guilty' – and does that right up to the trial – they would reward him by giving him bail, and by trying to get him a lighter sentence. Why would they want that? Because if he pleads 'not guilty' they can try to get me in court by pretending they need to use my tape.

So, after all that was said in the interviews, you can see now how I would be royally fucked off at still being charged, can't you? Even a civilian not familiar with the workings of the law or police procedure bullshit can see the common sense truth coming through there. How obvious is it now that, in charging me, the Met actually tried to finish off what Warnes had started? 'Hang him with rumours' is a phrase you use for what they were doing to me.

The big difference was that where Warnes had got hung by the truth, for me the truth would be a rope-cutter.

11. WHEN THE LIGHT AT THE END OF THE TUNNEL IS A BLOODY BIG TRAIN

Here we find out just how wrong you can be: and how they want to make an example of me.

Why do blind people wear sunglasses? Because they're flash bastards, that's why. Or as my nan used to say, 'You have to get up before the birds and crap on the doorstep if you want to see buffalo playing pinball in the spring.' Yeah, far too much cheese before bedtime there Nan, I'd say. Or 'The early bird gets the most drinks bought for her', that was another one of hers. See, they did do drugs in the old days. Domestos, gin and Mogagdon. Inhaling bleach, that's another one, that's why a lot of old people aren't steady on their legs.

Where was I? Blindness. We'll get to that in a minute.

What I also found out was what the wife, Kim James, had been put through by the police. When they first nicked her in June they already knew it was a fit-up by her husband using Warnes and the others, but they didn't tell her that until the others were arrested FOUR months later in September.

They made her go to court hearings and have Social Services visit to discuss taking her kid, because they wanted to do the little 'let them run' trick on Warnes. She could've fucking topped herself in that time, thinking she was going to get sent down and lose her son. What chance has someone like me got of getting a fair hearing from them when they treat a member of the public like that?

When they finally nicked Warnes for planting the drugs on her they didn't realise what a can of worms they were opening up. Or more like a nest of snakes. The Metropolitan Police started liasing with CIB3 over it. Now those two don't usually communicate too well 'cos the CIB3 boy's job is to catch their own kind – other coppers – so they ain't exactly welcomed with open arms by the normal Old Bill. (The Met's welcome mat to CIB3 says 'FUCK OFF' on it). And after three years of tracking Warnes, CIB3 had found that he weren't just a one-off. He was one of many.

Now correct me if I'm wrong, but if that came out it would be one fucking big news story, right? Correct. If someone on forensics is found to be bent, that means every case he's ever given evidence on has to be reopened. So you can see why panic would set in.

Not to mention Law & Commercial, the private investigations firm, acting as a Jobcentre for bent coppers past and present.

Listen, the reason there's so many officers working for CIB isn't because there's only a couple of corrupt policemen: it's because it is far more rife within the force than they want anyone to know. In 1997 even the Met's own boss, commissioner Sir Paul Condon, told the government that there was up to 250 corrupt police officers in his *own* force. And he was probably playing it down as well. That's a fuck load of bent coppers, ain't it? How many poor bastards have those lot fitted up?

It would have been so obvious to CIB from listening to the surveillance tapes on Warnes, and from the casual way the officers agreed to fake evidence, that it weren't the first time these geezers had done it. They didn't need loads of persuading, y'know what I mean?

In their job of catching a bent copper, Warnes – to show how good they were at fighting corruption – they found that their 'one bad apple' had suddenly turned into half a fucking orchard.

So they started dropping charges against the other coppers, maybe because they didn't have enough evidence to go to court. CIB3 discovered more bent police during their investigation of Warnes than they or the Met expected, and because they'd had Warnes under surveillance they were all caught on tape.

Now the Met knew that the first thing any half-decent lawyer represen- ting these coppers would do is object to the tapes being used as evidence. No tapes, probably no convictions. So, how about this – what if the police just happen to lose their legal argument in favour of using the tapes, which means the coppers can't go to trial? Would that be a pretty fucking good move on their part, do you think? To lose the legal argument, keep the other bent coppers out of court, and reduce the embarrassment to the force?

I'm only asking. It's just a thought. They can't do you for them y'know – having thoughts. Not yet anyway. We ain't got the Thought Police yet, but give 'em time. Fuck me though, if there was a Thought Police just who wouldn't be in prison? A few nuns and the Queen.

When I got nicked and learned that CIB3 and corrupt police officers were involved, my first thought was that the police would ask for a press ban to try and limit bad publicity. But now the trial was getting nearer and most of the others were being dropped out I just knew they weren't gonna ask for the press ban. For them, don't you think it would be better for it to be reported and show they've caught one bad copper; as well as give them a platform to hurt me by publicising lies and allegations that were being thrown at me? Yeah? . . . Make sense? I think so too.

Just a thought. Another one. I've been having a lot of those lately. No wonder I can smell wood burning.

This ain't me being paranoid about some 'plot' to get me. It does happen. It's happened to others. We've all heard of them. One thing that happened during this time was that I started to notice cases in the papers much more. It's like when you buy a certain car you suddenly notice all the other ones out there! Not being the biggest newspaper reader (unless it's wrapped round a fish) I got given reports that had been seen by other people.

I know, like the police know, that the number of criminals caught are only the tip of the iceberg. The big mass of uncaught geezers lie under the surface. Same with bent coppers. They catch a few, thousands swim free.

EXAMPLE 1: One of these stories was about something that happened about eighteen months ago. This geezer called Keith Pedder was charged with conspiring to corrupt a police officer, but he was acquitted because the evidence had been got by entrapment. So this Pedder complained to the Met's new commissioner, Sir John Stevens, and said that CIB3 had set him up to try to stop him publishing a book he had written that was critical of the police. *Get that!* Let that one sink in a second.

CIB denied it had anything to do with the book (what a surprise), but the commissioner gave the investigation to an outside force. Pedder had named police officers, some of them even in CIB, who'd had official complaints made against them but they'd never even been investigated. Even CIB's own boss, Andy Hayman, said the judge was 'justified in his criticism' of their case against Pedder.

This is the boss of the police force who police the police force confessing that, remember.

So you can see from that little example that the police know the power of a book, they know the power of the media, and they know that *I* know the power of the media. *Stop the Ride I Want to Get Off* was Virgin's biggest book all year, and I ain't saying that to brag but to make a point; which is that when *Raving Lunacy*, my second book, came out it got only a fraction of the publicity. Now who might have had a little word with newspapers and magazines to try to put a block on me getting press coverage? I'll leave that to you to answer. Phone a friend if you want. Even phone the commissioner of the Met.

Just a thought. And that's the third one this chapter. I'm on a roll!

The police even called Virgin and told them to cool the promotion of *Raving Lunacy* under the excuse that I was currently involved in a case, even though the book was about something else.

I think the Old Bill thought I'd want to keep it all low-key because of their accusations about me being an informant. But I didn't do that at all. Low-key ain't my style. The only people who go low-key in that situation are the ones with something to hide. I had fuck all to hide so I went fucking LOUD mate.

To one copper I said, 'If you put me in the same dock with Warnes I will knock him spark out in front of everyone.' He went, 'Yeah, yeah, yeah.' I said, ' "Yeah, yeah, yeah" nothing! Write down on a piece of paper that I asked to be separated from him because I will fucking attack him for what he's saying about me! And when I do I'll fall back on that bit of paper saying it's your fault.'

The mistake they made was trying to keep the geezer with the megaphone – me – roped into the case. We've already seen Warnes' statement, so the Old Bill knew I weren't anything to do with it, but they still won't let me go like they should, 'cos they can't bring themselves to 'let Dave Courtney go' when they've still got a chance of getting something out of it. Even if that 'something' ain't a guilty verdict but the opportunity to fuck with my reputation.

They should have dropped the charges on me 'cos there was no evidence. Then get Warnes to go 'guilty' and keep it out of the papers. When it's the police nicking the police they can do various things to stop bad publicity. They can drop the charges, give officers sideways promotions or demotions, or transfer them, or just get rid of them with early pension. Tricks that keep it all internal and limit damaging public confidence.

BUT they let it all go as far as the first court hearing at a magistrate's and as soon as that happens it's too late to change it. So then they couldn't drop me out of it like they should have. It's like when a footballer throws himself into a tackle and then realises he ain't gonna get the ball but he will get the geezer, but it's too late and . . . *bang!* Penalty.

Well I was the *bang!* in this little game. And the Old Bill know what I'm like when I decide to publicise something so their plan of keeping this low-key was well fucked. I am fucking good when I get in court. And I'm even better when I'm innocent!

The naughty one they had tried during the original police interviews still stood. Where I'd had to say about using Warnes in the past to pull a few strings for me and other people. And, get this, they immediately said, 'Right, we're charging you with that as well.' Cunts.

Then they said I might just be making up these cases where he helped me out, so they asked if anyone could corroborate it? I said I'd have to check it was OK with the other people involved first, that it was alright to mention them. So I did, and everyone said yeah, it'd be OK, 'cos they knew it was helping me. Until the police went to see them and said that by corroborating my statement about Warnes they were helping me, and if they continued to do that they'd be nicked for these old cases. So, of course, they all had to back out! Which I understand one hundred fucking per cent. They couldn't do anything else.

So the Old Bill were properly trying to fuck me in every way possible. The next fuckable thing that cropped up was the setting of bail conditions, but we'll get to that in the next chapter.

So, after everything that's happened up until now – me knowing Warnes, me using Warnes, me wanting Warnes to fuck off, Warnes and his mates setting up the bird for the husband, me agreeing to help Warnes so I get something on him, me taping Warnes, the arrests, the charges, the truth coming out that I weren't involved, me still getting nicked anyway – after all that crap, what did I think about it?

I thought that come the court case, when they start throwing around more shit than a sewage worker with epilepsy, I could completely understand people on the outside thinking, 'Oh Dave, that does make you look a bit iffy there . . .' (or at least people who don't know me well enough to know different might think that). Because I knew in court they would just announce Austin Warnes as 'a policeman', announce Jonathan Rees as 'a private investigator' and Simon James as 'the husband', etc.: but they'd announce me as Dave Courtney 'alleged police informant'.

That's definitely gonna get people who don't know me any better to go, 'Well . . . no smoke without fire', and all that. But you DO know better now, 'cos I've let you in on a few behind-the-scenes workings that the public usually don't hear about.

The Old Bill have been after me for the last twenty years, and especially the last five since Ronnie's funeral and since I started writing books. So they ain't gonna be shedding any tears about me being shown in a bad light. I would be very surprised if they weren't popping champagne corks over it, to be honest. Or champagne if it's coming out of expenses. Asti Spumanti if they've got to dip in their own pockets.

These things are sent to test us. Along with medium-sized condoms when Boots have run out of large. As they say, what does not destroy us makes us stronger.

You can see now that all of this is where my Man Bites Dog routine comes in. I refused to run away from the biggest police dog in the land – the Metropolitan Police Force – like they thought I would. I turned around and charged at the bastard.

And you don't even have to wish me luck here, 'cos luck is for those who don't plan ahead.

12. INNOCENT AS CHARGED: WITH BELLS ON

Heard the one about the geezer who went to court with headwear even funnier than the judges, with £50,000 in a bag, and punched a copper out?

So now I knew what the Old Bill were up to. They knew they weren't going to get a conviction for this one but they were charging me and taking me to court anyway. For two reasons. One – it gives them a chance to put me on remand. Two – they can indulge in some name-calling during the case and cause trouble for me that way.

Because I knew what they were up to it meant I could try to combat it. Like I said, the next fuckable thing was the bail conditions. Even though they knew they'd nicked me for something I ain't involved in, they also knew if they could fuck up my bail it would shut me up and get me on remand for a year. They did that to me in '96. They rated me as a high risk 'A' category prisoner and as a copper had said to me that time: 'As long as I can keep you as an A-Cat prisoner you won't get bail off any mug of a magistrate and we'll nick a year off your life.' Which is exactly what happened.

I worked out that over the course of fifteen years they've put me on twelve months' remand here, six months' remand there, another nine months somewhere else; and when you add them all up I've done over three and a half years on remand for charges that I was found 'not guilty' of. And three and a half years inside is what you'd serve after being given a seven-year sentence. Of course the police are happy with that 'cos they still get their pound of flesh.

So what they did here was give me a higher bail than any of the other four geezers charged. Warnes and the other geezers got what they call 'surety' bail. That means anyone with a house or a valuable asset can just sign it over on a bit of paper and they walk free. Dead easy. But my bail was set at 50 grand CASH, bond money! No one's got that. They know I ain't got it, so to them it's as good as banging me up inside on remand. Sneaky fuckers. Nobody gets asked for that kind of bail. Fucking hell, Warnes was only asked for surety bail – which means his wife or mum goes up and signs her house over as surety until the end of the trial . . . and that's it! Anyone can do that. But they wanted him to walk so he was free to spread lies and rumours about me – and put false dockets out on the street – and they wanted me inside so I wasn't free to tell the truth.

Luckily it got leaked to me that they were planning on doing this so I prepared. A very good friend of mine, Kevin Jenkins, who happens to be a very successful businessman (as well as a top shag – thanks Kev, I'll still respect you in the morning), supplied the £50,000 for bail. Which turned out to be a bit of a shocker in court. Let me tell you. Especially as they left it till nearly four o'clock before they told me it had to be cash, knowing I wouldn't have time to get to a bank. Courtney does a dummy and back-heels the ball between the goalie's legs! One nil!

Kevin did get some aggro for it though. He gave me the chance to produce the 50 grand bail – and they never thought I would – so he got a grilling for that and his company got put under scrutiny. Kevin and his business are totally legit and above board so nothing came of that. He got the hassle though, and was asked if he wanted to be associated with 'this character' (meaning me), but Kevin being the loyal, honourable man that he is, stuck by me.

I thought you nasty, nasty cunts trying to fuck me with the bail. They'd done it to me before so I knew what they were doing. After I got not guilty in '96 I tried to make a big stink about the whole remand thing but because the case had been and gone, and I'd been found innocent, no one listened! They just thought, He's got not guilty, what's his problem?

So now they were trying to do it to me again I wanted to highlight it before it happened. I did whatever I could do to drag attention to this court case: made flyers, posters, wrote about it, anything – which I couldn't have done if I'd been inside. 'Cos when it came to court I knew I'd have no hardship proving my innocence and I could ask the court, 'Why was I on 50 grand cash bail? When I've already been told I'll get a not guilty then please enlighten me why they hit me with such a bail demand?' And no one will be able to answer.

It's down to spitefulness and them abusing their power. I am not a police hater, but I need you to know that it goes on. They've nicked years off me. I've tried to point it out before but no one was interested so now I'm going to tell you about it.

Also, because of the proof on Warnes, would they go into his records and find how many people he's nicked for drugs before? Because there's now proof that he would have done that. So that means cases being reopened, and retrials.

I told them I was going to say all this. I even had leaflets printed about it, so they would be proper out-and-out fucked. My solicitor said that it was the biggest problem the police had had for some time, because they could foresee the damage that could be done to the public image of the police.

If it had happened quickly, fair enough, there's nothing they can do about it. Like if a fight breaks out next to you it might be Mike Tyson but too late, bang, you're in. But if the row was down the other end of the club, by the time you've run over there you've already had time to frighten yourself. Well, the police and Warnes had got prior notice that I was gonna rip the shreds out of them. So they let Warnes walk on bail to do whatever he wanted to try and stop it.

Despite all that, come the day of the bail hearing we had a fucking whale of a time anyway. Just listen to this.

A week before the hearing I went to *Front*'s offices to hand in my latest column. It was about 'An Audience With Dave Courtney' I'd just done in London, and very well it went too. I knew there'd be some undercover Old Bill there so when I went out on stage I said, 'Look at the person next to you and if you don't know him and he keeps talking into his lapel then he's probably Old Bill!' Apart from all the usual naughty people there was loads of celebs in the audience. All the *EastEnders* lot, the Stereophonics, Mark Morrison, Brian Harvey and Robbie Williams. Ha. Best bit was when Howard Marks got on stage to say hello. It was going to see his shows that made me want to do one myself. Howard is the absolute bollocks, really clever and funny. Top geezer.

Anyway, so the *Front* boys had had their usual hard day at the office, y'know how tiring it is tapping keys on a computer, sipping beer and looking at photos of naked birds all day. My heart bleeds. So we all nipped over the road to the Green Man for a pint. I was telling them about the court case and what a fucking joke it was, and how I'd decided to go in a court jester's outfit.

Then I thought, how easy could it be to find a jester's outfit for a fourteen-stone geezer with a 48-inch chest and size ten feet. Those court jesters are always played by tiny fellas, aren't they? I did get one though and it was the same costume used in the film *Shakespeare In Love*. Now it was gonna star in Courtney In Court.

By this time, though, I really thought it was a wicked idea. The Old Bill always knew I was the fly in the ointment on this case so why not make myself the joker in the pack as well, just to show what a fucking farce I thought it all was? I also had prior knowledge that the police had tipped off the press to be at the court; I think they thought I'd turn up quietly with a blanket over me or something. How wrong about me can you be?

Now usually when someone goes to court they put on their best I'm-so-innocent suit, get a never-done-anything-wrong haircut, have their nan in the court waving from a wheelchair, and then sit through the proceedings all meek and mild. Well my suits look like they could knock you out whether I'm in them or not, my haircuts range from bald to balder, my nan's busy in Heaven telling God one of her sayings ('Red sky at night – shepherd's on fire', that kinda thing), and I ain't meek and mild even when I'm asleep, 'cos I snore like a Kawasaki going through the Blackwall Tunnel!

So I'm just honest about being me and that shows I'm not afraid to tell the truth. And because of the charges about being an informer they thought I was going to go along quietly and try and hush everything up. But I'm innocent of it all so I do the opposite and go GET A LOAD OF THIS! – I went loud and proud, with loads of mates in suits and five black limos and dressed as a fucking court jester. Juggling!

Come the morning of the day, as is the custom when my company's been requested by the courts, all the usual suspects (i.e., 40 of my mates) turned up at Camelot Castle. Well, more 'turned out', as in 'turned out of bed'. 'Cos if most of these blokes are up before midday it's only 'cos they've shit the bed or are just coming in from the night before. Breakfast TV always existed for this lot, it was called News At One! So most of them stayed over at my house the night before.

I thought I had a big house until I had to find room for two dozen big geezers to kip! Every bed and chair was full, you couldn't move without stepping on a cauliflower ear or a shaved head and Mad Pete slept standing up with his eyes open (in case he fell over) – what a star! I even had one sleeping in the Wendy house in the garden. Which was a bit of a shocker for nextdoor's kids when they came round to play and found the Jolly Black Giant in there. But they're now in therapy so happy endings there then!

All these geezers being woken at 8 a.m. in the morning weren't a fucking pretty sight either. Thank fuck Jen had a cattle prod handy. Fucking 'ell, it was like Dawn Of The Living Dead 2.

We all fuelled up on tea, bacon butties and . . . erm . . . Red Bull! According to the adverts, 'it gives you wings'. So you walk around all day feeling like a pantie liner. Champion. For the next hour the door knocker was banging like a bunny on Viagra as everyone else turned up.

The roll call was Seymour, Brendan, Marcus, Terry, Matt, Piers, Dean . . . (the rest). All black-suited and booted and looking the absolute dog's danglers, mate. I was as pleased as Punch. Which is funny 'cos I fucking looked like him in my outfit! They all looked as cool as fuck and what was I wearing? A yellow, red and green jester's outfit with baggy pantaloons, pink stockings, pink pointy boots and a green and yellow jester's hat with bells on it. I always fancied that jingle-of-spurs that cowboys got when they walked. I had the ringing of little bells!

Why should the judge be the only one in court who looks like a prick? I thought I'd give him a run for his money.

You can tell I must have settled into my new neighbourhood 'cos when we walked out into the street, me like a jester and with an army of black behind me, none of the neighbours batted an eye! One geezer walking past just went, 'Morning, Dave.' Like, oh it's just Courtney going to court. Ha-ha! Wicked.

Our convoy of Mercs arrived at Bow Street Magistrates' Court for the hearing and we got out to find a pack of press photographers ready, armed and waiting. What a surprise. The press told me themselves that they had been tipped off by the police, and told to expect me to turn up with a blanket over my head. How wrong can you be? They took photographs of Brendan showing the £50,000 in cash he was holding in a carrier bag.

There was an even bigger surprise waiting inside for me, though.

In the court hearings before this one they'd made sure that me and Warnes appeared at different times, after what I'd said about attacking him for what he'd been saying. But when I walked in this time I saw Warnes stood in the reception hall. I couldn't fucking believe it. I truly didn't believe for one second he'd be there.

I took the few steps between us really quickly and launched a right hook that started somewhere in Peckham and ended up slap-bang on his jaw. (Afterwards people said they remembered two noises: the *smack* of the right-hander and the bells on my hat tinkling!) All hell broke loose – coppers jumped in, people started scuffling and all the blokes with me just saw fists flying and ran over like they were going to invade fucking Poland! (If it had been a film the soundtrack would've been 'WHO LET THE DOGS OUT?!')

A couple of plain-clothes Old Bill led me away from it all.

Now this is where it gets interesting (although it's pretty interesting already for a Monday morning in a magistrates'!) What I believe is this: The police knew I've already fucked them on the 50 grand cash bail trick so how else can they get me on remand? They know I've said I'll smack Warnes on sight, and they've deliberately kept us apart at the other hearings. So why do they suddenly produce him in front of me? Unless they want me to hit him, in court, on CCTV, in front of witnesses . . . then do me for assault and, 'cos you can't be on bail for two things at the same time, I immediately get banged up. Good plan – and it worked. Nearly.

Even as I went to smack him I was thinking: 'I'm going to prison for this but I'm not gonna get another opportunity to punch this cunt for a good few years'; and 'I can't beat him up but one good punch is all I ask'; and 'I'm really sorry, Jennifer.' All those things were in my head. But I did it anyway.

So as the coppers are leading me away I'm resigned to the fact I'm gonna get banged up for what I've just done. But fuck me, it was worth it.

But . . . third surprise of the morning is about to happen. What the Old Bill hadn't counted on was me turning up with nearly forty of the Dirty Dozen's even dirtier cousins! The filthy forty were all running amok in the magistrates' and there's only three or four coppers present, and two have got me. It was a really small reception area which made my forty blokes look even fucking bigger and badder. So the few Old Bill are proper panicking that it's all getting way out of hand.

One of the coppers in charge turned to me and – give him credit here for a good line – said to me, 'First off, Mr Courtney, good shot!' I thought, oh wicked, nice to be appreciated! Then he quickly went, 'We cannot have your lot running round here like a lynch mob after a policeman so let's say we should have kept you and DC Warnes apart, and put that one down to me!'

I said, 'Are you willing to say that in front of my solicitor?' He said he was, so my brief, Tokes, came over and they made it official. Touch.

I had another lightbulb over the head moment that second – pop! – and saw that this copper next to me was just like Warnes had been on

Plumstead Common that day; he needed to mend the immediate problem of forty geezers charging around so forget Warnes being punched for a second and mend this new, bigger problem RIGHT NOW.

So the one thing that saved me, and the thing they didn't plan for, was me turning up with my small army. 'Cos no one turns up forty-handed like I did – no one. And I love every one of my fellas for that. Really saved me.

Then it hit me that this whole thing had been planned to trap me otherwise that plain clothes officer wouldn't have had the authority to do what he did. I mean, fair enough, it didn't turn out as they'd planned and they could never have foreseen me bringing who I did, *but* he couldn't have the authority to deal with it going arse over elbow unless it was all pre-planned.

I know that one's a bit of a twisty one to take in, but it makes sense. The copper had thrown back at me such a quick-flowing sentence that it sounded prepared, like it was their own safety net if things didn't go to plan.

So now you know how you should turn up to any big occasion. Just take loads of naughty-looking geezers with you. My boys, by the way, are available for christenings, weddings, funerals, and court appearances at very reasonable rates. They're all house trained but they might shag your daughter. Sorry.

Knocking out a copper in court with a peach of a shot was, for me, like popping a couple of Viagra. So I went downstairs to the toilets and banged on off! – to the sound of bells ringing!

I'd also had some fun during the first hearing. I turned up in my white suit and with a copy of my book. Inside I stood it up for everyone to see. The judge went, 'What is that book, Mr Courtney?' I said, 'It's my autobiography, your honour, *Stop the Ride I Want to Get Off*, Virgin, all good bookshops.'

That didn't go down too well and I got a ticking off. Oh dear, I nearly cried.

The court officials were forced to re-arrange the schedule because I refused to appear alongside the other four geezers in this case 'cos they were fuck all to do with me. They did that 'cos they didn't want to see Round Two. Then they started debating on whether I should be let in court wearing my outfit. I thought that's a bit fucking rich, ain't it? There's judges wearing white curly wigs, black cloaks and probably suspenders and stockings and they can't decide whether or not I look too silly to be in court! Mirror for the judge, please.

Anyway, they let me in and the magistrate looked me up and down. 'I'm not too impressed with your outfit, Mr Courtney,' he said, 'however colourful.' Then he paused and went, 'Please remove the hat . . .' That's all he said. I've got pink pointed shoes on, stockings, baggy pants and bells everywhere and he said remove the hat!

He told me that if I wore this outfit again he'd do me for contempt of court. I said, 'Your honour, at 150 a day hire charge I will not be wearing it again I promise you!' That got a big laugh. Everyone in court couldn't believe it when Brendan opened the bag and showed the £50,000 cash. The magistrate said, 'This is a public court and everyone here now knows how much is in that bag. I do worry for your safety.' Which shows just how much faith he had in the safety of the court.

Because of some of the rumours flying around after they nicked me I tried to speak out about it and say that the court hearing before had unfairly shown me in a bad light to certain people. But before I could say any more the magistrate cut me off and said he was only there to hear bail applications. His loss.

By the time I came outside onto the steps of the court news had got round about what had happened so there was twice as many cameras there as when I went in. What a bonus. So I stood there in the full Technicolor jester's clobber – hat back on, by the way – I overcame my natural shyness and made my address to the nation! 'I'd just like to say that every time I lay eyes on that geezer I will punch him in the mouth. And I still have faith in the British justice system. Thank you.'

Although you could still only have faith through a triumph of optimism over reality. For instance:

EXAMPLE 2: Another case. A joint investigation called Operation Nectarine (catchy!) by Kent police and our old friends at CIB ended up catching half a dozen geezers, including a copper, who were charged with conspiracy to supply twelve million quids' worth of puff. Cannabis, to you. I bet the Old Bill were pretty pleased with themselves. Until the judge at Maidstone crown court threw the case out of court! He said there was 'Wholesale breaches of laws governing trial conduct and evidence preparation'; a failure to record and retain crucial material which was 'symptomatic of the culture of non-disclosure and non-compliance' (that's a fancy way of saying 'stitch up'); 1,700 pages of 'highly significant' police and CIB documents were not at first disclosed despite judges' orders; and a 'strong suggestion of financial inducements'.

Just your average day at the office then! Fucking hell. I think I felt a little waver in my faith.

So anyway, how did things stand at this point? Well I stand like this – slightly to the left, one hand on hip, one hand in pocket on duster and eyes straight at camera. But because I'd made such a big deal of publicising this case, and with good reason, to show I've got nothing to hide, it actually made it even more difficult for the police not to go after me. I'd made it very public with flyers and posters and press announcements. The downside is that I'm more wanted by the police now because of my popularity than when I was actually active in the criminal world. Figure that one out.

They cannot allow me to carry on going to court and coming out to a hero's welcome. They also could not now produce all the evidence that CIB3 collected when they were following Warnes because it revealed too much corruption. So, think about this one. Wouldn't getting me in trouble, or them dirtying my name so much that someone topped me, wouldn't that mend an awful lot of things? That would very quickly take the pressure off them.

The only thing stopping them from dealing with this police corruption case very quietly, and keeping it all low-key, is ME. 'Cos I'm pretty fucking high-key. I'm their shaven-headed, fourteen-stone fly in the ointment. The knuckle-dustered bee in their bonnet. But I won't buzz off.

In fact, I was thinking of changing my name to Sting.

They say it never rains but it pours. And the black cloud here was the death of Jen's brother John. John cut his knee on a nail while he was doing some DIY, went to the doctor's, took some antibiotics but within days he was dead from blood poisoning. Quick as that. It was awful. He was a lovely fella and everyone was devastated.

If it never rains but it pours then what happens if it gets worse – what happens after it pours? I'll tell you – your fucking house catches fire. Straight up, that's what happened. That night of the day of the funeral a fire started in the dining room at the back of the house. I heard the smoke alarm and jumped out of bed stark bollock naked, shouted everybody up and got them downstairs. By this time the whole of downstairs was full of thick black smoke. The kids were all elsewhere but in Genson's bedroom downstairs there was just one big problem, and that big problem was sleeping in the top bunk.

Of all the mates I could've had staying over for the night it could have been some normal-sized geezer couldn't it? (I do know a few.) But I had Mickey Goldtooth staying with me: this big, shaven-headed, sixteen-stone muscly lump unconscious on the top bunk. He was completely out, mate – gone. I managed to get him out the front door.

I ran back in and managed to get through the smoke, into the kitchen and throw some buckets of water on the flames. By the time the fire brigade turned up the heat had turned my body bright red. I was still stark naked so I pulled on some new pants and stood at the door like that, looking like a fucking lobster just jumped out the pan and straight into a pair of brand new white Calvin's. Even through the smoke I could see the firemen running up the path, tripping over Mickey, and looking up at me thinking what the fuck is *that*?! I think they thought it was the geezer out of the old Tango ads!

Anyway, after it had all died down and half the street where I lived had all gone back into their houses (after freezing to death in the street in their pyjamas) there was a knock at the door. I thought if this is a Mormon he's going spark out. I opened it to see the Old Bill. As prompt as usual when it comes to there being an emergency at my house. So it went something like this; I said:

Yeah?

We heard there was a fire.

Have you got a bucket of water?

Er . . . no . . .

Then *fuck* off!

(*DOOR SLAMMED*)

So, let me get this straight – it never rains but it pours, except when you need it to pour like when your house is on fire, but then it don't rain at all. *But* every cloud has a silver lining. So where does that leave us? Bloody confused. One thing's true though, like your mum always said, make sure you're wearing clean underwear in case you're in an accident.

The weird one though was this: on the same day we buried John, he saved our lives. Because when he was helping us decorate the house it was John that had put up that smoke detector. I'd seen it and said take it down 'cos it don't actually fit in with a castle theme does it? But John, and then Jen, had said it should stay. But the fact that it saved us on the same day he was seen off. Maybe there is another side. Or maybe I'd been to too many funerals. Just one or two . . .

13. TWO FUNERALS: PART TWO

The end of an era. The Duck of Peace.

This year was also a sad time 'cos it saw the passing on of both Reg and Charlie Kray. Charlie, the eldest Kray brother, died in Belmarsh prison. He'd been jailed in 1997 for his supposed involvement in a cocaine importation ring. Me and Charlie served our remand together at Belmarsh. I was banged up there for nearly a year in '96. We got on well and became quite close because it was a trying time for him, to be facing that kind of charge and sentence at that time of life. He was a top fella. Always a pleasure to make him laugh.

I beat my charge but unfortunately Charlie got sent down.

Me and a couple of other geezers later appeared as witnesses at Charlie's trial. I ended up stood in the same dock I'd been stood in a few months before when I'd been on the receiving end – so I knew exactly how Charlie felt. There was a lot of goodwill towards Charlie 'cos the general attitude was that although he had a couple of very, very naughty brothers Charlie weren't really like that himself. He'd had a double fucking big shadow to walk in all his life, cast by the twins. And that can't have been easy. What with him being the eldest brother as well. He really was misrepresented in his life. He truly was a victim of his second name. I cannot imagine a worse nightmare than if you are an older brother just ticking along nicely, like he'd been, a normal everyday kid; and then your mum gives birth to twins and they turn into Ronnie and Reggie Kray. Fucking hell. What chance have you got?

It was really sickening when he got given twelve years. Fucking hell. Twelve. You could live with that as a young guy, or maybe even as a middle-aged man, but he was nearly 70 years old when that was handed to him. It was pretty much the equivalent of a death sentence.

You'd only want to know in advance where you were gonna die if it was somewhere nice, wouldn't you? Like at home in bed with your missus by you. Or preferably on you. But to find out your last days on earth are gonna be in a prison must be absolutely fucking crushing. The very last place you would want it to end. It was probably that that killed him.

The fact that he had the surname Kray meant that the authorities pursued him till the end. Charlie was a prime example of one of my deepest fears: how you can become a scalp to get, or a feather in the hat; a trophy for whichever police force brings you down. They just want another fucking head to put over their mantelpiece. The difference is I'd spent most of my time stuffing *them*.

We spoke a lot during our year inside and he warned me of the jealousy of certain people in the criminal fraternity. I didn't know it to be true then, but I do now. The funeral was 19 April and Charlie was to be buried at

Chingford Mount cemetery with Ronnie and their mother Violet. Everybody met at my house on the morning in the usual fashion. Everyone knew the routine. It was ritual by now when another big funeral came around. My street would end up filled bumper to bumper with big cars and big fellas climbing out of them. The neighbours knew that either someone had died or we were having one big fuck-off game of pass the parcel.

About six month later, Reggie fell ill with cancer and was finally released from Weyland prison on compassionate grounds. Which could've been some sick joke by the authorities considering they'd kept him inside for more than the thirty years the original judge had recommended. No Home Secretary had the guts to release him because of the power of the name 'Kray'. It was a political decision to keep Reg inside. The only Home Secretary that could have released him without getting any flak – because the thirty years was up – was the one in office at the time. But that was Jack Straw, so enough said. What the fuck would you expect from that wanker?

Reg was transferred from Weyland to a hospital in Norwich. I didn't go to the hospital and I know some people who did genuinely care about him who didn't go, and a big fuss and a lot of malicious gossip was spread about what Reg did and didn't want, who he wanted to be a pallbearer and who he didn't. The genuine remorse that anyone had for Reggie going was lost in the arguments. The fact that he was the Kray brother who died last guaranteed him a big funeral – *if* it was run properly. And all his life he had *wanted to be remembered*. I am 100 per cent sure that the reason he asked me to do Ronnie's funeral was 'cos he knew I'd do a very flamboyant but professional job. He asked me to do his too, and told Wilf Pine he wanted me to do it, and he told Joe and Fred and Tony but . . . politics crept into and it didn't work out that way. Not that after Reg had died anybody actually *asked* me if I wanted to do it. They just assumed I would want it, which I actually didn't.

So, again, my neighbours got up one morning to find the street log-jammed with motors, and asked themselves that familiar question – 'pass the parcel' or 'funeral'. Bit of both, as it happens. Pass the coffin.

This was supposed to be one big fucking funeral.

The night before the big day my house was swamped again by a load of huge lumps.

By nine o'clock the next morning the whole army of 'em had scoffed a mountain of sausage sarnies and were ready for the arrival of the three original 1920s Huxmobiles cars we'd hired from 'Hooters' for the day. They were the absolute bollocks, old-fashioned cars with the wheel on the door, running boards, frog-eye lamps and massive mudguards. I had a white one with Piers and Mad Pete along with me, while Brenda, Brooklyn John and Seymour had the blue car, and some of the other boys took the green one.

Just after the cars arrived the wreath I'd ordered was delivered. We were expecting a four-foot white dove of peace, but as Julie the florist carried it out of her van we realised it was a bit on the yellow side; and a bit on the fucking 'duck' side as well! Now who has ever heard of a Duck Of Peace! No, thought not. Me neither. I thought, if Reggie is watching he's probably having a chuckle about it.

Could've been worse, I suppose. She could have misunderstood me when I asked for a dove and done a wreath like a big Ecstasy pill. That wouldn't have looked at all out of place on a hearse, would it?

Anyway, with all the people outside the house, the police had to drive past to have a look. Unfortunately the poor fuckers got caught in the traffic jam right outside my house! Oh dear, how sad, never mind. Ha! So, with my trusty Tommy gun in hand (only a replica, Sarge, honest) I went outside and began directing traffic with the gun. It must have been their worse nightmare. Imagine it – stuck outside Courtney's house surrounded by the Dirty Four Dozen and me directing them with a firearm. Love 'em.

So, off we went in the most scary-looking convoy since Hitler went shopping in Poland. By the time we arrived at W English & Son undertakers in Bethnal Green I had half a mind to drive on past and go on and invade Germany. See how *they* like it. But the old blue limo broke down in the Blackwall Tunnel. I mean of all places! That tunnel is jammed even when the cars are working.

A massive tailback built up. The driver of the car nearly had a heart attack knowing that he had a car full of naughty-looking geezers on their way to Reg Kray's funeral who wouldn't be too impressed by looking like proper silly cunts stuck in the middle of the Blackwall. And how right he was. Fortunately the boys just hopped out and commandeered Gilly's Merc and went on their way. Leaving one poxy old motor (which still looked the bollocks) in a cloud of smoke and blocking two lanes. Leave that one for a traffic cop to sort out, eh?

When we finally did arrive at the funeral parlour it was mayhem. Thank God I hadn't been offered the security job for this one. A lot of people had come out to pay their respects to Reg Kray, the last monarch of the old-style villains. And contrary to what the papers implied afterwards the security firm did a top job throughout the day and looked as professional as any I've seen. Not an easy job, as well I know.

We followed the horse-drawn cortège past the crowds to the church, but for some bizarre reason only half the church was open and I was allocated only eight seats. Having brought sixty-odd fellas (well, not all of them were odd) with half of them travelling over two hundred miles to be at my side for the day, who was I supposed to pick? I decided it was best not to go into the church at all, but to stay with the boys and take in a very slow drive over to the cemetery in Chigwell to deliver my duck of peace.

I say 'very slow' because these beautiful old motors go 25 mph. Get this – at one point the driver looked me straight in the eye and said, without embarrassment, 'I've had it go up to 36 mph once you know . . .' Oh, scary! I bet rice pudding skins were trembling the whole length of the country.

Anyway, at the cemetery they only let forty of the boys in, the rest had to wait until the cortège arrived. That pissed a couple of them off a little bit I think but no great dramas. Although Pete did want to rush the gates.

Some bastards walking past the wreaths threw some bread at my duck of peace! Wankers. It had already been fed.

It was a lovely sunny day as we gathered at the graveside and the priest said his bit. At Ronnie's and Charlie's funerals there have been rival groups of men who, without even planning a truce, stood together and paid respects to the brothers. That alone goes to show just how much respect these premier division naughty men had for the Krays. But at Reggie's not everyone turned up and only a few of the big names attended the service. It was a lot quieter than Reg would have wanted.

There was a bit of ill feeling among some very key players, which took a bit of the shine off the event and left a shadow over the day. I must say that Wilf and Flanagan did what was asked of them and did it well. Roberta and Bradley done what they thought best, and as far as I know, were very happy with the day's events.

After the service we left the cemetery and headed back to the Manhattan cafe pub in Plumstead for the start of a good booze-up – it looked like Wacky fucking Races with the old limos flying down the bus lane at warp factor three – or 25 mph. Ian Freeman, the world freestyle fighting champion, came home with me and Agent No 10.

I was as proud as fuck of the company of men I was with, every fucking one of them. I now owe my clothes shop, Short Stories of Commercial Way in London, a lot of money because they dressed lots of my boys and in a pissed-up state I'd said that I'd pay for the lot. And they've held me to it! Having said that, I now have the best-dressed bunch of naughty geezers you have ever seen.

All in all it was a very sad but memorable day. Ronnie's funeral was really too much of a spectacle to be sad, Reggie's was riddled with lots of inside problems and arguments which made it strange, and Charlie's was probably the saddest do of them all, I thought.

Reg could be very accommodating and sometimes during the prison visits you could almost call him an entertainer, when he was in a good mood, with all his bits of paper with reminders written down. I helped him get a page in *Front* magazine. It's important that each of us has his own platform, to get things across. Often we're painted to be very different than we are.

He continually had plans to give himself something to look forward to. Not that everyone would've looked forward to Reggie's schemes. Listen to these: he wanted to do a Scotch Porridge Oats advert (don't ask!), a Kray twin retirement home, the Kray Twin Fish & Chip shop (Ronnie on battering), the Kray twin taxi cab office ('No, you can't have a cab now – you can fucking *wait!*') . . . Make of those ideas what you will. The Kray twin retirement home is a proper blinder though, innit? Fucking hell, imagine trusting your granny to that establishment! How quickly would she become incontinent?

There was talk that I wanted the security contract for the day of Reggie's funeral, but I wouldn't have done that job for all the tea in China. In each of the security firms that had done the big funerals I could see in their faces that they were thinking exactly the same as I did when I did Ronnie's. But it was nearly seven years down the line now, and I knew that back then no one could have told me the trouble it would cause me, so who the fuck am I to tell anyone else?

Ronnie had been a very good friend of the English painter Francis Bacon. Ron used to do a lot of painting himself when he was in Broadmoor and one he did was of the crucifixion. The crucifixion scene was also the image that Francis Bacon became most famous for with his version, so Ronnie sent his picture to Bacon. Someone then regarded as the baddest man in Britain had done a painting of the biggest saint in history and then sent it to Britain's greatest living artist. What a combination.

Francis Bacon hung the painting and hid the name and had people guess who they thought painted it. Most of them guessed right and said 'a complete fucking raving lunatic from the looks of it!'

After the deaths of both Ron and Francis Bacon the painting passed on in the estate to Bacon's partners, John and Phil. Phil was a friend of mine and he gave me Ron's painting as a gift. He said he thought it'd mean an awful lot more to me and that I'd treat it with respect. Which I did. Even more so when I found it had an insurance valuation of fifty grand and even had some offers from America for it. I didn't want to sell it because I thought it should stay in this country, but I didn't really know what to do with it. Then Andy Jones got in touch with me to ask for mementoes from my life to put in his Crime Through Time museum. I gave him things like the top hat I wore at Ronnie's funeral, one of my knuckledusters – stuff like that – and this crucifixion painting by Ronnie Kray. Andy was over the moon until he found out that because of its value his insurance for the museum would go through the roof.

So it ended up, for safe keeping, in the safe of my good pal Kevin Jenkins. Originally, when I'd first been offered it, it was in a lost treasure vault in Leicester Square. I went up there to see it and made a film about it.

I also still have the letters that Reggie sent me from prison. And if anybody has seen Reg's style of handwriting you'll know how unusual it was. Actually it was almost unreadable on first sight, but as you got to know it you could read it straight off. One of the letters written by Reg, about me but to someone else, was one of the best testimonials I've ever had: 'One of the old school in principle and character . . . I would trust him with my life. There has been ample evidence in the past of his abilities as a fighter, he has a big following and is recognised throughout London as a main figure . . . I value him as a very close friend.'

It really is the end of an era. Now the brothers have gone. It's a nail in the coffin of all the old legendary villains, and that whole aura surrounding them. Villainy has changed so much now, in the modern day, just like policing has changed to keep up. We won't ever see the likes of the Kray brothers again I think. (Austin Warnes, my bent copper, had got off on doing a couple of jobs for Reggie.)

And if ever I needed reminding that for every one bent copper you have on the payroll there are three or four bent coppers trying to fuck you, that reminder came around about this time with a big story with the headline 'Corrupt Police Framed Three for Robbery'.

EXAMPLE 3: These three geezers had been fitted up for armed robbery on a jewellers. Two detective constables had planted a stun gun in one bloke's flat and falsified a palm print to convict these poor fuckers, and they'd been doing bird for it since 1995. It was interesting reading it 'cos I kept getting echoes of what they'd already tried on me and what I thought they'd try again soon enough.

Listen to this – the police raided this one geezer's flat (in my stamping ground of South London) in the early morning, but got the wrong flat! Then they kicked his door in, beat him up, planted the gun, cuffed him and nicked him. Fucking hell, if he hadn't been black I might have thought they'd mistaken him for me.

It took them seven months and three attempts to miraculously match a palm print in the jeweller's to one of the fellas they'd roped in. Whilst banged up – and in Belmarsh as well, funnily enough – the geezer put in a complaint against the Old Bill. They rewarded him by sending one of the investigating officers to see him; and the copper said, 'No judge or jury will ever believe that those officers fitted you up! You've just got to serve your sentence.' Sound familiar? How many times have I been threatened with similar by officers eager to try and fuck my life up.

Anyway, these three fellas would still be rotting inside if an investigation hadn't revealed a good percentage of Scotland Yard's flying squad to be a bunch of lying, conniving bastards. So the three got their appeal.

One of the innocent blokes was quoted as saying, 'There's a lot of other guys in prison going through all this who have been fitted up, and no one's listening. I just want to give all those people hope.' And there was a picture in the paper of the three outside the Court of Justice looking pretty fucking vindicated. As they had a right to. For the record the geezers were called Anthony, Kevin and Michael. So a big shout out to them for staying strong and scoring the winner in injury time.

With all them bent Old Bill out there is it any wonder me and my mates had a bent one of our own to try and even up the score!

Fuck me, though; it was enough to make you want to go on holiday. So I did.

14. FORTY BLACK SUITS IN SHADES: GANG WARS

Who'd have thought that trying to get away from it all could drop you right in it? Here I get sun, sea & World War Three.

Right, so you're in the travel agent's looking through holiday brochures and you see this deal for Tenerife. It offers sun and sea and guarantees you'll get thrown into the middle of violent gang warfare where your friends will be attacked and hospitalised, and someone will shoot at you.

You'd book that deal straight away, wouldn't you? No, neither would I. But that's exactly the holiday I got. If ever there was a case of 'But it wasn't what I asked for . . .' then this was it. (And that's the last time I ever take a holiday recommended by Charlie Bronson!)

Going away to Tenerife for a week wasn't exactly a case of getting away from it all, as holidays usually are, because it was a kind of working holiday. Oh, who am I kidding? 'Course it was a holiday – I'd been invited back to do another 'Audience With Dave Courtney'. The last one had been a few months earlier, when I'd had my birthday bash out there as well, and the show went so well I got a return invite.

This time I'd be doing a joint show ('joint' being the word) with Mr Nice Guy himself Howard Marks, ex-drug smuggler and now fellow book writer. Howard is the absolute bollocks, even if he is Welsh. He knows some of the sexiest sheep I've ever seen.

The show would be on a Friday, which was fine by me, until I realised I was supposed to be in New York with Tricky on Wednesday to meet Quentin Tarantino on the Thursday. Oh the horror of the jet set lifestyle! Fucking good problem to have though. Better than your signing-on day clashing with an appointment at the VD clinic.

A bit of flight-time juggling sorted things out. I'd go to New York on Wednesday for Thursday, then fly from NY to Barcelona on Friday and get a flight from there to Tenerife. I should make it with a few minutes to spare. I'd shave my head on the plane and just hope we don't hit any turbulence.

Like I say, don't let the bastards grind you down. Carry on with life regardless. The 'Audience With . . .' tour continued full pace. We were even going international now, New York, Tenerife, Peckham!

The tour gave me an opportunity very few people in my position have had before, which was to go directly to the audience. Not just talk about *Stop the Ride* . . . and my past, but things that were happening right now. The court case, police corruption and the fitting-up tactics of bent coppers were just some of the subjects between the jokes. I even played the film of me attending Bow Street Magistrates' Court in the court jester's outfit on the day I knocked Warnes out. You're welcome.

Anyway, before that I had a trip to New York to make. New York is the fucking bollocks, mate. Like the song says 'New York, New York is a wonderful town!' Or it was when I was there, 'cos this was before some cunts had decided to parallel-park a couple of planes in the World Trade Centre.

I was going to meet my old mate Tricky, record boss Chris Blackwell, and film director Quentin Tarantino, and we were due to do an 'Audience With . . .' gig slap-bang in the middle of Central Park! Fucking 'ell. Not bad is it for a geezer with no O levels from Peckham? (Yeah, I didn't know Tarantino was from Peckham either.)

The day before was the Fourth of July, Independence Day, so all the armed forces were home for the celebrations. An extra million people walking round Manhattan with fuck all to do. Then, suddenly, there's these English geezers – us – giving a free chat in Central Park. So that boosted our audience figures by . . . oh, I don't know – a couple of hundred *thousand*. I was fucked off I didn't have the hotdog concession!

And when US Marines get off ship they're not allowed to wear civvies so they were all walking around in these smart white dress uniforms like Richard Gere in *An Officer and a Gentleman*. It was a bastard 'cos no matter how dressed up and impressive everyone else was trying to look, you just can't compete with some cunt swanning around in a white suit and medals. And I *did* have my white suit on! Who the fuck thought I'd get upstaged? And, seeing all these gym-trained recruits in the audience, I did the whole show holding my tummy in. Nearly gave myself a hernia.

We had a wicked time, mate. Though they have so many rules and regulations over there about how you behave in public – no drinking, no *swearing* – which meant I was half fucked before we began. And everyone had said that my humour ain't gonna go down over there but they were either laughing to be polite or the Yanks have all got a bit more cockney in them than they're letting on, because they absolutely loved it. All I did was compliment them, 'cos they love that over there don't they? I said that compared to American gangsters ours were pussycats – Reservoir Mogs.

Quentin liked that one. Fuck me, *Quentin*, how did he survive school with a name like that? Must be tougher than he looks. Which it would be impossible not to be. I'm not saying he's got big ears but he shouldn't go out in a high wind without tying his legs to a gatepost, that's all I'm saying. He looked like the FA Cup's brother. If he wasn't a genius filmmaker with all the glamour that comes with it, *and* the millions of dollars, which does pass as confidence – without all that he'd be a proper geek. And he knows it. The geezer don't look like he's never paid his TV licence. He wears *sandals* for fuck's sake. At least Jesus had an excuse, they didn't have Barretts then.

But . . . the geezer does make shit-hot films, no doubt about it. He was aware of my film and *Stop the Ride I Want to Get Off*. His perception of crime is pretty far from the truth, but the films are entertaining. What he's actually doing is remaking old gangster films in a new way. Nothing wrong with that.

And nothing wrong with us all sampling the New York nightlife either, which we most definitely did.

Next day I had to leave to try to get out to Tenerife for my and Howard Marks' show on the Friday. Easier said than done, because you can't get flights from New York to Tenerife. No surprise there, though, 'cos the Yanks barely know where *Britain* is, let alone some little Spanish island. I flew back to Britain and then out to Tenerife, to meet Jen and the kids; Seymour and Bulldog and their families. A proper holiday.

Proper jet-setting lifestyle or what? New York – Plumstead – Tenerife. I was having a week that sounded like the side of Del Boy's van! Between flights I barely had time to shave my head, do my bikini line, change my pants and have a smoke, a shit, a shower and a shoeshine before it was time to fly off again. At one point I got confused and had a shit in the shower and smoked the shoe polish, but *fuck me* that Kiwi Black don't half get you high.

So eventually I landed in Tenerife. An hour before the plane. I told you shoe polish is a strong smoke. I had half an hour to get to the actual theatre before the show began so I was dawdling around the airport, buying the plastic donkey and the big sunhat, like you do. Like a prick, not realising there are *two* airports on the island.

So when I asks the taxi driver how long to get there, he went 'Over an hour'! I was actually miles and miles away. Oh, how I laughed. So I flashed my wad at the driver (the pervert), *and* gave him some extra money, and we set off on a whip-crack-away mad-dash rush for the theatre. Hi-ho, Manuel, away! At one point I leaned out and put the donkey on the roof, like they used to do in *Starsky and Hutch* with the blue police light. Funny thing is it even *sounded* like a police car – Ee-aw! Ee-aw!

Acting like a nutter has its advantages when you're in a cab. They always try and get you there that bit quicker. Ha.

I walked into the theatre as it was just getting to the halfway interval. Howard was just winding it up and I realised he'd done half the show on his own. What a trouper. That's showbiz.

Any road, as I walked in all the doormen grabbed me. I thought, Hang on, I don't even *need* a ticket . . . It's my show! They were just wanting to get to me to tell me about a situation that had occurred. They said that Mickey Goldtooth was upstairs surrounded by a lot of people that he owed a lot of money to, and they were expecting me to go and mend it somehow. Either pay them what's owed, or give the nod for them to . . . take it out of Mickey in other ways. Mickey's sat there charlied out of his head not knowing what to do.

I walked in, said hello to Mick and said we needed to have a little word. He suggested we go out on the fire exit but I said no, everybody needed to see it or he was gonna get seriously *seriously* hurt.

It was fucking serious 'cos he'd robbed them and they wanted to put a hole in him. Whether he was doing anything wrong right then or not was not the fucking point 'cos he's been a proper soldier for me, has Mickey. So I said leave it to me and I'll sort it.

Now Mickey was someone I'd instantly gelled with on meeting him. He was a prize-fighter with a heart of gold – and a mouth of gold, hence the name – and he'd give his all for you, if he thought you were someone worth giving it for. I was lucky enough to be one of those he decided was worth it and I could *not* have had a better soldier than him for a very long time. He was the nuts.

But, circumstances meant that he had ended up in Tenerife with free drink and drugs and the added bonus that people out there thought he was Dave Courtney. Straight up. He shaved his head and started smoking cigars and answering to 'Dave'! After a week of that he was addicted to it. And I don't blame him: I know the feeling – I've been addicted to being me for 42 fucking years! It's a hard habit to break, being me. But *I've* got an excuse. I *am* ME. (Mickey even ended up with a bird that thought he was me! I hope I was a good shag! Anyway, I took the whole thing as a compliment.)

Anyway, he didn't have the actual finances to back it up and eventually started taking liberties with people that, under normal circumstances, Mickey wouldn't have done.

I had to think on my feet. It was one of them 'cruel to be kind' times. Giving him a battering in front of everyone, (1) To let them know he weren't acting for me, and (2) To make it easier for me to bargain for his life. Meaning, I can then say let him come home with me and pay you back over the next year . . . OR you take him up to the mountains and put a hole in him if it makes you feel better, but you won't get any money.

Anyway, I'm afraid he did get a good clump, that dog. (After that I kept Mickey Goldtooth with me: I drove him out of there, took him to his flat for his clothes and kept him at my place for two days and sent him home. Maybe me and my lifestyle were too addictive and he wanted to run before he could walk, which is very dangerous in this little game. Very fucking dangerous. It probably wasn't pleasant for him at the time, but if I'd done nothing he'd have got taken into the mountains for another belly button. From Mickey Goldtooth to Mickey No-Head.)

This upstairs bit in the club, by the way, was visible to everyone downstairs so the whole audience had watched this event happening, gobsmacked. Which is why I made sure it was like part of the act. Then I immediately went downstairs, jumped on stage next to Howard, took the mic and said 'HELLO!' Howard just stood there looking at me in bemusement. He couldn't believe it. He said, 'It's like I'm tripping, man . . .

but I haven't HAD anything!' Fucking funny, mate. Even funnier in his Welsh accent.

Doing a show with Howard Marks was a bit of a dream-come-true thing 'cos it was Howard that sort of showed me the way in the 'Audience With . . .' shows. He's a proper entertainer. Anyway, after the little dramas the show went off fantastic. One of the best.

Then everyone went down to Marco's Place, Happy Daze and then Bobby's Bar for a booze-up. It weren't meant to be a late one 'cos we had the kids. We ended up in a crowd of all these other British skinheads that worked for a big face over there called John Palmer. We were still unaware of the severity of the power struggle between Palmer and this other heavy geezer called Mohammed for control of the island. Anyway, what happens next but one of Mohammed's relatives walks in the bar, a little fella, and some of these skinheads *immediately* run over and attack him, doing him serious fucking damage. All nothing to do with us and I, personally, didn't feel comfortable with it, so we left. There'd been enough excitement for one day.

After all, I'd already done the Central Park show in New York, left America buzzing, flew to England, no sleep, mad dash home, flew to Tenerife, wacky races in the cab, got to the show and found the Mickey thing, had to clump my pal, jump on stage, do a live show, and to top it all off some fuckers started kicking off in the bar we were celebrating in. And most of this, remember, WAS ALL ON THE *FIRST NIGHT*!

Little did we know then that things were just about to get a lot, lot, lot worse.

A lot worse.

So Jennifer and the kids, Beau, Genson, Drew and Courtney, had gone out to Tenerife in advance (before I'd got back from New York), along with Seymour and his lady Jackie, Brendan, Bulldog with wife and family, Andy Gardener, wife and kids.

And we'd ended slap-bang in-between John Palmer's 500 skins and Mohammed's 2000 do-or-die Muslims. So it was a bit of a no contest, really. Though given the position you've got to give credit to Palmer for holding out for a very long time.

So, all this gang fucking warfare was going on before we even land on the island. Fuck all to do with me and mine.

Anyway it turns out that the little fella was a nephew or cousin of Mohammed's. He was family, put it that way. The geezer was beaten so badly he slipped into a coma, but before he did he said that he was 'attacked by Courtney's boys'. Fucking hell. But this happens a lot. You get the blame for things you did do and things you didn't do. I could even understand the fella making the mistake 'cos it looked like we'd all been together.

Not forgetting that I had been out in Tenerife a few months previous for another 'Audience With . . .' show, mob-handed, with one hundred and fifty shaven-headed geezers of mine. And that was during the feud on the island and we did get a bit roped into it then. The fact that five or six bodies went missing the week we were there, and what with bombs going off, beatings, everything, didn't really help our image as a group of travelling nuns.

Anyway, now Mohammed's at the hospital with his nephew and still thinking I'm responsible. Loads of people were running around, vigilante-style, under orders to find Dave Courtney and his firm, including a black geezer with locks – meaning Seymour.

By now it's the next day and I am out with my firm. Trouble is it's a firm that consists of one wife (Jen), four kids (Genson, Drew, Beau, Courtney), one mate and his missus (Seymour and Jackie), another mate (Costas) and a *baby*sitter (Lorna). Not exactly the fucking Wild Bunch is it, or the Dirty Dozen? More like the Slightly Scary Ten. Little did we know we were now Tenerife's Most Wanted. So we just carried on as normal, walked back into Bobby's Bar for a drink.

And we walked slap-bang – *SMACK!* – straight into a fucking Tarantino film scene. As soon as we were spotted by these Arab geezers they started going fucking beserk. They ran over, shouting, and attacked me and Seymour. One geezer pulled a gun on me and shouted at me to back against the wall, and he's got the gun in my face, screaming at me, 'I'm going to shoot you! I'm going to kill you!' They're all shouting. The others start laying into Seymour 'cos he fits the description of the black geezer they're after. I've got the gun pointed at me. My kids and Jen are there. Seymour is outnumbered but putting up a *proper* fucking good fight, 'cos he knows he's fighting for his life. Fists and feet and headbutts flying. Then they tried to get him down – 'Get on the *floor*!' – and they were gonna shoot him in the fucking back of the head. But one bloke started going, 'No! Outside! Outside!' and they started to try and drag Sey down the stairs. There was blood all over the wall.

I turned and saw Jen and the kids and Lorna cuddling little Courtney, and Costas who was looking after us over there, and I thought there's no way out of this – I've got to do something. I said to Jen, 'I've got to go get him, haven't I? You know that.'

And she said, 'Yeah, yeah you have.' And I love her, absolutely fucking *love* her for that, 'cos 99 per cent of women in that situation would think purely of their own husband and fuck whoever he was going to help, and they would say no don't go.

Ever felt like you wished you'd stayed in to wash your hair? Or, in my case, polish your head?

I'd love to have some smart, intellectual reason for why I done what I did then but I don't have one, I don't even think of it as bravery . . . but I have known Seymour since I had a fringe – *that* fucking long – since thirteen, fourteen years old I've known Sey. And all that time we've been very, very good pals and been through some rough old times . . . and here they were trying to drag him off to shoot him. An eye for an eye, a tooth for a tooth and all that; that's what one of the geezers was saying to me – 'I am gonna kill your friend!'

By this time, 'cos it was all moving very fast, Seymour and the geezers round him have fought their way to the back of the club, but Seymour's been beat to his knees and I can see him hanging onto the belt of one of the blokes to stop himself going down.

This other cunt had the gun pointed on me to keep me in place . . . I thought, *FUCK IT*, got my bollocks in my hand and just started walking quickly towards him. He started going, 'Stop! Stop!', completely fucking freaked by what I was doing. He backed off saying, 'Stay there! I'm going to kill you . . .!' I said, 'No you ain't. You ain't going to shoot me.'

He shot one off at the floor to prove it weren't no starting pistol, and I heard it ping off the floor. Reflex made me turn around, not that I thought it'd bounce off my back! But your body takes over. And turned that way I saw Jen with her hands over her eyes. I could hear them still trying to drag Seymour downstairs but he was still kicking up a fight, the tasty bastard. I turned back and thought I was close enough now to grab the gun. I was talking to the geezer, doing the old mind game routine. Then I grabbed for it but I'd overstretched myself and he whacked me on the back of the head with the gun. Cunt. It actually knocked me on the floor. I just fucking got up and went towards him again, and I'm glad I did 'cos this time he saw me coming and in his panic he bottled it and just ran. He passed the other geezers who were now at the bottom of the stairs, and they stopped giving Seymour a kicking, looked up, thought *What the fuck?* – and then ran off after the other one.

As I went down to where Seymour was lying I was actually pissing myself laughing. I swear to God. Whether it was relief or what I just don't know. Fucking joy, probably, but I got to him and I was just wetting myself! Sey was looking up at me like, What the *fuck* are you on! But then he started to laugh as well, even though he's in big pain, 'cos I think it was just sinking in what we'd just been through. And got away with.

I threw some water over his face, because he's vain he wanted to know how bad it was.

I said, 'Well, your eyes need twenty stitches, your lips are fatter than normal, half your locks are on the floor, you're gonna have one fucking blue pair of bollocks tomorrow, and I will always regret looking at you but you're still better looking than me!' Did it hurt? Only when he laughed.

The music was still on upstairs in the club, and everyone was staring at us through the hole that led downstairs. We finished washing Sey's face, dangled his hair over his fucked eye, and he got up straight and we walked out through the club. Just to show we could fucking do it. We got into the

Space Cruiser people carrier that Costas had and as the door closed, Seymour collapsed on the seat . . . and everyone started crying!

I drove off with the right hump. I said, 'How the fuck can I make him be brave and not moan about his aches and pains if you're all crying. Stop it.'

I guess, though, that that was their relief. Mine was laughing. I know which one I prefer.

As we drove to the hospital I was thinking, fucking hell, if you're ever *ever* in a position to do it and do it right, then what better place than in front of your wife, your kids and your best friends. And if you're gonna fucking go . . . I mean, get killed, you know what I mean? One thing you can't really choose in life is how and when you die, you can't choose that. But I was pretty fucking close to being able to pick it right there and then. And I weighed it up in my head that if I had to go anywhere it wouldn't half have been a good little 'dot.com' at the end of my story to go out that way.

It weren't over by a long chalk, though. The nightmare didn't actually end there.

We drove to the hospital to get Seymour stitched. What we didn't know – 'cos we still didn't know what the fuck this was all about – was that Mohammed was inside the hospital still doing the bedside vigil with his cousin in a coma. He looked out the window and saw us pull up outside . . . And thought we'd come to finish the kid off! How much more mental can you get? I ask you. Fucking hell! Talk about out of the frying pan and into the line of fire.

Still we didn't know any of this. I got Sey out and we went into the hospital: not knowing that Mohammed's on the phone rallying his troops to go up there on a mad-dash rescue mission. The nurse asked what had happened and Seymour said he'd fallen down the stairs. *Ha*. She must've thought he lived in a lighthouse! Two hundred stairs high.

While Seymour was getting stitched I wandered back outside to see Jen and the kids. Just then, three black Mercedes came screaming round the corner, and about fifteen lunatic, shotgun-carrying, Uzi-toting Arabs jumped out, grabbed me and threw me against the wall. I thought, Fuck me, the timeshare reps over here are a bit tasty!

Ever get the feeling you're in the wrong place at the wrong time in the wrong country and looking down the barrel of the wrong gun with the wrong eye . . . on the wrong planet? In the wrong fucking universe.

I was flattened against the wall but I could see that they had Jen lying on the floor of the van with the kids. I had the barrel of an Uzi pushed up my nostril and fuck knows how many geezers screaming at me and spitting in my face. Costas got out and they started screaming at him.

Inside, meanwhile, the nurses were panicking and telling Seymour that there are some very dangerous men on the island and they'd already got his friend – meaning me. They told him to get out of the window but he couldn't even get his arm through it. The nurses were shouting at him to get out for his own health. Bit like being on the NHS in England.

Anyway, 'cos they don't build normal fucking sized windows in Spanish hospitals, Seymour had to walk out the front to us. These geezers went double mental then and started shouting more: 'YOU! You fucking dog! We will kill you!'

Then the police turned up. And I have never *ever* been so pleased to see Old Bill in my whole fucking life. Even though they were Spanish (or Olé Bill, as they call them). Fat lot of good that did us, though, 'cos even when these mental fuckers saw the coppers they didn't put their guns away. They just started talking like they were all pals. And you know what the police are like, they favour whatever side they want. So if they've got to stick up for an English skinhead and his family or some local Muslims armed to the teeth – no fucking contest.

See, Tenerife is like this – Tenerife is to the Libyans and Moroccans like Marbella is to us. Meaning that when it gets a bit hot for them in their country, police-wise, they shoot over to Tenerife to hide out, like our criminals do to Marbella. So on Tenerife you've got thousands of the naughtiest, nastiest fuckers you could want to meet. It's like Club 18–30 for naughty cunts, except the 'eighteen to thirty' stands for what sentence they'd get if they went back home.

Me and Sey were made to lie down by the wall. The armed gang members moved and stood back. I asked Seymour if there was anything wrong with his legs.

'Er, no . . . why?'

' 'Cos if I can get Jen and the kids safe, me and you can still fucking leg it, mate. Unless they've hurt you on the legs we're bolting!'

So picture the scene. In front of this hospital in Tenerife on a mad-hot day there's me in my shorts with a golfball lump on my head from the gun smack, Seymour next to me with an eye like a big purple fanny, double-thick lips, black and blue and with scabs on all his cuts, Jen, the kids and the babysitter flat on the floor of the Space Cruiser, an army of hyped-up Arabs circling us, armed to the teeth, patients and nurses looking out the windows or hiding under beds, and the local police just stood there watching. And – remember – *THIS WAS ONLY THE SECOND DAY OF THE HOLIDAY!* The second fucking day.

Even God didn't get that much done by the second day.

I hadn't even unpacked!

I felt like I was in a combination of a *Carry On* film and a spaghetti fucking western – *A Fistful of Traveller's Cheques*. I thought, Right! Next year it's Bournemouth. Fuck the suntan.

Then another Space Cruiser came round the corner, a white one with blacked-out windows. Seymour went, 'Right, this is it. They're gonna fucking top us.' Well, I ain't one to naturally look on the black side *but*, the police *had* turned up and seen the guns and done fuck all, and now they were chatting like old pals. So you could see his point. This looked like our one-way ride to a ditch by the roadside. And in a white fucking Space Cruiser.

I said, 'No, they ain't going to take us anywhere. They ain't shot you and they ain't shot me, yet. Like I said, we can still fight . . . if we have to.'

They were all standing there now looking at us, Mohammed's boys and the police. They started searching our Space Cruiser and Jenny and the kids had to get out. Me and Seymour moved nearer to the van and I got near to Costas so I could whisper to him; 'Grab Jenny and the kids, Costas, and take them somewhere, quickly.'

Now, people sometimes decide to do the bravest thing at the wrong moment, y'know: the right thing at the wrong time. So when Costas said to me, 'No, Dave, I'll stay here and die with you!' it sort of fell into that category. I weren't planning on dying *anywhere*, mate, so I think Costas was a bit gobsmacked by my answer.

'Listen, don't be a fucking idiot! We're gonna leg it but we can't until Jen and the kids are safe. So you take them away.'

Before it could get to that the police moved in and arrested me and Seymour. What for we didn't know – carelessly throwing our nostrils on the gun barrels, or something – and we didn't really care. At least it got everybody safe. Or as safe as you can be in police custody.

They took us down the station. They also gave the gang blokes our names and addresses and passport numbers – oh cheers! I was let out a few hours later but they kept Seymour in. They ended up keeping Seymour for four days.

In the meantime I tried to call someone that had come to Tenerife with me, but he'd turned his phone off.

So now I was in the position of having Jen and the kids with me and knowing that the police had given out our address to the gang. I got Costas to get me some armoury from somewhere on the island. Until this was all sorted I wanted something for me to defend everyone with; and something more than me just saying, 'Hang on a minute, there's been a terrible mistake.' In the time it'd take you to say that, you could be shot six times.

So we're all holed up in our villa in the mountains feeling like we've accidentally booked a week in Vietnam during the war. Seymour was still in the nick. What I didn't want was for him to come out and walk right into the arms of this gang.

They decided to have a court hearing. So for the next three mornings I drove us down to the courthouse. Jen and Seymour's missus, Jackie, hung around outside while I waited at the corner in the car, ready to whizz it up in front of the doors at first sight of him.

What actually made it a bit safer was the amount of media there. The courthouse was awash with TV crews and press, and even helicopters flying about. On an island that size this was massive, massive news. Mostly because the father of the Arab kid in a coma had gone on national TV and, while he was sat on the edge of the hospital bed (nice touch), he'd said, 'If this is a present from Mr Palmer then last night's casualties will only be the first of many.'

Fuck me. That's like advertising gang warfare on national telly! And check that out: 'will only be the first of many'.

Oh yeah, I almost forgot . . . then things got worse.

Much worse.

I have some people around me for novelty value. In a wide circle of friends you need a few jokers, and if I meet someone who is double-jointed, for example, and his party piece is kissing his own arse, or there's a bird that can tie her tits in a bow and blow fag smoke out her fanny then they can definitely come along and entertain us.

But these people should not be party to information that gets talked about in certain circles. But, everyone forgets at some point, particularly in moments of stress, like in Tenerife, and talks a bit too freely in front of these jokers.

There happened to be a gentleman on holiday there with us who is a world-class idiot, and I mean world class. But, he's fucking funny with it, and good val. Among other things, he goes around telling everyone he was the legal advisor to the Krays and also passes himself off as a spokesman for me. God fucking help me. Which is exactly the kind of help I wanted when I found out what this little prick had done in Tenerife. Walking through the town he'd just happened to see some of the gang members that were on the warpath. He approached them to do a deal and arranged for them to pick Seymour up outside the court! Not only that, but he gave them the address of our villa and said that I'd meet them up the mountains to collect Seymour.

In his fucking Idiot state he believed he was bargaining on my behalf for Seymour's life, when really what he'd done was sign his life away.

Now I didn't know any of this. Yet. In the dark once again. Par for the course on this fucking trip. In the dark so often I felt like Stevie Wonder. So what happened was that I got a message saying there was no need to pick Seymour up 'cos it had all been sorted.

Anyway, thinking that Seymour would soon be on his way, I ambled down to the nearby café for breakfast and met this geezer in there who was already having his. He said that he was the one that had got the message to me. I thought, hang on, I don't really know you. 'Wait a minute, mate . . . run that by me again. *How* did this happen?'

That's when I got the full story about the 'deal' the Idiot had done down in town. So now there's the possibility that this silly cunt had unwittingly set a trap that Seymour's gonna walk straight into. After all that fighting and fucking bullet-dodging we'd done, after all that, some little gimp we'd brought with us goes and fucks it all up.

I jumped in the car and flew down to town. I stopped off halfway there to grab this fucking Idiot along the way. And I battered him the rest of the journey, driving with one hand and smacking with the other. To be honest, I wanted to twist his legs together, drill him into the ground neck-deep and use his head for a penalty. But we didn't have the time. I said, 'You'd better pray that Seymour's okay 'cos if the worse happens to him I will fucking *bury* you on top of him.'

When we got there I was expecting the worse. I thought I could at least strap the Idiot on me as a bulletproof vest. Luckily the court didn't let Seymour out that day either.

So the Idiot got a clump for fuck all, but deserved it nonetheless. When you're a complete fool like this prick and you still think you're important . . . fucking hell, then you just become dangerous. This guy had gone past the point of being a novelty and become a pest.

Apart from that he's a funny man.

At the courthouse the next day there was about five, white skinhead geezers up for the charge of attacking the little Arab fella. These blokes were still scarred from the punch up, their heads looked like they'd been through a mangle – they had more stitches than my suit. And because Seymour didn't fit the description of the attackers – 'black fella with dreads' don't exactly match 'white geezer with skinhead' does it (even the Spanish police couldn't change that) – the court had to let him go. About time too. He'd been in jail from Sunday morning to Thursday afternoon. Some fucking holiday. Try selling that one on *Wish You Were Here*.

He was bailed and we got him out to the car, a very fast walk I can tell you. We went to a secret place that we'd all moved to in the meantime. It's called Belgium. No, actually Costas had found us another gaff on the island where we could lay low for a while.

You know them adverts for American Express and Barclaycard where they make a big play about sorting out all your holiday problems, 'Leave it to us, we'll look after everything' and all that crap? Well, I did wish I'd been with either of them just for the laugh of ringing up and hitting them with this one! 'I'm trapped on an island, slap-bang in the middle of local gang warfare, with my family, a beaten-up mate, two dodgy pistols and a sawn-off, and one of the gang bosses thinks we tried to kill his cousin. Oh, and I've lost my traveller's cheques.' Sort that one out.

Anyway eventually peace was made with everyone when Palmer realised that it was nothing to do with us and Mohammed realised it was nothing do with Palmer *or* us. So that was sorted. Don't you just love a happy ending? Yeah, so do I, shame we didn't get one. Because word also got back to us that all the attackers hadn't been caught yet, so there were still some vigilantes out there looking for likely suspects. And we still fell heavily into that category. That's one of the consequences of going on holiday with a bunch of people who look like they eat babies and pick their teeth with the bones. And that's just my kids.

As a result we had to swerve Bobby's Bar and places like that so the same kind of mistake wasn't made again. I think getting shot at *once* on any holiday is just about enough. Any more than that would be just silly.

Remember the geezer, one of our gang that I'd tried to get in touch with before and found his phone permanently off? Well I did manage to get through to him at last to get the message to him – be a bit wary when you go out and don't go in the wrong bars 'cos you might get hurt. As it happens, that message was the thing that brought him out, finally, to speak to me.

He came up to our hotel with too much swagger for someone that had let me down. He asked about the message I'd left.

I said, 'Wait a minute, let me get this straight. You know what's happened with me and Seymour, and that Jen and the kids were here as well, but the only thing that's brought you out to come speak to me is the thought *you* might get hurt . . . Am I right in thinking that?'

He said yeah. So I'm afraid I planted one on his chops. Another deserved one. It was a day for settling scores. One of them days.

Straightaway I told him that if he wanted to get the hump he could fuck off right now and then get embarrassed next time he saw me back home OR he could sit down and have a beer with me, 'cos in his heart he must know that he deserved that clump.

He sat down and we had a beer.

When we'd first been holed up in the villa, the police had given our address to the geezers that had been looking for us. The Spanish Old Bill had also quite blatantly showed them our passports before they'd taken us to the station. Which all goes to show that it's not what you know it's who you know. And bent coppers are the same the world over.

The little hotel room we now had was like the fucking Alamo. I'd got some weaponry from Mickey Goldtooth, who was still out there with us. I'd already had to mend that little problem with him, of course, but I love Mickey to bits. Andy was there with us as well, got to mention Andy 'cos he was there all the way. Andy, me, Seymour, Jen and Jackie, the kids, Beau, Drew, Genson, Courtney, the babysitter, Lorna, and my friend and his family. Like I say, it was supposed to be a sort of working/family holiday. We ain't gone out there mob-handed.

I think we'd seen more horror on this holiday than the bleedin' Addams Family. The only other holiday that came close was that time in Spain when we were attacked by marauding gypsies in a corn field and I ended up biting off a bloke's finger and being slung in jail. Remember that one? (Check out *Stop the Ride . . .*)

Any road, Mickey stopped in my hotel until I took him to the airport. I walked him through the whole thing and right up to the gates and saw him get on the fucking plane. No mistakes. He'd been on the loose over here for ten months but now he had a lifeline: go home to Britain and work off his money troubles; whereas before he was *definitely* odds-on favourite to end up in a hole in the mountains. And those mountains are littered with them. Remember, in the eyes of the police – No body = no murder.

By the time we left I'd never been so pleased to see a little, cramped, crap food, no legroom airplane in my life. We could've been flying home Suicide Airlines-dot.com and we'd have still taken a chance.

I still think they should sell bulletproof vests and hand grenades in duty free, though. You never know.

Anyway, apart from all that, it was a bloody good holiday. You should've seen the photos.

15. PORN IN THE USA

Here we go, here we go, here we go. Getting it on in England and getting off in Los Angeles!

We got back to England, at last, in one piece. Even the airline food couldn't finish us off. *That's* how determined we were to get home . . . Soggy chicken in a plastic tray? Bring it on.

The trial had been set for 6 November, so there was about four months to go. The speaking tour carried on. Onwards and upwards. Upwards to a little country retreat I know in Nottingham, actually. Nottingham, that's where Robin Hood lived with a load of other blokes and they all wore tights. No wonder they called them the Merry Men.

In *Stop the Ride* . . . I talked about the first big security gig that I did at a place called the Queen Mother Reservoir Yachting Club, or Queens, as everyone called it, down near Heathrow Airport. It was a great club but spoilt by all the trouble they had there, which came from this massive gypsy site nearby. For travelling people they don't travel very fucking far. They're a bloody good bunch of fighters, though. A proper force to be reckoned with.

I took on the job that no one wanted of trying to keep the peace there. I used to drive down to Queens from London in my black Austin Princess Hearse with my crew in the back. Belting down the motorway at over a 100 mph, we were the only 'undertakers' who overtook everything. On the back window we'd spray 'JUST BURIED'.

We got in some real wars there – fights, stabbings, shotgun shootings, ram raids, door-charges, petrol bombings (and those were the quiet nights) – before we eventually got a lid on it. One of the best things to come out of that experience, apart from the fact it was like a Fight Club to polish your combat skills, was meeting the owner of Queens, a gentleman named Vinoo. Vinoo was probably the best guv'nor I've had, or any doorman could ever have. He'd protect you 100 per cent. He'd come to court to get you, put up your bail, vouch for you and pay you three times as much as anyone else. He did expect more back in return, but we gave it.

Fuck me, that was fifteen years ago now, when I think about it. How time flies when you're being naughty.

Anyway, Vinoo took over this country place called Stoneyford Lodge. That's where me, Jen and a substantial part of Courtney Crew of London headed for my 'Audience With . . .' evening. It'd been a few years since I'd seen Vinoo so it was absolutely wicked to see him again. We really got into the old reminiscing mode, like, 'Oh remember when the gypsies set the telephone poles on fire to cut off our phone line!' and 'What about when the windows were blown out by shotguns!' Y'know, touching little memories like that.

Nottingham being in the middle of the country meant it was easy for people to come there from all over. It was sold out. We had people from Leeds, Manchester, Liverpool, Birmingham, Sheffield, Derby, and Coventry. Yeah, not one place where anyone talks normal. It was like the National Accent Awards. Hearing a Brummie, a Scouser and a Yorkshire geezer have a three-way conversation is fucking baffling, mate. I was lost in the Bermuda Triangle of accents.

Stoneyford Lodge is this pub/club/restaurant/hotel complex in the middle of the country, so they hadn't seen anything like it when four hundred people descended on them all at once. Just the sight of the geezers who turned up scared the local cows into not giving milk for a week.

The 'Audience With . . .' on the Thursday evening went blinding and I ended up talking for much longer than other ones I've done. It was nearly three hours, but I got on a proper roll and they wanted me to carry on, so I did. (I think the gearbox went on my voice box and I got stuck in fifth doing 90!) Enlightening people about some of the workings of our lovely police force is always a buzz for me; and I played the film of me on the court steps in the jester's outfit, just after I'd belted Warnes, saying 'I still have faith in the British justice system!' If everybody hadn't already realised how bent the Old Bill can be then they would by the end of this tour. And the tour never ends.

Afterwards we had a book-signing session, a going-to-the-bar session, and then into the club next door for a dancing session. Because there were rooms at Stoneyford for people to sleep everyone hit the bar big-time. There were some proper funny people there as well. This Yorkshire bloke told me he'd been arrested more times than anyone I knew. I said, 'I doubt it. You don't know who I know.' Another one told me he was a street trader. I said that must be fucking hard work, buying and selling streets. I mean where do you store them? He must've had one helluva big lock-up somewhere.

It doesn't happen often, but occasionally there's someone at these gigs that wants to have a go. Especially when they've had a few. There was this one geezer who, for a start off, had got the night's Fashion Award for Best Supporting Prick. He was wearing a proper stripy 70's tank-top with nothing underneath. Which is a good look for a court appearance if you're going for a 'diminished responsibility' plea. Any jury would've looked at that tank-top and immediately recommended an open prison with regular therapy. Apparently he'd taken offence at something I'd said during the talk: about how when you get arrested you can stick to 'no comment' if you want – unless you've got a fucking good reason not to (like I'd had when the Old Bill had questioned me) – and if you decided not to speak don't let them bully you into speaking. Which is all fair comment.

What I didn't know is that he'd been nicked recently and thought he had to answer every question, and he'd gone and dropped himself right in it.

Anyway, it got to the point where he offered me outside – for 300 quid! Get that. I said that I didn't want to take advantage of him when he was drunk and told him to come back tomorrow morning when he was sober and I'd batter him for free. Special offer. Can't say fairer than that.

We were up bright and early the next morning considering we'd gone to bed just before dawn. Fuck me, though, isn't the countryside noisy? Cocks crowing, cows mooing, tractors starting, fucking birds doing the dawn chorus. I thought it was supposed to be peaceful. I get less noise in Plumstead.

It was nice being away from London for a while. I had some more work to do as well – finishing the manuscript for the next book *Raving Lunacy* – and here was a good place to do it. Reading and writing aren't exactly my forte; I went to school so little the teachers kept forgetting what I looked like. Doing the books didn't half sharpen me up quickly, but trying to work in London at Camelot Castle was a bit of a nightmare. I couldn't have had more people coming in and out of that house if I'd had a revolving door fitted and two judo experts stood outside throwing people in.

So out in the Stoneyford Lodge gardens in the bright sunshine I got down to my homework. It was good having Vinoo on hand 'cos he reminded me of loads of things that had happened that I could put in. It was at Queens that I met my good mate Wolfie.

At one point during the afternoon I went off to stretch my legs. Well, I've always wanted to be taller. Next to the beer garden I saw these two country ladies sat on their horses having a chat. As you do. Nothing unusual there. Happens all the time in Plumstead. If you're hallucinating. So I went up to say hello. These horses were fucking huge, mate. I mean proper big, handsome beasts. One of them with this little lady perched on top. She must've had some fucking dynamite thighs to control that between her legs. Have pity for the husband, I thought!

She jumped down, or 'dismounted', as horsey people call it. See, I'd only been in the green bit of the country for a day and already I was speaking the lingo. She patted its neck and went, 'This is a half-cross Appalachian Blue. There is none better than this.' That was good enough for me so I asked if I could have a go.

Christ, when you get up there it's a long way down. The horse is big, but then you get on and add your body length on top . . . and you feel two stories high. Anyway, no backing down, so I set off up this path on a canter, turned him around at the top and decided to go into a trot coming back. How clever was that? 'Not very' or 'very not very'? Actually, what was happening was that 'cos the stirrups were set higher for the woman's feet I kept digging my heels in the horse's side and accidentally telling it to speed up!

It took off like a rocket. I saw the two little wide-eyed ladies and a big green hedge behind them heading towards me at Warp Factor 2. I thought, right, you big cunt (the horse, not me) and pulled back hard on the reins. It skidded to a halt like something in a cartoon.

Oh, the fun of country life. It occurred to me that it'd be a brilliant stunt to turn up for the first day outside the Old Bailey, on the back of a fucking big Appalachian Blue. What do you think, bit over the top? Not like me at all then.

Everyone else had gone home by now so the last night at Stoneyford was just for me and Jen. Which is a rarity that there ain't a million other people around us. We went into the bar that night and the barman looked at me funny and went, 'I don't know if I was seeing things but did I see you fly past the window this afternoon on the back of a big horse? . . .'

Next morning – trouble. We woke up at 9 a.m. and Jen suddenly remembered that I was supposed to be best man at the wedding of John and Kathleen at a South London registry office at eleven! Ooops. By the time we'd got ready, thrown everything in the car and said goodbye to Vinoo it was 9.30. I had an hour and a half to do 135 miles. I knew if I did 100 mph for the first hour that'd leave me half an hour for the last 35 miles. But that would be going across London where traffic is always a cunt. Better then if I went, say, . . . 120 mph.

One of my sayings is 'Don't tell me – show me'. And I'm a 'practise what you preach' kind of person. I think most people wouldn't have even tried to make it – it was an outside chance – and the few that would try would fail through not trying for it 100 per cent.

We were in this Cherokee Jeep of Jennifer's but it had a decent-sized engine so, chocks away! I came off the on-ramp and entered the M1 at 90 mph. Start as you mean to go on, I say. It was a fucking big shock for everyone else on the motorway though, 'cos I was going too fast to move over between cars so I thought, oh fuck it, and moved onto the hard shoulder and stayed there for about five miles at 120 mph. Undertaking everything on the way. Actually they're quite easy those hard shoulders you know. It wasn't hard at all.

The traffic spread a bit and I got over to the fast lane. Which isn't rightly named because no one was doing over 90!

That set me off on an hour and twenty minutes' worth of overtaking, undertaking, weaving, dodging and hard shouldering. Not a thing overtook us 'cos nothing dare. I passed Cosworths, BMWs, Porsches and one Ferrari. Every now and again some driver would get the hump that his new BMW had been overtaken by a Jeep, but when we stayed at 120 mph for a few miles he'd suddenly think, Do I really want to lose my licence, and back off. I thought there was no way we wouldn't get clocked by an unmarked police car. Even if they couldn't keep up they would radio ahead.

We were getting nearer but time was moving on. I'd covered a fuck-load of miles in the last hour but traffic was starting to build up already. I knew we needed a little unlawful impediment to the marriage. It's amazing what the right accent can do so I rang a mate of mine who does a good Irish one, and asked him to go to the nearest phone box. I said that when he got there if he wanted to ring the registry office and suggest there was an explosive device in the building then that was entirely up to him and God forbid that I would think it a good idea! Cheers.

He rang me back five minutes later and said he'd been overwhelmed with a sudden feeling of naughtiness and made the call. Cheeky monkey. Kids today, eh? Fucking idiots. I BLAME THE PARENTS. Got that, officer?

So we burned on down the foot of the M1 leaving a cloud of brake dust and cigar smoke behind. 'Burned down' being pretty accurate, more like 'burning up' to be exact. There was a fucking awful smell from the clutch, which meant it was on its last legs and the brake pedal was having less and less effect. By now everyone would be at the church. The groom, John, family and friends. Kathleen the bride and her family and friends. All waiting for it to begin. All those fucking awful hats hired for the day!

We came off the M1 and hit a typical London logjam, which meant more 'creative' driving. That's what I call it, 'creative'. 'And what exactly did you think you were doing, Mr Courtney, when you went straight across the roundabout on two wheels and slid sideways down an alley?' Being creative, your honour. Yeah, I was just getting in touch with my inner wanker.

Sixteen run-through red lights later we were getting near. I'd called the registry office a few times but there was no answer. Good. God bless the Irish. And the devil could fuck the Jeep 'cos the brakes finally went. Nothing. Flat to the floor. I had to start stopping it off the handbrake. The clutch smelled like an asbestos pot-pourri. That was fucked as well. We finally managed to get over Vauxhall Bridge before the whole fucking car burned out and gave up the ghost. We were only two miles away and it was 11.15. I freewheeled along and bumped it up on the pavement, right outside a taxi office as it happens. Touch! Oh, yes – God was smiling. He can't have even been bitter that they weren't getting married in church.

We slung the bags in the cab. For some reason I got an immediate earful from the old geezer driving about how he'd known all the old villains, and this face and that chap; who he didn't fucking know is nobody's business. I asked him if he knew Dave Courtney. 'Oh, yeah. He's alright he is. Nice fella.' Hand on heart; I swear that's what he said. I wanted him to say I was a real *tasty* bastard – so I didn't tip him. Ha.

I jumped out the cab halfway up the road after we got stuck. I came round the corner and crossed the road to the registry office just as the police's yellow barrier-tape was being taken down. That's always a special moment at a wedding, I find. Everyone was outside on the pavement waiting for the all clear and they looked at me as if to say, 'cutting it a bit fine weren't you?' So I just held up my hands and went, 'Ready?' And we all walked in. Even I couldn't believe I'd timed it so well. But one mile per hour slower, one minute less on the hard shoulder, one less mate who couldn't do accents, and I wouldn't have made it at all.

Someone even came up to me inside and said it was a good job there'd been a bomb scare or I wouldn't have made it. True.

Anyway, there was loads of people there, everybody happy and it made it all worthwhile. I would've really, really hated to let them down. Even though it cost me a car.

During the ceremony, when it got to the part where the registrar says, 'Is there anyone here with any lawful impediment to this marriage? . . .' there was such a long silence afterwards that couldn't I resist it. I said, 'I think I can hear ticking.'

No, listen, it went down a bomb.

So even though the Old Bill like to feel they've got their finger on the 'pause' button in regards to your life it don't mean your life has to stop, and I was totally, 100 per cent proof, solid-gold, 24-carat absolutely fucking positive it weren't gonna have that effect on me. I'd carried on with the 'Audience With . . .' tours (including video film of the court jester appearance), gone to Tenerife and done a show, gone to Charlie Kray's funeral, popped over to New York to see Tricky, and written a new book! I was packing it all in. If I could've appeared on *Who Wants To Be A Millionaire* and the *Tweenies* I would've done.

Do not let them grind you down.

Next stop? . . . Los Angeles in the good ol' U S of A. Let's try there, shall we? Make a change from Plumstead anyway. Less drive-by shootings for one thing. I decided to do a piece for *Front* magazine about this English geezer called Miles who is quite big in the blue film industry. In fact he's quite big everywhere.

Miles was looking for English girls to work abroad, and because of the links with the fetish and sex club scene I knew of quite a lot of suitable birds. There's also a good friend of mine out in LA called Guy who works in Sin City in Hollywood.

The money the girls could earn from working out there was an awful lot more than back here, maybe three times as much per day. So I got some people to go out and work with Miles, and I went out there as their minder for the week they were looking for somewhere to stay and trying to find their feet. I thought they should try looking behind their heads because that's where their feet usually were, but what do I know.

LA's wicked though. If you've never been you've got to go. Forget Ibiza for one year and go clubbing in LA. It is full of Americans but you can't have everything. No, actually, I like them. I like that positive attitude thing, that's right up my street.

While I was there I saw the large financial possibilities of the blue film industry. It ain't exactly difficult to spot 'cos it's a billion dollars per year business. Something like every one in four video tapes rented in America is a porno one. Who'd have thought it – they're even bigger wankers than us. That ain't Alaska above the States, it's one massive used tissue.

Anyway, the thing that got me was how the blue film industry over there is not really frowned upon in the way it is in this country. In fact, we're probably one of the few countries left where it is thought of like that. In LA, where they make all the blue films, it's all above board and professional. Some of the big budget blue films are like proper films and a lot of the film technicians like camera and lighting men work on blue films when they're not making ordinary ones. They do these porno rip-off versions of Hollywood movies. They've got wicked titles, *Shaving Private Ryan*, *ET – The Extra Testicle*, *Forest Hump*, and my favourite, *The Bare Tits Project*. Let's hear it for 'Pornywood'.

We went on set to watch the films being made. Sort of 'Lights, camera, hard-on!' Now, I thought I was broadminded . . . but I had to walk around and pretend I wasn't shocked. There was like this big aircraft hanger and in all four corners there was a set built with four different blue films being shot – a gangbang with midgets, a lesbian scene, a three-blokes-on-one-bird scene, and a dialogue scene in a bar. Fuck me, I didn't know where to look. Actually, I did. The dyke bonkfest.

I'll tell you what, watching these films being made makes you very suspicious of any woman's orgasm 'cos these birds faked it so well. You'd be stood there watching them full at it, moaning, groaning and going 'Oh yeah baby!' and then all of a sudden they all stop and one gets up to go to the bog! or the make-up lady walks over to dab some powder on. Fucking weird. While that's going on the geezer stands there wanking so he don't lose his hard-on. The bird comes back, takes a bite of her sandwich, has a drink and they start again. And she picks up moaning where she left off.

I was like, 'Wow!' It shocked the bollocks out of me. It made you realise that it's purely a job to them (don't go looking for it at your local Jobcentre though). You have to witness it to fully get it; the complete lack of inhibitions or desire for privacy, the fact that no one gives a fuck about being naked or being watched doing something that's usually private (or just between you, your wife and the goat).

I thought it was all really cool, actually. The professionalism of it all. It ain't at all tacky. They all have AIDS tests every thirty days, and when they go for a film they take their passport for ID and bring their new test.

The shagging part don't mean anything though. It really is just a job. Bloody good way to earn a living if you ask me. Some of these geezers had non-stop hard-ons – fucking blinding! – although Viagra may play a part but no one is saying. So some of them can shag all day but they can't come. That's when they bring in what they call the 'stunt cock'. Get that. The stunt cock. Fancy having that on your passport under 'occupation'. When the first geezer can't come, or he's got none left in him after doing it all day, they bring the stunt cock fella in.

Now listen to this bit. The stunt cock comes in and strips off. The other geezer who's banging the bird pulls his cock out and the stunt dick moves in and stands beside her for the come shot. But the first bloke who was shagging her, he puts his hand on the stunt guy's cock as he comes! I couldn't get my head round it. I mean I know they can't have two different-looking hands on the film, but fuck me . . . they were actually using different cocks. I couldn't believe it. It's just part of the job to them though.

So they wrap up the shot, the stunt dick gets his fifty dollars or whatever it is, and rides off into the sunset the conquering hero. Although I don't remember John Wayne letting another geezer wank him off, to be honest.

An interesting thing was watching how a man/woman relationship worked once the sexual bit was removed. It was like the sexual side wasn't there because they were too familiar with each other. And once that little bit in your head that says 'Yeah I wouldn't mind' has gone, and the man's sitting there stark naked talking all day long to a woman who's stark naked, then they actually get on together. Men get on with women! They're both on a level and no one's trying to disguise the sexual bit because it's already been and gone. Once that's not there you understand women.

And if it means shagging loads of women to get to understand them then all the better! (There, I've gone and spoilt that touching little 'understanding' moment, haven't I?)

Seriously, though, I could see then why everyone was so laidback and friendly. It was because the sexual tension side of things had gone. Which is ironic, considering they were porn stars. Doing it all day every day to order must take some of the excitement away. Seeing a woman getting shagged up the arse three times by lunchtime must but a dampener on things. The fantasy goes out the window once you've seen it all: her stark naked for three days being fucked up the arse by five midgets dressed as jockeys. See, once your imagination has been spoilt then it gets past all that.

I did actually get to fulfil my fantasy on a blue film set. And no, this is one time when I am gonna let your imagination run riot. I'm not doing all the work for you! All I'll say is it involved a blonde nun, twin cheerleaders, a pint of baby oil and an egg whisk. Let me tell you, everyone likes to think they could do the old porn star job but it's a lot harder than you think, so to speak. When you're surrounded by twenty people with cameras, microphones, talcum powder, bottles of Coke, lubricant, dildos, scripts and a spatula. Fortunately for me the nun's habit and cheerleaders were enough to kick-start my imagination.

You can't do it for a living if you're a normal bloke though. The geezers who do it for a living are deformed, mate. It's like they've got three legs and you're stood there feeling like a nine-year-old!

Word got around that the real fella that Vinnie Jones' character in *Lock, Stock and Two Smoking Barrels* was based on was in town, so I had meetings with film people and got the red carpet treatment. Well Vinnie's quite big out there now so that's had a knock-on effect with the Americans getting interested in the British scene; and the Madonna connection to Guy Ritchie can't have hurt either. I got another call from Quentin Tarantino's representatives and had a meeting with them. They must be into the Brit scene more, because Hollywood even remade *Get Carter* with Sylvester Stallone.

One of the English girls out there with us really wanted to get famous and she had this idea about coming home and selling a story to the papers about her doing a lap dance for Vinnie Jones. It was a bullshit story so I put a stop to her doing that. I know more than most what an effect it can have when the papers start printing lies about you. Which is something I was going to find out a lot more about when the trial date started getting near (you'll see what I mean later).

Anyway, I ended up with some press following me around and I did some interviews for LA radio stations about the book and the British scene and moving into films and all that. They are enthusiastic Americans, though, aren't they? I do like that.

I met up with a couple of Brits out there, Chris Paul and his missus Zoe. Chris is a DJ that used to play at my raves years ago. Later he moved to LA (working at my gigs could have that affect on people!). He heard about *Stop the Ride* . . . so I'd sent him a copy and mentioned him in *Raving Lunacy*. He was really kicking it off over in LA, running his own rave company and DJing at the private parties after the Oscars. His missus Zoe used to be a Page 3 girl in Britain, but in America she's gone on to act in films and model for *Playboy*. That's one of the best things about the States, they don't hold your past against you like they do in England. She probably couldn't have gone on to act over here 'cos the Page 3 thing would've prejudiced people against her, but in LA she could model for *Playboy* and do the acting as well. And, get this, she was also applying to join the LAPD! Fuck me, being arrested by an ex-*Playboy* model would certainly take some of the sting out of getting nicked. If you don't believe me check out her website – www.totallyzoe.com.

So our little troupe of Brits went out clubbing. It is nice to meet some of your own when you're away though, ain't it? Y'know, people who talk proper like what we do! We went to the Viper Rooms and met Johnny Depp. Then we ended up at a club where Chris was DJing. He introduced me to the crowd and held up his copy of *Stop the Ride* . . .! We met more promoters at the club who were planning on doing a massive rave with Paul Oakenfold. It was all wicked, mate. How could I not love every minute.

Hollywood is so plastic it's fantastic. It really is. And it's really funny – but it is true – that everyone does believe in the American Dream, or at least the ones who end up in LA do. They promote it so much that everyone there is on their way to another career. Or so they believe. So the bloke that parks your car is a budding Tom Cruise, the taxi driver thinks he's the new Ricky Martin, your waitress thinks she'll be the next Julia Roberts. And if they play it long enough they become it. They're all living the part hoping that someone will discover them.

It does happen. There are so many stories where someone was discovered like that. Harrison Ford was a carpenter and was spotted when he did some work on this film producer's house. In Hollywood all that kind of madness and dreaming and the people who believe in it is all condensed into a small space. Everyone who's like that moves there. And everyone exaggerates whatever they are, so the bodybuilders look more like 'bodybuilders' than any others you've ever seen, the porn stars look exactly like what they are, actors try and look starry, even the hookers look like they think they're a film about hookers.

They do like an individual, someone who has a flair in whatever it is they do. Whether it's a singing road sweeper or a bodybuilding bellboy. What's different about the attitude there is that they encourage everyone to show off their ace card, whereas over here they expect you to keep your ace card hidden up your sleeve. Playing ace cards – especially my own – is my forte, mate. I ain't even gonna try and be shy about that one. And in LA just being real is enough to set you apart.

There is this one geezer over there called Ed Powers, who makes these gonzo style blue movies with girls off the street and out of clubs. Shag Your Neighbour, stuff like that. And like I'd make thousands of flyers to promote a rave, he does that with his line of work, makes loads of postcards and posters and advertises himself everywhere. He's a brilliant self-publicist and really, really funny. He has his own series of videos called *Ed Powers' Debutantes* and does his own porn show with things like 'Slut Of The Week'. Blokes ring up and put their wife or bird on it! Top.

Some of the blue movie people have since been over to this country as well and seen my little operation that I set up with a partner. Jen helped out making a few films. Not being in them but helping out with the auditioning, which is always fun.

But in LA everything is exaggerated. The whole town is fucking wicked. You can tell I came back a proper convert, can't you? Coming back on the plane, just thinking about some of the things I'd seen gave me a hard-on. It was a bastard trying to balance my food tray on it. Mash potato everywhere.

When I got back though I had bigger chips to fry. In fact, the Old Bill had both a frying pan and a fire lined up for me. Hoping they could get me to jump from one into the other.

If it was a film you wouldn't believe it.

16. DEATH BY PAPERWORK

Scissors cut paper, rock smashes scissors and paper wraps rock (but arse wipes paper). And how to kill someone with 10p.

Bullets aren't friendly things, especially when they're coming at you. But a piece of paper dropped in the wrong hands can be the thing that actually gets the gun cocked.

When the police realised their mistake in not dropping the charges against me, and when they realised I was gonna let loose in court, they knew they had to do a 'damage limitation' job on me. That is, try and discredit me by painting me as a grass. At the very least people would turn against me, and at the worst I would get shot.

That's when the Met began their campaign and this started months before the court case began. Documents found their way on to the streets and into the papers – these were fake documents that Warnes had made up when he was lying about where information came from, and from when he was getting information off the police computer for me and my friends. But the documents didn't look like they were fake, of course, because Warnes had to make them look real. I mean that was *the whole fucking point!* – fake up a document to use to get *real* information on what the police had on me and my pals.

I've already told you about how Warnes let slip all these techniques the police use, putting fake paperwork out on the street, so I wasn't exactly surprised when they started using them on me. It was only a matter of time. In fact, I would have been more surprised if they hadn't tried to use this weapon in their armoury. It is one of their most powerful tools because if it works the person they target gets another belly button . . . end of story.

Now because there's been over a year between the arrests and the actual court case the police had time to investigate what my involvement was; and what they found out was that all along I'd been using Warnes to get info rather than the other way around.

It must have fucking riled them to realise that over all the years they'd been trying to nick me I'd actually had my own bent copper, one I'd used to undermine their investigations. That's got to have really fucked them off, ain't it?

So, looking from their point of view, what would've you done in their position? Try and paint me as a grass? Anyone can see that's the next step they would take. And they did.

Now the people that know me, and know all about how Warnes was used by me and mine, don't have any doubts. But it's fucking difficult to personally visit every single fucker that gets wind of an accusation and explain everything you're reading about in this book.

The police know the power of the grapevine better than anyone else because they have the biggest grapevine in the world. The police are the biggest gang in the world. And just as a grapevine can be used for good – like to get warning signals – it can also be used for bad – like to send false information.

That's one trick certain coppers use. Force-feed the grapevine with the right lies to help make something come true that they want to happen. And between the arrests and the trial verdict I was a victim of that trick.

They kept trying to find excuses to make me look like the thing they wanted me to look like. So when I complained about them deliberately trying to endanger me by fucking around with police paperwork, they turned around and tried to make me go on the witness protection programme. Which would have just helped them out even more. They even said they'd had a moody phone call about me. The call was, surprise, surprise, 'anonymous'. Meaning someone from their own nick only has to spend 10p in a public phone box. Then that call is put on a police log. Once it becomes 'official' in that way, the press can then write about it as if it's gospel truth and print a story about how Dave Courtney is getting threats. Even though I never had.

What they are actually trying to do is undermine any solidarity that we might have and make it look like we are fighting amongst ourselves. That is now an established police tactic. It's a combination of 'Divide and conquer' and 'Throwing a spanner in the works', with a little bit of 'No smoke without fire' thrown in for good measure. Then they stand back and watch the fireworks.

For instance, I got a call from that DC Tyson, the one that interviewed me, saying they wanted to talk to me about some death threats. I said I didn't make them any more but I knew someone who did. He didn't find that very funny. I was at Virgin Books at the time (I *am* an author!) and told them to come there. So Tyson and another one comes down and starts telling me they've had 20 death threats made against me. Supposedly. I said, 'I don't believe you. Not for one fucking second. Why would they call you?' I said, 'Why would someone tell the police? If they were gonna threaten me they'd ring me wouldn't they?' He didn't know what to say to that. 'And were these 20 calls from 20 people or just one?' He said it wasn't 20 people, just one he thought. 'So one geezer's rung you 20 times!? I don't believe you, mate. I think you're lying.' It was just utter shit.

See, this was all part of the same con to try to make me look guilty. They knew I'd never *ever* take up an offer of some fucking Witness Protection scheme, never in a million years – stupid cunts. So what had they done? They'd waited till I was out the house then gone round to see Jen and tried to scare her with the same stories. Nasty bastards.

Anyway, back at Virgin: on me I had a copy of the fake informant docket that had 'mysteriously appeared' on the street. This copy had been passed on to me by a mate called Mark. So I said, 'This is a fake document, you *know* it's fake 'cos you've actually nicked Warnes for *faking them!* So it could only be the police that's putting them out on the street couldn't it?' That got about as good an answer as my last one. Just total shit.

Despite all that crap being deliberately flung in my direction, little of it stuck. Under normal circumstances though, being called a grass, and the police leaking out info that made it appear true, would be enough to get you bang in trouble. The Old Bill must have panicked a bit when they saw that because of what people know I'm about, and what people know I stand for, that was enough for them to doubt the police information more than doubt me. Which, of course, they were right to do.

That kind of rumour would normally get people shot but I was given the time to vindicate myself.

However, not everyone was onside. There's always somebody with an axe to grind and they don't care who puts the axe in their hands, even if it's the police, as long as they get a chance to chop you down.

The really ironic thing is that the few people who did believe this stuff about me actually ended up doing the police's dirty work for them. Get that! They were tricked into doing shit-stirring and suspicion-spreading on behalf of the police. How fucking ironic IS that? Fucking hell. The people who believed the lies and called me a grass were actually working for the police themselves, albeit by accident, and in ignorance of what they were doing.

The wiser ones didn't get sucked into the Old Bill's game.

At the same time I didn't underestimate the power that the word 'grass' can have on people. Because it is such a fucking big no-no it can make people back off, even people who should know better, because they're playing the old 'better safe than sorry' game.

So life went on. We carried on regardless. 'Don't let the bastards grind you down' and all that. Fucking good philosophy, I say. It was business as usual back at the ranch. And like my favourite film cowboy, John Wayne, used to say, 'Fill your hand you sonuvabitch! . . .'

17. 'THERE GOES THE KNIGHTHOOD!'

Here I decide you can't fucking well please everyone . . . And my head gets nicked!

Did you know that the Queen has her own Royal Appointed bra maker? No neither did I. And neither did she until Prince Philip walked in on her one day and caught a geezer with both hands on his wife's tits. Thinking quickly she said, 'I'm just being measured by my bra maker, Philip. So, if you wouldn't mind . . .' and waved him away with a little gloved hand. So Philip sloped off for a kebab, a pint of bitter and a game of Kick The Corgi.

And the geezer caught with the Queen left Buckingham Palace with Her Majesty's tit fitting – two bowler hats held together with a curtain rope.

Which reminds me. Remember when that geezer broke into Buckingham Palace about ten years ago and the Queen woke up to find him sat on the edge of her bed? He said to her, "Please, Your Majesty, can I feel your tits." And she replied, 'Certainly not! I shouldn't even be giving you a wank . . .'

When I sign my name now I always put 'Dave Courtney OBE' (which stands for either 'Order of the British Empire', 'One Big Ego' or 'Ole Bald 'Ed' depending on who you ask).

The trial date was set but life goes on and I was doing a book signing and another one of my 'Audience With . . .' shows in Brighton, so I sent an invite to the Prime Minister. As it happens, my show in Brighton was the same day as his – the Labour Party Conference.

I got a reply saying 'Blah blah fuck off!' basically, but the best bit was that it was addressed from 10 Downing Street to 'Dave Courtney OBE'! Wicked. Now does that count as an official acknowledgement or what? I think it fucking well does, matey.

I'm not saying the Old Bill were still listening in on me, but my ears were burning so much if I'd had hair it would've been permanently on fire. When we set off for Brighton we had the usual convoy. Which means that when I'm followed by unmarked police cars there's usually so many cars behind that my mates can spot the Old Bill tailing me. One car follows you for a while and then turns off and is replaced by another. My mates see that it happens in my wake. Like when I walk through London I just see people walking towards me looking normal, but my mates see them turn back and look when they get past me. Well, the following-car thing is the same.

On the way to Brighton we got in a traffic jam. My mates had already rung me on the mobile and told me which was the unmarked car behind. I got out the Rolls and walked back to it. It was funny seeing them not really want to look as I approached. I tapped on the window.

'Excuse me, officer, can you tell me the best place to park in Brighton? Where you parking yours?' He said he didn't know what I was talking

THERE GOES THE KNIGHTHOOD!'

about. Oh, yeah. 'That earpiece you're wearing is for Radio 4 and not Scotland Yard then?'

I do love to fuck up their day. So the wagon train rolled on.

Because of the Labour Party convention there was tons of police there. And our convoy turning up started a proper ripple of concern. They'd already approached the owner of Bar Centro, where the 'Audience With . . .' was gonna be held, and suggested he cancel the show. He said he wouldn't. They also asked him what sort of blokes he was expecting me to bring down. The answer was – very big ones with not much hair and slightly unusual names. Like Wish, Mad Pete, Mickey Goldtooth and Warrior. I think that gave them a flavour of the nature of our party!

Bar Centro was slap-bang opposite the place where the Secretary of State for Northern Ireland was going to be having dinner.

The book signing was at Ottakars in Chatham (with my two favourite sisters), and was a roaring success, even if I do say so myself. The gold pen, given to me for my very first signing session by my good mate Kevin, got another thousand put on its clock. The whole of Chatham's CCTV cameras on the walkway were trained on the shop that afternoon. There were probably as many undercover police in there as punters. After we'd left we learned that Ottakars staff were questioned about what I'd said and who I'd taken in.

The police tried to stop my friends and guests at the top of the road leading to Bar Centro. They said they needed to block the road at both ends 'cos the Northern Ireland Secretary was having dinner there, or that was their excuse. Block off the road 'cos he's having dinner? His after-meal farts must be fucking outrageous if they need to clear the area. 'Was that an IRA bomb attack, Sarge?', 'No, Constable. The Northern Ireland minister's had the bean curry again!'

The police tried to set up this temporary checkpoint and say that everyone had to give their name and address before they'd be let through. Can you see my lot putting up with that? The only personal details Mad Pete would volunteer is an imprint of his. The Courtney Natives definitely started getting pretty fucking restless, so everyone was let through before it kicked-off.

We parked up. On the pavement. If I got a ticket it would go to whoever the Rolls is registered to. The mayor that used to own it, I think. I hear he's gone bankrupt because of all the speeding fines.

We saw loads of people in this massive queue to get into the Party Conference. Jennifer noticed Stephen Lawrence's parents halfway down. We said hello and shook hands. It always struck me when I saw them on TV what really dignified people they seemed in the face of what had happened.

There was all these protestors outside the conference centre waving placards and shouting stuff like 'Save our hospitals!' and 'More pay for teachers!' I started up a chant of 'More weasels in Parliament! Nature must have its say!' I just couldn't resist it. Sorry.

We had hundreds and hundreds of those flyers for my up-and-coming appearance at the Old Bailey, so we walked around handing them out. Cars were jammed nose to tail, so we went on a windscreen blitz! There was a gang of over thirty of us in black suits strolling down. My little travelling troupe aren't all naughty men by any means, but all stood together they do look that way. Everyone thinks 'Dave and his henchmen' but most of the ones in the public scenes are normal fellas! It does help that there's always a few fully fledged 'members' in there as well, though, like Mad Pete, Big Mark, Big Mick (Coventry), Rees, Huxford, Jerry, Jamie & Mark, Wish, Tucker, Lone Wolf, Big Marcus and Baz. Baz is this big black geezer mate of mine who wears a bowler hat, and looks wicked in it as well. He was pulling back windscreen wipers, putting a flyer on the glass and then letting the wiper snap back – *smack*! Smile! All the police cars and police vans got proper flyered as well. In fact anything we passed that didn't move fast enough got a flyer stuck on it, or rolled up and stuck in it (fuck me that poodle did yelp).

Right outside the conference centre there is a zebra crossing and it did the old beep-beep-beep noise as we got to it. About fifteen police motorbikes all pulled up side-by-side across this wide road. So I stopped on the little island in the middle, took my jacket off and held it up like a starting flag. I was going, 'Wait for it! Wait for it!' They were actually laughing, bless 'em. Then it went green and they raced off.

Oh, get this. A copper came up to me and asked me to sign a bit of paper. He said it was for a policewoman who was too embarrassed to come over, and pointed her out. I said 'course I would and asked her name and what message she wanted. 'Oh whatever you like . . .' he said. So I put 'ALL COPPERS ARE BASTARDS, LOVE DAVE COURTNEY OBE' and then folded it up and gave it to him to give to her. Don't look back, that's my advice!

I came up with the idea of hitting the pier. Mad Pete liked that idea 'cos he said he'd never hit a pier before. I said no, I mean we *go* to the pier, Peter. Honestly! I do love our Mad Pete. If he ever has any kids I hope they get his eyes. That would be one fucking scary baby, mate. Imagine a tiny Hannibal Lecter in a romper suit.

We walked to the pier to do some more flyering. I couldn't feel it 'cos I was buzzing but I knew it was freezing cold because everybody was telling me and the girls' teeth were chattering like maracas. But they soldiered on loyally. Well, not that fucking loyally because afterwards Jen told me that they'd all been looking at her like, 'Go on, Jen! Talk him out of this – *please!*'

Jen said she'd been thinking, 'If the IRA do bomb here they'll go for the most populated area to create maximum mayhem, which would be . . . the pier. And if you didn't die in the bomb-fire you'd die in the sea.' Happy thoughts! Anyway, as we got closer we saw that the pier was cordoned off. One of the coppers said there'd been a bomb scare. Jen said, 'Wicked! Now will you tell that skinhead over there?!' pointing at me. (And I promise, that bomb scare wasn't down to me.)

So we gave him a flyer and went back into town to set a world record for how many big geezers you could squeeze into a tiny seaside tearoom. Turned out to be 25 including the six sat on pensioners' knees. You should've heard the bones crack. It was like gunshots!

In the evening we descended on Bar Centro for my 'Audience with . . .' show. Before it started another blinding thing happened. Me, my brother Kevin and the club owner were in the foyer near the door. This motorbike cop pulled up outside, walked in and started asking me, Kevin and the owner if we knew about this Dave Courtney. Obviously a lot more than he did. I said, 'Yeah, I know him. The cross-dressing Buddhist dwarf, that Dave Courtney?'

Asking *me* about *me* could lead to a very long and very one-sided conversation, y'know what I mean? 'Well, it all started when I was about thirty seconds old and I gave the midwife a good right-hander for slapping me . . .'

The show went blinding. It was a particularly good one, for some reason. We all just had a wicked time.

After the show we went out to an array of different nightclubs followed by a contingent of plain-clothes policemen. We went to a selection of raves and had a proper jump around. And if there's ever a place where you can spot an undercover Old Bill it's at a rave! Everyone else is on a level, all peddling at the same speed and giving it loads of *that*; and then there's these two who don't know whether to do nothing and look odd, or try and join in and end up dancing like Mr Bean.

They've actually got undercover police who specialise in doing the nightclubs so they do blend in. They're wicked dancers, they can fake being on one . . . well, I say 'fake'. Who knows? But the Old Bill that follow me around have got to go wherever I'm going, bookshops, down the shops, nightclubs, 'Save The Whale' and 'Ban The Bomb' meetings. (Actually, I've started a group called 'Bomb The Whale'.)

At the 'Audience With . . .' shows these undercover geezers have to look like they're enjoying themselves. Which I hope isn't too much of a strain. And when I go raving they have got to rave. Which is where you pick 'em out.

Which brings us nicely to the launch of my second book, called, funnily enough, *Raving Lunacy* (out in paperback). The subtitle, 'Clubbed To Death', might give you a hint as to what it's about, if you haven't already got it, you cheap bastard. Yeah, it's about all manner of naughtiness around the club scene, and a lot of naughty things do go on around clubs. As you well know. If you don't, you will after you read *Raving Lunacy*. Fucking funny and enlightening it is too, even if my mum does say so herself. I haven't been able to keep her in the house since she read it.

Before the book came out I got a call on my mobile from Charles Bronson. Charlie was calling from Wandsworth prison on the pay phone and he called my mobile! How much did that fucking cost in ten pences? I had this image of him with the phone in one hand and holding some poor cunt by the ankle with his other, shaking him upside down for coins. Anyway, we had the usual funny chat that you have with Charlie, which includes philosophy, art, appreciation of apple pies and a rendition of 'What A Wonderful World'. All in the space of five minutes.

Before he rang off I told him about the new book I'd just finished. He asked me what it was called and when I said *Raving Lunacy* I thought he was gonna come – 'Ohhhh . . . WHAT a title! *What* a fucking title, Dave!' Big praise from the original.

We had the launch party for *Raving Lunacy* at my mate George's place, the Tardis Studios in Clerkenwell. It's a wicked venue.

We had the usual people from villains to lap dancers, mates and their ladies, musicians, actors and actresses (and real people), photographers, models, clubbers, promoters, publishers, schoolteachers, lawyers, press people, maniacs, lunatics, Buddhists, and three TV camera crews filming it all. Sky news, James and his crew from Channel 4 and Tony and his crew from Channel 5. It was a race to the finishing line between them to see who could get their documentary about me finished and out first. But they both had to wait for the finale of the up-and-coming court case. Neither of them wanted to miss that.

All the chaps attended. Well, almost all. We were one short. Very short, actually, about five foot one. The sculpture of my head by Bruce Reynolds' son Nick from the Cons to Icons exhibition was back out on display for the night. And fuck me if someone didn't go and nick it! Bleeding cheek. We figured he must have been very drunk, very brave or very stupid. And probably a Pisces.

The next day George went in to the Studios to work at his office. He got a knock on the door and a delivery from a cab driver. He said he'd been paid in advance to drop something off and handed George this big cardboard box. And inside, sure enough, was my head! (Yeah, that cab driver really knew how to give head.) Back safe and sound with a little note taped inside. It said: 'Really sorry about last night. My mate got drunk enough to think it was a good idea to nick the sculpture. He realised afterwards it wasn't a good idea; especially when we found out it belonged to Mr Courtney. Apologies to Dave. (My mate said he actually thought he was nicking Ronnie Biggs.')

Double fucking cheek! Ronnie Biggs? He's thirty fucking years older than me! What was that cunt drinking who nicked it anyway, pints of absinthe?

So I got one head back, but there was still another certain bunch of blue-uniformed boys who really wanted the head of Dave Courtney. No apologies.

Above Happy families in Marbella: my mum, my sister Sue, Jen and Sue's husband Wayne

Left Jen held my jewels throughout our wedding in Las Vegas

Below The big day itself

Left Me and Terry with a special guest at our One Nation do

Below With Chris Penn on a weekend bender

Below With Bruce Reynolds and Ronnie Biggs at Ronnie's 70th bash in Brazil

Above Guy Ritchie at the audition for Snatch – in my back garden

Below One half of my biker friends – off to a book signing

Above left On tour with Howard Marks

Above right Home sweet home

Left With Brian Harvey, ex E17 star, at my radio show

Right Me and the chaps, just posing

Top left Gathering on the morning of Reggie Kray's funeral

Middle left Wrapping up my movie, *Hell to Pay*, at the Aquarium nightclub

Bottom left 'Avin it large in Cannes

Right This was for a film, too. Honest – you can always trust a vicar

Below Hell to Pay. From the left, Charlie Breaker, Malcolm Martin, Lou Schultz, Billy Murray, Mickey Pugh, Garry Bushell

Left 'You can't have a tank, Dave, it'll blow the budget.' 'Budget? What budget?'

Below I thought I looked great in this outfit, but the judge didn't. How we all laughed

18. THE TRIAL – BRING 'EM ON!

*The audience take their seats, the curtains go up, and the cameras start rolling –
'Action!'*

So on Monday 6 November the trial finally began in Court Number 8 in
the Old Bailey. I was in good and bad company with some of the other
trials that were being held there.

In one court was a hearing about David Shayler, the bloke who used to
work for MI5 and who'd tried to write a book on the dirty tricks that the
security forces and the government get up to. Which they had slapped a
ban on pretty sharpish – surprise, surprise – and also slapped the cuffs on
him as soon as he left France and came back into Britain. It wouldn't do
for them to let the truth get out, now would it? Shayler talked about MI5
ignoring an IRA unit that carried out the bombing of Bishopgate; MI5
ignoring bomb warnings, and using agents to assassinate people; and
intelligence services bugging confidential interviews between clients and
their lawyers in Belmarsh high security prison. Which is what happened to
me when I was there.

And in mine, me and the other co-defendants had already been up and
pleaded not guilty. Warnes had gone up first, earlier, because they were
keeping him separate from me (wise move), and he finally pleaded 'guilty'.
Like he should have done months ago, but he decided to cut a deal and
help the police try to stitch me up. That was also a clever move on their
part 'cos him going 'guilty' meant that I couldn't call him as a co-defendant,
and my brief couldn't cross-examine him and prove him a liar. So they had
turned that to their advantage. But I turned it back; it also meant that I
could say my piece and he couldn't jump up and object.

Him going guilty would also have opened the door for him to do a deal
with the police to get a lighter sentence. No one could be in any doubt that
that would happen. That's how they operate, scratching each other's backs.

There had been a massive build up to this case for everybody involved
and everyone connected to them – like Jen and my family, and Jen's family,
and our friends; the other accused, and their families and friends as well, I
expect; the police and the press; the jury, I'd guess, must've been pretty
fucking hyped-up as well about it all (I know one of them was 'cos later he
told me he was actually reading *Stop the Ride I Want to Get Off!*)

But for me when that first day came it was a relief, I must admit. I just
couldn't wait to get in and sort out this fucking stupid 'informant' bollocks
thing they were trying to hang around my neck. I felt I was never in trouble
with the actual case but there was actually two juries sitting here. One was
the lot in the courtroom; and the other was the unseen 'jury' outside on the

streets. That was the one the police were really trying to influence into thinking of me as guilty. Getting a guilty for grassing meant you get shot.

I pulled off a bit of a coup on the first day, as it happens. Remember that film I told you I was making where I was playing a judge? Well, on the very morning that the trial started in the Old Bailey the *Daily Sport* ran a page 2 article on me playing the part of the judge, complete with a photo of me in a wig and robes and under the headline 'Dave's A Good Judge Of Character!' Fucking get *that*. What timing! Coincidence? I think not. (By the way, what do you call a judge with no thumbs? Justice Fingers.)

That wasn't all. The prosecutor, a Mr Holden, brought the judge's attention to my flyers. These flyers were A4 size, much bigger than normal. On one side there was a colour picture of me in the court jester's outfit on the steps of Bow Street magistrates' court, surrounded by knuckledusters and 'The Court Jester – Dave Courtney OBE' written underneath. On the back was a photograph of me kneeling next to the little gravestone I have outside my front door which says, 'Dodgy Dave Courtney – One Flash Bastard But A Nice Flash Bastard: Born 17.2.59, Died – Never'. Just your usual household ornament. Around the photograph the back of the flyer was covered with the following words:

DaveScape 2000

NOT GUILTY YOUR HONOUR.COM
6th November 10am till kick out
10 on the door/5 with this flyer

The venue – Court No 1 THE OLD BAILEY
(Don't panic if you can't make the 1st show as the fucking thing goes on for 9 weeks!)

Don't miss this spectacular court case. Attractions include: A selection of pompous blokes in wigs (probably wearing suspenders), Dodgy Dave getting a not guilty (Hooray) and the copper going to prison (eh?). I do have complete faith in the British Justice System.
This court case will once again show how Dodgy Dave outsmarts the Old Bill by bravely playing them at their own game.

Advance booking – call Scotland Yard on 999
(Free from any phonebox)

Dress code – no jeans, trainers or hats and
all guns to be left at the door.
The Old Bailey doormen reserve the right to do whatever the fuck they want, so please bring ID to gain entry.

Out in February in all major bookstores
that Dave has 'convinced' to sell it!!!
Why not buy the new book *Raving Lunacy*
out October 19th by Virgin Books

What's wrong with that? Not an untrue word there, and I think the only thing I got wrong was the number of the court!

So on the first day the prosecution tried to get the judge to do me for contempt of court and get my bail taken away. On the *first day*! I was fucking stuffing it to them already and we hadn't even broken up for tea. Start as you mean to go on, that's what I say.

We'd been handing the flyers out outside the court to everyone going in, coming out or passing by. To coppers, briefs, court clerks, even some of the jurors might have got them. And had a fucking good laugh I bet. The judge said, 'Would the flyers stop if Mr Courtney was jailed, because he doesn't actually print them himself?' Holden said that he wouldn't really know, so the judge gave me a contempt of court warning and play was resumed.

One nil, I think.

The second day was even better. We all had these headphones – me, the other co-defendants, the jury, the judge and the lawyers – for listening to the surveillance tapes that CIB3 had made. Now because much of the first half of the case was absolutely fuck-all to do with me whatsoever, and was just everyone going over these tapes, it turned out to be pretty boring. So when I got up to leave at the end of the second day I nicked my set of headphones (they were proper flash little sets with an aerial stuck out the back). What I didn't know was that Holden, the prosecutor, had seen me do it.

I went home and had a laugh with them, putting them on this skeleton I've got at home wearing a policeman's helmet. Usual childish behaviour! Anyway, the next day I walked into court and noticed that Holden was looking at me. I thought, he looks even more fucking smug than usual today. Then he stood up and said something like, 'If we need any more proof of what this character Mr Courtney is like may I direct your honour to the fact that last night he stole a set of the court's headphones!' Gasps from the court – not at all. There were a few chuckles from my mates up in the public gallery, though.

The judge didn't take too kindly to what I'd done (and he'd probably had time to think about the fact that on the flyer I'd called him a pompous bloke wearing suspenders). So he took away part of my bail: the part that covers me being able to move freely around the court. (One all!) Which meant I had to go in in the morning half an hour before everyone else, go down into the cells beneath the Old Bailey, and then go up into the court afterwards. Then spend dinner back downstairs and wait an extra half hour before I could leave at the end. Which was all a bit of a fucking drag, to be honest. After a couple of days my brief persuaded me to write a letter to the judge apologising and saying there was no malice in nicking the things.

I said I'd taken them as a souvenir because I had no intention of ever being back in the Old Bailey ever again.

So my brief left the court, called Jen, and she sent the headphones back to court in a cab. Twenty-five quid that cost! Anyway, there were pop-studs on the side of the headphones holding the covers on and one of them had popped open. It weren't broken or anything. But when the prosecutor, Holden, picked up the headphones between his thumb and finger he held them at arm's length like they were about to explode. Then in that Lawyer's Voice that they all have he said, 'Oh yes, they are returned . . . but they are *broken!*' Fuck me, talk about over-dramatic. Even the judge didn't buy that one.

Anyway, my first little letter did the job 'cos the restriction was lifted.

When I was still under that restriction, though, it meant I had to get up even earlier in the morning than I had been doing. In fact, the whole routine of travelling to court everyday was a pretty big eye opener for me. I actually turned into a commuter! The horror. My life is very, very far from being habitual. Anything but. Everyone who knows me knows that and accepts it, down to a very understanding ex-wife who knows I can't get to see my son and daughters at the same time every week.

I just cannot do the 9 to 5 thing. Regular routine and me just don't mix. Last time I lived like that would've been in Belmarsh nick in '96. And before that it would have been back in 1980 when I was done for the Chinese waiter thing. You can see a pattern emerging can't you? Prison is the only thing that gets me into bed at night and out of it in the morning. High price to pay for a regular sleep pattern though, ain't it?

I can do 95 on the motorbike but not 9 to 5 in my life. Speaking of the bike, I travelled to court most days on it. When I used the car I got stuck for two hours queuing for the Blackwall Tunnel. I had to re-shave my head by the time I got out the other side.

Every morning I was getting up at 6.30 a.m.: I'd put my suit and tie on, have breakfast, have a bath and a shave. Then I realised it'd be better to have the bath and shave first, then put my suit on.

Every day I'd pull up at the lights next to the same motorbike and cars I'd seen the day before and go 'Morning' and they'd go 'Morning' back. Everybody going to work at the same time every bleedin' day. Or I'd weave through traffic to get to the front and go past cars I'd clocked before . . . ah, there's that one again, nod and smile. Or I'd see the same young geezer on a moped, same bird in her Corsa, same businessman in his Merc, same bread van, same hearse – different dead guy. Every day.

I tell you, it was fucking awful being normal, just awful. How do you people do it? I felt like a stockbroker. No stocks just broke!

So if during any of that time you saw a geezer in a wide variety of different coloured suits, suede slip-ons and no socks, on a big black and chrome bike saying morning to everyone . . . that was me, that was.

One day I even took the tube. Fucking hell – it was like Dawn Of The Early Morning Brain Donors. It'd been years since I'd been down on the underground. I'd forgot that you're not supposed to smile or look at anyone.

I remembered Warnes describing the way the Old Bill relish the fact that if someone's on bail then their life is sort of on pause. It's not a nice feeling. Some of the police love the fact that they're causing you so much fucking grief. I went out of my way to not show any of that. I didn't want them to see that. On some days I had the bike taken home for me and I got picked up outside the court by a limo, or a pony and trap, or a Chinese rickshaw. Or, one day, an armoured car.

See, because I live a public and very hectic life, and my house is like Base Camp One for everybody, me being in court every day meant I missed the usual round of visits and house meetings. But, I was getting home every night to phone calls or really nice messages on the answerphone.

The Old Bailey can be quite an intimidating place for most people. The courtroom is a really high-ceilinged room, two floors high really, because the public gallery is up above you. That's up on the right. For some reason they'd blocked off the front row of seats with police accident tape. Funny, it almost looked like a crime scene. The dock for the defendants was at the back of the room, set above the floor. Sat there was Simon James the husband, then Rees the PI, then Rees' colleague Cook, and then me on the end at the left. I weren't too fucking happy to be sat next to any of them. I'd never even met them until court day.

In front of us, down on the floor, sat the legal teams at their tables. Eight of them. Two prosecutors and six defence briefs, two for each co-defendant apart from Cook, who didn't have any legal advice. His wife actually sat in court every day representing him. Everyone thought that put Cook bang in trouble to begin with but I later found out – and I'll tell you later how I found it out – that his missus being there actually counted in his favour big time. My legal eagles were Mr Lithman from Ralph Haeems, who've handled all my cases, and David Haeems, Ralph's son. David's defended me a few times and he is very much a chip off the talented old block. His youthful looks sometimes make people underestimate him, which they learn to their cost. He's the bollocks, mate.

In front of the legal teams, and sat higher up than every other fucker, of course, was the judge. His Right Honourable Whoeverthefuckhewas, in his wig and gowns. In fact there'd probably never been so many bad wigs in one room since Elton John, Terry Wogan, Charlton Heston, Cher and Lily Savage all got invited to the same party. It was like Rugs R Us.

To the right of us was the witness box, and right over to the left was another raised bit with two long benches where the jury sat. It's a weird one with a jury. Do you *not* look at them, and then hope they don't think that looks guilty? Do you look at them, and hope you don't look intimidating? Do you smile at them, and hope you don't look like a nutter? I can form a very, very good opinion of someone within five minutes of speaking to someone, but just by looking at someone? That's different. I'm a firm believer in don't judge a book by its cover, 'cos if you tried to analyse me by looking at me you'd be wrong.

So it was like that for me with them when they walked in. Six men and six women; mixed ages and races. I weren't gonna get a chance to speak to them so I just hoped they were OK. I'd heard some horror stories in the past from people who'd sat on juries about how some jurors don't give a fuck about the case and the evidence and just wanna get home or back to work. But as I saw it, whatever they thought of me personally, the law would make them find me not guilty. Getting a 'guilty' was out of the equation. To me, getting found not guilty was the only dead cert. Everyone else didn't think that, though. The only worry was how much of the truth and the evidence that counted the jury would get to hear. Sometimes you get fucked by what the judge in his 'wisdom', for want of a better word, decides is admissible.

I knew the police weren't bringing me into court to convict me of this charge – 'cos they knew it was bollocks – but to get me convicted out on the street of something they thought would bring me down. Two juries, remember? In fact, because there was no evidence at all that I was involved in this thing – there was loads of evidence to the contrary, saying I weren't involved – I was quite intrigued as to how they were gonna justify me being there at all!

What I didn't know at the time was exactly how much evidence they had to prove that I *wasn't* part of it – reports from other police stations saying Warnes had rung up and used his position to get me and my mates out of trouble, making it obvious that we were using him and not the other way around. But did they let that be admitted as evidence? I think you'll find they most definitely did *not*.

An awful lot of the trial for the first three or four weeks was just listening to legal arguments, or wearing the headphones and listening to surveillance tapes of conversations that I weren't in. (I had the 'broken' headphones of course.)

So I took the opportunity to write loads of letters to people and answered some fan mail. I did most of my Christmas cards from the dock. I wrote to Charlie Bronson in prison, 'cos Charles sends me letters and amazing drawings; my mate Warwick who is also banged up, and numerous others living at Her Majesty's pleasure; Outcast Phil, Wilf Pine, Brendan, Seymour, my kids, Chelsea, Levi, Beau, Courtney, Drew and Jensen; Sue and Bal, Marcus, Richard and Dean, Birmingham John, Albert Chapman, Patrick, Wayne, my mum, Andy Jones of CrimeTime Museum, Agent No 10, Ronnie Biggs, Cowboy, Lone Wolf, Dave the Builder, Kevin, Gary Bushell, Howard Marks, Jocelyn Hogg, Posh John, Kevin Courtney, Big Mel, Guy in America,

Website Steve, Pat Brogan, Steve McFadden, Pard, Steve Low, Vinoo, Val and Ron, Lou. They weren't all 'what I did on my holidays' type essays; some of them just postcards saying things like, 'So far so good' or 'Have the helicopter on the roof by six'. That kinda thing.

One day I looked up into the public gallery and amongst my usual die-hard supporters – Seymour, Jackie, Matt, Animal, Jacket, Paul, Paul, Paddy, Mick Colby and Louise, etc. – there was my mate Eoin, the deputy ed at *Front* magazine. Top geezer, considering he's a roller-blading transvestite. But don't these magazine people go far to make sure you get your work in on time? Even down to visiting me in court! But it did remind me that I still had a deadline to meet. Fuck me, I don't know . . . work, work, work. So I wrote my next column, which was about attending Reggie Kray's funeral.

I also wrote my regular thing for Terry Turbo's clubbing magazine *The Scene* called 'Dodgy Dave's Funny Page'. It went like this:

Hello my little sucklings . . . I knew you'd be back! Welcome to the weird & wonderful mind of Dave Courtney. I'm sorry it's a bit empty but I've had a good clear out of all that old shit you seem to keep, now there's fuck all of any practical use left at all. Which brings me nicely to my dinosaur theory . . . that is that they were all out their fucking heads 24-7 on 'ganja'! It's fucking true I tell yer. It's a fact that the weed plant was around at that time, they've got fossils to prove it. It was very very hot back then & the plants were 6 to 7 times bigger, and seeing as about half of them ate plants (the wankers of the bunch that is) they must have been out of it all fucking day! The lucky bastards. Weed & puff have been legal for about 10 billion years, but in 1922 someone made it an illegal substance. So it's only been a nickable offence for about 80 years! What poxy fucking luck, aye?

Where was I? Oh yes. My court case started at the Old Bailey on 6th November, so book a seat now before it's too late. It's going on for 9 poxy weeks . . . all them new suits I'll have to buy. Once again I will demonstrate how to completely fuck them right up in the courtroom! And come out triumphant. But the icing on the cake to this little story is – that lying little prick of a bent copper, 'my old pal' Austin Warnes, who will get a lump of bird for trying to set some woman up. Please, please forgive me for pissing my pants laughing and gloating but I can't fucking help it . . . ARSEHOLES. And as my old Nan used to say, 'You have to get up early in the morning to paint the lilo black if you want to see the buffalo play pinball in the early spring' . . . silly cow that she was.

Didn't we do well in the football? What has a three-pin plug and the England football team got in common? They're both useless in Europe.

My offer still stands to any mug who's stupid enough to try, to come down my local pub, the Manhattan cafe in Woolwich, and play me a

50 game of pool, playing with one hand (for real). Flash cunt! I know, I know, but if you can walk the walk there's fuck all wrong in talking the talk I say!

Apparently I upset some readers with my last page. Well, even by sending me a letter complaining you've obviously mistaken me for someone who gives a fuck. If you don't like it then turn the page and look at an advert for half an hour. And if you do find it informative, interesting and witty then you're a sick fuck as well!

My trip to New York and Tenerife last month went according to plan. I can't remember fuck all – no change there then.

A big HELLO to all my mates in Her Majesty's Prisons at the moment. It's fucking horrible in there in summer, you actually wish it would rain every day. It does in Scotland. And did you know that if you put 3 grams of whizz and one E in a goldfish bowl with 2 fish in it, one called 'Tonker' and one called 'Tyson', they would die and float to the top by morning. You just can't get the fish these days! I remember getting the ping-pong ball in the bowl one time at the funfair & I won a fucking 2-foot pike in a black bin liner! Now you get a fucking sandwich bag with half a dead excuse of a goldfish that can't handle its gear.

What is this world coming to? You'll be saying you've got faith in the 'Great British justice system' next if you're not careful . . . only kidding! Don't forget to look out for & keep a hold of the flyer for the court case. It's 2 off if you show the flyer on the door. See ya there! Just in case you didn't know, I'm the bald geezer in the dock cracking up laughing all the time.

By the way, me and Terry Turbo are gonna start up a readers Pets page, so if you've got any snaps of you and your pet performing sexual acts please send them in & the winner will get a free blow job from Rolf Harris at any park or zoo in the country. My pal had an unusual pet once; it was a tin of salmon. Pink salmon though.

I wonder whatever happened to that Jill Dando bird? You don't see her much on the TV these days do yer? Pity that.

Remember this – If the cap fits . . . run off with the fucking thing and nick it! See you soon, Dave Courtney (O.B.E.).

I got so pissed off at one point that I even started doing Biro drawings on some napkins that I'd got with my sandwiches. Proper little works of art they were as well, even if I do say so myself. And I do. If they'd only given me a ladder I could've done a Michelangelo and drawn over the whole fucking courtroom ceiling.

I didn't have to write 'Dave Courtney woz 'ere' on the desk because I knew I was going to leave my mark in this courtroom another way.

19. THE TRUTH, THE WHOLE TRUTH & THE BITS THEY DON'T TELL YOU ABOUT

Even I never thought I'd end up in pantomime with the judge, the jury and the executioner. But someone's got a blunt axe . . .

I got well into the routine of pulling up outside the Bailey, parking the bike over the road on the pavement, and walking in helmet in one hand and big black bag in the other. This bag that I brought with me every day had nothing in it but crap, absolute crap – Guilty/Not Guilty signs, musical lobsters, wigs, handcuffs, books, champagne, just loads of rubbish. Everyone else was walking in with their smart black briefcases full of case notes, or whatever, and I had a bag of what we might politely call 'amusing nonsense'.

As I went into the Bailey every morning there's this door that opens and shuts behind you. Then another one buzzes open in front of you and lets you in. Glass in front and glass behind you. They put your bag on these metal runners to go through the X-ray machine and there's a woman sat there watching a screen. She might be watching breakfast TV for all I know. Well, when they X-rayed my bag it was just full of all this stuff.

I knew, as they put it on the runners, what they'd see. I'd walk forward and the security guard with this electronic wand would sweep it up and down my body. When I knew the bag was coming on the screen I'd start having a laugh and a joke with them all, which weren't difficult 'cos they started it as soon as I walked through the fucking door – 'Oh, what you wearing today?' and all that. So I'd banter back – I'm wearing this one for you; got the diamonds on today! Ain't the judge a cunt – that kind of thing. So every day the bag went through without ever really being looked at. Plus, an extra distraction was the fact that with all the bits of metal on me, like earrings, rings, shirt collar tips, bracelet, chains, metal headplate etc., the electronic sweeper-wand was buzzing its little head right off. I think I gave that device a dozen multiple orgasms.

The police and prosecutors couldn't believe it 'cos after the first week all the court ladies are going 'Morning, Dave', like they're all my aunties or something. It was wicked. There's no substitute for being friendly. It actually inspires more loyalty than fear, believe me. I've tried both.

It is funny, though, when you get in a routine and see the same people every day. The sandwich man in the court would give me a sarny every day and say, 'Go on, son!' to wish me well; the bloke in the pub opposite, Irish geezer, lovely fella, set up a tab for me behind the bar (I think he got stung more than some that got guilty verdicts!); and the court ushers and clerks usually came up for a chat and a joke. One of my mates even told me that when he was upstairs in the public gallery one of the court ushers, a middle-aged lady, ended up sitting next to him and telling him that she was reading *Stop the Ride . . .* and was rooting for me during the trial! I thought, fucking hell, that's nice.

I took a corkscrew out and opened the champagne in court one day, a couple of weeks into the proceedings, keeping it out of sight. But the lady Group 4 security guard saw me doing it. She didn't say anything 'cos we used to chat anyway, and by that stage of the trial she'd already said she couldn't see why I was even there. So I mixed the champagne with Red Bull in little glasses and passed them down the dock. It was really funny. By the end of the day I was hoping they'd hurry up and finish before I started pub-style singing.

Actually, what was a bit of a cunt for me was because Cook, Rees and James had never met Warnes before all of this, so they really believed the police's version of my place in all this. They weren't in any position to know any different I suppose. They'd all only dealt with whichever part of it concerned them. But it meant they were all very much on edge at the first hearings 'cos I didn't want to get in the dock with them, and then when I did knock Warnes out it can't have really put them at ease much.

I wasn't at all happy, to say the least, about being sat in the dock next to people who, for all I knew, were properly involved in the plot – as the husband and the private eye seemed to be (Cook, I wasn't sure) – when I knew I definitely wasn't involved.

So a lot of the time I kept getting up and walking out of the dock. This was during the actual trial. You're not supposed to do that unless it's something like a toilet break but I covered myself by saying I was recovering from flu and had a dicky tummy; then I'd disappear for an hour!

There's two doors. One at one end where you walk into the courtroom and one at the other end where you went out to the toilet. The door to the toilet also led downstairs to the jailer's bit so I'd go down there. There were some people in the cells I knew and some of the screws knew me from Belmarsh, so I'd have a cup of tea and a chat. I'd walk back into the court with a drink and a newspaper under my arm an hour later. But ain't that constipation a killer.

So like I say, the first weeks were the prosecution presenting their cases, which of course didn't feature me, 'cos they had fuck all on me. The other three, though, looked bang in trouble. Considering all the evidence presented against Rees, James and Cook, secretly recorded tapes and video films etc., I thought they must have been given the worst legal advice ever for them to plead not guilty. But then Warnes had thrown everybody by going not guilty initially and only changing his plea at the death. By not saying anything they'd protected him by protecting themselves, though he didn't return the favour.

Every day in court I had my little mascot out on the long desk we sat behind. It was a little pot pig dressed as a policeman (given to me by

Sheffield Ben). Subtle, eh? But what did you want me to have, a fucking Furbie? Well if students can have a mascot on *University Challenge* I didn't see why I shouldn't have one in the court of the Universally Challenged.

All part and parcel of showing that the bastards aren't grinding you down. They'd made pretty fucking sure that this time when they did pull me in for something it was, to say the least, the most embarrassing thing and, to say the worst, quite possibly fatal thing they could think of. That I was a grass. So I was not going to play into their hands and act that way.

I had to relieve the boredom some way. One day I stuck a ponytail to the back of my head. The judge couldn't see it but the jury and people in the public gallery could.

A wicked clothes shop called 'Short Stories' made me loads more suits to go with mine; a different one for every day (and no, they didn't know the trial would go on six weeks!). On one of the mornings when I walked into court the judge looked me up and down, as usual, and said, 'Are you still having your own personal fashion show, Mr Courtney?' I said, 'I am your honour and today I will be wearing beige!' Ha-ha. And he couldn't say a thing 'cos he'd fucking started it. Well, if I can bring a little glamour into their dull, dull lives . . . (it was funny, though).

The prosecutor used these antics to come out with a sneaky little one. He obviously wanted to get out that I had previous convictions and experience of being in court before but he can't do that directly 'cos it's not allowed. So he said something like 'Mr Courtney seems very relaxed . . . almost like he's done this kind of thing before.' Clever little bastard.

A lot of the barristers really do think that we are stupid, y'know, the punter they have to deal with day after day. They really do think you're a div if you're not one of them. They look at us as the minority. Because life is a series of habits, the way they act in court is the way they act outside it. They talk in that Lawyer's Voice way all the fucking time, even in the canteen when they're asking to pass the salt. And because everyone they know is like that they have no reason to stop. Same with any closed shop, like when raving first began, for example. Every raver thought everyone was like them, and they were right, so they didn't feel odd about dancing like a complete nutter while off your head.

I've been for meetings with barristers in the past and he'd start talking to me like he was addressing a jury – 'I do firmly believe.' I'd go, 'Hold on, we've only got half an hour. It's gonna take you that long to get to the end of your first fucking sentence. Talk *to* me not *at* me.'

The courtroom is an alien environment for most people. 'Alien' being the word 'cos some people feel they've been beamed down onto another planet full of tubby little geezers that sound like they're all talking underwater. So when they have a banter with each other they think we don't understand. For them it's a home from home because they've been in this environment for twenty years. So to them it's like having an argument in their own front room! That's why they're so relaxed. Like when you're at home arguing with your missus, or fella, you proper fucking go to town don't you and use every trick in the book to win that argument?

The trick is to try and think of it in that way. I've never really looked on these people as anything but geezers that do a job. They ain't special. Just like any copper that puts on a uniform. In fact, if anything they're more ordinary because they've had to get a job where they're told what to do all the time.

So, practising what I preach, I looked on that courtroom as my other living room for the next few weeks. Which weren't easy, 'cos the Old Bailey carpet is shit, there's too many coppers there and I wouldn't let one man let alone eight wearing white curly wigs walk through my front door. But then half the people who are usually permanent fixtures at my house were up in the public gallery anyway. Cheers.

One of the reasons why the other three decided to plead not guilty might have been down to what they thought of the taped evidence against them, and by that I mean the quality of the recording. The evidence that's gonna be presented in court against you has to be given to you pre-trial so you can prepare your case. OK, now listen to this, 'cos this came straight from the bent horse's mouth: if, when making copies of the surveillance tapes, an officer just switches on a mobile phone and lays it next to the recording equipment it causes a buzzing noise (same thing happens when you use a mobile next to an ordinary phone that's being used). So when the defendants get their copies of the tapes they don't sound too clear or distinct. And as there has to be 'beyond reasonable doubt' to convict, the defendants start thinking, 'Well, I could be saying something else there, something that sounds similar. Maybe I can fight this.'

Then they spend hours poring over the tapes and written versions, changing words to sound more innocent.

The trouble is that come the day in court the police produce their original, crystal-clear, Dolby stereo digital Surround Sound version of the tape, which leaves no fucking doubt whatsoever about what was being said. But by then it's too late because you're already in court wondering what's hit you.

So when Rees, Cook and James got up to testify they looked pretty fucking shocked at the sudden clarity of the tapes, I can tell you. They'd had nine months to prepare what they were going to say they had really said on the tape. They had typed out transcripts of what was said on the tapes, and they took those into the dock, as well as their prepared version of what they said was said. However, when the tapes came on they were just fucking distinct. As a result when it came out clear as a bell – 'That amount of class A's should get her banged up' – and they're stood there planning on saying they said something stupid like – 'That Amanda's classy, eh? You should bang her one'. You can see why they got slaughtered.

It was awful to watch 'cos they fucking died; they just had to stand there and wither under the glare of it all. I thought crucifixion was a slow death until I saw them getting nailed in the witness box day after day.

Simon James, the husband, got roasted over a spit in there for three days. By the end of it he couldn't even hold his head up or catch anyone's eye. Afterwards when he saw me he asked me how I thought he'd done. I said, 'Don't ask!' He went, 'But you only need three in the jury to hold out.' I said, 'You'll be lucky if you get three in the whole fucking building, mate.'

James, and Rees the private eye, both looked like they'd been caught bang to rights to me. James Cook, though, said that when he'd been told by Rees to put the 'gear' in Kim James's car he'd assumed 'gear' meant recording equipment. Bugs not drugs. He couldn't actually say he didn't break into the car because they had it all on videotape. Which they played in court. TV monitors were brought out for the judge, the jury and the court.

Because the Old Bill had already been bugging the private investigators office, due to some other bent operation they suspected him of, they stumbled onto this plan and were right on it from the beginning. They knew exactly when Cook was going to plant something in Kim James's car, so we all sat there with our headphones on (mine were broken!) and watched this video surveillance film made at night of him breaking into her Fiat. Or at least trying to.

It weren't supposed to be funny, but I was just cracking up 'cos this geezer took seventeen minutes to break into the fucking car. It probably didn't take Fiat that long to build the bleedin' thing. He had a go at the locks on the doors, then the hatch, but still couldn't get in. I've met sixteen-year-olds that could rob a Porsche in thirty seconds and be back home having their tea in under seventeen minutes.

This video just went on and on. I half expected there to be an interval for ice creams and popcorn. Cook finally gave up on the break-in after fifteen minutes and walked off. Then he came back from his own car with a dirty great big screwdriver, jammed it into the top of the door and actually bent it open, reached in and pulled the button up. After he opened the door he leaned in under the dash for about five seconds. It looked too quick to actually put anything there. Then he tried to shoulder the bent door back into shape! Fucking hell, I'm telling you, it was like watching Mr Bean on *Crimewatch*.

The video ended and everyone took their headphones off. Cook was sat next to me just dying. The judge looked up and came out with a little cracker. He said something like, 'Well, I think perhaps the Fiat motor company might be interested in that it's a rather good advertisement for their car security! What with these films around called "Gone In Sixty Seconds".'

Around about the last quarter of the trial something really important happened. Seymour and Matt, two good friends of mine, had come out of the public gallery because the session had ended for lunchtime. They were both outside the courtroom when everyone came out. A police officer called Mr Critchley, who was the one in charge of the case, emerged smiling, looking all smug about what was going on. Seymour couldn't let it pass and he said to him, 'Dave's gonna beat this, you know.' Critchley went, 'We've already beat Dave in the newspapers!' Get that. Talk about blatant. What Critchley was referring to was the court reporting that had been out about me being an 'alleged informant'. Seymour and Matt told me what he'd said during the lunch break.

It didn't in the least bit shock me because I already knew what they were trying to do. It was actually a sign of how satisfied they were with the job they were doing. And he obviously knew I would be told what he'd said.

I thought, fuck, we just can't let that one pass. That's got to be mentioned in court. My brief wasn't having any of it, though. He said that much as he'd like to raise the point, he'd get blown out for doing it and it would be classed as 'not relevant'. But just 'cos he had to do things by the book didn't mean that I had to. 'Cos me and him obviously work by different books.

Well, when we reconvened for the afternoon session I waited until everyone had sat down and then I stood right up and started telling the judge exactly what had been said outside court. The prosecution jumped up and objected, the judge told me to be quiet and when I wouldn't he instructed the jury to be taken out. They were escorted out by security. I carried on until I'd said my piece.

I didn't expect anything particularly favourable from the judge in response but his reply was fucking gob-smacking. He said something like he was sure it was just jovial banter and not to let it hurt my feelings. Jovial banter! Those were the words he used to dismiss it. It wasn't 'jovial banter'; it was a senior police officer admitting exactly what my case was about. Exactly what was at the heart of them wanting me there in court.

At first I'd thought that Critchley had just cockily said it and revealed the truth because he'd been caught in an off-guard moment and didn't think of the consequences. But it wasn't that. He already knew there would be no consequences – that my brief would say he couldn't mention it, and even if I tried to mention it I'd be told to shut up and the jury removed. Which is what happened.

But it was a much bigger thing than the judge knew, or cared about, or would admit to. It was a massive thing for Critchley to actually admit. It was everything, in fact. Yet it was just brushed under the carpet. There were so many things being brushed under the carpet that you would've needed a four-wheel-drive Hoover just to get over the fucking hill.

What Critchley had said was exactly what I'd been going on about and trying to explain to some people. Me being in court for the last few weeks and the bad press about me that had followed was, to them, a job well done. A job fucking well done. They had achieved precisely what they'd set out to achieve – to discredit me to the point of putting my life in danger.

Can you see now what a bastard it was for me to sit there in that courtroom for weeks on end and know all this? It was a proper cunt, mate, I'm telling you. To sit there and have to take that. Even the methods at my disposal for trying to combat it and set the record straight, like writing about it all in *Front* magazine, were actually blocked to me 'cos you can't do that while a trial is waiting to begin. 'Hands tied', and all that.

This had been the second time the jury had been asked to leave because of something I'd said. Earlier on, about three or for weeks into the trial, something else happened.

One day during a break in the court I'd rung Jennifer and she told me that she had been talking to a friend of hers, and this friend had said she'd got a moody phone call advising her to stay away from me because I could be in line for getting hurt. As a direct result of what they were saying about me in court.

Anyway, that was still in my head, how they dismiss so many things as irrelevant. I'd asked for the judge to be told that I wouldn't mind any of the press reporting if I was given equal opportunity to say my piece. Y'know, so there was a balance. But he said he couldn't do anything about it.

So again I told my brief about what Jennifer had told me about one of her friends getting a warning, and what was happening as a result of what they were saying. Knowing the law like he does, he had to say that he couldn't bring it up in court. That fucking word 'irrelevant' again. Funny how it's always stuff to do with the defendant's case that's called 'irrelevant'.

After that call I made to Jen the court resumed in the afternoon. The prosecutor, Holden, just couldn't use the word 'informant' enough in connection with me. He just kept laying it on thick. I sat there listening to him thinking, you spiteful little fat cunt. Because I knew that he had seen all the police's evidence – or complete lack of – regarding me, so he knew as well as they did that it was all shit. What was that my nan used to say? 'Better out than in'. Call me old-fashioned, but I agree. So I stood up.

In court everyone sits, apart from whoever's speaking. So when I stood up all heads turned to look at me, everyone probably thinking the same thing, what the fuck is he doing? I pointed at the prosecution. 'Down to that cunt down there my wife is getting moody phone calls!' The judge told me to be quiet and speak through my solicitor. I said, 'You be fucking quiet! Down to that cunt there lying and you lot pretending to believe him my wife's upset about her friend!'

The judge ordered the jury out and as they were being led away I carried on. 'I'm telling you that if he carries on doing that and you carry on letting him I'm gonna jump over here and batter him!'

And for that they gave me another contempt of court. What a surprise. Pretty accurate though 'cos 'contempt' was just about right.

Anyway, that was the first time the jury got kicked out, and then later on me bringing up Critchley's comment was the second time they got the boot. Which must have really pissed them off, come to think of it! They'd sat through all the more boring legal arguments and then every time the fireworks began the judge threw the poor fuckers out. They must've been sat in the back fucking fuming.

One funny bit (well, I thought it was) was when one of the coppers in the dock was trying to describe me. He said, 'I am from CIB3, we are known as the incorruptible and we catch the corrupted. And he (meaning me) is the corrupter! These are the people that make the public lose confidence in the police force. He has put his hand deep into the force and ripped its heart out.'

I said, 'I've got to go guilty to that!'

Fucking hell, talk about over-dramatic. Pass the Oscar. But 'the corrupter!' Try saying that and not sounding impressed with yourself. And no one can try and tell me that the Old Bill haven't got it in them to be vindictive towards me; I mean, are you fucking joking? When they're using phrases like, 'He ripped out the heart of the force'! That is proper emotional stuff they are using there, ain't it? Don't tell me that don't make them sound desperate for a result against me. They couldn't have tasted me more if I'd come in their mouths.

I was supposed to get up in the box and give evidence. I'd been looking forward to it. Relishing the thought of it, in fact. I've never not got up during any of my court appearances 'cos I know me better than anyone and I can defend me better than anyone. And the single most important thing when you're on trial is this – to introduce the human element. That's the one thing that gets lost among the legal arguments, the points of law, the posh-voiced briefs in wigs, the judge's comments, the legal precedents that are read out from law books, the evidence – all of it, in fact. Just the whole fucking dry, formal legal process takes over and the people whose lives are at stake get lost in the middle.

I saw that early on in my dealings with the law and I thought I would never ever get lost in the middle. I'd make sure everyone knew exactly who and what I was about. Which means telling the truth about the bad bits of you – or what they consider the 'bad' bits – and not being afraid of doing that. I did that during the importation trial in '96. I got up and said:

'You all know me and I am actually worse than you may think, but I treat you with enough respect to know you can look at me and know what I am. I've done most of the things you might have heard of – debt collecting, beating people up, even burying people – and been pretty fucking naughty in my time. But I haven't done this.

'And because I'm good at what I do, the people who don't like that don't like me, and they've roped me into this. I've been visited in my cell and told that they don't think they'll get a conviction for this but if they can steal a year off me on remand then they will do. And you never know, maybe if things go a certain way on the day and they make me sound bad enough to you, I might even get a "guilty".'

Now how much of that sounds familiar and still rang true? Every fucking word of it. Mind you, since that case I'd cracked it off big-time in the media world so that was unlikely to endear me to the Old Bill now, wasn't it? It kind of makes sense for them to rally round and have another push at getting me. I guess for some of them they just look on it as part of their job to act like a bunch of vindictive cunts.

Anyway, my day (or, more likely, days) in the witness box were something I was looking forward to, so I could set the record straight and bang out a few home truths. Fire a few volleys across the bows and put a big fucking hole in their already sinking ship. Fuck the *Titanic*, I wanted to be the fucking iceberg, mate.

While the court case was going on though I was informed that it was quite possible, and more than likely, that the prosecution had advance warning of what I was going to say. Now that's a big fucking bombshell. It didn't suprise me 'cos I'd always suspected it, but to get confirmation of it was something else.

How it happened was like this. Because it was the run-up to Christmas there were office dos and works parties going on everywhere. For the legal profession as well as everyone else. During one of these parties for legal people, held on a boat incidentally, one of the other lot (who I've been told I can't name) was overheard saying something by a legal person known to me (who I will protect by not naming). What was said was that because my house was still under surveillance they had been able to listen to me preparing my case, my defence. Now that is about as illegal as it gets! You have a right to confidentiality over that matter. Everyone does. From a shoplifter to Fred West. That's why you have closed meetings with your brief, even if you're in a nick or a police station.

The general feeling picked up from what was said was 'Oh Courtney thinks he's so clever, but he doesn't know that we know what he knows.' That was the gist of it, like they were one step ahead of the game. Things had obviously been planned by the prosecution on the back of what they'd heard me talk about in the run-up to the trial.

So someone was still taping my house. Even when the fucking trial was going on, probably. The Met and CIB3 aren't allowed to do that by law – they wouldn't be given a warrant – but even if they decided to obey that, which is debatable, they get around it by saying that 'another agency' is doing the surveillance – Customs and Excise, the Inland Revenue, the Flying Squad, or whoever else they can put up. All it would take would be another 'anonymous' phone call to Customs saying I was involved in smuggling something and Customs would get a warrant for surveillance.

And however naive you might be to the everyday dirty working of the law do you really think for one second, one solitary second, that those agencies are not gonna talk to each other?! Or if the Metropolitan Commissioner requests access to the tapes he is gonna be refused? Congratulations, you've just won a million quid 'cos the correct answer is 'No fucking way would they not do that.'

Now we get to one of their 'edges', those little advantages that everyone tries to get for a fight. From a boxer with the longer reach that uses his jab more, to a copper calling on his colleagues to back him up. Everyone does it. Any professional fighter wants the edge when they go into battle, which is what a courtroom is, a battleground.

The edges have changed down the years. First of all, before tape recording, they'd just verbal you up. That's what they called it, 'verbal' you up. Meaning the coppers would just completely lie about you making a confession about something. Plain as day they'd say, 'He admitted he did it, Sarge.' If you argued and said, 'No, I never!' they'd just say 'cos you were now trying to change your statement it proved what a liar you were. And that edge worked, because in those days people were more liable to believe in the police.

Tape recording put an end to all that so they started holding people for hours or days on end and grilling them without a solicitor being present. Some people would crack and sign a confession. Eventually that came to an end. Mostly. There were so many high-profile cases of innocent geezers being released after ten, fifteen, even twenty years inside. I think most people wised up to what their legal rights were in a police station.

You can bribe a judge – I've seen it done – but you can't bribe a jury. So little tricks were developed to get the jury on the side of the law and against the defendant. One of them you've already heard about – a copper phones a bloke's house when they know he's out and leaves an incriminating message on the answer machine, something like, 'I need another two kilos of gear from you, get in touch.' That tape will then be played in front of a jury without them knowing that it's a copper that made the call.

That could sway a jury towards a guilty verdict and all for the cost of a 10p phone call.

One they used to discredit what they call career criminals was one they used on me in 1996. They come up with some excuse to beef up security around you in order to make you look bad. Again, all it takes is an anonymous 10p phone call to a nick saying, 'I think Courtney's gonna escape, just overheard it in a pub!' Which is fucking laughable stuff, really, but it's all they need to throw a ring of half a dozen armed guards around you every time you go to court. The jury take one look at that and go, Fucking hell!

That's how they operate: get the EXCUSE first – the convenient 'anonymous' phone call – in order to justify getting the thing they WANT to happen.

When DNA evidence came in everyone thought that would put an end to innocent people being convicted, but what people didn't realise was that if a bent Old Bill planted DNA evidence against you it was actually more likely you'd get sent down. See how they move with the times. One step ahead.

Then a few years ago they went and outlawed the 'no comment' part. Well, I ain't gonna go no fucking comment here about this. I think you know my view on that. What a fucking coup that was for them to pull off: 'What did he say, Sarge?' 'Erm . . . nothing', 'Oh, he must be guilty then!' Fuck me, talk about loading the dice.

Yeah, they've definitely worked out a little set of rules for themselves in the courtroom. If a defendant is being questioned and the prosecution lobs in a difficult question which he can't answer, or he answers in a way which makes him look bad, then that's how it goes. He's got to live with that. But if a member of the law comes under fire in the witness box they can refuse to speak on the grounds of national security or that it may endanger a colleague, or compromise an ongoing investigation or reveal a valuable source. There's loads of things they can pull out of the hat when they're in that situation, but the only one that me and you had, as civilians, of going 'no comment', they even outlawed that! They've even made that practically fucking illegal. If that don't teach someone something about the way things are going in this country with the law enforcement agencies . . .

Anyway, when it came to me and my brief questioning the police about the continued surveillance of my house during the trial they came back with another little 'edge' that they occasionally pull out of the bag. They said they could not confirm whether or not another agency is listening in, as it may compromise other investigations that are ongoing. Which is basically the old 'national security' bullshit answer that governments give whenever they're caught out spying and lying; spying on people and then lying about it – suddenly everything becomes a matter of 'national security' so they can't talk about it. Pretty fucking convenient.

I got the same smokescreen thrown up in front of me. But they didn't outright deny that I was still under surveillance, so I could use their little trick. The old 'anything you fail to mention now . . . may later be used against you' argument.

For them to listen to a man preparing his case is fucking outrageous, ain't it? Talk about a millennium dome-size diabolical liberty. Someone else would probably go the European Court and get hundreds of grand compensation for an infringement of their human rights. But me? What could I do? I just took it on the chin, leaned back on the ropes for a second, shook my head to clear it, and then went back out into the middle of the ring swinging the fucking corner stool! (In a boxing match you can't do a great deal about the ref being against you, but if you knock the other fighter spark out there ain't a lot even a bent ref can do about that!)

So I made the difficult decision and decided not to get into the box and testify. It burned me not to do it, to be honest, 'cos the one thing you can take comfort from in these situations is that you will, literally, get your day in court. And explaining me – and what I'm about, what I do and won't do and why – that is my forte. To miss that chance hurt me, but at the same time I didn't want to give them the satisfaction of walking into what obviously was a very carefully planned attempt by them to discredit me, even more than they were trying to do already.

The morning of my supposed first day in the box I walked into the Old Bailey. Everyone was stood there, the six defence briefs, the prosecutor, the other three co-defendants, the court ushers and security guards. Everybody just milling about waiting for the session to be called. I happened to walk by one of the prosecuting team and as I passed he made some little sarky comment like 'Good luck today, Mr Courtney'. I just turned and went, 'I ain't testifying . . .' His expression said it all, really.

You see I hadn't told anyone, not even Jen, that I was gonna do that. What with the surveillance carrying on, I couldn't afford for that to be known and spoil the surprise of me dropping it on them as a little bombshell.

The knock-on effect was that the two or three days they'd planned on having me in the witness box were suddenly available now for other witnesses of mine. So they were brought forward early. This was another thing I'd planned on, because I knew it meant that the prosecution would've been banking on those days to do preparation work on those witnesses. Now, while they were still getting their heads around what I'd said, they were faced with having to cross-examine witnesses earlier than they'd planned. Like I said, it's a battle in there. A proper little war. That's how they look at it so that's how you've got to look at it, and plan your strategy accordingly.

It wasn't till near the end of the trial that I got the chance to call my witnesses. First up was Ian Tucker. I'd met Tucker years ago when we were both at the height of our debt-collecting skills. It seemed natural to team up so we did, and went on to more success. One time we even got back a golf course that had been stolen (which came up in court). A feature on me called 'Fun Lovin (Ex) Criminal' appeared in the first edition of *Front* magazine three years ago. The editor Piers Hernu interviewed me in a casino I took him to in Leicester Square, and then I dropped a big surprise on him by introducing him to Tucker. Tucker was on the run at the time and had been on *Crimewatch*.

Tucker was one of a few people that the prosecution were saying I'd informed on. And all of the others were – get this – friends of mine, funnily enough! See a pattern emerging here? All along I'd said that the fake paperwork on the list of people I'd supposedly 'informed' on was, actually, a list of people who I was using Warnes to help. The fake informant thing was just the smokescreen to get info from the police. Remember this – in any other normal court case these people would be called by the prosecution to use *against* me, but here they were appearing for the defence. Why was that? Because they wanted to help prove that I'd actually *helped* them, not grassed them up! And they certainly wouldn't be called by the prosecution because what they had to say proved I was right and the police were wrong.

So these witnesses, which the prosecution thought were gonna bury me, actually ended up being called by me to completely fuck up the Old Bill's twisted version of events!

Over the years Warnes had tried to convince me that various friends and associates of mine were informants. That's the old divide and conquer technique. Trying to create unrest in the enemy camp. They'd tried to do to them exactly what they were trying to do to me – paint me as a grass. I hadn't fallen for it.

One of the fake information sheets that suspiciously found its way onto the streets – though that wasn't anything to do with the police now, was it?: I wonder! – was one saying I'd informed on Tucker. They wanted to start that rumour off, knowing that Ian was a very, very notorious naughty man, and if someone like him thought that about you you'd be well advised to be seriously worried. Which is exactly why they picked him. It'd be no good them trying to get me in trouble with Julian Clary. Most I'd get is a slap on the cheek.

That little plan didn't work 'cos despite all that, Tucker knew the real score and got up in court to say that. And he did an absolute blinder. Ian, looking every inch the seriously naughty geezer that he is, got up in the witness box and immediately the jury, and everyone in court, were under no illusions that he was anything other than what he is. I doubt they mistook him for my local Help The Aged shop manager.

He said he'd swear on the Bible but seeing as everyone else – the prosecution witnesses and the Old Bill – had been lying on it all day he'd rather just say that what he had to say came from the heart. He said he knew I weren't involved in all this, no way was I a grass and he wouldn't still be a friend of mine if he thought that. The prosecution replied, 'Well, let's see if you're still friends after this . . .' and then they produced the docket that supposedly 'proved' I'd grassed him up.

This was their big moment, their big Courtroom Drama Scene that they thought was gonna shoot me down in flames.

Tucker just went, 'Yeah . . . what about it?'

'Well, this is where Mr Courtney said where you were in hiding when you were on the run!'

Tucker said, 'I think you'll find that's absolute cack! 'Cos when I was on the run Dave was the only one who knew where I was and I was never caught. I actually wanted to have more information on what the Old Bill had on me so Dave got Austin to check it out for me! He was actually helping me.' Which is exactly what I'd done with everyone else through using Warnes. Now that little revelation coming from a geezer like Tucker stood up there in the box put a proper damaging hole in the side of the prosecutor's and the police's battleship. And rightly so.

In his statements Tucker said, 'Dave Courtney has got information for me on numerous occasions. If my name is on a docket it's 'cos Dave was receiving information *for* me. I've sent people to Dave when they were in trouble with the law. People who want help go to Dave because he knows contacts. Warnes was valued as a corrupt policeman. Dave said he had this bloke by the bollocks.'

So that was that little misconception cleared right up! Bang. Bring 'em on! They then started pulling out more 'examples' of me supposedly doing the same thing, and every time Tucker shot them down in flames with the truth – 'Oh yeah. Same thing there. I was being investigated, and I knew I was, but I didn't know what the fuck they had on me. So Dave used Warnes on that one.'

On the golf course story. About when this geezer temporarily signed over his half of a golf course to his partner for safe keeping, but then his partner just forgot the 'temporary' bit and decided to keep the golf course all for himself. All four million pounds' worth of it. Tucker made it really funny the way he told it: 'This geezer tried to steal a golf course and me and Dave allegedly went down there to try to get it back. Later on this bloke's windows were blown in with a shotgun in the middle of the night. Now just 'cos a big bent-nosed geezer and another fella with a bald head and a cigar were seen driving away, in a car with the same registration as mine, the Old Bill thought that WE were something to do with it! Fuck knows why!'

It was really, really funny how he did it and the jury were falling about. See, all the time, as well as the truth coming out, the human element had suddenly been put into the trial. That's worth its weight in gold. And the golf course story was another example of how I used Warnes. 'That's when we wanted some information on how far they'd got with that case and Dave went and got it. There's the proof in the thing, and here I am telling you.'

So that was that one dealt with! After about twenty minutes the prosecution wouldn't talk to Tucker any more, they just weren't having it! They were scared of bringing up another piece of what they thought was 'damning evidence' just for Tucker to completely piss on their bonfire. They wouldn't talk to him any more 'cos he was just too damaging in proving that it was actually me that was using Warnes.

IMPORTANT BIT HERE – another witness they wouldn't let me produce was a Detective Sergeant Gary Theobalds. Theobalds was the investigating officer on a case where Tucker was on the run because of an alleged attempted kidnapping. Tucker's picture even appeared on the *Crimewatch* TV programme. (Tucker actually rang in himself and told Nick Ross that he could send them a better photo!) I got Warnes to ring up and try to find out how much information the police had on Tucker so I could get it to him and help him keep one step ahead. So Warnes rang Theobalds. This is what Theobalds later said in his Witness Statement report – 'The context of the conversation was that Warnes wished to assist the investigation and that he had an informant who might be able to help. Specifically, he wished to know where officers believed Tucker was hiding. He also wished to know what evidence police were in possession of. The impression gleaned from the information requested was *not one of an officer keen to assist but more of an officer bent on obtaining information for his own purposes.*' No shit, Sherlock! 'His own purposes' being to pass it on to me so I could warn Tucker. You can see now why the police didn't want to let me produce stuff like this as evidence . . .

Then it was Jennifer's turn in the witness box.

Jen could back up all the things about Warnes that everyone knew were true. She knew all about how the information thing worked and had been with me when I'd taken people to Warnes so he could get information to help them out. All that stuff she knew.

The effect Jen's evidence had was she also put the human element back into the trial, big-time. More than anyone. Because the case was something that was very dry and legal, and complex and hard to explain. And I wouldn't have blamed the jury for nodding off at certain points because I nearly did (fortunately I took a travel alarm!)

You couldn't have scripted Jen's bit to any more devastating effect. She was just so obviously a woman whose husband was being really wrongly done by. Just as when someone else praises you it always sounds better than if you praise yourself, well if someone else describes the wrong done to you it has more effect than if you describe it. So it was with Jenny.

There was a real undercurrent of underhandedness in court when I brought my witnesses up, like they were trying to rush everyone through before they'd had a chance to speak. Which, of course, is exactly what they try to do. The defence asked Jen what my state of mind was on the day we went to the meet on Plumstead Common. She was going to answer that she knew exactly what my state of mind was 'cos we'd already talked about the possibility of Warnes trying to stitch me up, but the judge jumped in and said, 'You can't ask Miss Pinto that question.' My brief argued that he should, but the judge said it was hearsay, and he wouldn't allow it. So he moved them onto something else.

Jen's take on it was this – 'Just like Kim James was a victim, and they didn't tell her what was going on, Dave was a victim as well. What they did with Kim James – not involve her in the trial – they should have done with Dave. He was in the same position!'

She talked about how on that day she witnessed Warnes admitting on the tape that I weren't involved in it. The judge kept butting in, which didn't go down too well in Jen's book.

'I think you're bang out of order and rude, actually, keeping interrupting me. I'm giving my account of things and you're cutting me off and I'd rather you didn't do that!'

He said, 'There are rules and regulations and things are run according to that.'

Jennifer said, 'Yeah, you are right there when you say that, it is "run". This whole thing is run by you. It does feel like you're "running" things but I thought Dave was entitled to a fair trial. There's nothing fair going on here. But you're right it's being "run".'

The prosecutor quite quickly realised he was on a bit of a loser with Jen, like 'oh we've got a live one here, back off' kind of thing. Jen's not one that you can really score points off. But then usually your defence comes in and asks you 'leading' questions, y'know, to give you the chance to say the things you want to say. Trouble is, what with everyone bantering with each other Jen just saw all these Blokes In Gowns In Wigs and dished it out to all of them, even Mr Holden, my brief. It was like at the fair when you shoot at the ducks. To Jen, in this courtroom anyone in a wig was getting it, mate!

So I stood up, pointed at Mr Holden and went, 'This one's on our side, babe, and that one ain't!' Everybody laughed except for the judge. He said, 'That is highly irregular, Mr Holden, the defendant talking to the witness!'

It was as good as me being up there because she said what I would have said and with as much passion as I would say it. I've always said she's 51 per cent of me. She dropped the human element into that courtroom like a grenade with the pin out. Everyone was sat up that day, I can tell you. First Tucker and then Jen: the atmosphere was fucking charged, mate. She said things with as much passion and disregard for the law and order rules and regulations of the courtroom – what's the 'right' and 'wrong' way to say it (in their view), and what you can and can't say according to them. And she was right, mate.

When you're saying what they don't want to hear they try and hit you with the 'just answer "yes" or "no"' thing. But if there's any two people who are less than likely to be intimidated by that it was Ian Tucker and my Jennifer. Jen said to the prosecutor, 'If you cut your questions down to one word, then I will answer with one word.'

No one else in the world can do that for you 'cos no one feels about it that way except you and your missus. And how lucky I am that I don't have an ordinary missus that's all quiet and shy. Mind you, even a missus like that, if her husband's life was put in jeopardy, would probably find it in her somewhere to jump up and have a go.

I run my life by the 'human element' and Jen hit that bang on.

Still, as good as you might do when you're up there in the box, most people come out feeling there was so much they weren't allowed to say. Even Jen. Still, afterwards she told me she'd felt elated at how things had gone.

Brendan McGirr and Lee Smith were also called and testified in the same manner: they said that in order to help them I used Warnes to *get* information not to give it. Brendan's Witness Statement: 'Warnes was known in our circle. He was impressed by criminals and police. He had a sales pitch about getting information. He worked both sides, there's a nasty streak in him. He was in awe of Dave Courtney. He wished he could be in our circle permanently. Dave only kept the relationship with Austin Warnes for his friends' benefit and for other people too. Dave was uneasy that Warnes could turn on him. Warnes would let everyone know what he was capable of. Dave was actually tapping the establishment via Warnes for everyone that knew him and what he was doing, Dave put himself up to get help, and if anything went wrong only he'd pay the price.'

And then Lee Smith's Witness Statement said: 'Me and Dave Courtney used to run raves. I gave Austin Warnes £500 p.w. for information to let us know if we were to be raided. Warnes kept saying he shouldn't be seen here, so he once asked me to sign as an informant to make the meetings look OK.'

I hate to sound like a stuck record but there's only so many ways you can say the same thing, and I needed to get the witnesses out that could tell the truth. Especially after the prosecution had had the first six weeks of the trial to say what they wanted without anyone in the dock being able to reply.

From the big witnesses of mine right down to the little ones they ruled most of them out when they saw what they had to say. Like Lee Brown, a reporter from the *South London Press* that I'd told about Warnes trying to entrap me with drug deals he'd offered, which I'd always told him to fuck off with. In Lee Brown's Witness Statement he says – 'Dave Courtney said there had been one guy who was annoying him who was a police officer at Bexleyheath Police Station. He told me before that he had officers who gave him information.'

I had all these people that they said I'd supposedly grassed on lining up to say the opposite – that I'd helped them. But after the damage done by Tucker and Wolfie and Brendan these other witnesses of mine were deemed to be 'not relevant'. Yeah, get *that* – all the rest of the people that the prosecution were trying to say I grassed up but were actually people I'd helped out, and were willing to get up and say so, were not allowed to be produced because of the prosecutor's objection on those grounds of 'not relevant'. Very fucking convenient. They were relevant to proving I weren't a grass, but then the police wanted everyone to believe I was, so that was a result for them. Other witnesses that proved my case but were refused were: Kevin Suma, Phil and Des, Roy Shaw, Saskia and Christian.

But, the good thing was that the more the trial had gone on the more there had been a real feeling about the place that no one believed the police about this case at all. No one. You could just feel that. Even when Jen came out from testifying and she was talking to the court photographer. This geezer is there every fucking day, official Old Bailey snapper, and he definitely wanted a picture of Jen 'cos she's so distinctive-looking. He told her that he'd been at the trial from day one and before the end of the first week he realised what they were trying to do to me. He said he was glad to see I walked out the front doors every day, head held high, and not out the back way, like some do. Jen said, rightly, that if that option had been offered I would've said 'No fucking way!'

So it was nice to come out and hear stuff like that, but it just pissed me off even more that the Old Bill had had the fucking cheek to try and pull it off. Still, I thought the police were guilty of underestimating me, the jury *and* the general public. Mind you, like I say, they were really banking on the old 'Throw enough dirt and hope some sticks' routine.

Little did they know that my aftershave's made by Teflon.

20. JUDGEMENT DAY

Some guilty, some not – some day. And a very, very unusual set of drinking partners . . .

Even though we were in the last week of the trial there was still time for me to get one more bollocking for contempt of court. Holden, the prosecutor, said he 'felt compelled to bring to his honour's attention' that my website was displaying a copy of Austin Warnes' own statement to the police in which he said I wasn't involved.

Holden asked for my bail to be taken away! He went on to say that my website had been checked every single day of the case – which I wish I'd known before 'cos I'd have left extra special messages on there for them – and although there was nothing there they could moan about when they'd looked before, last night when they checked they'd seen the statement. The judge asked if there was any evidence that I had personally put the statement on the site and Holden said there wasn't. Holden really played on this one, like he'd done with the headphones, but even the judge didn't buy it. So I just got another warning and we had to say we'd take the page off. Bit late as it had already been round the world a million times! It was already up in cyberspace being read by astronauts.

I got loads of letters and messages of support on my web page and me and Jen sat up at night answering them all. The Internet's fucking wicked though, ain't it? I'm a real convert. It's like global graffiti – you can quickly write something about whatever's just happened and get it around the country, or the world, in a few minutes. That's why the law and the authorities still get twitchy about the Internet, because it's one of the few areas left that they haven't put a complete fucking stranglehold on yet.

The last days in court were set aside for the summing up speeches by the barristers and the judge. Parts of it were quite funny. In the summing up by Simon James's brief he said, 'For a very long and complex court case it has been made more colourful by Mr Courtney's wide array of suits. He has more suits than Imelda Marcos had shoes!' Everyone laughed but the judge. The next day, after he'd obviously thought about it, he said, 'Your comment on Mr Courtney's suits and Imelda Marcos' shoes . . . it was reported in the papers that she fell off one of her high shoes and broke her ankle!' Well, thanks for nothing. If that was a joke then no one but the barristers laughed, but in their case every joke the judge makes is funny.

My brief, Mr Lithman, was by far the best brief there. Most probably the most expensive, but also the best. Then again, mine was the most obviously bullshit case out of the lot. The other three co-defendants' briefs did have an uphill fucking struggle with what their clients had been caught doing.

The summing up bit is pretty valuable, especially on a long case. To be honest, I thought that if we'd asked the jury for their verdict then and there, before the summing up, it would have been 'not guilty' for me. But you know the prosecution is gonna really lay it on thick in his summing up so you need your brief to do his bit as well.

Mr Lithman did his summing up on the case against me and hearing him put it all together, like they do, in one long description – the late date that I was dragged into it, the complete lack of evidence, the bent copper's own admission, the fact I ain't met anyone involved in it, the stacks of proof that information passed from Warnes to me not the other way around, etc., etc. – all of that and more, really drummed home to me what an obvious below-the-belt punch it was for the Old Bill to get me here. Basically, weeks of a trial about something that was fuck all to do with me just so they could try and paint me as a grass. I suppose it was worth it to them. What had they got to lose? They hoped that even if I got 'not guilty' then some of the mud would stick.

My brief picked up on the maliciousness of me being prosecuted at all for this. At one point he leaned on the guard rail in front of the jury, and pointed at me: 'Can you imagine how much the police hate that man? Imagine being a police officer and seeing Mr Courtney driving past in a Rolls Royce smoking a cigar!' or on TV talking about my book, or making films, or giving 'Audience Withs . . .' across the country (and the world), and openly talking about police corruption. Or any of the other hundred things that make certain sections of the police want to see me brought down. Because, knowing full well the power of the media themselves, they don't want to see someone else use it against them.

From the outside looking in the judge's summing up probably looked just about fair. But sometimes what you see is not what the defendants get. What can happen is this. A judge can really stick it to you through all the weeks of the trial, just on little decisions he makes about what can and can't be heard, which witnesses can and can't be called, which legal arguments he wins and loses. All those things, which people don't see unless they're there in court every single fucking day.

So when it comes to the last week, people come in, see the judge's summing up and go, 'Oh that weren't too bad was it? Quite fair in fact.' What they've missed is the hundred rabbit punches and low blows you've suffered in the past however many weeks.

Another thing you might not know is this, that any appeal by the accused against their verdicts (in any trial) can only be on the basis of a complaint against the judge's summing up. It's on that you get your appeal. The briefs are sat there with their pens at the ready to write down any points for an appeal so the judges take it easy during their summing up. They leave no points for an appeal because of the final word, but that won't make up for any damage they might have inflicted during the trial.

The amount of evidence that I wanted to present which was ruled out as not relevant was amazing. The one thing they didn't rule as 'irrelevant' and 'having no bearing on the case' was the one thing they should have ruled out – me.

The summing ups went on for three days, starting on Monday. The judge did his on Wednesday and then the jury retired to consider their verdicts. During the decision-making time by the jury I had to go downstairs to the cells to wait for the verdict. This was because during the trial we were supposed to leave the court fifteen minutes after the jury but on one day, right in the last days, I left only ten minutes after the jury. The prosecution reported me! So I got another order from the judge saying I had to stay in custody downstairs while the verdict was being deliberated. It also meant that when I went in the morning my bag was searched manually. So they ended up pulling out all the usual crap in there that I took along. It was funny at the end of the day when I had to get it all back and they were signing out 'one musical lobster, one small bottle champagne, and one policeman/pig statue.'

By the end of play Wednesday afternoon we got a call saying that the jury were coming back in. Everybody assembled in court. That's over thirty people what with the jury, the judge, all the defence counsel, the prosecution team, typist, ushers, guards and us lot, the defendants, plus all those in the public gallery. Most of which were my lot.

The foreman stood up and said that they were undecided on one of the four defendants. They weren't allowed to say which one. Though I had a fair idea. At one point the jury had come back in because they'd asked to look at some evidence again. So we all came back into court! (I was up and down those stairs like a geezer with his braces caught on the banister.)

The thing they wanted to see again was the film of Cook, the private investigator's colleague, breaking into Kim James's Fiat. Yeah, that film, *Not Gone In 17 Minutes*! And during the judge's summing up I noticed that he was particularly careful about how he'd mentioned Cook's bit. Y'know, saying they had to be sure that they thought Cook knew it was drugs and not a recording bug in the package he put in the car. I mean, the geezer weren't saying he never broke into the car, how could he when it was on Widescreen, Dolby Surround sound cinema! He was just saying he didn't know what was in the package.

So no verdict came through on the Wednesday and everybody went home to wait and see what happend tomorrow. Some to sleep easier than others, I'd suppose. Me, I slept like a log and snored like someone sawing one in half. I could tell the next morning by the cracks in the ceiling plaster.

Next day was a big day. For little Courtney anyway 'cos it was her third birthday! Not that I had anything else to think about. But she did say, 'Daddy's going to the Old Bailey!' Kids today, where do they get it from? You know who I blame . . .

I had someone drive me in to court because I didn't want to go on the bike and not be able to celebrate when I came out. There's confidence for you. While I was down in the Old Bailey the pub over the road, Seamus O'Dell's (I love those Welsh pubs!), was again full of people waiting for the verdict – Jen, Seymour, Matt, Brendan, Marcus, Wolfie, Ray, Jackie, – etc., etc. – the bar tab in there must have been bigger than Salman Rushdie's take-away pizza bill.

The jury still didn't come back in all day. Then we got the call again late in the afternoon, about four o'clock, just before the end of play. I honestly thought it was another false alarm and they were gonna resume again tomorrow. That is until I saw a load of prison officers coming up the stairs with us, so this was it. Whatever I thought about how shit it was that I'd ever even been brought to trial or how pathetic their 'evidence' was, seeing those prison guards could still make you feel awful. It's like when a cop car pulls up behind you at the lights; even if you know you've done fuck all and everything's in order you still get a twinge. I fucking hate them for that.

The public gallery was full. The courtroom was full. Everyone present and correct.

The foreman stood and spoke. Simon James first – 'Guilty'. Then Jonathan Rees – 'Guilty'. James Cook next – 'Undecided'. Then me.

'Not guilty'.

Everybody in the public gallery cheered, which I understood, but really what could I celebrate? The fact that they hadn't managed to fuck me over? It was like having a goal disallowed, losing the match, and then the video replay afterwards shows that the ball did actually cross the line. Big fucking deal. It don't change the result. But the good thing is that at least everyone knew the truth.

So I weren't elated but I was happy for my family and friends who had lived with my embarrassment about this whole thing, and with the insinuations that I was a grass, for as long as I had. I was pleased for them. I was pleased for my Jenny and my kids. For my mates as well, because being Dave Courtney's mate was a proper fucking bonus until about six weeks ago. No one knocked you for any money, you got laid for nothing, you didn't pay to go in anywhere, you got to go to openings and premieres if you wanted, that kinda thing. Then it hit the papers about the trial and all the propaganda that went with it and suddenly being Dave Courtney's mate might not be as good a thing as it was before. And this is where you find out who your mates are.

It was sort of mixed feelings for me 'cos I was happy because everyone else was happy, so I was happy for them.

I felt . . . vindicated. That was the word. I felt fucking vindicated.

Rees and James were taken down to the cells immediately. They would be sentenced tomorrow along with Warnes.

Because I was actually still technically 'in custody' I had to leave the dock the other way and go back down to the custody suite to be registered out.

Still playing it slippy to the end the police said they could offer me a car at the back door. I told them to FUCK right off! As if I was going to miss walking out of the front door to what I knew was waiting for me out there – mates, family, a mass of press photographers and two TV camera crews. I was ready for my close up, Mr Director.

Still, they kept me hanging about for ten minutes waiting to get signed out. Eventually I came up and walked through the court lobby and up to the entrance. I could hear the racket through the glass doors. It was just turning dark outside so I could see this mass of people. Jen was waiting for me first in the entrance with Courtney, so it was hugs and kisses all round, thank you very much. Then we walked out into the TV camera lights and everyone started screaming and cheering and the photographers' flashbulbs all started popping off like strobe lights. I was getting hugs and backslap from See, Wolfie, Matt and Mad Pete and the others. To the tune of 'Who Let The Dogs Out' Cream started chanting, 'Who let the Dave out! Ooo! Ooo! Who let the Dave out!' and everyone joined in. It was fucking mad, mate. Cars were stopping to watch. To walk out to that reception was wicked.

Like I've said, I wasn't exactly jubilant at the 'not guilty' and now you can see why, but I was really buzzing 'cos I could see that everyone around me was relieved.

Flashbulbs were still blasting off everywhere and someone from behind one of the TV cameras asked how I felt. I couldn't resist it – I said, 'Thank fuck the trial is over . . . because I was running out of suits! And I really do now have faith in the British justice system, and even less in the Metropolitan Police!'

The whole crowd of us moved off over the road with the photographers and camera crews in tow. We walked into the pub to find even more people inside, all clapping. Even the bar staff. They must've thought there would be at least a drink in it for them. Well, there was! We cracked open a dozen bottles of champagne and any other drink for any other fucker who wanted one. Every other person was either on their mobile telling their missus or their mates, or taking calls on their mobiles from people checking up if the verdict had come through. People were firing questions and congratulations at me from all angles, or mobiles were being passed to me to say hello to other people who couldn't be here. Blokes and birds were coming in off the street just to see what was going on and be part of it. James and Tony from Channel 5 and Channel 4 were buzzing around, trying to get the best footage for their documentaries.

Word came through then that the jury decision on Cook had finally come through. Not guilty. I think that was the result of the day, actually.

So we were all just fucking buzzing, mate. More than anything I was getting off on them all getting off on it. It was infectious. It was like a street party in a pub!

Then the oddest thing happened . . .

It was now about ten minutes since I'd come out of the Bailey, and I turned around and fuck me if the jury weren't all walking in the pub and coming up to me to shake my hand! Hand on my heart – the fucking jury walked into my party! Fucking hell, I'd never heard of that before. Neither had the geezer running the pub. He later told me he'd been there five years and seen just about everything, but he'd never ever seen an acquitted defendant get congratulations and 'best wishes' from the jury – which immediately told me exactly what the jury thought of my part in the trial as well.

I don't think the photographers could get their heads around it either, so the old camera flashbulbs got a proper hammering for the next ten minutes. It was kind of amazing though.

We all stayed in there for the next six hours, the rest of the drinking night, actually. My mate Eamon, the little diamond, got his credit card battered behind the bar and actually paid for all the drinks. All eight hundred quids' worth. So big, big, big thank you to Eamon. And I know there are several alcoholics who were in there who'd like to thank him too. From the bottom of their livers.

So for the rest of the night everyone was talking ten to the dozen about everything that had happened. And I do have a lot of fucking good talkers and storytellers in my crowd so every part of that pub was jumping. The jurors told me that when they came out of the Bailey and crossed the road for a drink, they did hesitate a bit when they saw that me and mine were inside – a sort of, 'How will this look?' moment – but then they thought, Oh fuck it, we found him 'not guilty' so what's the problem?

No problem at all. Come in and take a seat. Let me entertain you. And you enlighten me. I didn't question them about what went on, but then I didn't have to because most of them were just happy and eager to talk about it all.

Oh, and get this – they started telling me that they had already decided by the end of the first week of the case that they knew I was nothing to do with it. More than that, from then on the more of the case they heard – and with less and less of me in it – the more they thought why is Courtney here at all? Same thing as I was fucking thinking, as it happens! I mean, I was confident all along that it would turn out this way but even I never imagined the jury would rule me out in the first week of the trial!

If only I'd known that then I could've relaxed more; but they could hardly give me a wink in the courtroom could they? No, they couldn't, I know 'cos I asked! (Joke, officer).

So the rest of the six weeks of the trial they spent deciding on the other three. They also said that their 'Why is Courtney here at all?' question gradually got answered over those five weeks, when it became obvious to them that what I'd said in my outburst was true. By 'outburst' I mean when

I stood up and accused the prosecution of fanning the 'informer' flames they were trying to light beneath me. The jury came out every night, remember, and saw whatever newspaper reports were out at the time. Then they applied that to what they heard in court and saw for themselves the difference between the two.

I know, actually, that that was the real heart of why they came in the pub. Forget all the congratulations bullshit, it weren't that. The heart of it was that after they themselves realised in the first week that I wasn't involved, they then had five weeks of watching the Old Bill, and the prosecution on their behalf, try to say exactly the opposite. So coming in the pub was really a way of showing they knew that, and were showing that. A couple of them actually said they hoped I wasn't in as big a trouble as some of the newspapers were trying to make out. I could see that they wanted to let me in on the fact that they were now aware of what was going on in the press.

But be under no illusion, because I wasn't, that if they had thought me guilty they would have found me guilty. Without a shadow of a doubt. And knowing that made it even better that they hadn't. Because they hadn't done it for me – I meant absolutely fuck all to them; they don't know me or owe me – they did it for themselves, to know that they did the right thing. They were not the kind of people who could live with themselves for doing anything else. Y'know what I mean? You could see that straight off. They were decent people who took it all very, very seriously. And thank fuck for that.

You see, you can't bribe a complete jury. You can bribe a judge but you can't bribe a whole jury. They make their own minds up.

The judge, like the ref in football, can't score a goal for you but he can give a penalty one way or ignore it the other. Match-changing decisions. So if, for instance, an awful lot of the evidence against a man was taped telephone conversations and the defence argued it was inadmissible, if the judge agreed to let the jurors hear it that would be a big bonus. From then on the judge could afford to be seen to be very 'fair' during the rest of the trial because he's already done his damaging bit.

All that would be unseen to the jury and everyone else watching.

Tell you what though, if the judge in my trial had been nobbled you could tell it most certainly fucking didn't come from my side! If it had, from the way he behaved I'd have definitely wanted a full refund. Ha!

I tell you what, though, it was fascinating getting to talk to the jury, especially just fresh out of the trial, because you learned things you couldn't possibly hear anywhere else. They learned a few things too. They couldn't believe it when they heard about what evidence and witnesses I wasn't allowed to call (another one of those 'edges' the Law has). The jury only see part of the evidence, so they learned that; and they learned what was said in court after the judge had ordered the jury to be taken out. A lot of major decisions are made behind the jurors' backs. That's what the Americans call giving information on a 'need to know' basis. Well, we're given information on a 'need to know fuck all' basis.

Tell you what, we really wised each other up on that old 'need to know' shit, and on what we'd been shielded from. And the jury came to their decision without even seeing all the stuff that the police held back! How good is that?

On the other side of things, they said the testimonials of my friends really stuck with them. That's the human element right there, at work. As Bob Marley said, the truth is an almighty sword. Which is why it hurts like a cunt when you fall on it. Amen to that.

We ended up staying in the pub all night. I won't name them individually, but out of the ones I talked to most there was the foreman, a really decent smart guy; a young fella who you might have thought naive but he was right on it; an older chap (the one reading my book); a lovely lady from Malta; a geezer who was sharp as a pin; a middle-aged black lady; a young Asian girl; and this tall librarian fella who you might have put down as someone easily swayed but he was anything but, mate, even I couldn't have changed his mind. Yeah, and the older fella when he'd walked in the pub, he took a paperback of *Stop the Ride I Want to Get Off!* out of his pocket. Straight up.

He said that when he'd told his son which trial he was doing, his son went, 'What! Dave Courtney? I'm reading his book!' And then he lent the old man his copy. He'd actually been reading it through the trial! So he said when he'd first walked in the courtroom with the book in his pocket and seen me sat there he didn't know what to do. I said I thought it would've probably been the wrong time to ask for a signed copy. But it would have been fucking funny though. (I signed it for him there anyway.)

A strange thing came out of it: one of the jurors said that he would know more about the case than even a lot of my friends 'cos he'd been doing it as a job 8 hours a day for six weeks. I thought, fuck me, that's right. I couldn't sit down and go through it with everyone I know. Another thing that came out was that when they first retired to come to their verdicts they all sat down around the table and decided to go at it from the most innocent to the most guilty. The foreman told me that I was rated as being not involved at all, the husband and the private investigator were rated as most involved, and Cook, the PI's assistant was in-between. Which led to the initial 'undecided'. So, the foreman said, in the time it took them to take off their coats, sit down and say 'OK. Dave Courtney first. Votes for not guilty', twelve hands went straight up. A unanimous, hands-up 12 to 0!

'So that was you done and out of the way,' he said, 'In about two minutes flat.' Then they took not too much more time to decide that Simon James and Jonathan Rees were guilty. Which was obvious. And most of the rest of the time, in fact, was spent debating James Cook and whether he knew the package he put in the car was drugs or thought it was just a bug.

The younger fella said two really interesting things. One was that the evidence of a police officer (from a CIB3 department that specialises in searches and surveillance) stated that it would take a minimum of fifteen seconds to properly plant something in a car dashboard. But when the jury looked at the video of Cook breaking into the Fiat (which is why they asked to look at it again) he only leaned into the car for something like five seconds. That raised doubts in the jurors' minds about Cook's involvement. So the copper's evidence helped acquit him! Touch. What a result. The other thing, and this was the biggie, was that because Cook didn't have legal representation his wife actually appeared for him in court. And that show of loyalty and trust and belief from his missus had an effect on the jury that was massive. It even surprised me, the effect it had on them, and I know human nature. Again, that was the human element at work.

Believe me, go for that human element all the time. And when I say that I don't mean use it as a trick or something, I mean sometimes you have to get past the image and show people who you are and what you're about. People are more alike than different. You've got to show that.

They said they had too many doubts about whether Cook knew what was in the package to be able to convict him. And when his wife cried with relief at his 'not guilty', as she did, the young fella said they'd rather have seen tears of relief than a woman crying over a guilty verdict they couldn't be sure of.

See what I mean . . . it was fascinating, mate, getting an insight into all this. And it was all volunteered. No one asked them to come over to the pub or quizzed anyone about legal arguments or things like that. Because the whole thing was over, everyone was on an equal footing and talking like people discuss what went on at the office. Well, for those six weeks the Old Bailey was the 'office' for me and the jurors. We both had a lot in common in that we'd been sort of dragged out of our normal lives and thrown into this.

So the night in the pub was like a big office party! And it was 14 December, only eleven days to go till Christmas, so we threw in a bit of Christmas spirit as well. Quite a lot of spirit actually. Thank you Eamon, Champion! Again.

I just happened to have a load of posters of me in the boot of the car, so a good old signing session followed. I bet not many jurors end up with autographed pictures of one of those they acquitted. It is mad, though, ain't it?

I was too busy to notice but someone saw some Old Bill pass the pub and look in at what was going on. They'd seen me get not guilty, their own bent copper get sent down, and the jury join me and my party in the pub to show their solidarity. Oh, mate! . . . can you imagine? Can you even begin to imagine how much the police must have loved me at that point.

Yeah, I'll bet they were just about ready to love me to death.

21. THE LENS IS MIGHTIER THAN THE SWORD

The Old Bill try to get me twice! Dave Courtney's Underworld *hits the TV screens, but there's a twist in the tale just waiting . . .*

What happened next surprised even me. But we'll get to that in a minute. First the part that didn't surprise me – little men in blue uniforms putting me at the top of their shit list.

The Old Bill must've thought they had a proper little plan there though, mustn't they? A proper plan and a half, mate, fucking hell. Their thinking obviously went like this – 'Let's get Courtney in court and even if he gets "not guilty" we'll still tarnish his name by leaking stories to the press.'

The first bit hadn't worked 'cos I got 'not guilty'; the second bit had worked to a degree because some press stories did muddy the waters around me. But if that wasn't enough, to top it all off the police then immediately charged me with something else. Listen. First they'd nicked me for the conspiracy thing against the bird. Then when that didn't work and I got not guilty they turn around and try and nick me for conspiracy with the bent copper!

Remember when I said they were trying to put me in that position when they interviewed me? I had to say what I'd used Warnes for in order to prove that I was getting information from him and not the other way around. Which I did. Well now they turned around and said, 'Right, we're nicking you for dealings with a corrupt police officer'! Now if that ain't having two bites at the cherry I don't know what is.

As I've said, right at the beginning of all this, before the Old Bailey trial, my brief went to the police and said they'd better make their minds up what they were nicking me for, because one charge contradicts the other. Y'know, either they thought I was an informer OR a police corrupter. Well they had the evidence to prove I weren't an informer but they went for that charge anyway (for reasons we all now can see). Then when that one didn't come off they returned to the charge that even I didn't deny – that I'd used a bent Old Bill! And now they were trying to do me for that!

Warnes, Rees and James were sentenced on the Friday and got four years, six years and six. Which were, considering the charges, more than fair. Especially Warnes – surprise, surprise: don't tell me a deal hadn't been struck there. Hardly anyone could believe that he'd only been given four (more of that later). He'd be eligible for parole in two. Even though the judge had described Warnes as 'a disgrace to the Metropolitan Police service' and said that even Rees's own lawyer had been 'unable to disguise the unattractiveness of his client's actions' he still handed down light terms.

And even though the plot, in the judge's words, would have 'permanently and perhaps tragically damaged two innocent lives'. Meaning those of Kim James and her son. No doubt, he deliberately neglected to include me on the list of people whose lives would have been fucked up.

The geezer in charge of CIB3, DCI Nicholson, said, 'Given the severity of the crimes we are surprised at the lightness of the sentences. The CPS will consider what grounds there are for appealing against them.' We'll pretend to believe him there, shall we? This is the same CPS that decided to proceed with the charges against me, charges that were so 'justified' that a jury saw through them only a few days into a six-week trial and found me innocent within thirty seconds of their deliberations. *That* CPS. So they obviously know what the fuck they're doing.

Well, actually, they do. It weren't no accident or slip-up that I'd ended up there on trial. If there had been as *little* evidence against any copper as there had been against me do you think the CPS would have proceeded with charges? Answers on a postcard to the European Court of Human Rights. Or should that be Human Wrongs.

See, barristers talk to each other, always in the same group, all together; and sometimes defence and prosecution from one case end up working together on the next one. So they tell each other about the last job like mechanics talk about the last engine rebuild or dustman about the heaviest bin – the law: it's just a job like any other, you've got to understand that. Forget the justice and the wigs and the gowns – to them it's just a job. And we know for a fact that deals are done between barristers, between the police, and it's so fucking *obvious* from the light sentence Warnes got that he'd done a deal to try to turn attention away from him being the bad copper – and all the bad publicity that brings for the Met – and turn it round and try to make me look like an informant (which is all the Met were *EVER* gonna get out of this). They already knew – and I'd already been told by them – that I wasn't guilty of the actual charge!

And remember they already admitted in the Old Bailey, on transcripts, that they had nearly five years of surveillance tapes of Warnes, and evidence of me using him for my own ends (and for others), so they *knew full well* what the score was. But some little twisted genius saw that all they had to do was flip it over from what it was – me getting info off Warnes – and turn it into what it wasn't – me supposedly *giving* info to him. Simple but effective. Cunts. It's no accident whatsoever that they chose one of the two subjects that makes people back away from you: grassing and child abuse. On those things some people don't even want to give you time to explain you've been stitched up, y'know what I mean. And that's exactly what the Old Bill bank on.

They did actually say well before it got to the Old Bailey, when we were still in Bow Street Magistrates, that he'd be the first serving police officer to get a recommended sentence. That was obviously said by someone not up to speed or in on the plot because not long after that Warnes was given bail! Which is absolutely ludicrous considering what they had on him. And if you see how hard it was for me to get bail, and the different circumstances that everyone was given, you can see that one of their main targets was *me not getting bail*.

So everyone had expected something like an eight or ten stretch to be handed down to him but because he'd helped them along and lied about me being 'his informant', supposedly (which then gives them enough reason to say it in open court whether it's a lie or not), then all he got was four fucking years! Of that he'll do two, if that. And no one could get their head round that. That's why I know how devious they can be. So I went fucking mad about it, and I've written to the CPS, the Home Office, and CIB3 asking them questions about it. Saying that unless you can explain why he only got that I'm saying that it's obvious he helped them along with their intention to fuck me publicly.

They were being so *blatantly* naughty to me now, so blatantly 'one rule for us and one rule for you' that it was almost unbelievable, and I said that in my letters; that if they *hadn't* done a deal with him to give him a lesser sentence then I – and a lot of other people – would like an explanation why.

Still waiting for that one.

Since the Old Bailey's finished I've started a 'Let's tell the truth' game about this little lot here and they know exactly what I know, they know how big the coup was; and they're not even answering my letters, which is something they'd automatically do for anyone else just as a courtesy.

Anyway, on the same day that Warnes, Rees and James were sentenced the *Daily Express* ran a page on the trial with a picture of Kim James and one of me giving the old V-sign to camera:

> *Yesterday, Courtney, 41, saluted the jury as he was acquitted of conspiracy to pervert the course of justice. The gangster said his official status as a 'grass' was simply a way of disguising his corrupt relationship with Warnes. Courtney was still under investigation last night over alleged crooked deals with Warnes and other officers.*
>
> *He left the court smoking a large cigar and went to a nearby pub to celebrate.*

You fucking better believe it. Actually, I left with a large cigar, fifty friends, twenty photographers, ten journalists, two TV camera crews, one wife, a raging hard-on and a partridge in a pear tree.

Sunday 17 December, three days after the verdicts, a full-page report on the trial came out in the *Observer* with the headline 'Corrupt Police Split Reward Cash With Fake Informants – drug addict detective fabricated tip-offs, sabotaged court cases and planted evidence'. Catchy title, eh? It certainly made my Sunday breakfast go down a lot better to actually read a newspaper report that nailed down the facts and didn't just deal in rumours and lies. I'll give you the highlights:

Corrupt detectives across Britain are pocketing tens of thousands of pounds by sharing reward money with a network of 'fake' informants, the Observer *can reveal.*

The scam involves the recruitment of crooks who confirm that they provided tip-offs. They then got their reward, which can range from several hundred to several thousand pounds. The money is later split with the detective concerned.

And didn't I know it after throwing loads of people in Warnes' direction that used him in that way.

Austin Warnes, a long-time cocaine addict, had agreed to assist in a plot by passing false information to local police that Kim James was involved in high-level drug dealing. The plan failed because anti-corruption detectives had been monitoring Rees' agency, following concerns that he had been making illegal payments to a number of serving officers in return for confidential information.

Following his arrest, Warnes had originally claimed that the tip-off about Kim James came from his registered informant, Dave Courtney. At the Old Bailey trial, Courtney revealed that, far from being an informant, he had been involved in a '100 per cent corrupt' relationship with Warnes for 15 years, which involved recruiting fake informants, obtaining information from the police computer and sabotaging numerous court cases.

Gotta go guilty to those last three!

An investigation by the Observer *has revealed that Warnes' unscrupulous practices went far deeper than those admitted during the trial. Officers in other forces, including Essex and Greater Manchester, have been investigated for allegedly sharing rewards with informants.*

Warnes fed his own drug habit by regularly stealing drugs during raids. Warnes also assisted Courtney and dozens of other professional criminals in the south London area to avoid capture and evade charges by providing them with information about police investigations. In order to cover himself and not face questioning about why he was accessing police files, Warnes would say one of his 'informants' had knowledge relevant to the case.

I do hate to say 'I told you so' but . . .

'The information he provided was invaluable,' says Mick, a one-time armed robber and one of those who benefited from Warnes' corruption. 'He would

be able to tell you what statements the police had obtained, who they had interviewed, which properties were under surveillance, which phones were tapped – the lot. Worth its weight in gold.

And you know how I like my gold!

Documents obtained by the Observer *show that, in one case, Warnes intervened after an attempted kidnapping. One of the suspects, an associate of Courtney's, had gone on the run. Warnes telephoned the officer in charge and said he had an informant that might be able to help in the case but would require all the information. The officer in charge of the kidnap later noted: 'The impression gleaned from the information requested and questions asked was not one of an officer keen to assist but more of an officer bent on obtaining information for his own purposes.'*

'Bent' being the important word. That last bit is obviously when Ian Tucker went on the run and I used Warnes to get information for Tucker. Then they tried to bring Tucker into court and make it look like I'd grassed him up! The police themselves knew that wasn't true, and look, one of them is even quoted there in the paper saying he was suspicious of why Warnes was getting the information. But that officer weren't produced at the trial 'cos it would've proved what I'd been saying all along was true. And they couldn't have that could they?

Warnes would regularly brag about 'fitting people up' and applying pressure to ensnare people. He said he collected cigarette ends – you can get DNA from traces of saliva – to implicate people he didn't like.

The Old Bailey heard that Warnes had bragged about his help with matters concerning 'the IRA, drugs, driving offences, anything'.

Rees and Simon James were convicted and sentenced to six years. Warnes was sentenced to four years. James Cook and Courtney were both acquitted of all charges.
Courtney said outside the court, 'I have always had faith in the British Justice system. That not guilty verdict was both for the charge I faced and the accusation that I was a grass. I have never been an informer.'

Right, now, back to the bit that even surprised me . . . wait for it, wait for it, you cheeky monkeys! You know I'd been followed around by two TV documentary film crew for the best part of a year, one documentary for Channel 5 being made by Tony Jackson and one for Channel 4 by James Cohen. There was a little bit of competitiveness there between them, as you can imagine, but that's a good thing. But a year is a long time to have two lots of ugly bastards with cameras, microphones and lights in your fucking house! No, actually they were all top blokes. They do start early though, those film people. Some mornings I'd wake up and find them all sat at the foot of the bed chatting amongst themselves waiting for me to get up! I do like people to make themselves at home but seven of us under one duvet was just a bit fucking much. Especially when I was trying to have a wank.

One of the best compliments I've had was when I was talking to the geezer who was in charge of editing the Channel 5 film. I said that after filming me for so long they must have loads of stuff that they wouldn't have room for in the film. 'Yeah, there are diamonds on the cutting room floor, mate,' he said. Wow. Fucking good line or what? Diamonds on the cutting room floor. I like that.

So what started out as something like 'A Day in the Life of Dave Courtney' grew into something more because at the eleventh hour I was arrested for the conspiracy charge. That meant they couldn't show the film until I'd been to court and they didn't want to miss that so they just carried on filming. And filming. And filming. They witnessed the court jester escapade, the 'Audience Withs . . .', me making predictions about what would happen, the trial, the aftermath of the trial, me describing how the trial wasn't there for me to be found guilty but just as a platform for them to try to discredit me – and they saw my predictions coming true. They actually got frightened for me because they saw the things I'd described actually happen. And my last prediction was that the intention was to assassinate me.

Anyway, on Monday, four days after the verdict, I got a call from Marcus asking me if I'd watched Channel 5 recently. I said I hadn't 'cos I think it's shit (joke, Tony). He said he'd just seen an advert with me in and I was on TV tomorrow, Wednesday and Thursday nights – *Dave Courtney's Underworld*. Fucking hell. You could've knocked me down with a Spam fritter.

So we switched the telly on and sure enough, half an hour later, there I was. Now even in my wildest dreams I didn't think they'd get it together that quickly. The original idea to make one programme had grown into making three (some of those diamonds must have been picked back up off the floor) and they were gonna be shown three nights in a row. Even *Coronation Street* don't get that. Only *Who Wants To Be A Millionaire?* is shown consecutively. Who Wants To Be a Villainaire?

So that got me on the old phone making a billion phone calls. Turned out that everyone but me had already seen the adverts anyway. See, when you're making telly you're too busy to watch it. That's my excuse anyway.

What had happened is that Channel 5 had got wind that I might get nicked again (as I might get rearrested for admitting I'd used a bent copper) and they knew that would put a hold to the film – again. They didn't have the budget (or the stamina!) to follow me for another year so in their panic they found the nearest slot in the schedule to put the documentary out. And 'cos they're a newer channel they were more flexible with the schedule, not like a BBC or an ITV where things are planned a year in advance.

Channel 5 didn't do it to deliberately trick the police, but that's what happened. They had their own personal reasons for putting it out quickly but that worked fantastic for me. 'Cos if the Old Bill had had the chance to vet it I'm sure it wouldn't have gone out like it did, but Channel 5 bypassed that. The police knew I was being filmed but they couldn't have imagined for one second that it would come out that soon, y'know, only one week after the court case finishing! It caught everyone on the hop. Even me. Usually only the news comes out that quickly.

Channel 5, in their beautiful little wisdom, putting the programmes on TV so quickly completely bamboozled the Old Bill. It must've been a nightmare for them when they thought they had a clear run at promoting their own propaganda.

There was another clever little move done by the two fellas that made the films. The one thing that you're not allowed to do when making anything about the criminal fraternity is glamorise crime. So what these fellas did was say they were making a film about an EX-criminal making it famous as a celebrity. That got around that, and they said it was going to be called *Dave's World*. Which it was, right up until a few days before it was transmitted when they added one more word and made it *Dave Courtney's Underworld*. Clever little move. And on the day it was due to be first shown one of the filmmakers flew off on a break to New Zealand in case there was any heat.

Even some of the *TV Times* were still fooled. In one paper it said 'Channel 5, 11.05 *DAVE'S WORLD*: Comedy about parents struggling with the demands of life'. What!? I think if you asked my mum she'd say it was no comedy struggling to bring me up.

The first part, on Tuesday night, began with the Channel 5 announcer giving a warning: 'Now we enter Dave Courtney's Underworld and encounter strong language throughout . . .' Strong language? Fuck me, no. It's colourful language. Blue.

It opened with a shot of about twenty of mine gathering outside 'Camelot Castle' with the voiceover saying, 'It's September 1999. Courtney has brought his boys together for one last job. It could make him a very rich man. Trouble is the police are following his every move.' Which was just a funny way of saying the 'job' was the first book signing I did for *Stop the Ride* . . . at this massive Waterstones' shop in Oxford Street. The police 'interest' was deadly serious, though. God knows how many copies we've sold to undercover coppers who've bought one just to try and 'blend in'. (There must actually be some expense account invoices knocking about Metropolitan Police HQ with 'Copy of *Stop the Ride I Want to Get Off* – £16.99' written on them. And don't I just love the thought of that!)

This first episode covered my background and interviewed my mum. Or as the voiceover said, 'His mother says she struggled with his behaviour as a boy but early efforts to reform him failed miserably.' Just about bang-on. They even interviewed my favourite old schoolteacher, Mr John Edwards. He was the teacher that all the naughty boys loved, for some reason, although (as I said in the programme) that might not be the best recommendation he's ever had.

It also gave me the chance to talk about some things I'd only ever written about before. 'I have done what would be said in the Bible is the most cardinal sin and taken someone's life on more than one occasion, and I felt justified in that it was put upon me – it was a him-or-me situation. Now that doesn't happen to normal people in normal everyday life but on very rare occasions in my way of life that did arise.'

It ended with me outside English & Son's funeral home telling the story of doing security at Ronnie Kray's funeral: 'It was the biggest funeral since Winston Churchill's. I was responsible for the security. One of the most memorable conversations I've had was with the chief of police at the time. I was being a bit cocky, like I normally am, saying my security could do anything the police could do. He said, "One thing you can't do is deal with the possibility of snipers; and one thing we've got that you haven't is firearms". I said, "You're wrong there. The one thing you've got that we haven't is licences for firearms. But we've got the guns". He didn't find that funny at all.'

So, all in all, it was a good little opener to the week's events. And the phone went mad, with people ringing up saying they'd just seen it. I tried to get through to the commissioner of the Met but he was engaged. That's what it said on the toilet door anyway.

Part two was another cracker. It began with me and loads of the fellas on a rooftop in south London (just opposite where A Clockwork Orange was filmed, funnily enough) being photographed by a Channel 5 photographer. Or, as I put it, 'We're all registered childminders and this is our Christmas card photo!' It also began by explaining how the Kray funeral job had brought me to prominence with both the public and the police. As I say, from then on the police 'decided to systematically shut down every avenue that I was earning money at'. Which they did.

Which is also when I went off into the media world and the film followed my exploits through that. They interviewed Piers from Front, Ray Mudie from Virgin and filmmakers like Nick Moorcroft, who I'd made two short films with and who was also writing a full-length film of me in LA. My mate Tricky appeared as well, in New York, talking about the record we made together with some of the other chaps, 'Products Of The Environment'. Proper gangster rap.

One part of the programme was funny to me because there always seemed to be another camera crew in shot. One geezer, a documentary director called Paul Wimshunt, says, 'Every time we've met him there seems to be someone from Channel 5, or Channel 4, or reporters from GQ, or film producers trying to make a film of his life!' And that's 'cos I say 'Yes' to everyone. At one point, the voiceover even says, there also appears to be another film crew filming him. They say they're from ITV and he has promised them exclusive access to make a documentary about him!' I thought that was a funny little one for Tony, the Channel 5 director, to put in. 'Cos he'd worked out by then that I'd said the same thing to him!

They also filmed me on a sunbed talking about the real life incident I was involved in that inspired Vinnie Jones' scene in *Lock, Stock and Two Smoking Barrels*. Except this time I was relaxing on the sunbed and not punching someone on it. Much easier. But this bit did give the chance to point out what all along I'd always thought was bleedin' obvious – 'I can only act this way because I am no longer active. You can't do the driving-around-look-at-me-I'm-a-villain bit if you really are still a villain.' Ain't that obvious? You've got to retire before you hit the fucking book circuit! Well, you try telling that to the police, 'cos I have. With no success.

Anyway, the big ending part two was this – 'At the end of 1999 he is called to Bow Street magistrate's court and charged with conspiracy to pervert the course of justice. If he is found guilty he faces a lengthy prison sentence and the end of his celebrity status – And to find out how that turns out join us for our third and final part of *Dave Courtney's Underworld* tomorrow night at ten-fifty.' Which would have been a proper little cliffhanger for the people who didn't know what the result of the trial had been. I think most people in London already knew, but outside of that the papers had reported the actual trial more than the outcome.

My programme was followed by *Late Night With Jerry Springer*. I met him at China White's. There's a picture of me and him together in *Raving Lunacy*. Like I say in the book, he's the only man I know who's seen more violence than me! I really liked his last show, 'I Slept With My Own Transsexual Mother – Now She's Pregnant With Her Own Grandchild!'

Over on the other side, on BBC1, at the same time I'd been on, was *Watchdog* with Anne Robinson. That's one scary little woman. And ginger-haired to top it all off! Fucking hell, Anne Robinson. You are the freakiest bint, goodbye.

Now the first two parts of the programme the Old Bill could probably live with – me being a cocky cunt, me on camera, and me being a cocky cunt on camera – nothing new there then. So they probably thought that the third part on Thursday night was gonna be more of the same. I think not, boys! They never would've guessed how it turned out. In fact I had to guess 'cos I hadn't seen the chuffing thing either. But who would have thought that only seven days after the court case had finished there would be me on telly talking all about it? (Yeah, as it happens, I did guess it would be about that.) But they didn't. Shocked? I'll bet a squirrel's nuts they fucking were.

So, part three: start as you mean to go on. And picking up on what had gone before and what I knew was to follow, I began – 'I succeed in most of the things I try to do, and it will take someone shooting me or locking me in prison to stop me being a celebrity now. I'm bound for Hollywood, and that's where I'm going!' Yeah, take that. Then the voiceover kicked in with more extra drama: 'Unfortunately for Courtney, prison is now a very real prospect. He has been charged with perverting the course of justice in a police corruption case.'

Cut then to Bow Street and 'A large crowd of unpleasant-looking men (cheeky, but true) are gathering outside Bow Street magistrates' court. They're here to offer support to Dave Courtney who is here for a pre-trial hearing. His appearance does not disappoint.' And that's when I appear in full court jester's outfit – red and yellow pantaloons, pink stockings, pink pointy shoes, and green and yellow pointy hat with bells on.

Juggling.

And with £50,000 in blocks of cash in a carrier bag. I dropped all the juggling balls but that wasn't as big as the bollocks dropped by the police when they put Warnes within punching distance of me inside the court. Or as the voiceover put it, 'On entering the court and seeing the policeman who has implicated him Courtney proceeds to punch him in the face . . .'

Unfortunately the TV cameras weren't allowed in so it didn't end up on film. My exit from the court did, though. That's when I did my 'I've always had faith in the British Justice system' speech.

The next shot in the film was one that I'd actually forgot about. It was at my home the next morning after the court jester thing. The commentary went, 'Dave is a little concerned that punching a policeman in court might have repercussions.' Oh, I absolutely LOVED that line! It's so fucking English and restrained, aint it? Y'know what I mean? Anyway, it was true enough for me to stick a note on the front door of my house, and the camera zoomed in on it. It said:

Good Morning officers!
A little bird told me you lot would be calling around this morning.
Please don't be spiteful & pull the place apart & have the fucking
door off its hinges. Just knock & I'll open it for ya without waking
the kids. Let's be fair, you lot are not the prettiest sight at this
time in the morning!
DAVE COURTNEY OBE.

Inside the house it showed me and Jennifer surrounded by the day's newspapers looking at reports of the court appearance: 'See, the papers don't want the public to think that I've retired. They find it more romantic to think that I'm still doing it and showing off about it.'

Cut to me and everyone in a snooker club, at the tables, with me playing while they interview me: 'It's not the era to be a criminal 'cos they have got you trapped every way you turn. They can look at you from the fucking moon. My friends have been nicked from photographs taken from satellites. Before the police had so much money to get high-tech surveillance equipment you could pit your wits against the police, and if you were clever you won.

'When I was active, crime actually consisted of an awful lot of other things than narcotics. But now crime is basically 'drugs'. And they have no morals.

'You can actually get someone shot for about ten grand and a professional hit for twenty grand. So if you're doing drug deals for five hundred thousand cash, a million cash, y'know? I know people who'd wipe out . . . Stoke . . . for two million!

'I've been in positions where I've had to put a hole in someone to save my own life and, given the same position again, I'd do it about a second QUICKER.'

The programme rightly pointed out that 'his impending court case is preventing Courtney getting media exposure'. Mostly for *Raving Lunacy*, which had just come out about then. Not that the book was anything to do with the court case so there shouldn't have been any knock-on effect. Not that I'm conscious of the police's influence with the media or anything like that. What, me?

This one also covered another Kray funeral, Charlie's. Loads of us gathered at my house to prepare for going down to pay our respects. And for me to set the record straight about something. It's very hard 'cos I've had some people suggest I shouldn't go to the funeral if I'm trying to say I'm not like that no more. But the fact I'm not like that no more don't necessarily mean I can't be respectful to a friend I've had for years. I was in prison with Charlie for a year during a very trying time for him. I felt quite close to him. And the fact that I'm trying to turn over a new leaf . . . it's very unfair of people to put on me that I shouldn't go to his funeral.

'What happened to Charlie would be a prime example of my deepest fear. He became like a scalp to get. He was always going out and introducing people to people and it don't matter how innocent you are, if you're second name is Kray, or in my case "Courtney", then you're thought of as guilty.

'I do know there's some fellas (in the police) out there thinking, "We cannot allow Courtney to walk around and glorify the underworld as much as he does".'

Then it showed me driving to Bow Street magistrates' court for another hearing, this time with just the other three co-defendants present. No Warnes. Lesson learned there then, I think. I was just so used to the camera crews being around now and someone hovering about holding a microphone above me. Though that is difficult in a car, even one with the headroom you get in a Roller: 'They are obviously worried that not only am I gonna get a "not guilty" for this, but also that I'll come up smelling of roses. So, damage limitation, they think "Now we've got Courtney in court, what can we do to him?"

'I'm actually on trial for perverting the course of justice with a bent copper, but this policeman is saying I was an informant in a case where a woman was arrested for drugs. This is the police's last onslaught, their last onslaught to do me any harm.

'I don't think they'll get the conviction out of it but whatever harm they can throw my way to hinder my new future . . . I'm sure they will.'

And, like all the more serious points I said during this film, that last one was a proper heartfelt statement. I think what had happened was that when I went forward with the new lifestyle the Old Bill probably thought that they could bark and bite at me even more, without any fear of me having a snap back. Difficult not to, though, that's the trouble. And why shouldn't I? I thought. Why should I just stand and take it from them? That's exactly what they want, as it happens. Exactly what they want. They just love it when they've got you in a position where they think you've got too much to risk to fight back. Well, they were trying to kill me by spreading lies so I had fuck all else to lose by telling the truth.

The bit of the film that came on next I hadn't seen (well, I hadn't seen any of it really, except in rushes); but this I hadn't even seen being filmed 'cos it was Jen talking one night: 'He just wants to relax. He don't want to do the old cat and mouse thing with the Old Bill any more. But the more they do it, if they do it and he don't retaliate it's like showing them that they're winning. But we're alright. They can throw whatever they want at us – truth. But it does shadow me. Makes me want to cry. I look at him sometimes when he's asleep and I bawl. Just out of . . . I just feel sorry for him 'cos I know he's trying to do his best; trying to do the right thing.'

That's when it really fucking guts you that what the police sometimes do to people don't only effect just one person – 'cos I can actually live with it – but the people all around you, and most of all those close to you. And especially your missus. Which is why I am so very, very lucky to have such a one-in-a-million lady. But this last programme was turning into a proper golden opportunity for me to put my side of things across, and exactly a week after I'd got a 'not guilty' as well, just in case there was any doubt.

'The court case has been changed (by the police) from a conspiracy to pervert the course of justice with a bent copper, to "Is Dave a grass?" That's what the court case's main aim is (in the eyes of the police). And if I lost that argument I get shot. And rightly so. If I come out of the Old Bailey and everyone believes I am a grass I deserve to be shot. 'Cos I would rather not be here than have someone walking around and think I was. How's that for confidence for ya? I'll even lend you a gun!'

Every word of that was spot-on. That sound you can hear is hammers hitting nails right on the head. Every time. The same hammers that had knocked the first and last nails into the coffin lid of the police's supposed case against me. That 'case' had been in intensive care before it got to court, had died in the first week, and was now being buried with the little dignity it deserved. Rest In Piss.

I didn't know if my mates knew that I knew what effect the whole thing was having on them, but I did know. Like I say, family and friends being affected hurts more than if it's being done to yourself. So I had to make that point in the film.

Remember, I'd had to sit through six fucking weeks of SHIT – of no fucking evidence, of nothing but sly innuendo and downright lies and snide comments – six weeks of that and not say a fucking thing. So thank Christ I'd at least set a few records straight on film.

'This is a proper argument I'm having. A highly publicised one with the Metropolitan Police that, win or lose, I am not a grass. That's a proper argument, a proper set of stakes! Now . . . fuck money . . . if I lose I die.'

Then it cut to outside the Old Bailey on the verdict day, or what the film called 'The day of reckoning'. Da-dah! Nice and dramatic. So for the first time I saw film of what was going on outside when I was inside, waiting for the jury to come back in; everyone waiting in the pub, and the photographers and crowds gathering like storm clouds outside the Bailey doors. I tell you, it was fucking weird watching myself emerge from the doors. Especially as they did it in slow motion! I thought, I know I was savouring the moment but I don't remember walking that slow!

It did look dramatic though. Because it was dusk, the light was dropping so all the flashbulbs going off in slo-mo looked wicked. And with everybody cheering. I learned afterwards that they couldn't use the bit when Cream had started singing 'Who let the Dave out!' to the tune of the song 'Who Let The Dogs Out?' because the record company had asked for ten grand to use it! Wankers.

Brendan got interviewed on the pavement outside the court:

'The main thing that should become apparent here is that not only has Dave proved his innocence, he's also had the prosecution admit he was not a police informer.' And outside Seamus O'Dell's even Mad Pete felt moved to put himself on camera. 'Dave's got a copper nicked for being bent and they've counteracted that by nicking Dave for something he hasn't done; and in the media they try and portray him as a grass, hoping that some other villain will come along and plug him in the head with a gun. The man is innocent.'

I was there when Pete gave the interview and I'm telling you, Pete's bit in the programme was the severe edited highlights 'cos he went on for about ten minutes. He was wicked. In his speech he even managed to rope in Tony fucking Blair and implicate him! (Even I hadn't done that.) Most people speak eloquently about what they're most passionate about . . . and Pete is passionate about THE POLICE. Or the police's sometimes dubious methods, shall we say. So Pete really did himself proud that day. (And somewhere there is an editing room at Channel 5 re-wallpapered with the out-takes.)

The cameras had hung around for ages afterwards and even caught the jurors coming in to see me, but I don't think that was allowed to be shown. That would've just made me look too good.

The final scene was filmed with me and Jen having 'bubbly' bath. That's one where you sit covered in soap bubbles drinking champagne. As we did back at home. And the last thing I said to camera was, 'One of the nicest sounds you'll ever hear is someone saying "Not guilty". It's the closest I've ever come to a premature ejaculation!' Then there was the *pop* of another champagne cork. 'Hello Hollywood – Goodbye Peckham!'

The final shot was me sat with Jenny stood in front of me covered in bubbles, and me grabbing her beautiful little bum. THE END, in other words.

As the credits were rolling the Channel 5 programme announcer's voice came on, sounding a bit flustered, 'Well, after that, if you are still able to concentrate on what I'm saying . . .'

So the third and final part ended. Not with a bang but with a 'Not Guilty'! And so, with that, 'ole Courtney scored a hat-trick! I felt like Geoff Hurst at Wembley, 1966, stuffing three goals past the Germans to win the World Cup. They think it's all over . . . it is now!

Well, not quite, because they still had something up their sleeve for me. The wrong arm of the law, as it happens.

22. WHO POLICES THE POLICE WHO POLICE THE POLICE?

Good question I think. Fucking difficult answer, though.

Yeah, good question. Who the fuck indeed? All enquiries on a postcard to The Commissioner, London Metropolitan Police Force, Scotland Yard, London W1 1EE. Let me know if you get an answer 'cos I've never had one.

Oh and while you're at it ask him why hamburgers never have any ham in them. And why the fuck did Kamikaze pilots wear crash helmets? That's another puzzler.

EXAMPLE 4: I've got another one for you. Right now one of the police's top brass, a geezer called Andrew Trotter who is the Deputy Assistant Commissioner, is investigating whether the CIB themselves conspired to pervert the course of justice by withholding evidence during the committal of two other coppers. Get that! The police who investigate the police are under investigation themselves. Which is a bit like an ambulance coming to pick you up after a car crash and then crashing itself on the way to the hospital.

So if CIB3 are willing to use those tricks on their own officers do you think they'd give a flying fuck about using them on a high profile, flash bastard ex-villain who writes for magazines, tours the country slagging off the Old Bill and turns up at court in a jester's outfit and knocks a copper out? I think you'll find the answer is that they definitely wouldn't give a double-flying fuck about using those tactics on me. As they have proved.

And these cases I've mentioned are just ones you could have read about in the papers, never mind the ones that don't make it that far. The police are fucking good at the propaganda war because they've been doing it for years. They do it better than us. They have the media and they know its power. They know what a few well-placed newspaper stories and leaks can do.

Which brings us back to what was said to Seymour outside the courtroom in the Old Bailey – 'We've already beaten Courtney in the newspapers.' What's unusual about my situation is that I've got more access to the media myself than most of the other chaps in my position. I've got the TV programmes and the magazine column that I can use to try and right the wrongs.

All credit to the police though because, as plans go, theirs wasn't a bad one – 'Get Courtney into court for something we know he'll certainly beat but then use the case as the opportunity to try and destroy his name.' Good plan if people fell for it.

What they couldn't bargain on – and what was the icing on the cake for me and the fly in the ointment for them – was not only that I'd come out to a hero's welcome but also three nights of documentaries on national TV! They'd done what they thought was their best shot, which was to call me a grass and then sit back and wait for the grapevine to do its work, and someone with a shooter to do his. But I came back smiling. I think the Old Bill misjudged my popularity and the amount of time I would be given to vindicate myself.

The reaction from the general public to the documentaries was fantastic. To them it was all very theatrical, y'know: the build up, the acquittal, the cameras filming everything. Like some of the letters I get . . . I get a lot and some are from kids doing loads of things to support me. Writing 'Dave Courtney Is Not Guilty' outside police stations and sticking my flyers through the station door. Then they send me pictures of them doing it! Can you believe that. I don't even know these people. What a wicked compliment.

But I have to say that when it came to the outcome of the court case, to people who knew me they wouldn't expect anything less. It was business as usual. Like me, friends were relieved more than anything and knew it was difficult to really celebrate, considering the circumstances. In the same way they didn't really make a big scene when the charge was first laid against me because they knew what the score was and what the police were trying to do.

The shrapnel from all this was this: I'd played the cat and mouse thing with the Old Bill for a long time. They're the police, I'm the baddie; they're supposed to try to put me in prison, I'm supposed to try to escape. That kind of thing. But then they overstepped the mark by a mile and marked me out for something far more grievous. They had overstepped the mark to the extent of thinking, 'Fuck prison, let's get him shot.' They'd done their best in the media to paint me as a grass, but I had enough outlets to tell my side and enough mates who knew the truth to stand by me.

Now, I could either sit back on my laurels and let the Old Bill get away with that, and wait for the next wave of attack, or go back out and hurt them.

So now I felt like this – that they had thrown their best shot, a big right hand, and it wobbled me. The problem (for them) is that it didn't knock me out and so now it's my turn.

The thing about someone getting you on the ropes is that you might seem like you're backed up, but you can actually use the ropes to get extra speed into your attack. That's why they made that move illegal in boxing; fighters who fell back on the ropes bounced back off them with knockout punches. Sounds good to me! Fuck the Marquis of Queensberry's rules.

The fact that I'd been up against all the Met (the straight and bent ones) and their legal dogs meant that it weren't exactly a fair fight, so fuck the ring manners. I was coming off the ropes, mate, with a fucking piledriver of a punch, knuckleduster inside the glove. And my counterpunch was to sue the Met for malicious prosecution.

So I decided to nick the police. How's that for a Man Bites Dog scenario? That a big enough dog for yer? I wanted to hurt them as much as I could, as much as they'd try to do to me. And I'm not an idiot thug who drives around randomly picking them off one by one. I want to crack that part of the system that they use to crack others. I wanted to give them sleepless nights like they have tried to do to me.

The only way I can do that sensibly is to learn from my peers that the pen (or camera lens) is mightier than the sword. I decided to use the press, the TV, and write letters to my MP, the Prime Minister, to the Old Bailey complaints board, to CIB3, to the Citizens Advice Bureau, High Courts of Justice, to the CPS and anyone else who should know. And make it very public what's happening to me.

I decided I was gonna nick the Crown Prosecution Service for taking me to court. If the CPS hadn't given the police the firing post to tie me to, and to do it so publicly, then I would never have got to court; and they had enough evidence in front of them to show that it was nothing to do with me – Warnes' statement, witness statements, even police officers beliefs – and yet they still pursued it.

So I nicked them and CIB3 for saying I'm an informant, which even they know I'm not. I've sent a 23-page letter ('Full Disclosure Bundle') to the Home Secretary Jack Straw – and put it on the Internet! – with all the details of everything that's happened: the informant scam run by bent police, what I believed to be CIB3 and the CPS's malicious prosecution of me, me and my family's harassment by the police, Warnes trying to set me up, and corrupt officers' dirty tricks. I did that, sent that letter, so that even if anything happens to me I still feel like I've won.

I also sent letters to Tony Blair, CIB3, the Metropolitan Police, the Crown Prosecution Service, the Old Bailey Complaints Dept: all outlining what had gone on in the case.

Serving the writ was fun, though. I met Bill Murray, the actor who actually plays the bent copper in The Bill. He's also in my new film Hell To Pay playing my brother (more later). Anyway, we went up to the Royal Courts of Justice on the Strand and the press were all there, out in force. Not one to waste an opportunity, I said, 'I've lost one bent copper but as you can see I've brought another one along!' Then I explained exactly what it was all about.

On the claims form it said that the case against me wasn't dropped because of a 'conspiracy to allow a case with no evidence to be brought to the central criminal court for the sole purpose of discrediting the claimant's name to the level where it is believed it would endanger the claimant and his family's life'.

I paid the three hundred and fifty quid court charge and served a writ for £50,000 damages. Which would be £49,650 profit if I kept the winnings, which I wasn't planning on doing, it was gonna go to charity. I wasn't doing it for the money; I just wanted to hurt them back. When we came back out I told the press that any money would go to the prison widows' fund. I also said that the police had put an excuse out in the public domain to get me shot.

Serving the writ made the news big-style and even went into the top ten headlines on Teletext (why have they got top ten headlines anyway?! It's the news, not a bloody pop chart). The headline they gave this one was 'Police Wanted Me Dead'. Hm, catchy little title.

You'll like this next one. I applied for legal aid to the Legal Services Commission and filled in one of the usual boring forms, though it was a lot less boring because of my answers. In TYPE OF CASE I ticked the box 'Actions against the police'. Then under PART 3: OPPONENT'S DETAILS I had to write details of who I was suing: like *Name* – 'CIB3', *Job* – 'To police the police', *Relationship to client* – 'Very Bad'. Ha, what an understatement. Then PART 7: COURT DETAILS asked *Purpose of next hearing* – 'To continue to sue and expose them'. The part of the form about human rights cases asked if there was any part of my case where the human rights issue is significant, so I put: 'I don't know yet. But I'll try it next time if you fuck me off'.

PUBLIC INTEREST CASES: *Please state why your claim has significant wider public interest* – 'My name is Dave Courtney, so what do you think?' and 'the public will want to know the truth – that they tried to manipulate my death'.

Then under PERSONAL INJURY it said *Please explain the nature of the incident and the basis of the client's claim* – 'Tried to get me shot'; *What injury or loss did your client suffer?* – 'Sleep'; *Give details of what caused the incident* – 'Corrupt police officers'; *What is the name of the group this action forms a part of?* – 'The Police Force'.

Under EMERGENCY DETAILS it said *Give us a brief description of the proceedings and the words you used for them* – (police/CIB3) 'were knowingly involved in a conspiracy with the CPS in an attempt to endanger my life'. Then STATEMENTS OF CASE: *Give description of events* – 'Read disclosure bundle'.

Then I sent it with one of my With Compliments slips which has a photo of me pointing.

See I'm not doing this because I'm concerned the police force is corrupt or because I deliberately want to throw down the gauntlet and start a fight with them on my own; that would be a fucked idea, 'cos they're the biggest firm of them all. But I would say that them trying to get me shot is about as blatant an act of throwing down the gauntlet that you can get. It don't get more upfront and nasty than that. And that's what they done. So taking them on wasn't something I did lightly or for the fun of it, I done it for survival: and sometimes attack really is the best form of defence. Much better than waiting for some fucking no-brain to actually believe the police's crap and do something about it.

Whatever you've learned about me from my books you must know that 'waiting around' just ain't my style, is it? You *know* that. I'd rather go out fighting than in my sleep. It's just like if you were a boxer and the other geezer spent the first round doing every dirty trick in the book – rabbit and kidney punches, low shots, thumbing you in the eyes, head butting – by the next round you'd be pretty fucking sure you were gonna get the cunt back, whatever it took. And quite right too.

Listen, three years ago I was being filmed for a programme by London Weekend Television. I asked this geezer from LWT called Lee to film me making predictions about what I thought the authorities would try to do to me in the near future. How they'd try to discredit me. He filmed me and got it all on tape.

So a couple of months ago, when the little ploy to try to discredit me first kicked off, and when the first bit appeared in the papers calling me a grass, I rang Lee and just went 'Well . . .' He knew immediately what I meant. He'd been watching it all unfold in the press and said he'd gone back and watched the film he'd made of me predicting how the law would go after me. He said he couldn't believe what had happened in my life since I'd told him that.

Because someone telling you something is one thing, but actually seeing it come true is another. That's when people that know me, and that have known the truth about this from the beginning, sometimes get worried for me 'cos they see my predictions coming true. Because the police have always got more people in their corner than we have, haven't they? Than you and me have.

What they've tried to do to me they've already done to Kenny Noye. This is a whole story in itself. Listen to this. Kenny Noye was, I'm sure you'll know, the geezer involved in the road rage stabbing incident. He was caught, tried and found guilty of murder and given thirty years. Now really it was at worst manslaughter in self-defence, and you'd get no more than five, ten years for that. Really they wanted to get him for something he did years ago, which was killing a copper in self-defence. The jury at that trial believed him and he was found not guilty.

To justify giving him a big lump of a sentence this time they also circulated that he was a registered informant. Yeah, that old trick. The police do like to use that one because they know it's the one thing people least want to hear said about themselves. And the one thing most guaranteed to turn other people against you. The first time they said it about him was before he was caught, in the hope that it would goad someone into flushing him out; and, sure enough, someone passed on information about where he was. Then, secondly, to help justify the sentence.

It happens as simple as I'm gonna make it sound – the *News Of The World* gets a direct information leak from the Met saying that Noye's supposedly a registered informant. Now the only one who is saying he ain't is Kenny Noye, from a prison, in solitary confinement, through the bars on his window. Which don't count a lot against ten million people reading the crap they print every Sunday. And that's down to a senior copper picking up the phone and making a call.

It was exactly the same with the IRA bomb scares in the 70s. There were times when the IRAs popularity was really high and at those times it was murder for the army literally. So when an IRA bomb was next planted in a shop or whatever, they'd ring in their warning but the authorities don't give the warning out. Civilians are killed and suddenly support drops for the IRA. Afterwards they say they gave a warning but no fucker believed them. But there's army guys now who admit to all that kind of behaviour and feel guilty about it.

The police, the army, the judges – it's all 'Queen & Country' with them. Everything's a war. Everything's a fucking war-zone.

It didn't stop after Kenny Noye's imprisonment either. Remember how a couple of months later a geezer got shot? Well, that was the fella that was a key witness at Noye's trial. What did the papers say about the killing? Only that Noye had ordered it from inside prison!

Oh, really? What, even when Kenny Noye was the only person in the country with an interest in keeping that geezer alive.

No two ways about it, Kenny Noye wanted that geezer *alive* not dead, because if he was dead he couldn't retract his statement. It was someone else who wanted him silenced. So some geezer on a bike with a blacked-out visor pulls alongside and bang bang. I didn't notice any all-out, full-scale, countrywide police search for that killer, like with Jill Dando.

What they do is this: when there's an outcry after a high profile murder they adopt a certain game plan. And when you've been in my game you learn to look at things a little differently than everyone else, but things like this go in a pattern and you start to see the way that they, the Old Bill, play. And when there's a big murder they do all their investigating and sometimes they can find no one. By the time they nick someone a year down the line – and they've started doing that a lot more lately, nicking some geezer way, *way* down the line – they've had enough time to plot how the evidence scans out; whether it really relates to the suspect or not. And the longer they investigate you, the longer they've got to fabricate evidence and set you up. It happened with the Rachael Nickel murder on Wimbledon Common, they got an undercover bird to meet him, plant seeds of evidence, try and sway things round just enough to get a jury convinced. That time it didn't even convince a *judge*, which is lucky for the suspect 'cos on an off day a jury might go with the police.

Whenever there's a public outcry for justice and the police can't be seen to be doing nothing, they just nick another idiot or outsider or some loser with no power and no way of standing up for himself. They did it with the

Birmingham Six and loads of others. Proven. And pressure just pushes the bad seeds of the police to the surface.

I know it's a massive thing to try to comprehend. And go to any newspaper with that story and they will bury it. Whether they think there's any truth in it or not, they will bury it alive.

It makes no sense whatsoever for Noye to want to get rid of that geezer. He hadn't even had his appeal yet. Which is another thing. After the bloke was shot, the papers ran stories on Kenny Noye ordering it, and that totally guaranteed a massive prejudice against him at his hearing. It fucked two birds with one dick.

So me thinking that they might try to do the same to me don't sound so divvy or paranoid. It fact they'd already planned my assassination with bits of paperwork. But because I think about the long-term I looked at all this, and everything running up to the trial, and I thought 'I will win': but it cannot be left at that. The whole system is geared to 'crime don't pay' and 'police are good', and if they will go to such extremes as to turn the nation into traitors, through TV programmes, then they will stop at nothing to fuck up one person. I'm under no illusions about that at all.

So far I've weathered all they've thrown at me. The arrests, the charges, the trials, the surveillance, the harassment, the attempt to blacken my name, the attempt to manipulate people around me, the name-calling, the kicking my door in and dragging my kids out of bed, the interference with my new career. Everything. And like my barrister said to the jury, 'Can you even begin to imagine how much the police hate him?'

I've even taken them on in the public domain of the media world and more than held my own, which is fucking saying something when you're faced with the power of the state's machine. I don't think I did too bad, considering. I like to think I've been a worthy opponent.

Behind all the jokes is the truth. And it's a shit truth, I know, which is why I've thrown in some jokes and stories as air-freshener to try and take some of the smell off it.

See how it's gone. For instance, I knocked out the copper whilst dressed as a court jester. They think, 'Let's keep it hush-hush. Oh, we can't. Courtney's got a video of it and is showing it around the country at his speeches!' They can't hide the bad copper away and keep his face out of the papers 'cos I've put it all on a flyer and handed ten of thousands out. Plus everything else. The whole kit and caboodle. Whatever the fuck that is. What is a caboodle? (Sounds good, though.)

The thing is, because I'm so far in it, this little war with the police, the only way I can get out of this safely is to go the whole hog. If I stopped now they would fucking want me for a long, long time. Like they wanted Charlie Kray till he was in his seventies. If I let them get away with this they will fucking hound me. And I'd end up hanging around waiting for the time when they'd do the DNA Fag Butt trick, or the Drugs In The Boot con, or the False Witness scam. And I'll say, 'But they fitted me up!' and people won't listen. Or some people will listen, the ones who have listened to me, but what could they do?

But, having said all that . . . I'm fucking winning it, and they've never had that. They've brainwashed so many people that anyone and everyone who's not a 100 per cent model citizen must be nasty and bad. The media is one tool they use to keep that going. Although through some magazines, I've got my own soapbox to shout from now. That's not been done before. The editors at newspapers still knock back stories, though, however good they are, because they're unpalatable. The line they'll take is, 'I don't care, as a journalist, how entertaining you find Courtney, as your editor I'm saying NO. Next!'

The authorities won't be seen to be threatening or warning anyone not to go near me or use me, y'know, I mean publishers, magazines, and film companies. They won't be seen to do that.

Trying to explain all of this, or any of this, to a geezer you're sat at the bar with would be fucking difficult. Ordinary people do do things they know are not right in order to get the bigger picture they're after. 'The end justifying the means' and all that. The law does it as well: and these are leaders of the country. They do it at a higher level. During the Falklands Margaret Thatcher could've said no we won't attack, but she was coming up to an election so . . . policewomen get shot by suspicious looking geezers supposedly in the Libyan embassy; we go off to war in the Gulf over oil; the 'Shoot to kill' policy in Northern Ireland.

The British police force is really part of MI5 and MI5 go around the world killing people. So if they've got someone in their own country blowing the whistle on bent police practices what do you think could happen? This flash cunt with a cigar, showing off, writing in magazines, appearing in his own documentary, writing big selling books, making films, all that and everything else. I guess they'd think 'Shut him up and worry about the civil liberties aspect later! We've tried to put him in prison; we've tried to call him a grass. It hasn't worked. Yet.'

So, I'd get a suspicious pop in the back of the head. The public wouldn't say 'It was the police that done it'; they'd say, 'An underworld killing'.

Which brings up an article in a paper from the end of last year: EXAMPLE 5: It said, 'In a magazine article four years ago, then former chief constable. John Alderson, warned that British policing had been "poisoned" by methods first used in Northern Ireland and the miners' strike of 1984–8. The dangerous blurring of the distinction between terrorism and civil disobedience was exemplified by the murky role of MI5 and Special Branch.'

In a book about MI5 Jack Straw said, 'More recently the services skills have been harnessed in support of the law enforcement agencies tackling serious crime', and 'There are no circumstances in which a Home Secretary will tell which actions of particular groups are under investigation.'

So, so much for me trying to find out from the police if they still had me under surveillance before the trial and while I was preparing my case. They've always got that convenient little word 'security' to hide behind. Now that the cold war with Russia is over these government spy agencies have fuck all better to do than spook around with the lives of their own people. And I don't just mean from the criminal world, either, so don't think you're immune. You'd only have to go on some protest march that the government didn't agree with to find yourself on their shit list. They've got billions of pounds' worth of unused surveillance equipment now at their disposal. That's not counting over 2.5 million CCTV cameras in this country, which is the largest network in the world. Pretty soon you'll only have to go for a slash to get a round of applause.

You'd be surprised how little you can get away with without them knowing. Like I said on the documentaries, it is the wrong era to be a criminal. And if they can't get you legally there's a good percentage of them that will get you illegally.

Things do happen. What I'm saying is that I'm not off my head. There's no one less paranoid than me, believe me. But don't tell me that it won't have occurred to them that it would be very fucking handy if I got run over. And you know if you can think something then someone else can think it. They must have been thinking it over like I've been thinking it over. Now that they've got me, the joker in the pack.

After that day in court what are they supposed to do? Just let me carry on as a hero. If someone stabbed one of my doormen and then carried on going out to nightclubs, I'd get it sorted out. If someone broke a footballer's leg in a tackle his teammates would kick the geezer responsible out of the park. Human nature.

One of the ways of trying to stop me is the one already put into action, of throwing so much shit about that it clouds what I have to say. Sometimes lies stink stronger than the truth. That's the power of lasting impressions. It don't have to be right, it just has to last. Like David Beckham can play a blinding seventy minutes but kicking that geezer and getting sent off is what's remembered. Shutting the door after the horse has bolted is not what they're about. Here's a geezer – me – that knows about corrupt policing and is gonna get it out. The only thing that would make that not count is if I was that bad a person (according to them) that nothing I said was worth listening to. But I would not have invited the world to my court case if I'd had anything to hide. I didn't want a press ban. I wanted a press caravan!

The thing that will save me is me putting it down on paper first so everybody's heard it. Message received, loud and clear. I ain't saying nothing that ain't true, just stuff that's difficult to believe. But that's different. And I'm not saying 'I am a police hater'; I'm not saying there's only one thing to blame; I'm not saying they're all like that, but . . . please acknowledge the fact that these things I've mentioned do really happen.

When I had fifty doormen working for me I could vouch for them all. They were all known to me and hand picked. But when I had three hundred geezers working for me, a quarter of them I might not have even wanted in the club. Which is exactly how it's gone with the police force because it's grown so huge. They're so desperate for people to apply they keep lowering the levels, 'cos they're undermanned as it is. So out went the minimum height and while we're at it let's make the intelligence test less difficult. So, if I'm nicked these days it's likely to be by a divvy dwarf! Fucking hell, please don't tell me they're like Sherlock Holmes these days, more like Eamon Holmes.

And the police *know* the extent of the corruption inside their own gang but they can't make it public. How could they? Then they'd get either nobody applying to join the force or just loads of iffy fuckers hoping to cream off the backhanders. Not to mention the loss of public confidence. It's got too big to rectify it, so they can only try keeping it out of view. Bit like that trader geezer Nick Leeson who lost billions and bankrupted Barings Bank; at some point he must have thought 'Fuck it, it's too big to admit to now – I'll have to try and bury the cunt.' Or words to that effect. (You can see I'm familiar with the language of financial institutions, can't you? My favourite thing to hear in a bank was always, 'put the cash in the bag and no one will get hurt'.)

If the force ain't so corrupt why are there so many internal police in CIB investigating their own? And if it don't run so deep then why do even CIB themselves end up getting investigated!? You know, it would be funny if it hadn't almost led to me getting fitted up in court. Larf? – I didn't think I'd stop for three or four *seconds*.

Let me ask you a question. Do you still believe that the British police force wouldn't lower itself to pursue a personal vendetta against someone? . . . well, that's funny, because even the police themselves believe it. And admit it. Check out this little headline that was in the newspapers at the end of January of this year: 'Met Finds Itself Guilty of Vendetta'. Pretty conclusive that, I'd say. No beating around the bush.

It was all about how the Metropolitan Police arrested this man 37 times! He was charged eighteen times, only got convicted of one, and even that was overturned on appeal. And he was subjected to 52 intelligence reports. After the bloke complained about his treatment, as he had been doing for years, the Met did an internal report on itself – which sounds painful. (Now that's a bloody miracle in itself, to get them to even investigate themselves.) Anyway, it showed them up to be a bunch of vindictive bastards that had harassed this guy and his family for years, so they refused to publish the report!

Anyway, the report on their treatment of this geezer did get out eventually. The newspaper article said: 'An explosive report by the

Metropolitan Police into allegations of a vendetta by officers against a black activist has recommended he should receive a public apology. Senior officers initially refused to publish the report, which criticises organisational failings in the Met, after its findings caused a row in the force.' I'll bet it fucking did! And I know why.

It caused a row because inside every force there always is, and always has been for years, a good number of police officers (but not all of them, I have to say to be fair), who think it's part of their job to get at people. Even innocent ones. And these officers have got used to their superiors either encouraging it or, at the least, turning a blind eye. So you can be sure that that report into the Met caused a fucking big row. (1) Because senior officers know they have to criticise their own so it at least looks like they're doing something; and (2) 'Cos it made loads of coppers go, 'But, Sarge, we've been doing this stuff for years! Why is it wrong now, all of a sudden?!'

At one point this geezer they'd been hounding was arrested by the Met for 'sucking his teeth in the presence of a police officer'. No, it's true. They nicked him for that. That was the charge. Fucking hell, I guess I was lucky then when I was nicked in Manchester and got out the car with my pants down! I dread to think what charge of 'sucking something' they could've come up with there if they'd put their minds to it. You can just see the copper reporting back – 'Well, Sarge, I observed the defendant, Dave Courtney, alighting from the vehicle with what looked like a weapon in his hand. In fact, he turned out to be in the possession of unregistered hard-on. I asked if he had a certificate for it but he just laughed.'

Fuck me, what next? They'll be nicking George Michael for sucking a Fisherman's Friend.

Anyway, the fella and his family have decided to sue the Met for £1million damages for all the years the vendetta has gone on. Good luck to them. I hope they win. And I hope they get a better response than I did when I put my writ in.

So you can see that when they are on the receiving end of some of the bigger problems that I've presented them with, (1) Getting famous for the thing they're trying to stop, (2) Making it look like a career option, (3) Admitting I'd shot someone after I got a 'not guilty', (4) Taking the piss out of them, as I have done for years, (5) Using their own bent officers to help me and my mates, (6) Highlighting police corruption during the recent trial, (7) Being found innocent, as I should have been, and then making an even bigger stink about it, (8) Suing them for malicious prosecution; – after all those things, and more, you know that certain sections of the London Metroploddingtan Police ain't gonna think twice, matey, about coming out all guns blazing to try and discredit me. Them thinking about it once would be enough.

And if that means they try and get me shot by my own side, by someone fooled by the propaganda, then don't think that they haven't thought of it.

See, by this stage of the game, all of us, both sides, were in it too far not to go all the way. Following it to its logical conclusion. Which is one of two things: either they win and fuck up my life, or even end it. Or I win and come out smelling of roses.

Now I ain't saying I am a rose, but as far as they're concerned they think of me as one big fucking thorn.

There was no point along the way in this whole thing where I could have gone 'Hang on! It's gone too far – stop it now.' It really wasn't ever a possibility, this time, to say, 'Stop the ride I want to get off.' I had to see it through, even at the risk of some people thinking wrongly of me along the way, in order to get to the point where the truth could come out and I could show them for what they are.

23. ROLLING, ROLLING, ROLLING

One way or another there's gonna be . . . 'Hell To Pay'.

Because they'd tried to fuck up my life I was even more determined to not let them get away with it. And what was the best way to do that? Well, carry on regardless. Don't let the fuckers grind you down.

So what to do next? Let me think . . . oh yeah, I know, I'll make my own movie: a feature-length, wide-screen, fully-loaded, blood-coloured, double-barrelled, triple-whammy, 100 per cent beef steak, villainous epic of a gangster film. With cheese on top. And bullets for chips.

How it came about was like this. I had meetings with Quentin Tarantino's lot about making my book into a film but he wanted to buy both books and make one film. Now I think there's enough stories in *one* book for *three* films, never mind putting the two fuckers together. So that weren't on. Also, I said I wanted me to play me. But Tarantino said that the geezers who control the purse strings in Hollywood wouldn't risk twenty million quid on a leading male that weren't already an established actor. Fair point. As I always say I ain't the best actor in the world but I play a *fucking* good Dave Courtney. I play a good me. God's honest truth! If there's a better Dave Courtney out there please stand up 'cos I' m fucking good at it.

While the Yanks were still umming and ahhing about how they wanted to handle it I started thinking about making my own movie. Just by luck a mate of mine, Malcolm, who is a reporter for *Combat* magazine and also the Sky boxing presenter, was partnered up with a fella called Ross, from Brighton. And Ross was a young filmmaker who wanted to make a movie. So us two got together. We met in Cannes when I went over there to check it out and see about getting my about-to-be-made film in their film festival.

The way I looked at it was that this was also an opportunity for me to make a film to show that I could play a major role, and someone could work out from it that I could play myself in a *big* film. So it was gonna be like a showreel as well.

The thing that I brought to this film, apart from me playing me, was that I could pull a thousand strings to get things done and call on hundreds of people to help out. But the one big thing that made it unique was that every character was gonna be played by a real life version – so doormen were playing doormen, street fighters playing street fighters, prostitutes playing prostitutes, nutters playing nutters and villains, boxers, lap dancers, pimps, drug dealers, porn stars, etc., were all played by the real thing. So in the film the whore is a whore – and then she's mine (*and* her sister *and* her aunt, and I'll even have a go at her cousin if he has a shave).

I was creating a new kind of film – real fiction! The only thing we couldn't get was real policemen because the bribes were beyond our budget. Boom boom. We did get our own special Bill, though.

So this was gonna be a film made with my mates, using my house, my car, my guns, my duster, and starring me as a geezer betrayed and lied about by a bent copper.

We had only two or three months to make it, which ain't a lot, is it? Fuck all really. But throughout my life one thing has been true: all I need to get something done is make a rod for my own back; and if you put yourself in a position where you *have* to do something then you *will* do it. That's why pressure has never really fazed me. In fact, I thrive on it. Every man should love a challenge.

My challenge was this; making a full-feature-length film on a shirt buttons budget with one digital XL1 camera, a first-time director, no script apart from what's in my head, mostly non-professional actors, limited time and, as an added bonus, the threat of the police trying to shut me down. All that *and* trying to get it in the next Cannes Film Festival. Bring 'em on!

The kids were all packed off to their grandma's and everyone on the film team started living in my house. It became Base Camp One for the *Hell To Pay* crew. Nothing new there then. On no one day has my house *ever* had less visitors than went to the Millennium Dome. And 'cos I live just up the road from the Dome I think that was part of their problem. If they'd put a turnstile on my front door their figures would have doubled.

Anyway, I quickly realised that things weren't going to plan. Ross came part and parcel with a young fella called Brendan, a kung fu expert, and they came with another fella called Jacob, lovely geezer but he was down to play the hitman; and with the calibre of genuine naughty geezers in this movie no way could this little fella every get away with playing a hitman. Four or five days into it I realised I couldn't grab anything out of the script that was gonna sell me well.

Ross, love him, really nice fella, just wasn't the man for the kind of job I wanted done. You can be too nice, y'know what I mean? After a week of living in my house some of the crew were still tentatively walking around like 'Oh shit, it's Dave Courtney's house – better be careful'. Which is nonsense 'cos everyone who knows me knows I don't eat the kids until filming's *over*. Otherwise the funerals fuck with the schedule. Silly.

I mean, for instance, Jen walks round the house half naked, half the time – which gives me no end of pleasure I can tell you (love the hot pants, babe) – so I was gobsmacked when I got back one day and found that Ross had just shot off out the house because, apparently, he'd accidentally walked into the bathroom when Jen was having a shower. So he shot off 'cos he thought I'd go mad about it and he wouldn't come back until his mate rang me to see if it was alright!

But when I saw him asleep on the bedroom floor and afterwards when I said why didn't you sleep on the bed he said, 'Because your coat was on it.'

I thought, fuck me, if you can't win an argument with a *coat* . . . how can you be on my team and deal with the kind of real characters making this film? No disrespect meant 'cos I love the little fella, but he knew he was out of his depth with such a big project. It was an amicable split though and those that went were still mentioned on the film's credits: Darren, Ursula and Phil.

But this weren't a wait-and-see situation, y'know what I mean? We just didn't have the fucking time to see if things worked out, they had to work out, right off the bat. I already had two screening times booked at the Cannes Film Festival in France in about two months' time.

As they say, you've got to learn when to hold 'em and know when to fold 'em. That can be the hardest thing in the world, knowing when to quit if you're a natural trier. But I cut my losses and everyone went; the cameraman went, the director went and even the fucking script went. Everyone went but me and Malcolm, and he and his wife was a rock for me in this little venture.

I'd met Malcolm first at a kick boxing do. I told him about the conversations with Tarantino and all that. It was Malcolm's story that was made into the first script and even though we changed it I still owed him for that. And for finding Ross for me as well, for even though he went it all played a part.

Anyone that goes out on a limb for me or takes a chance, or takes a risk, whatever you want to call it, anyone who does that for me then I definitely notice and will always remember. And to finish this project Malcolm had to give up his job for a while, earn no money as a journalist, and live down in my house on the off-chance that we're gonna make a masterpiece and all become rich and famous. And his missus, who happens to be a prison officer and a lovely lady, actually said he should go ahead and do it. He was really pleased about that, and he should be. A woman who backs you up and supports you is worth a fucking army, mate, let me tell you. Worth an army.

The team I had around me in the end were completely different from the young boys I began with. The boys had the enthusiasm but the second lot had the knowledge. Andy who I'd met at Sky TV, put me into Rob Gomez and I arranged to meet him on the same day I was doing a photo shoot. So Rob turned up and he was wearing a yellow anorak but because he's a six foot six skinhead I thought he was one of the lot there for the photo shoot; and I told him off for wearing a fucking silly yellow anorak when he should've been in black! Rob said, 'But I'm only the cameraman, do I really have to?'

Then Rob went and got another geezer called Austin, another very good cameraman; and Austin jacked in his job at Granada to do the film and I love him for that.

So I said *right*! We're gonna start making a new film tomorrow. I said I'd give everyone their script for the day *on* the day. Meaning, that I had it all in my head and they'd get it on a 'need to know' basis. Ha – *need to know*, fucking handy phrase that when you're making it up as you go along. 'NO . . . you don't *need to know* yet!' Otherwise known as the In The Dark theory. Another thing I was relying on here was this – the ability of a man to think on his feet and lie for England. Meaning, if I came up to you with my missus beside me and said, 'Didn't I sleep at yours last night, down there on the sofa, at your house? Tell her': and you would go, 'Fucking right he did.' And then we'd ad-lib it so well that she'd believe it (and that would be in *one* take, with no chance to do it again). That's a man's natural ability to instinctively lie his way out of a ten-hour, screaming and crying ear-bashing session. And because my film was full of genuine naughty but very talented geezers who were used to coming up with quick alibis for the police, lawyers and judges (as well as for their missus), I knew they could improvise very well during the film.

Because the film story is about the life that we are all involved in . . . or some of us are involved in . . . or *HAVE* been involved in (fuck me I've got to watch myself there and use the past tense), then I knew my geezers would be good at making it up. As a criminal one of your best assets is your ability to ad-lib. You have to be good at talking, 'cos it's alright doing a job and making a clean getaway, but it's when they come to you and land a hand on your shoulder – bang! – and say you're nicked, *that's* when you're expected to turn round and say something to get yourself out of trouble. And something that will be later repeated in court in front of the judge and jury. You've got to be fucking good at telling stories and *Hell To Pay* ended like it was up as a result of that. It's full of . . . how can I put it . . . *criminal invention.* That's it.

So, after the initial toe-stub we were now all ready to start the proper shooting of *Hell To Pay!* Thank fuck. The new story was this: The age-old power struggle between good and evil once more proving there are good baddies and bad goodies. Or straight villains and bent coppers. Top story or what? Remind you of anything.

My little string pulling exercise had also got us the actor Bill Murray from *The Bill* to play the other male lead role, the part of my brother. I'd also got Martin Hancock who plays Spider in *Coronation Street*, the model Jo Guest, Gary Bushell, Ronnie Biggs' son Mickey, boxer John Conteh, John Altman who plays Nasty Nick in *EastEnders*, the other Nasty Nick from *Big Brother*, Helen Keating, Andy Beckwith, Robbie Williams' dad, my mates Big Marcus and Dave Legano and Scot Walls who were in *Snatch* and *Lock, Stock* . . ., and loads of stars in their own right from the criminal fraternity – a couple of whom had to be in disguise on camera 'cos they were still on the run! In fact we had half of fucking *Crimewatch* as extras. Next time Nick Ross says, '. . . And do you recognise this man?' all my film crew are gonna think fuck me yes, he was in *Hell To Pay* playing a nun!

So we spent the next month filming in London and Portsmouth, staging bareknuckle fights, murders, car explosions, sex scenes, and gunfights. We shot more blank bullets than film. And what a fucking buzz that is – staging your own fights and deciding you'll *win*. It was mad. Time was zooming on and we had to stay on schedule. I've never been up *so* early, *so* many mornings of my life probably since the last time I was in court.

Can you imagine the scene, though? I had this mad posse of nutters, hardnuts, geezers on the run, fighters, actors, models, lap dancers, cameramen, lights, soundman and technicians all driving round London in Mercs, black BMs, my white Rolls and me on the Harley; shooting in the streets and at real places; blowing things up; staging gunfights: and giving the general public more causes to call the police than they knew what they could do with. It was *fucking wicked*, mate. Don't let anyone ever tell you that making a film is boring. They must be going about it the wrong way. We had a riot. And caused a few.

Oh I've got to tell you the baguette story. Get this. We moved down to Portsmouth to film the big finale, the gun battle. We were filming it in an old submarine wrecker's yard that I'd hired. I'd heard of car wreckers' yards before but not submarine wreckers. I mean what do they do with the old periscopes – sell them to dwarfs? Anyway, so there was me and the film crew, the other main actors, and about sixty other geezers to make up the two gangs, all descending on the coast.

Now it was winter so Portsmouth was as empty as a nun's womb. Fucking desolate. The only people at the hotel were some blokes there for a conference, and that was so small the hotel only had a skeleton staff. Bony cunts. So there was fuck all happening in the hotel and then Dave Courtney and eighty odd of his finest turn up – all black-suited up – and take over three-quarters of the rooms. I'll just say one thing – the mini-bars got well and truly hammered, mate. In fact one geezer took his mini-bar home for his bedroom (which didn't please his missus; especially when he charged her for the Ferrero Roche and the mini brandy she had during the night).

Anyway, filming the gunfight was absolutely wicked, running round this breaker's yard straight out of James Bond, shooting the film and each other. During this scene we also burned out a couple of cars, one of them a Rolls Royce. Not mine. I did feel sorry for the owner of it. Whoever he was. (Next time switch on the *alarm*, you silly bastard.) We put so much explosive in this car it went into orbit and just missed a Jumbo jet.

The local police and fire brigade got called out because they'd had reports of very large explosions going off and that 'all hell had broken loose', which was very apt. (Anyway, half the time they weren't actually explosions, just Mad Pete going off on one.) The police came skidding round the corner into the yard and I was stood there on top of a tank with a gun in each hand and a burning Rolls Royce behind me. They asked who was in charge.

I said it looked like I was! I said sorry for the exploding Rolls but we were just wiring the radio up.

I had a problem during filming that I bet no other director's ever had. And no, I don't mean trying to find a tart in Portsmouth. We took our own. No, the problem I had was this – all the geezers and the little firms involved in the film didn't all see eye to eye in real life, but for the sake of the film they put their differences to one side. But filming the gun battle brought them all out again. So it went something like this (names have been left out to protect the childish):

> 'Right, so you shoot *him*, and then *you* get shot by *him* and –'
> 'Hold it, Dave!'
> 'Yeah?'
> 'That cunt ain't shooting me!'
> 'What?'
> '*That* cunt ain't shooting *me*.'
> 'Erm . . . what d'you mean . . . he has to . . . you've just killed *eight* people!'
> 'No way, Dave.'
> 'He's *got* to shoot you – that's what happens here!'
> 'No. *Or* . . . wait a minute . . . he can shoot me if he shoots me in the back.'
> 'In the back?'
> 'Yeah . . . five times.'

So I goes over to the other geezer, who's stood the other side of the yard with his gang members, and he says:

> 'What? I ain't shooting him in the back! What am I, Dave, some kind of back-shooting *cunt*!?'
> 'Nobody's saying that. Oh, *stop* it. *Shut* up. It's a fucking film!'
> 'No way.'

So I walks back over to my first geezer:

> 'He says he ain't shooting you in the back: what is he, some kinda back-shooting cunt?'
> 'I ain't saying that, Dave. OK . . . what if we . . . shoot each other at the *same* time?'
> 'Yeah, *very* realistic.'

So it ended up with them both wanting to draw at the same time, shoot each other in the head, and fall down dramatically still firing and killing people; and then their ghosts carry on fighting it out in the afterlife as well, most probably, for all I know. Fucking hell. I thought they were gonna start arguing about the size of their hotel rooms next – 'Yeah, why ain't *my* room got hot and cold running lap dancers?'

Because your room ain't *my* room, that's why.

Anyway, in between shooting, looting, tooting, filming, fucking, fighting, car-exploding and general larging it, we also managed to go out clubbing as well. One night we went out to this little club – Paul's place, 'Time and Envy' – and, with this not being London, it shut at two o'clock. Which is about the time when we're generally just getting into our stride, nightlife-wise.

Outside we'd all parked our cars as close as we could get them to the club (like we usually do) but, again with this not being London, they'd all been fucking clamped. Not only that but the two geezers were still there clamping the last few! *Touch.* Lucky for us. Not for them. And because we were still buzzing, and a lot of my lot still had their props with them (in shoulder holsters), I'm afraid to say that a gun did get pulled and cocked and pointed at a clamping fella. And a voice did say:

'OK. Take that clamp off . . . and *that* one . . . and *that* one . . . and that one . . . *aannd* that one . . .'

Twenty-five clamp removals later we all got back to the hotel. Then we got to the thing that's gone down in local history as the infamous Baguette Incident. Now don't that sound serious! So, we returned to the hotel, bedtime's come and gone a long time ago and everyone's walking round the hotel at night having a good time. And out of this lot I've got one geezer on the loose – a six-foot some, tattooed, bodybuilding skinhead in just his boxer shorts and socks who was still wearing his shoulder holster and gun, off his head and roaming around the corridors trying to find someone to talk to at four o'clock in the morning! Fucking fearsome sight. As someone found out.

Next morning I got up – and felt like I deserved a medal for doing that – and went down for breakfast. The hotel manager came over to me looking a bit odd, or a bit odder than he normally did.

'Mr Courtney, can we have a little chat? We've got a bit of a problem.'

'Oh, sorry, mate; what's happened?'

'Now . . . I know *you're* alright . . . but we've got a seventeen-year-old night porter who works here who is very distressed; and thinking of calling the police.'

'Why? What happened?'

'*Well* . . . he said he was accosted by a semi-naked six-foot skinhead with a gun and ordered into the kitchen to get . . . a *baguette.*'

'Fucking hell.'

'He's still quite distraught.'

'I'll bet he is.'

Ha! A *baguette.* How fucking serious is that? And at gunpoint! I bet he was going, 'Prawn, prawn! I want a prawn baguette.'

Anyway we smoothed that one out. We lifted the night porter out of the walk-in freezer, defrosted him, and explained how it had all been a terrible misunderstanding; and how the large skinhead in question didn't hold it against him that he'd mistakenly got cheese salad. There. Sorted.

What we couldn't sort was what happened next. Everyone's mobile started ringing like mad with an army of even madder wives and girlfriends on the other end. Turns out the two wheel-clamper fellas had run off and phoned the Old Bill about being held at gunpoint, and given over everyone's number plates. We were still down in Portsmouth, of course, but every fella's missus got the early morning Door Kicked In and Dragged Out Of Bed routine. The early morning spin. So if you can imagine the sound of one missus with the hump, and then times by fifty, and all screaming down a phone . . . proper murders, mate . . . and oh, fuck me, the *language*! I swear I've never heard swearing like it. I fucking swear. (And I pity any Mormons or double-glazing salesmen that called at those ladies' houses that morning. More murders.)

But then again, let them get kicked out of bed for a change. Get your fair share, ladies. You've been to all the weddings, now have a bit of the funerals. You know what I mean? No, actually, anyone who's read my books and knows in what high esteem I hold the women of naughty geezers knows I'm joking there.

Come to think of it, the funniest comment came from the hotel manager. He rang me at 4.30 in the morning and said, 'Mr Courtney, we've had two complaints about the noise already . . . and if I get any more I'll move them to another room, okay?' Top line. See, don't silence the noise, *move* the complainers. Nice touch.

Just the making of the film was very funny, though not without its little problems. Like having an official budget of -- what they call in the film industry -- absolutely fuck all. Technical term that. I mean fuck all compared to the usual. What we were spending wouldn't keep Hugh Grant in batty girl blowjobs for a week. For instance, at one point I owed ten grand by five o'clock to continue the shoot. At three o'clock I did not have the *slightest* idea where I was going to get it. I couldn't stop to panic though 'cos I needed to use every daylight hour for filming.

At four o'clock Johnny McGee turned up with a lifesaver of ten grand, so I could pay the geezer who was sat there waiting for it and he never had any idea of how close we were. Until now.

We only had enough money to book everyone in the hotel for a week, and in the last few days it started raining so we couldn't film. We never had time to reshoot or fuck about, and towards the end I realised I was actually getting very, very close to realising a lifetime's dream of mine – to make a film. And that's something that ordinary people are not supposed to do, y'know, not really – not take on the big boys and do it yourself. Believe me, half the time these people that run the arts and media, and companies and big businesses, all want you to think it's a lot harder than it actually is. One, it justifies them getting a fuckload of money, and two, it stops you doing it yourself and making them redundant.

So how difficult is it to make a film – and how easy as well? Both of them are true. The problems are actually silly little things, but the actual making of it is not half as big a deal as you might think. We were doing it on a really tight schedule and non-existent budget as well, so if you had the time and the dosh that you get in Hollywood it would be a doddle. Again, believe me, you don't know what you can do until you do it. Don't let anyone stop you or tell you otherwise.

Finally we got the whole thing in the can (as they say in the film biz) and shot it off to the editing suite for editing, surprise surprise, and added sound effects and music. We'd been editing it as we shot but we still needed to put in a full week at the end to polish it off. There was just enough time left for one spectacular fuck up. I gave the editing suite a week to put it together, and they did. But in the wrong order! Easy. Don't panic. We can rebuild it. And we did.

I knew what I wanted and I ended up with what I wanted. With the amount of films out and the kind of technologies about it's very, very hard to actually make a different kind of film from everyone else, but I think we did and we did it by doing it raw. And every scene that the film people told me not to do 'cos they were difficult to pull off well – hand-to-hand fight scenes, a love scene, people dying, getting shot, long speeches – we did anyway and did them our way. For instance, I was advised to do the boxing match with the fighters wearing boxing gloves 'cos it'd make it easier to film them having a go at each other. So we filmed it as a bare-knuckle bout with enough blood, snot and bone crunch to turn Tarantino green.

I made a different film in a documentary way. I might not be the best actor in the world as I've said but I do a good Dave Courtney in documentaries, and I can play a good Dave Courtney in films.

There are five people that started the film but ain't in the finished thing. 'Cos they got nicked and are now in prison. And the governor wouldn't give them time off for filming. What a fucking liberty – jailing my actors! How dare they. Just 'cos one geezer had gone and done a post office job. He was just getting into *character* (even though he was only playing an ice cream van man; it was on a tough estate). Fuck me, haven't the courts ever heard of Method Acting?

Anyway, do they give an Oscar for Best Supporting Bank Robber? Or how about Best Squeely Tyre Sound Effect Made by a Getaway Driver?

You can be sure, though, that if they gave out an Oscar for Biggest Pisstaking Bastards it would go to the Metropolitan Police. I had to drop my case against them because, listen to this, if I couldn't prove that I could pay for the damage if I lost (and they know I can't 'cos through bugging me they know my financial situation) then I have to drop the charges against them. *But* they refused me legal aid! They didn't refuse me legal aid when they wanted to get me in court to throw all that shit at me in the hope that some of it stuck – but they did refuse it this time when I wanted to sue them for malicious prosecution. Funny that, ain't it? I got a stitch laughing, and then nearly burst my stitches.

I sent them a letter asking why I was granted it last time and then not this, when everything about my circumstances was the same. The only thing I'd changed was my pants and the blade in my head razor.

Another thing I was missing was all the property of mine which was in the hands of CIB3. The reason I ain't still got it back being that it's two videos and some tapes and photographs of me with bent coppers, including Warnes. The police have had them since Brendan brought it up to them after I was arrested. After they hit me with this 'informant' crap I got Bren to bring up the proof about what really had been going on. Brendan signed them in and I thought, right, that's it, I'm going home.

But when I got not guilty they should actually give me my property back, but 'cos I turned round and nicked *them* they say they've lost my stuff! As blatant as that. I had proper letters accusing them of things and predicting things that were gonna happen to CIB3 . . . and they say they've just lost them. It's impossible they've lost them, but they would actually stand up in court and say that. And what can a judge do? But they obviously won't give me back my evidence, the same evidence that I would use to nick them with.

Brendan's solicitors sent off letters to the police asking if it was because their client signed the letters in so Mr Courtney couldn't sign them out, but they just never replied to them. Never even answered. And there ain't a lot you can do when someone just shuts up shop and won't reply.

Then they waited until I was on holiday before they tried to contact me. That's another clever little one of theirs, that one. They really do that. They know when you're at home, so they fucking well know when you're not. And they know when you're out the country as well.

I went down to CIB3 offices to ask for my stuff back and I took a photographer, Sian, from the *South London Press* to take pictures of me going in there to ask for it back. I've written to some people to try to get attention to it but nothing's happened.

Best of all I sent a twenty-three page fuck-off letter to Jack Straw explaining the full extent of police corruption and asking for some explanation of the whole thing, the scam, the cons, the cover-up, and the unfair ways in which the courts are used against people. Didn't even get a reply, surprise sur-fucking-prize.

So I put it on the Internet! *Ha* – try 'losing' that letter, Sherlock!

Fucking hell, it was nearly enough to make me want to take a coachload of nutters to France and premiere my new film *Hell to Pay* at the Cannes Film Festival! In fact, it was *more* than enough. So that's exactly what I did . . .

24. PREPARE FOR LANDING!

Rev up the bikes — WE INVADE! Me and my gladiators conquer Cannes, Russell Crowe and the undercover police.

I was really proud of the film we'd done. I thought it was a proper classic, even though I say so myself. And like I'd always planned we got it placed to be shown at the Cannes Film Festival in May 2001.

I'd had a proper uphill struggle getting to where I was going because the authorities are in no hurry to have great big posters of Dave Courtney with a couple of guns over his shoulders plastered up and down the high street. If they were in a position to either help that project along or kill it off then they would kill it. Obviously. And so would I if I was them. But I say to them: don't talk to me like you're not doing it. They can't be *not* doing it 'cos it's their job to do it!

Like, for instance, 24 hours before we got to France, the hotel we were booked into rang up and said they needed deposits for *everyone* because they'd heard some things about who was coming. Then the coach company rang up and asked for all the money up front, cash, and a hundred quid deposit on top because they'd been tipped off we were a gang of hooligans. Suddenly the editing suite wanted £39,000 or they wouldn't let the film out the building for us to take with us! *And* I was taking the head of the editing company with us to Cannes as a thank you! Get *that*. And the best bit was – after we'd paid it he still fucking came with us. Bloody cheek.

So it was a genuine, undermining attack on my transport to get us there, an attack on our accommodation if we got there, and an attack on the film I was selling if I got there. Attacked from all sides – repel all boarders!

Sometimes there has been a proper press halt on Dave Courtney products. I've had people come up to me and say they couldn't understand why they hadn't seen any promotion for a book or a film. Well I can understand it: it's the moody handshake lot. The 'unofficial' word to put a lid on something.

Nearly all the TV companies that work with me are approached afterwards by the police. Even if it's just to ask questions it acts as a warning. Most straight-goers are shitted up just to get spoken to by the police. They approached Channel 5 about their documentary. *Front* magazine have been talked to, and now the Old Bill were saying they were gonna bug me until they actually caught me saying something.

The latest one was trying to get me with the Inland Revenue because they read I'd said the film cost under a million; so they're now running round with their heads up their arses trying to work out where I got a million quid from. What they didn't realise I meant was that if I'd had to *pay* for all the favours I called, all the strings I pulled, all the stuff I blagged, all the people who wanted to do it for free, all the real props I got, all the locations and cars I used, all the catering I got given, all the actors and actresses, all the generosity I was given and all the stuff we nicked then it *would* have cost about a million. Probably more. The prawn baguette bill on its own would've been fucking colossal! (thanks due there to the little night porter).

Fact is this: I can live my life penniless. I do not need money. Whatever it is you need money for . . . I *get* – Rolls Royces, holidays, trips to America, in and out of clubs, drinks, my clothes and cigars, petrol for the cars, and work done on my house. So I don't need money as such 'cos it's like . . . a club.

The police and the taxman are tearing their hair out trying to work that little one out. *Ha*! They've never had anything like it so they don't understand it. But my people would stand up in court and say *why* they done it for nothing. Like if a mate in the motor trade gives me a car, he knows I'll pay for it ten times over by sending enough people back to him to buy their cars. If someone VIPs me at their club they know I'll get them the same treatment at one hundred more.

See, *we* have got our networks and methods and ways to get things done; which is why I know so well that *they* – the authorities – have got theirs for getting things stopped and blocked and fucked. Same thing in reverse. Big fucking negative influence. If they can deliberately stitch up innocent people and bang them up for years – we all know it happens – then everything else is a doddle to fix.

But 'We shall overcome!' as I used to sing at Sunday school, while I was shagging the vicar's daughter in a cupboard. Onwards and upwards. As she used to say.

Next stop – France! Oh, mate, you should've seen our convoy. We had the freakiest fucking coach party since the Krays, Charles Manson, Hugh Hefner and Billy Smart's Circus all went on holiday together. A coachful of the most unusual band of characters you've ever seen in your life. We had villains, porn stars, boxers, bodybuilders, lap dancers, DJs, bank robbers, publicans, strippers, housewives, drug dealers, dog breeders, hash growers, actors, skinheads, scarfaces, forgers, giro cashers, three millionaires, a geezer on the run, a black transsexual, a white dread, page 3 girls, photographers, a camera crew, a suspect from *Crimewatch*, four Rastafarians, and a parrot.

(On the day we set off the parrot could say 'Who's a pretty boy?' and 'Give us a kiss!' and by the time we came back it was saying '*Shut* up you cunt', 'Anyone got any Rizlas?' and 'I is *well* mashed, aiiiee!')

Nothing short of nuclear war or some cunt draining the Channel was gonna stop us from getting to Cannes, mate. You *know* that. We'd even dropped a couple of Viagra in the coach's petrol tank to guarantee staying power. Fuck the unleaded, we had lead running *right* through us.

Even the parrot had a hard-on.

We also had our own chauffeur, cameraman, barman, spliff roller, and flight bag full of money. Oh, and a top tart. All the women sat down the front, and for 23 hours she entertained the chaps at the back. *And* fucked the parrot. It was a bit like a school trip in fact. But only if you went to a fucking strange school.

The coach driver freaked out right from the start when he saw who, or what, he was going to be carrying. The first thing he said was, 'No smoking! No drinking! No eating!' Just as Charlie Breaker was getting on carrying a pallet of cigs, beer and sarnies. Then he saw the bags being loaded on board with strange things hanging out of them and freaked out more. So he's stood there at the top of the coach with the pilot's hat on (nice touch), already standing in puddles of beer, and he goes, 'Right. The emergency exits are here and here.' I said, 'What about the big window?' He said, 'No, noo . . . if you smash that an alarm goes off and we have to drive for miles with *beep! beep! beep!*' Oh, dear. Never mind the fact that there'd be no glass and everybody would be getting blown to fucking bits! Good one.

On the way there, though, he was a proper cunt and only allowed ten-minute toilet breaks. Then when we got to Cannes he got completely lost and spent an hour and a half looking for the hotel. And everyone said is that what the rush was all about, 'cos you knew you'd fuck it up at this end? Could hardly blame him, actually, 'cos by the time we got to Cannes this driver was half off his head – pilot's hat now at a funny angle – just from passively smoking what was wafting down the front from the back. Even the air conditioner got stoned and went oh fuck it and packed in.

We'd needed one hotel with 38 double rooms, but we couldn't get one near the front so I'd plumped for one further out where the hotel guy had said they'd provide two drivers 24 hours a day to ferry us back and forth to the front in our coach. That swung it for me so I'd said OK and booked it. When we got there though our driver freaked out even more – I think it was catching the parrot having a wank on the back seat that did it – and just fucked off with the coach! Along with some vintage champagne that was on board, a kid's passport and some guns. He just high-tailed it out of Cannes. With all the windows open.

So now we were trapped. One cab to the seafront was fifty quid and there's more than sixty of us. And no coach. There was fucking murders going on, mate, let me tell you; everyone was going fucking nuts. Nice weather though. We were fucked off but getting a tan.

At least I had the Harley Davidson. Yes, *the Harley*. Not my motorbike, that was still at home: this was another one. I borrowed this wicked Harley to use in *Hell To Pay* from a Harley showroom called Dockgate 20 in Southampton. The shop is run by two top fellas called Bob and Steve, and the big boss is a fantastic nutter I call Mad Aussie. (Later I did an appearance at a wicked open day they had at the showroom with lap dancers from *For Your Eyes Only*. How easy was it to have a good time that day then? The hard-ons come free.) So they lent me the Harley on the strength of it being featured in the film. When the Cannes trip came around I rang them up to ask if I could bring it out with us as the ultimate prop but they told me that this geezer, Doug Bodingson, had heard about it being in the film and bought it because of that! I felt chuffed. And bikeless.

I rang this Doug and said I'd pay for him and his son to come out with us if we could take his bike. He said okay. He was an absolute diamond this geezer Doug, a proper good fella.

So at least I had that to use now that the coach had gone. You can imagine what a buzz it is cruising along the seafront in the South of France in the blazing sun on a big, fuck-off, chrome-piped Harley – all sparkly and loud and turning heads. Never mind the multiple orgasms, I nearly spontaneously combusted, mate. Even *I* wanted to fuck me. And the bike played its part in helping me pull off one of our biggest coups. Listen to this.

First, let me tell you what the press photographers are like at the Cannes Film Festival. They hunt in packs, like wolves wearing trainers, and they eat *everything* and then decide later whether it was worth it. They literally *stampede* towards you because they know that if they're not the one at the front getting the photos then they'll be the one at the back missing it all. Hoards of them roam around like vultures, still picking bits of Lady Diana out of their teeth.

Now when we pulled into town one morning and I saw a huge mob of photographers on the other side of the street I didn't think anything of it. They thought about us though. I saw every one of them turn away from whatever or whoever they were photographing and turn to look this way. Can't blame them really. There was me – white suit and black shades, no helmet or socks, gold and diamond duster in one hand and fat cigar in the other, roaring up the street on a bike that sounded like a male lion's orgasm and looked like a silver, glittery gladiator's chariot. I pulled up onto the piazza, right in front of the British Pavilion covered in Union Jacks, and there just happened to be over forty very naughty-looking geezers in black suits and shades all waiting there to greet me. What a *touch*. So lucky! Thank fuck I arranged it.

This mob of photographers paused . . . and then just *burst* over the road towards us and left behind this geezer sat in a chair that they'd been clicking over. Anyway, by now I'm surrounded by people, the camera clicks sound like applause and I'm sat on the bike proper buzzing away; answering questions, signing autographs, giving out flyers and posters for *Hell To Pay*, handing out copies of *Stop the Ride* . . . and my bike posters, and generally making the absolute fucking most of an opportunity that few people get. And was I gonna waste it? . . . Oh, *stop* it! *Shut* up. It was my duty – my *duty* – to enjoy it to the hilt.

Then this geezer appeared at my shoulder and congratulated me getting the film shown and asked me to sign a bit of paper (apparently he'd already asked Doug, my Harley man, who was I and what had I done and Doug had filled him in). So I said yeah, sure, who's it to? He said, 'It's Russell . . .' I went, 'Okay, mate.' Then I noticed everybody looking at me oddly, or even more oddly than normal. Then it dawned on me, and I looked up and saw it was Russell Crowe, Mr Gladiator himself. I put the pen down and said that I hadn't meant that disrespectful, y'know, but I *genuinely* hadn't clocked him. Which I hadn't. 'Cos I hate all that 'pretend you don't recognise the famous person' nonsense. If I see someone that I think is the bollocks then I'll say hello and tell them. Like you should. And I told Russell that I thought *Gladiator* was an absolutely wicked movie – best of the year (which it was) – and he was really wicked in it.

So we chatted for a bit, and he's a really nice geezer and all that, and it felt it bit odd that I'd drawn all the press attention so I said: 'Here, Russell. You are the nuts, mate, *but* where you're going wrong is this . . .' – and he leaned in to listen, and so did everyone else – '. . . all those gladiators made you look the absolute bollocks, but then you've come out here all on your own! But me, see,' I pointed to my chaps, 'I've brought *my* gladiators with me!' And in that second I could feel forty British chests behind me just *swell* out with pride. All the flags stopped fluttering for a second 'cos so much air had been drawn in!

He just laughed and we chatted a bit more and that was that. He was dressed really casual in T-shirt and jeans and trainers, and how many photos of that can fifty photographers take and still find interesting? Especially when me and mine pulled up, pulling out all the stops. But without a leather skirt on, a sword in each hand and a few dead Christians round his sandals, he didn't look like Russell Crowe, he just looked like 'Russell'.

A lot of actors these days want to be more anonymous off screen. Why? Get a job in a bank. If I'd played a part like gladiator Maximus I'd turn up on a fucking chariot. Oh sorry, I did. The Harley. God bless Doug.

Not the warmest form of transport though, the Harley, 'cos even in the South of France it's cold at night. Especially up in the mountains. No, I don't know why we ended up in the mountains either. Don't ask. Actually, it was because it took us a few days to get our bearings and find the right way back to the hotel. One night I made the mistake of allowing myself to believe that Lenny, the geezer driving the van that brought the bike over, actually knew the way home. Half an hour's night driving later me and Brendan – riding pillion – were looking around thinking, This fucking country's getting a bit on the hilly side, ain't it? Where's the sea gone? Is that a mountain goat? Why can I hear cowbells? Is this what frostbite feels like?

I thought, first I'm gonna freeze solid, and then the bike vibrations are going to smash me into little bits. Like the geezer in *Terminator II* .

Turns out Lenny had taken a wrong turning or two (hundred) and we were fuck knows where at fuck knows what altitude at fuck knows what time in the morning, both wearing suits on a motorbike, with the temperature fuck knows how many degrees below zero. I never knew snot could freeze that fast. At one point I shouted back, 'I think I've just seen a fucking penguin!' Then Lenny decided it was a good idea to clean the van windscreen, which meant we were dead in line behind for the spray to shoot over the van roof and come down on us. As hailstones.

When he finally pulled over at the lights, as I pulled up alongside I heard him say, 'It's alright, Dave. Follow me!'

'Lenny, we *have* been following *you*, mate, which is why we're halfway to fucking Switzerland! I keep expecting to see Julie fucking Andrews come over the next mountain singing "The hills are alive with the sound of music"!'

And the moral of the story is never follow someone who has just had their first ever gram of whizz – they've no idea where they're going but they're *fucking* determined to get there. I came down out of those mountains with a head like a snowball and balls like hailstones. They had to lever me off the bike with a crowbar and a blowtorch.

Next morning I did my postcard and letter duties, sending them out to the usual suspects, the Met, CIB3, the CPS, Tony Blair and Jeffery Archer, saying 'Wish You Were Here – but glad you ain't'. I also sent a full letter to the Met, 'cos I'd recently learned that the CPS had stuffed me on the writ I served against the police, ruling it invalid by saying that unless I could prove in advance that I could pay the legal costs if I lost then they were just going to drop my case against the Old Bill! Very fucking handy.

The letter went something like: *Hello Chaps, it's me again. Just a quickie to let you know it's all going very nicely for me out her in Cannes and it's one step further in my plan for world domination. Russell Crowe don't look like much of a gladiator without his leather skirt on and a sword in each hand. Anyway, you must know legal aid was refused. And you still haven't given me my property back (tapes, photos, etc) have you? Maybe I'll just stay here in the sun, out of the country, considering what you tried to do to me. I'm off now to have lunch with Brad Pitt and Tricky. Wish me luck, love, Dave Courtney OBE.*

If you ever get the chance to go to the Cannes Film Festival then do go. It's absolutely wicked. Once again, I saw it as my duty – to you my loyal readers – to have a really, really good time. I mean what did you want me to do, have an early night? Or go to a yacht party held by *Playboy* magazine? My choice. *Stop* it.

But before we got to that we had to get down to business.

As well as *Hell To Pay* having its premiere I was also in another British film that was being shown called *Daddy Fox*. This was the film I first told you about in *Raving Lunacy* where I played a high court judge. Good casting! On the very day the court case had started at the Old Bailey one of the tabloids had run an article on the film with a photo of me in the gowns and wig. Perfect timing. *Daddy Fox* was picked up for world distribution at

Cannes. So somewhere out there there's a probably badly dubbed Spanish version of it with me still moving my lips ten seconds after I've finished speaking. No difference there, then.

So, in Cannes, on one side of the street I was in my film playing a villain and on the other side of the street I was in a movie theatre playing a judge, and also in a porn film. And one thing I forgot until I saw the film proper, during the filming of *Daddy Fox* I snuck a knuckleduster into the courtroom and hung it from the royal coat of arms. No one noticed and it stayed there through all the scenes. My little infiltration, you might say.

The showing of *Daddy Fox* was a funny old day. It was fucking red hot actually, and we left the hotel about two in the afternoon to go to this showing of the film. All the cinemas there have these specially built pavilions in front of them covered in flags and red carpet for gala openings and premieres. Like the British one covered in Union Jacks where we did our photo shoot. Anyway, we get to the town, me and Seymour Brendan, and somehow ended up in the pavilion area for the wrong film – a much, much bigger film, obviously, than ours. So I'm actually on the red carpet outside the Plaza, next to all these stars. I ended up walking past what I thought was a band, 'cos they were all in uniform with braiding and sashes and peaked caps. But some of them started looking over at me in not too friendly a way. I thought this lot look a bit lairy for musicians.

One of them peeled off and came over and when he started questioning whether I was in the right area I realised they weren't a band but actually a gang of local police, all dressed up for some honorary awards thing. I truly thought they were the band. So this French Old Bill goes, 'I theenk you are in zee wrong area. You must get on zee uzzer side or you could get shot.' I said, 'What with? A trombone? I thought you were the band, mate.'

I was gonna get elbowed out any minute so just as they posed for their group photo I stepped in and pulled the duster out *just* as all the camera flashes went off! Spot-on timing. Frame that one, Inspector Clouseau.

There is a fuck load of security around there though. Most of them with some tasty looking sub-machine gun slung over their shoulder or a pistol in a holster. But most of the robbery in Cannes goes on in the cafés and restaurants: yeah, their daylight robbery is called 'the bill'. Ten quid for a poxy coffee. You order a few with some mates and it's like getting in a round of whiskey pints back home! So then you need a stiff drink to get over the shock of paying ten quid for a fruit juice and the bill for the stiff drink makes you go fucking limp. No wonder there's no bank jobs done over there – they just open fucking cafés instead. Gram for gram, coffee beans must be worth more than cocaine in Cannes. Fucking difficult to snort though. You can always tell them coffee bean snorters – they have to breathe through their mouths 'cos their nostrils are full of beans.

After the *Daddy Fox* premiere we went out clubbing and Brendan ended up, at the end of the night, going off on some sexual adventure, as usual.

Quite a funny one. He'd ended up propped up against the bar at about four in the morning with the staff practically sweeping up around his feet. He'd said to this bird, 'Are you coming back to mine?' She'd said, 'For business?' So, he's pulled a tart. How difficult is that. He bartered her down to twelve hundred francs – how romantic is that – and he knew that she thought she'd got some nice, easy, drunk English geezer, off his rocker, who'd shoot his bolt in ten seconds or fall flat asleep before. What she didn't know was that Brendan had just thrown two hundred mill. of Viagra down his neck.

So as they were leaving the club to get a taxi Brendan took her hand and put it on his crotch and she looked at him like, 'Oh fuck, this is gonna be a long night.' And, apparently it was. By nine the next morning when he was still going strong this bird was saying, 'Not normal! Not normal!' *Ha*. He does know how to get his money's worth from a brass, does old Bren. Not so clever with the taxis though, 'cos that one with the tart cost him fifty quid! Mind you, if you got a taxi *anywhere* in Cannes it was always fifty fucking quid. Even for the shortest journey possible. If they parked on your foot and you asked them to reverse off they'd charge fifty quid for it. Anyway, all in all, with the extras, Brendan's holiday romance cost him two hundred and thirty quid.

The morning after we went out on the yacht that the *Daddy Fox* film team had hired. Brendan met this posh bird that he'd been trying to get off with the day before; then she'd asked him if he was looking for a nice girl and he'd said no, he was looking for a tart. So now she asked him if he'd found a girl, and if she'd been nice:

'Oh yeah,' he said, 'two hundred and thirty quids' worth nice.'

Talking about getting overcharged for a shag, every time you went in a café you got fucked. The worse one was when we first got there and me, Jen, Bren, Helen, Anjela and Phil 'Real Deal', sat down outside this place and had three brandy and Cokes, three Cokes and three toasted ham sandwiches. Before the bill comes Brendan asks the waiter if he can cash some money. The waiter, a real snotty bastard, says, 'No, you can't cash. Here is what you have to do – run across the road to the casino, change it into change for you, bring it back here and I'll change it into notes. But you have to start the process.' Yes, sir! So Brendan did all that (luckily he'd been taking notes) and came back with sixty quid in francs. Then the bill came and it was *one hundred and twenty quid*!

Brendan went, 'It's one hundred and twenty quid!' See, it takes a good one to get past Brendan. I said well don't look at me like that, I ain't ordered and ate another fifty sandwiches while you were gone!

We now haven't got enough in francs so when the snotty waiter came over I gave him two English fifty pound notes. He looked a bit put out.

'Have you got francs?'

'No, Frank's paying for his own.'

'Sorry?'

'No, we haven't. But here is what you've got to do. Run over to the casino, get the change, come back here and pay yourself. But *you've* got to *start* the process. OK?'

That's a bloody big bill for a few drinks and some toasted ham sandwiches though. I've got married for less. It's a wonder Ecstasy dealers aren't moving out of that scene and into the old toasted ham racket. It'd make the news interesting – '*And today drug enforcement officials raided a local butcher's and found pig carcasses, uncut, with an estimated street value of twelve zillion . . .*'

Next day we had a bit of a problem with the Harley Davidson. How can I put it? It was sort of like the kind of problem you get when a twenty grand motorbike is stolen . . . that kind of a problem. Very much like that actually, 'cos the bike got nicked. One day we were sat there looking at it from across the road whilst we all had breakfast. People were taking pictures of it, as usual. Then this van pulled up, looked like it was unloading for a shop or something, and blocked our view of the bike. Next thing I knew I heard it kick to life and by the time we'd stood up it had shot off one way and the van shot off the other. It was all to do with the fact there was a Harley Davidson rally in Cannes at the time, and as well as attracting all the Harley owners it had brought out all the Harley nickers as well. Over two hundred Harley Davidsons were stolen in seven days at Cannes. All Heritage bikes like ours. Or Doug's.

So that put a bit of a damper on things. I put on a brave face about it. And then went behind a building and went, '*Aaaargghhhh!!*'

Brendan ended up going down to the police station to report it with another geezer called Ricardo, who speaks a bit of French but, unfortunately, with an Italian accent. No copper in the station spoke English, or they didn't want to, and Ricardo's struggling attempts at communication involving three countries – England, France and Italy – weren't helping anyone. Then this skinny little geezer came in, who turned out to be a detective and could speak a bit of English. But only enough to say, 'Ah, you're from England! Where *Fawlty Towers* comes from!' That was his only connection with England – Basil Fawlty. They were trying to explain to him about the bike and the copper's going, 'Deed you see zee episode where Manuel . . .'

Then came the big day for the premiere of *Hell To Pay*. I called a press conference. I'd been to a few already to see how they went, and from what I could see all they seemed to be was a posh room hired by the filmmakers and then filled with journalists ferried over by limousines. Then the filmmakers would get on stage, bare their jugulars and go please like me, please like me, don't slag off my film: that kind of attitude. I thought *fuck that*. That was just not the spirit that our film had been made in. It was more . . . defiant. Yeah, we defied the odds, the police, the weather, the fuck all budget, and the warnings and still got it done.

So during my press conference I said, 'Ladies and gentlemen, if you've come to this marquee to get loads of free booze you can go fuck yourself 'cos I've got sixty mates with me and friends come first in the queue. And, to be honest, I don't give a fuck whether you like my film or not 'cos it's already massive in my house! One more thing, if anyone would like to tell me who's got my motorbike I will give them five grand.'

One of the reporters jumped up and said, 'We're all here for this press call, Mr Courtney, you can't leave it at that.' I said, 'OK. If anyone gives me the name of the guy who stole the bike, whether it fucks up my career as an actor I will chop his fucking hands off. Thank you.'

The actual showing of the film went brilliantly. We had a full house and *Hell To Pay* went down even better than I expected. We had cheering and a standing ovation at the end. Afterwards we went into the British pavilion and had a good old drink or twelve.

So, in Cannes, we held up the British end in the reality stakes, which made me really proud in a silly, romantic way. Me and mine – all 62 characters – were a huge fucking dose of reality in that little dream world they create there every year. I think half the people that ran into us thought we were putting it on, 'cos we were so genuinely larger than life. The truth is, most people would seem that way if they lived the life they *really* wanted to live. Do you know what I mean? Think about how you'd live your life if you had less fear of stuff like being judged and being embarrassed and what people think of you; and no fear of failing (that's the one that does it, mostly) and all that other bollocks that fucks you up. All that stuff. Think about it – *then* get rid of it – *then* do it without.

Some people, mostly the ones that critcise me writing books – and most probably the ones that have never read them – think that I'm using the old 'be like me' message to say people should go into crime. That ain't it at all. I wouldn't be big-headed to say 'be like me' in any way except two: (1) Do things your way – as I've done things mine, and (2) Don't let the bastards grind you down. Oh, and just one more thing: leave 'em smiling.

Even your enemies. Especially them. And if that don't work shoot first.

The yacht parties over there were a big buzz. We don't get a lot of them down our way – Plumstead, South London. And not a big yachting area, Peckham, is it? So we missed out when we were kids. Having said that, remember in *Stop the Ride* ... when I accidentally nicked the British Olympic team yacht from outside Queens Reservoir Club? It did look a bit odd outside my gaff in Peckham.

At the film festival we went to Jennifer Lopez's yacht party for the launch of her movie. She weren't there though, but Brendan did look for her – high and low. Mostly low. He even got a bird to go to the toilets with him to help him look.

If you can spot the flakes and quiet nutters in a crowd then you can have fun with them and get your money's worth. No harm there. If it weren't for me and Brendan noticing them then an awful lot of lunatics would go totally unappreciated. Some are easier to spot than others. There was these two New Zealand geezers there who were just fucking out and out conmen. That's all right, each to his own, but the worse thing was they weren't even very good ones.

They were cracking on that they were a couple of high-powered Public Relations guys. They'd done it but they'd already managed to convince some people that they'd get them into all the parties. I was watching them thinking, you two are working a coup, you two are. I can see it going down. Then when they'd first spotted me they'd come over immediately like they smelled a chance to get in on something profitable. Giving them the benefit of the doubt (well, you just never know – but I usually do) I'd thrown them a little task as a test – to get fifty photographers to go to a certain place the next day: a place where we just happened to have breakfast every morning, as it happens! So, if no photographers turned up, no big deal: and if, against the odds, they did turn up, then I'd have an improvised press call and photo shoot. Guess what? No one turned up to take a picky of my bacon and eggs. What a surprise.

We were out the next night having a laugh and bumped into these geezers again, the Bill & Ben of the con men. They were still working the room, playing it, you've got to give them that. I didn't mention the phoney photographer thing. And this night they looked even fucking dafter than usual. Both had bits of wire hanging out of their earholes as if they were connected to earpieces, but the wires didn't go anywhere! Just hung there. And they'd obviously nicked a couple of those big, padded menus with gold tassels on from a local restaurant, and they were trying to pretend they were fancy little folders with invites inside. Fucking funny. Especially some of the chat:

> 'Okay, mate. Here's one for you – I want to go to the big premiere tomorrow at The British Pavilion.'
> 'Right, Mr Courtney, I tell you how we handle this one . . .'
> 'Yeah?'
> 'I've been a doorman . . .'
> 'Oh, yeah?'
> '. . . And I know what it looks like when forty people walk towards you, especially if *you* – *Dave* – were, like, at the front, and we all just . . . we all just . . .'
> 'Yeah?'
> 'We just . . . *walk straight through!*'
> 'So you're not actually doing PR; you're just telling me what *formation* to use to gate crash? I don't need anyone to tell me how to do that, I did it for fucking years.'
> 'Okay. But I can get you press out here.'

'Who do you know?'
'Well, I don't actually know anyone.'
'So how you gonna get me any press?'
'I . . . can . . . *think of stories!*'

Oh not the old 'think of stories' routine. Why didn't I think of that? The old thinking bit! So I said look, you silly-looking cunt with your ear-wire and your bleedin' menu, don't try and bullshit a bullshitter 'cos I'm a fucking good one and I've nothing against bullshitters, but don't try and have me over like some soppy tart you're trying to nail 'cos for one thing your photographers didn't turn up, which I don't really mind 'cos we didn't expect it, but fuck me mate, give it a rest.

Then he said: 'What I was going to say, Dave, was this. Can you give me a half a dozen of your guys tomorrow to walk beside this open-top car for a PR stunt we're doing for this American woman?'

Fucking non-stop or what? Ha. What a trooper. So I said yes, he could have six of my boys, tomorrow, at eleven, just where you want them – walking like bodyguards next to an open-top car on a sunny day with an American lady in it. On one condition. That she wasn't related to President Kennedy.

We went to Hugh Hefner's *Playboy* party on this huge liner. Well, y'know, we were asked, and you've got to make the effort to get out now and again. The ship was just overflowing with *Playboy* birds walking around half-naked in tiny fancy dress outfits like Indian squaws and cowgirls, with nothing more than cowboy boots, a bow and arrow and a smile. And they were saying to all the men what can I do to make you happy sir? Bending over the back of the sofa would be a start, babe.

There was a life-size ice sculpture of a naked woman on the ship's deck. Brendan tried to get off with it. Talk about how to prove you're English without saying anything! Then I heard the familiar sound of a shotgun coming from the back of the liner.

For a second I thought Mad Pete had decided to gate crash but, get *this*, it turns out they had a proper clay pigeon machine set up back there. They were firing them out over the harbour, off the back of the ship, and blasting them. Like you do. I thought I'll have some of *that*. So me and Bren announced ourselves as the British contingent, by Royal Appointment, and stepped up and got our guns. Then we shot up just about everything in sight. Well, hitting those clay disc things is piss easy, but you can use them as an excuse to follow them down with the barrel and shoot . . . oops, there goes a buoy, there goes a jet ski engine, there goes a little dinghy – pop! – and there goes the head of the ice sculpture.

There was this one bird on board who couldn't speak. Something had affected her. I don't know what she was on but when she opened her mouth all she could do was fucking yodel! She must've had an Ecstasy tablet shipped over from Switzerland. She was properly fucked up, mate. *Yodelling*. That's one side-effect that'd really scare the youth right off drugs. You *know* that.

And things just got better. We met this American woman, Jackie O'Nasty! Oh fuck me, what was she like. We just saw this THING tottering towards us – she must've been 58, pink miniskirt, stilettos, orange tan, false claws, pumped lips, false tits – looking like a melted Barbie doll on the prowl. She looked like she'd been mugged by a plastic surgeon. Fucking scary. *I'll* talk to her:

'Hello, babe. Looking good.'

'Hi. Oh *hi*! I'm Jackie O'*Nasty*. Producer, porn filmmaker, and I *star* too.'

'Star? What, in your own movies?'

'Yeah. Uh *huh*. I'm *natural* as well.'

'Really.'

'You'd better *believe* it, honey!'

'Natural' if you happen to live with the Addams Family, have sex with chimps and gave birth to your own mother. Michael Jackson kind of natural. These are the kind of people that give each other new heads for Christmas. And, another thing, her teeth moved. I swear to God. I heard them clicking first and thought what the fuck's that noise? Oh fuck, it's her bleedin' teeth. Brendan sobered up for a second and, with his usual restraint, went, 'Oi! *Your* teeth moved!' Honestly, you just can't take him anywhere. She didn't seem to hear him, and we were busy dodging all the spit flying out of her every time she spoke. Fucking hell, catch your teeth, girl!

She started handing us business cards with all her phone numbers on and these PR releases for porn films and stuff, all this *shit*, and, best of all, she gave me a calendar full of pictures of Betty Boop (the cartoon character) but underneath she'd written her own name, 'JACKIE O'NASTY'. The fact it was done in green felt tip was a bit of a giveaway.

Then again, it's not everyone who can say they've met Pamela Anderson's grandma. Five years after she died. Anyway, Brendan shagged her. No I'm joking. He just got a blowjob. With the teeth out.

So we're strolling round the yacht, taking it all in, going down well with the Brits and most Yanks on board 'cos they get the jokes, but the rest . . .? This camp French geezer slides up to me and goes, 'Oh, you theenk you recognise me, *no*?' I went, 'You're right . . . *no*.' He said, 'I am a famous 'airdresser!'

Now *I* wouldn't know a famous French hairdresser if one bit me on the arse and another one sucked out the poison. I mean who would? So I said that I was only looking at him 'cos I was thinking that he needed a fucking good haircut. That went down like a lead life raft.

See, my humour's wasted on anyone foreign. It's wasted on anyone normal, actually. (Like when we were in Monaco and met this geezer who had just been left five hundred million dollars. I said that I'd shag him for half. And we'd been getting on pretty well right up till then. Weird.)

The day after the *Playboy* party we ran into Bill & Ben the con men again and they looked a bit pissed off. They asked me what had happened to the half dozen blokes I was supposed to supply for the stunt. 'What happened to them?' I said. 'Same as your fucking photographers.' Then to show there was no hard feelings I tipped them off about this hot, American Pamela Anderson lookalike that we'd met who needed promoting.

I gave them her number and told them to just ask for Jackie O'Nasty.

25. 'FUUPIIFINNGLY-*FRRUUFFF!!*'

Stay 'Firm' and don't give a fuck. We come home . . .

The journey back to Britain was always going to be interesting 'cos I knew we had some serious police-dodging to do. I knew that they'd know I'd been out the country, and I knew they'd want to pull me when I got back in. One of the funny things on the the way out to Cannes was how we'd totally bombarded the Cross Channel Ferry with flyers for *Hell To Pay*. We plastered them everywhere.

Our coach was a few miles behind with everyone on it, but me, Brendan and another geezer were in a van carrying my complete wardrobe for the trip, loads and loads of suits, and piles of books, posters and PR stuff: oh, and the guns in a big bag. I know the Old Bill and Customs will be waiting to try and pull me in and anyone with me to create absolute maximum inconvenience. That's what it was. They must already know I'm not divvy enough to try bringing anything in when I'm under surveillance so the only reason for stopping me is to try and fuck me off.

I was half preparing myself for it but was also on the lookout for a way round it. Before we got there I got a bit of luck by the fact that near the port these people from Margate spotted me and came over to say how much they'd all liked *Stop the Ride* . . . One of them had bought it first and then passed it round. I said thank you very much but could they all buy one *each* next time, the cheap bastards! and I told them they'd enjoy the next one even more 'cos it was gonna be a colouring book (I mean doing a dot-to-dot book would be just silly).

Anyway, I let them in on the situation we were in and they said they were more than happy for me to ride through Customs with them. Ha *ha*. Result! Take me to my people. The pen *is* mightier than the sword. And God bless *Stop the Ride* . . .

So I was sat there in a big fuck-off Shogun with smoked windows and Brendan's in the van with the driver, waiting in another queue. The Customs officials were getting nearer and the van driver said to Bren that he didn't want to get involved in it all so Brendan said that was alright and took over the driving duties. Then the driver went, 'Er . . . so how will we handle this?' Brendan said, 'Quite simple really – you don't say a word, mate. I'll handle it.'

The Customs geezer asked Brendan what was in the back of the van:

'Oh a couple of shotguns, a few machine guns, two automatics, fifteen suits, three wank mags, a chocolate éclair and a hand grenade.'

' . . . Sorry, sir?'

'You've just asked me what's in the back and that's what's in there.'

'Get out please. We're going to have to search it.'

Suddenly, when he got out the van, a dozen armed security guards appeared. Well he obviously didn't like the sound of that chocolate éclair, did he? Probably contravened some European hygiene law on taking fresh cream products across the border . . . with a hand grenade. Just a guess. Remember, you should always store food and weaponry on *different* shelves in your fridge.

So they throw the back doors open and the van really is full of all this stuff – all the weaponry for the photo shoots, and my suits and all the promotional gear, and loads of complimentary *Playboy* magazines. Now they don't really give a toss about that 'cos they're actually after me and they can't quite believe I'm not there. They started pulling up the carpet and emptying boxes, asking Brendan if he was absolutely sure there was no one else with him. Brendan said, 'Yeah, positive. I've even checked the ashtrays and everything.' (And Brendan does a really good 'pretend innocence' as well; he just comes out with all this *shit* but keeps a straight face.)

The Customs officials were pissed off now. There's another van full of about a dozen Old Bill sat behind in the queue just watching, casually pretending this is nothing to do with them; and they're just waiting to pounce but they can't 'cos I ain't turned up. I'm sailing by over the other side in the Shogun, with the respectable-looking Margate people. Brendan knows the police are fucked so he starts getting a bit cocky, waving at them. Actually there *was* a bag there with some food we'd got for the journey, most of it had been scoffed but there was – as it happens – a manky looking chocolate éclair left over!

Brendan dived in the bag and went, 'You don't mind if I finish this off, mate? I'd share it but I'm a greedy cunt.' The Customs bloke hesitated . . . and you could see that for a split-second he was seeing headlines like EVIDENCE CONCEALED IN CHOCOLATE ÉCLAIR! (I mean, they're trained to think like that, aren't they? That a nun's tampons might really be disguised joints.) But in that split-second Brendan crammed it all in in one go. Then he said something. Or tried to. What he tried to say was: 'Mmmm! Surprisingly fresh!' But, afterwards, he told me it just sounded like, 'Mmmm! Fuupiifinngly-*frruufff*!!'

I was watching from the Shogun so I couldn't *hear* it, but I could see the mouthful of pastry and cream spray that came flying out with '*frruuff*!!' Fucking funny. I was absolutely wetting myself. The people with me were loving it as well 'cos they'd never been involved in anything like this before and they felt like they were smuggling me through. They'd gone off for the weekend on a usual shopping trip and come back as the International Gang for Smuggling Authors. (And as a little thank you to those people here they are in the book. Cheers.)

So we all got back home to England in one piece, just about, with everyone pretty well chuffed that our own little homemade, no budget, no frills, raw, blood and guts gangster movie had been over there in Cannes batting with the big hitters. And . . . Made In England. Everybody made an effort, either in making the film, helping out making the film, promoting it, financing it, coming out to Cannes . . . y'know, just everything. I'd like to thank every single person involved. Ian Tucker just picked up his family, Debs and the little girl, and drove out to Cannes to visit us for *one* hour. Is that a pal or what? Thanks very much.

I was still buzzing when I hit Plumstead. I used the speed bumps as launching pads and banged everybody's heads about twenty times on the roof of the Rolls. It now looks like a car with mumps. So, despite all the non-stop partying and the driving and the not-sleeping, the sheer buzz I got off the whole trip – and the thought of seeing my Jen, of course – put an even *bigger* spring in the old Courtney step than usual. I could've entered the fucking triple jump and got a gold.

Yeah, you could say I came home surprisingly fresh.

And just in time for the launch of *The Firm*.

In *Raving Lunacy* there's a really wicked photo that's probably one of the best photos that I've been a part of. It shows me and thirty of the boys all suited and booted and lined up across a bridge in Tenerife. It's the absolute nuts and it made a wicked poster (I know Scotland Yard appreciated their copy). Anyway, that photo was taken by Jocelyn Bain Hogg, who was a geezer who'd been almost living with me for eighteen months, putting this book *The Firm* together, about me and the people who walked through my door. For the first six months we thought he was Old Bill! The only pictures he got were back of head shots. No, actually he'd been travelling with me and mine for over a year taking these pictures, and taking pictures of all the chaps in London too. And even though our world's a million miles away from his, Jocelyn fit in really well . . . for a posh, six-foot clumsy bastard!

Jocelyn's photos were all collected together in a book called *The Firm* (by Westzone Publishing). It's a big black fuck-off paving slab of a book with a gold knuckleduster on the cover. I nearly came when I saw it. It just looked so fucking *naughty*. It looked like it'd beat up every other book in the bookshop, nick the day's takings out the till and run off with the best-looking shop assistant. It is the absolute bollocks, mate, believe me. Beg, steal or borrow a copy. Or, as a last resort, *buy* one. There's an introduction by Bruce Reynolds and interviews with me, Joey Pyle, Seymour, Welsh Bernie and Mickey Goldtooth. In my interview bit it was the first chance I'd had in print to set the record straight on the whole bent copper saga. Seymour told the tale of Tenerife. The publisher went bust afterwards and – listen to this – the unsold copies were bought up at auction by an unknown buyer. Coincidence?

The book looks like a proper orgy of naughtiness; there's pictures from Reg Kray's funeral in the East End to us lot out in Tenerife, and everything in between. Inside there's more hard nuts than on a coconut farm, more shaved heads than a Buddhist monastery, more gold than Beaverbrooks, more chaps than a cowboy convention, more tits and arse than is strictly necessary (but no more than we need!) and, to top it all off, a picture of me with bells on – stood on the court steps just after I'd knocked the bent copper out. What *more* could you ask? What do you want – a pop-up version!

More than just being a book about villainy, it's actually about people who know how to enjoy life and wring every last drop out of it. When you look at the pictures, as well as thinking, 'He's a handy looking bastard' or 'What the fuck are they feeding *him* on!' you also think these people are just having one fucking good time with life. Erm . . . apart, of course, from Reg Kray (but the pub buffet was wicked).

Borders bookshop held a launch for *The Firm* – the book weren't published it was just let out on bail – and they also got a panel of people in the shop to have a debate about glamorising crime. Bit of a non-starter that debate though, 'cos I walked in with the model Jo Guest in a skirt no bigger than a belt buckle, Andy Beckwith from *Snatch*, ex-world champ boxer John Conteh, Seymour, Ian 'The Machine' Freeman, big Wish and clubland Lou; and all of us still in full gangster attire from doing some publicity for *Hell To Pay*. So I'm supposed to walk in like that – in a silver suit, by the way – unpeel the model from my arm and go, 'No . . . crime does *not* pay and it ain't glamorous!'? *Stop* it! How the fuck could I?

What I did do was jump up on stage, grab the mic and say, 'Well, ladies and gentlemen, the whizz has just kicked in . . . anyone fancy having a chat?' That went down like concrete kipper so I burst into song with my rendition of the Kylie Minogue classic *I Should Be So Lucky*. Ha, just to see the looks on the faces of everyone else on the panel made it all worthwhile. It was fucking funny, mate. It got better when questions from the crowd started. I was thinking of such good answers (*I* thought) that I not only answered mine but everybody else's questions as well. I was spewing out bullshit at a thousand miles a minute, but it seemed like sense at the time, like it does. It ended on a high note, though, when I combined two questions, one about lap dancers and one about female traffic wardens and came up with the answer to why men prefer pussys to dogs.

Then we all went on for a drink in Soho, got even more out of it and shifted into turbo. By 4 a.m. I fancied a jog home but everyone else wanted a cab. In the taxi I made even the cab driver look like a mute – not easy with a London cabbie – but I knew that after all this time if I stopped talking all of a sudden the whiplash would fucking kill me! Just the *shock*. I think at one point I smashed my feet through the cab floor and did a Fred Flintstone manoeuvre with the car – I fucking *ran* it home. By that time I was about in the same condition as that fucking chocolate éclair so I quietly slipped into a semi-coma (I was gonna go for the full coma but I was too tired) and had a little catnap . . . for three days.

Never again. At least not until the next time.

Which reminds me of when we were late for this book signing up in Liverpool 'cos we got stuck in traffic on the fucking M6 – it was a logjam of car thieves and joyriders leaving Liverpool! So the bookshop lady rang us up saying there was already two hundred people there waiting for me. I said send someone out to buy twenty boxes of teabags, babe, put the kettle on for everyone and we'll be there soon.

Now, we were in my mate Leon's Merc and a proper fucking tool of a car it is too, but a tool of a car ain't worth nothing without a weapon at the wheel . . . so I took over driving duties and immediately swerved us onto the hard shoulder and floored the cunt. Strange, it was almost as if I'd done this before . . . oh, yeah I have. Anyway, 120 mph down a hard shoulder covered in stones and bits of tyre rubber and debris and fuck knows what other shit off the motorway did nothing for Leon's confidence in my driving abilities. Matters might not have been helped by the fact I was wearing a World War One leather flying helmet – Chubby Brown style – and shouting, '*Damn you, Red Baron!*' Brendan was on Old Bill lookout duty and as soon as we spotted some we dived back into a lane until we could dive back out again. Easy when you know how. And easier if you don't really give a fuck.

Sometimes all you've got to give is not give a fuck.

Especially when you find yourself in the odd position of trying to do it honest and legal, like I was with the films and media stuff, and *still* finding that the police are getting the hump with you. But they're more right than they think 'cos if I was a policeman I'd worry about what Dave Courtney's doing with the media: so they think 'Right we'd better start pulling some strings'.

They can't get to everyone *but* like I know all the main players in all the main cities and they themselves get down to everyone, so the police play it the same way with the people they can call on in other walks of life – politicians, newspaper owners, magazine editors, TV company bosses. They don't ring every journalist 'cos they don't have to, they ring the editors instead.

I know what's been said to the editor of *Front* magazine about me 'cos I write for them and the editor is a friend of mine, and a ballsy little fucker he is as well, because right from the start he got stick for employing me. If I ever get blocked out at *Front* it will only be because it's come from above. I usually hear it straight from the people that have been called and warned off. So when I was trying to line up distribution for *Hell To Pay* and there were people who were happy about it and then, all of a sudden, they're backing out . . . y'know, forgive me for being fucking suspicious. And also a bit dubious about everyone else, 'cos when you sign a contract over to someone to distribute a film they then also have the rights *not* to sell your film. I've seen it done with boxers. I know people that have done it with boxers – they buy a certain boxer and put him in a certain stable and then deliberately not give him fights so he don't end up clashing with another boxer that they're grooming for the top. People mistakenly think that money and power just gets you things done – but it also gets you things *not* done as well.

Eradicate your opponent through silencing him. The best generals are the ones who completely fuck up the prospect of their enemy even fighting in the first place.

One example: a little while back the *Sunday Express* ran a full page piece with the headline 'Fury As Crooks Are Turned Into Heroes', and it was topped off with a photograph of me and one of Ronnie Biggs. It said, '*Those in the war against organised crime have nothing but contempt for the way killers are portrayed on screen*' and '*The head of the fight against organised crime has stepped in to try to stem the rise of the new crop of gangster movies, which he believes have helped fuel a rise in violent underworld enforcement*'. By that they mean a geezer called John Abbot. '*Abbott, Director General of the National Criminal Intelligence Service, has long been a fierce critic of the film industry's gangster chic. He has attacked the film* Lock, stock and Two Smoking Barrels.' And then it went on, '*Reformed gangster Dave Courtney has written several books lifting the lid on his escapades. His latest venture is working alongside cult film director Quentin Tarantino.*'

Now they happen to be talking about films there, but you know they apply the same attitude to books, or magazines or CDs or any media that they want to control. I mean look at that for a second – that's the Director General of the National Criminal Intelligence Service who has supposedly 'stepped in to try to stem the rise'. The rise of what? We're talking about people writing books and making films. That's called something very simple – *free speech*. But in their eyes it ain't free speech it's 'a rise' and they have to 'stem' it. They're not even hidden about it, they're blatantly, openly saying 'We won't stand for this – we want this stopped!'

So on that side of the battle you've got the government, you've got the highest-ranking members of the Metropolitan Police Force, you've got judges, you've got newspaper owners and newspaper editors from the *Daily Mail*, the *Express*, the *Telegraph*, *The Times* etc., you've got Conservative MPs, and you've got all the favours they can pull and the old school pals they can call – and all that mob are throwing their weight behind trying to stop people like me writing and speaking and making films. And, funnily enough, trying to stop us earning what they would call an honest living.

Then on *my* side you've got the owner of some local radio station, or the editors of magazines that are frightened for their jobs, or pub and club owners that don't want to lose their licence, or filmmakers who don't want to lose publicity for their film, or writers that have no power over their editors, etc., etc. – all the people who want to let people have their say but they just ain't got the power to resist the other mob. People that it's easy to bully into not using Dave Courtney, or anyone else they think doesn't live they way they say we should.

And that *Sunday Express* article is just one of many.

One of the ways they use of putting a lid on my activities is to target the people that want to put on my 'Audience With Dave Courtney' shows. They get singled out for a visit from the local boys in blue to get asked if they are really sure it's such a good idea booking Dave Courtney, and do they really know what I am. Course they fucking know what I am, that's why they want me at their gaff pulling in punters, making them all laugh and then helping the bar bill to go through the roof. Pub owners in London that I know have had their licences threatened for advertising me doing a show there.

Think about this: it cost a hundred grand and fuck knows how much time and effort to get Ronnie Biggs to come back to Britain – but the authorities thought it was worth it. Not because they really gave a toss about him serving out his sentence, but because of the way they knew it would switch off a million lights. Meaning, Ronnie Biggs is the one who did it, who really did the classic Great Escape to the sun, took his dosh, stuck two fingers up to the police, and sent a postcard saying 'Fuck You' from Brazil.

Proper movie style stuff, but for real. That's like a beacon light for men who dream of doing the same. So, they brought him back to snuff out all those lights at the ends of all those tunnels for all those prisoners. And to finally kill off the great myth that you can ever get away with it or that you can ever beat them. Even after thirty years.

Me? I'm saying 'Fuck You' from Plumstead.

Ten miles from Scotland Yard.

26. A DIFFERENT WICKED

You've got to watch yourself 'cos if you don't there's always someone else who'll do it for you . . .

Everybody's got a gift. James Dean, for instance, great actor. Fucking terrible driver, but great actor. Michael Jackson: good pop star, bad babysitter. God gives everybody a gift, and whatever it is I don't know 'cos it's different for everyone, but I know I was lucky enough to be given the ability to tell a story well, and to tell it funny. And in saying you can make people laugh also means you're not shy, and those two together means that if you choose you can put yourself forward as the life and soul. That's actually a kind of position of power that most people wouldn't know how to use if they had it. But they haven't; I have.

What this has done for me, and I thank God for it, is that because of the way I can talk and what I can actually make someone say, it's given me the ammo to be a fucking good judge of character. How that's come about is this. If you can get on with people and tell a funny story or two and make people laugh then they relax, and then they don't mind telling you their stories. People reveal things during the moments when they least expect, 'cos they're off guard. What I've learned to do is see what a man will do in *one* situation and read him from that. And from his reaction in only a few situations I can completely read the man. His story might've seemed not that important but in it you can see the character of a man's personality and then project, well, if he'd do that in *that* situation then you can be sure he'd react *this* way in *this* situation. It's all there to see, plain as fucking day, if you know how to look.

As I've said to you before but I'll say it again, life is formed by habits. Very early on in my life – and much earlier than others usually get into it – I got into the habit of looking at and watching and reading people and remembering. And fuck me if that asset hasn't been the one weapon that's stood me in good stead; even more than the knuckleduster, and that's saying something!

So, 'cos I'm the sort of person who would work out a character like that I would very, very quickly get to know what his thoughts were but never put the man in the position where his thoughts might affect me badly. I'd have the geezer around me for what his abilities were. I ain't gonna go to someone, 'Fuck off you're a wanker' 'cos like I say everyone has some gift. What I have to do is fit that person in to do whatever he does best.

It also helps me spot what friends are friends and what 'friends' are enemies. And, because what you give to someone else you take from yourself, that old saying comes into play: 'I've taught you all *you* know but not all what *I* know'. I am 100 per cent sure the establishment is terrified of the truth.

Then when you can read people you can place them and get the best out of them. Long-term I can, and have, done that. The most obvious example being the copper, old Austin Warnes himself. I made sure that me and my mates got the best out of that bad apple while the getting was good. That's learning from the police's own tactics and using it to manipulate the police. Where it can get a bit dodgy is when people on your own side who are bit too simple in the head to see the beauty of the ruse, get hold of the wrong end of the stick. Then you have to deal with that shit.

The element of doubt is very important. Your missus can be 90 per cent sure you're having an affair but she'll cling to that other ten. Human nature, and it's one you can play on. The Old Bill play on it when they get caught out being bad, just like anyone else would. You have to *not* forget they're only human and I know it ain't easy sometimes.

This is how I analyse someone: first I'll make an impression of someone and then, knowing that you rarely catch someone out for sure, I'll go on the balance of the odds. Or what I call, in my head, the Scales Theory.

Now it has actually been seen that I treat everyone in exactly the same way, everyone; whatever you are, whatever your job is, whether you're black, white, blue, green, fat or skinny or bits of all those rolled together (Christ, sounds like my first parole officer!). Kids, old people, people in authority, bin men, judges, whatever, I meet them all and treat them all equal. And 'cos I do that what happens is this – because *I'm* the same all the time, it allows me to see people as they are, and what their disguises are. I don't confuse things by being different with different people, like a lot of people do.

So, even if I have some thoughts about someone and what they might or might not be, I will now imagine in my head a set of scales; and from that day on I will put on one side of the scales everything that that person does that *confirms* what I think they are, and on the other side I'll put the things that might prove me wrong. And 'cos I don't show I'm doing this and they don't know, they carry on being themselves until I know one way or the other. Because in life you can't always find the exact thing to prove something, so you have to go by elements of doubt and a collection of little bits of proof. Then when there's too many weights on one side . . . you will know.

And how many coincidences does it take to be too many coincidences? The same as the Scales of Justice used by British law. If the situations are not there that might show someone's true colours then you make up the situations yourself, and put the geezer in a scene you've created to see how he reacts. It's easily done. Bit like directing a film, and I've done that. Except one person don't know it's not for real. You throw them a task and then read their reaction.

Sometimes they just happen. Like when the geezer crashed my Rolls Royce outside my house and then ran inside and fell on the floor crying in front of me. That collapse showed me exactly what he would be like in a police station under questioning. Jelly.

And there is a definite set pattern to how people behave. You can work out whole personalities and box people off with it. Then you never ask too much of the wrong person and put them in a position when they might end up being a liability to you (like the Rolls Royce crasher ain't no car thief – fucking hell, he ain't even a pencil sharpener!) That's one use of the scales – for placing people. The other use is in spotting your enemies.

Because I've used the element of doubt theory throughout my life to get out of trouble when I needed to I realise it works 100 per cent and there must also be other people that are good at it. The police use it! There's always an element of doubt in what they do – like planting the evidence, or making the 'anonymous' call – so they can't get in trouble if it all backfires.

If you get good at spotting the truth you also get good at spotting disguises, seeing the line that runs down someone where the disguise begins. People that are a certain way try to do certain things to hide it and I've learned the props that they need, the dress, the look, the laugh, the choice of company and places to go. Then when I see that I start my weight process, my scales theory and . . . often I don't *mean* to, you know what I mean, but it's a habit of mine and one that I'm glad I've got.

And I've done this for years and years and years, mate – this watching and waiting – so I'm *fuck*ing good at it. And I've sometimes waited years before I've decided on someone because that's how long it's taken for the truth to come out. It might not get to the right amount of weights on one side for five/ten years. But it will get there.

That's the difficult thing for most people who try this – the waiting. Most people can't be fucked with waiting and rush in before they know. Which is *exactly* what the police hoped people would do with me during that whole trial and the accusations that were flying around before. But time always tells, and it has: and by the time this book is out I'll be even more vindicated than ever.

Listen, I'm *always* fucking right about me – it's only ever other people who are wrong about me. It's true though, innit? You are always right about yourself.

Weigh it all up and put the stuff that proves your point on one side of the scales, and stuff that don't prove it on the other. The longer you watch and wait the more accurate it is. Do it over a week and you can't really bank on it. But when you've done it for *years* you learn to trust time. Years don't lie, know what I mean? They do *not* give a false reading. Patience. Slowly, slowly, catchy monkey.

I was using coppers that had gone bent to get advantages for me and mine, BUT that still meant the much bigger numbers of straight coppers were still against us and after us and wanting to nick us.

There was another geezer, though, who had *properly* turned over to the law's side. One foot of his was slap-bang in their camp, and one in ours. I knew it but couldn't prove it; but the scales proved it. And cunts like that are in very, very strong positions – 'cos it means you get full-on protection from the police, like their own Get Out Of Jail Free card, because the police want to keep them as their information giver. Which is all the proof, if any more proof is needed, that the charges they trumped up against me were just so fucking obviously fake. Because the *first* thing the police do with their *genuine* informers and plants is keep them active by *protecting* them. Not take them to fucking court! That kinda blows it, don't you think, and shows it up for what it was.

Okay. The police, if they have prior knowledge that they're gonna arrest you, will say to themselves 'If we arrest him now what could he say to get himself out of it?' Then they shut all them angles, even if it means them putting off giving you a tug for two years. And if they're gonna do something naughty to try and get you then they put the excuse in first for it, wait a while . . . and *then* do it. Like if they wanted to plant a bug in my gaff they'll do the old pretend tip-off call to themselves from a phone box down the road from the station saying 'Courtney's got a gun in the house.' That gives them legitimate reason to raid my house, handcuff me and keep me in one room, 'search' the place, plant the device, admire my butterfly collection, and then fuck off back to the station, job well done.

Fuck the idea that the tapes will be inadmissible 'cos they didn't have a warrant for surveillance, because they don't give a toss about taking the tape to court. They just listen in for three, six, nine months until they've got enough to *ambush* you! As policemen their job is to sit there and listen to geezers coming up with a million different ways of getting off with things, so they can't help but learn what works, what doesn't, and how to get away with things themselves. That's what their thing is, and that's what this double-agent's geezer's thing is. Both pissing in the same pot.

Jesus knew who his Judas was, and I know who mine is. But even Judas had his part to play in the scheme of things. I have an awful lot of people who jump to my defence, people known to me and some I don't even know. I'm lucky in that I put that down to me developing another habit over the years of dealing with people in a certain way, a right way, even down to the little people. We've got people who'd ring up and tell us who was a policeman and who ain't and their details. The details would be got from the coppers' own cards – 'cos policemen get money-off discount from certain places when they show their card. (Bit like when I go to confession and flash my duster and the priest always gives me less Hail Marys.)

So I do get tip-offs from people trying to balance out some of the dirtier police tactics: civilian workers in police stations, for example, like cleaning ladies (fuck me, you would not believe what cleaning ladies get to see and hear), or other uniformed workers that have police contact, and even some senior officers themselves, of course. Then there's the traffic warden birds I mentioned before. Even coppers' ex-birds and old ladies. Now that is a very, very deep well of dirty knowledge that those ladies have. Which is why we're now doing a book by women who've been in policemen's lives, 'cos those are the ones that really do get to hear the true shit. And how enthusiastic will the police feel about that one?

But after years and years and years of people-reading and using the ability, thank God, of being able to do that, I can see the reason for a man and see what's in him. What that means, though, is that the *genuinely* bad men, and the ones who are clever enough to see that they can be seen through, they don't want men like me around.

This 'gift' thing, y'know, some people have got it in reverse. They've got it arse-backwards – they've just got a talent for nastiness. I know a lot of really, really wicked people, as in good 'wicked'. I've known and still know the other kind of wicked as well.

Speaking of which, I was watching a documentary the other day about that geezer that got shot in bed by the police last year. An unarmed, completely naked fella at home in bed, when the police burst in and shot him to death. It's only just come out because they put reporting restrictions on it. Wonder why?

What people don't understand is that the police are like governments, they think long-term, they decide where they want you and what manipulation they're gonna have to do to get you there. So they do the old 'make the excuse first' routine, meaning: if you want to get away with a situation which you know is gonna happen in the future what you do is this – you first deliberately cause the situation to happen *now*. Right now. Then you cope with the shit that comes from it by making a law that leaves you free to carry on doing it in the future. I mean even the police need a reason to run into your house and shoot you point-blank in the head – in bed – in front of your missus – painting *her* tits with *your* brains. But how would they get away with that? Okay, what if this happens – they choose someone likely for a raid, do it, shoot him, sit back and wait. Next, the copper who killed the guy in bed goes on full paid holiday leave. Touch. Then a judge sits down to decide if it was okay to shoot the geezer. They put a reporting ban on the case and a gagging order on the wife for reasons of 'security'. The judge decides it was all okay – surprise, surprise – because of 'evidence' from the police that they felt their lives were in danger (like the guy might've started a fatal *pillow* fight with them), and that's one nil to the provisional wing of the Metropolitan Police.

And all forces do have their extremist elements. Like the army have the SAS and the Paras, and they bring them in to wipe people out, like we know they do – shoot first and ask questions afterwards. Or shoot first and worry about it being an unarmed twelve-year-old afterwards, like in the case of Bloody Sunday.

So if the Old Bill do enough of these 'shoot to kill and protect' cases it pretty soon gets to the stage where such a legal precedent has been set that they don't even go to court any more, it's just referred to the CPS or the police complaints authority, and they decide. Whoopee. We'll all sleep much safer in our beds now won't we? – y'know, in that bed you bought from 'Armoured Beds U Like'. The one with the Kevlon duvet.

They make the excuse, test the waters, deal with the result, make the law. Whether you want it or not. Now, I know *you* don't think that applies to you – and maybe something that extreme don't – but they use that same technique, the 'test the waters' technique, to slowly nick certain rights off you, one by one, year by year. And they do have the years, mate, they think about the effects twenty years down the line. Long-term thinking.

Don't be in any doubt, *any* doubt whatsoever that this National Identity Card idea will eventually come through. They can already track you from one end of the country to the other anyway, because they've done that same little by little/year by year introduction of one surveillance technique after another. Till we've got to this stage, and now it's too late for everyone to go, 'Wait, hang on a minute! Where's this gonna end?' It ends up in the future with you farting in bed one night and thirty seconds later there's a computer surveillance record of what flavour it was – *'Chicken vindaloo, lager, tobacco and traces of cocaine: Cocaine is against Illegal Substances Act (authorise house search warrant); Alcohol reading indicates more than legal driving limit (check subjects in-car CCTV records for evening)'*. Slight exaggeration maybe but somebody's gonna live to see it!

Anyway, so now you know to be suspicious if I get shot in mysterious circumstances. Like coming out of the baker's with a French breadstick – 'I thought it was shotgun, Sarge, honest! I feared for my life.' Which is why I only ever carry de-activated and imitation French breadsticks! You know it makes sense. (Actually that ain't even a joke any more – last year a geezer was shot dead by police marksmen after he was reported having a gun in the street. When they searched his body it turned out he was carrying a chair leg in a plastic bag.)

The reason I'm now winning this battle is 'cos over the years I've learned the importance of choosing the right weapons, and this full-on war I was in with the police couldn't be won with the usual duster, sawn-off or 76 hardnuts. I was using the courts, using the law, using statistics, using the press. And they have no defence. It's like when an attacking football team gets attacked themselves they're fucked 'cos they've got no defence. And the police are all forwards and strikers; they are the aggressors – they arrest you, trick you, bug you, plant things on you, lie about you, take you to court and prison – and they haven't had to put the brakes on and go into reverse in a long time: and if you don't do something often then you are no longer good at it. They haven't had much experience of someone turning round to them and try putting them in prison and saying prove this and prove that.

Even at the expense of upsetting a few people I'll acknowledge the false informants scam con, and I won't be too embarrassed to say that I was involved in that little coup 'cos it helped a lot of people out and got us into coppers we could use.

Somewhere along the line everyone usually stops and thinks, hang on, you can't really piss the police off too much 'cos they'll fucking crucify you. Well, that don't apply to me 'cos they've already tried that by dragging me through court for fuck all, in the hope that some of their shit would stick, and in the hope I'd get fucking shot. So what the fuck have I got to be worried about them liking me or giving me a rough time? *Fuck* them. I've got a loaded microphone and I know how to use it!

So when they are nasty and spiteful and dishonest and try to cover it up with the old 'closing ranks' technique, I can make it very public what they do to people and what they tried to do to me.

Imagine the satisfaction I got when I tried to nick them, when I decided to charge *them*! And then just to be extra, mega-fucking cheeky I offered them a deal! If they go guilty on the charge of maliciously prosecuting me with the intention of doing me harm, then I would drop the attempted murder charge. Fair play. I'm not an unreasonable man, just a fucking pissed off one.

And you know what . . . they didn't even send me a Valentine's card! They love me so much it hurts. But they actually want it to hurt *me*. Sorry, boys.

27. LOCK, STOCK AND TWO SMOKY BACON, PLEASE

Shark fishing, sperm banking, fetish partying, Djing, wheel clamping, Mike Tyson talking, Trisha baiting and doing crime big in Italy.

Okay so I didn't succeed when I applied to enter for Lord Major of London a while back, but only because they screwed me on the admissions policy. As you well know. They found some old hidden-away clause saying you couldn't be Lord Major if you were a good dancer! Well that was me fucked. Ain't you seen me break dance? Yeah, the number of dance floors I've *broken*. When I was younger, though, in the kind of places I used to go you couldn't get through a single night without some dancing breaking out on the fight floor. There's always some that's got to spoil it for the others. And back then you had to have a girl home by eleven – no, *on the same day*, you cheeky monkeys. That's right, home by eleven; so the last shag had to be at about ten to.

The whole Lord Major campaign did have its bonuses, though. For instance, round about that time I had to go up and visit a friend of Charlie Bronson's. She was coming out of Derby prison and I went up there with Lee in this Rover.

On the way back home, not far out of London, the car fucking blew up. We were going 120 mph at the time but we did have a following wind. Luckily we were near an off-ramp (or 'pissed off-ramps' as they're known if you have to come off early). We ended up steering the car – which was smoking like an old boiler (Gladys I think her name was) – off the motorway and trundled it into the nearest petrol station. It was banging like a clown's car. I half expected the doors to drop off.

Bit more luck, there was actually a garage workshop next to this petrol station. *Touch.* Trouble was we didn't have a brass farthing on us, not a fucking penny, mate. I said to Lee watch this. We freewheeled it up to the garage and I got out with armfuls of these flyers, posters, photos and advertisements about me running for Lord Mayor of London that I took everywhere; and I started chatting to the geezer who ran the place. I gave him loads of the stuff (whether he wanted it or not!) and signed a copy of 'Stop the Ride . . .' for him, which he most definitely did want.

He looked over the car and it didn't look good. It wouldn't have looked good to Stevie Wonder. You could smell how fucked it was. So I asked the fella what he had for sale and he said nothing 'cos they were all repairs, and all he did have was his own car. I told him I'd give him a couple of hundred quid more than the grand his car was worth and he could drop the Rover back down to me next time he was in London. He said okay.

So we loaded everything out of ours and into the new car and went to the office to get the documents. The bloke said that'll be a thousand pounds then. I said well I obviously haven't got a thousand pounds *on me*, but when you bring my car back I'll pay you then. And I can't exactly run away 'cos I'm running for Lord Major and you know who I am! So is that okay? And he went . . . er . . . yeah. Double touch.

We drove down the road me and Lee just wetting ourselves. Even I didn't think it would work. On the way back we were still laughing so much that we didn't notice, when we were coming up to this roundabout, that this little old Morris Minor, which looked like it was gonna shoot out, suddenly thought twice and braked hard. Well we smacked this little Morris up the arse *so* hard that it went flying straight across the roundabout flowerbeds and the two back wings just flew off . . . like a *proper* clown's car this time! The people were okay but the car was on the top of the critical list and not allowed visitors.

The geezer we'd left the Rover with never called, but then he probably realised it was worth more in spares than the cheapie that he'd given us. More so because the car he'd given us ended up with a Morris Minor's rear bumper jammed in its grill.

I've started doing live interviews and Q&A sessions on the Internet with members of the public. It's wicked. One of the things I was asked was:

Question – 'Does crime pay?'

My answer – '**You'd better ask the geezer who services my Rolls Royce 'cos I wouldn't know about that.**'

And the geezer who does service my motors is a fella called Jimmy at Tills Motors in Charlton. Go there, he's blinding. Jimmy and his son have kept me on the road for a very, very long time. He don't charge me after my recommendations have sent people there and he's now got probably the scariest-looking clientele list in South London: the Jobs Board looks like a list of a *Crimewatch* Top Ten. Anyway, one time Jimmy was doing some work on this geezer's car and it ended up coming to more than the this geezer thought it would, about two grand two hundred quid. So the fella went beserk, said he weren't gonna pay and started threatening Jimmy. Now Jimmy's only a little fella, lovely bloke, works there with his wife and son 'cos it's a proper little family firm.

Someone in the garage rang me up while all this was going on. I only live nearby so I got up there. That's exactly what I am all about, actually, helping out the little people (and I don't mean short!) if I've got the chance to do so. I really can't help that bit of me that wants to do the old Robin Hood bit. I do get off on that.

So I shot up there to Tills and this fella was just threatening Jim with *me* when I walked in the door. (Number of times that happens, people I don't even know using my name. Fucking annoying when it's the Inland Revenue!) So I set about the bloke and gave him a fucking good hiding, and while he was still half out I took most of the money for the bill out his pocket, 'cos he happened to be carrying a wad. Then we lifted him into his car, put my telephone number on a piece of paper on his steering wheel and told him he still owed six hundred quid. It got paid. I think he must've thought I'd gone through his pockets and got ID of who he was and where he lived but I didn't. If I'd thought of it I would've done! However, he thought I had, so same difference.

One of the funniest things I've ever seen was with Jimmy. Jimmy and his family went shark fishing with me off the Maldives. I was out there with my mates Gary Ditton and Ray – Ray don't do fishing, he just jumps in the sea and nuts the fuckers unconscious – and I'd just passed my diving course and was trying to get my instructor's course. Jimmy didn't want to do the diving so we went shark fishing. Now Jimmy's so small that they couldn't tighten the old harness up really tight, like it should be. But then no one likes the belt on too tight, do they – like when you're on a plane you don't give a toss how tight the belt is 'cos you never think anything's gonna happen. And even if it did and you rammed into a fucking mountainside, what the fuck good is a seat belt going to do?

The geezer on the boat keeps stressing that you've got to hang on to the rod, got to hang on to the rod; there's even these little knuckleduster-type grips on the handle so you can actually put your hands in them. You've got to *hang on to the rod* but no fish is going to drag you out of your seat is it? Ask Jimmy.

First bite he got – and this cunt must've been *Jaws*' brother – yanked Jimmy and the rod straight out of the chair! We couldn't believe it. One second he's there, next second there's just his trainers: all eight stone of the geezer went flying out that chair and plopped into the water like a Tom and Jerry cartoon. Just *ripped* him through the harness. We looked into the sea where he'd gone under, thinking he'd come back up there . . . but he popped up fifty fucking feet away, still hanging on to the rod! Talk about obeying the instructions about not letting go. We all started yelling, 'LET GO OF THE ROD!' Everyone was screaming at him.

Anyway, when Jimmy reached Dover . . .

Talking about sharks, I've had my fair old run in with wheel clampers. The one during making *Hell To Pay* I've already told you about, I think that lot are still getting over it. In fact I heard they had a change of profession and set up a crèche! Then it happened when I was up in Manchester filming *Men & Motors*. The car got clamped outside the studio. Probably because it was parked in Ken Barlow's space off *Coronation Street*. No, tell a lie, we actually parked *on* Ken Barlow. Fucking hell, was he livid, some of them actors can get quite arsey when they want, can't they? Any road, we did have to pay to get this clamp off.

By the time the geezer came back to do it I'd decided to take a nap on the back seat and had fallen asleep. So this little Pakistani geezer from the clamping firm looked in and saw me, turned to Brendan and went: 'Is that that Mr Dave Courtney fella?' Brendan immediately saw an opportunity for a piss-take and he *took* it with both hands, as always:

'Oh yeah, that's that Mr Dave Courtney alright!'

'Can you . . . wake him up so I can . . . jack up the car?'

'Oh *no*. Oh dear, oh dear. Fucking hell, mate, I ain't waking him up. No way!'

'But you *must* wake him . . . please.'

'*You* tell him. There is no way I'm waking Mr Courtney, I can assure you!'

'I have been sent for the clamp though . . .'

I'm obviously awake during all this shit and just having a quiet laugh listening in. So the geezer started to jack up the car very, very slowly and ever so quietly. Brendan's going, 'Oh dear, I really wouldn't like to be you, mate, I can assure you.' Brendan and his fucking assurances. He's assured people of totally *shit* all over the world. And he's bloody good at it, let me tell you. It's almost an art form.

I don't know how long it took this fella to slowly jack the car up, but I nearly fell back asleep it was that long. You've got to make them earn their poxy seventy quid, that's if you give them it at all. Next time it happened was when I was at the bank making a deposit. It was a sperm bank, as it happens, and my deposit ended up in a test tube. I even took it there in a sack. Not the first time I've come in a bank, but this time the alarms weren't going off. Which was a novelty.

It was all part of an article I was doing for *Front* magazine. Everyone else had chickened out of doing the sperm bank story 'cos they didn't want to end up being called a wanker so I stepped in, hand on cock, and said I'd do it. For the men. What I didn't tell them was that I took along Jenny, who was just wearing a thong underneath her fur coat, to give me a helping hand. Well, a helping blowjob to be exact.

We came outside and, what do you know, the fucking clamping gremlins had come along and done us, clamped the Roller! There is something sadder about seeing a Roller clamped than a Fiesta. Bit like putting Nike trainers on the Queen. It don't fit. Now there was the geezer from the magazine taking pictures of everything and I thought what a cunt of a time for this to happen. So I rang the company and the bloke said, 'Oh yeah . . . er . . . you've got something on the back seat.' He was right.

I had a toy policeman's helmet, a duster and a gun from the film. The usual. He said, 'Who am I talking to?'

I said, 'You're talking to Dave Courtney, listen . . . (and at this point I'm thinking if this don't work and he says "fuck off" I'm gonna proper mug myself off in front of the cameras and everyone). I went, '. . . listen, I've been five years trying to make my wife pregnant and I've brought her down here to get it done and tried to make it as nice as possible, Roller, champagne, and now one of your dopey cunts has come and clamped me!

If I were you I'd quickly get down here and take it off.' Which they did. That's another one they lost.

But you can't win 'em all, as Frank Bruno used to say. Another one who hasn't won 'em all but come fucking well close is Mike Tyson. And even when he loses he still gets his dinner out of it. Ask Evander Holyfield down on the Ear, Nose and Throat ward. That's probably the only thing that me and Tyson had in common as boxers; when I knew I was getting beat I went for the deliberate disqualification as well. Corner stool round the back of the head usually worked. And the ref weren't usually out for long.

When Tyson was fighting over here I was invited up to the suite with Joey Pyle, Mark Morrison and Prince Naseem. There was Tyson's mascot there, that geezer called Crocodile who dresses in army gear and shouts a lot. I don't know how strong he was but the geezer fucking stank, he was very strong in that area. I've never seen hotel wallpaper curling at the edges before.

My impression of Mike Tyson was exactly what you'd expect it to be if you came face to face with the geezer – he just looks like this big mass of trouble squeezed into skin and waiting to burst out. He came over to shake hands, with no shirt on, and it was as if he'd put on armour, that's what it felt like, like his skin was pulled round his body like a balloon and it was *rock* hard. I thought that's the last time I feel *his* tits! Anyway, I weren't having all that so I thought it was about time I showed him my duster! That went down well, I don't think he'd seen a gold and diamond-encrusted one before. He sat there playing with it and we had a little chat. Difficult getting a smile out of the geezer, though, but the duster did seem to please him. Maybe it gave him some ideas about how he should handle his next fight – do the old Laurel and Hardy trick and put a horseshoe inside the glove.

Tyson was in London to fight Julias Francis. Julias's a mate of mine and has worked for me in the past so it was an odd night watching the fight. Now, I should imagine that even if you're in *perfect* health, fit as a fucking fiddle, right on top of your game and proper up for it, even then getting into the ring for Round 1 and just having to walk *towards* Mike Tyson must be fucking hard! Y'know what I mean? That alone would floor most people even before a punch had been launched. Just seeing that ear-chewing, flesh-ripping ball of muscle banging its gloves together is a natural laxative. Julias not only took him on but also – even after he got smacked in the mouth, got knocked down, and got back up (and by then he *knew* he was only half-cocked and that Tyson had tasted blood) – even after all that he still walked forward. That takes proper arsehole, mate: proper bollocks. And Julias must have a pair big enough to fill Pamela Anderson's tit hammock. Imagine – bad enough not to be able to hit *one* Tyson but to get up off the floor and see *four* of him – fucking hell – and still have a go! That puts Julias Francis in the 'hero worship' league for me. So I was more than proud when he was in my film *Hell To Pay*. Playing a transsexual Tupperware salesman.

Brendan got loads of shags out of the making of that film. He'd promised so many birds a part in the movie that I had enough extras to shoot a crowd scene in *Gladiator*! They'd turn up on set and say things like Brendan told me I could be in the film . . . am I late? I'd think yeah you are a bit late, babe, 'cos Brendan obviously did you last night. Brendan's casting couch needed re-upholstering twice.

Funny, though, how loads of Muslim geezers are top of the old violence league. Tyson, Naseem, even Ali. Whether it's with their hands or as world leaders, all the tasty cunts are Muslim. Any cunt that can punch you in the head five times in a second becomes Muslim. In fact I'm thinking of starting a Muslim fight club called 'Ramadan-a-Ding-Dongs'. Not sure if I'd let one park my car though; it might end up going through next door's front window.

That's the good thing about those Chinese rickshaw pedal taxi things, you can't really have a high-speed crash in one. They are funny, though. One night me, Brendan and Charlie Breaker came out of Sugar Reef and decided to hire one of these pedal taxis. Well Charlie Breaker on his own weighs four people so on a seat meant for three there was barely any room for me and Bren. We were practically sat on his knee like Bill and fucking Ben the Flower Pot Men. The skinny geezer who was supposed to pedal it couldn't even get the thing moving! He was just standing on the pedals, straining and going red in the face. So we put our feet down and helped push him off and, fair play to the little skinny fella, once he got it moving he really put his back into it. Shortly before he put his back *out* (we did visit him in hospital). At one point he took a wrong turning and when we went NO, it's *that* way! – you could see his face go *Oh fuck*! Charlie was shouting out careful for the speed cameras up there, mate.

Game little geezer though, so we had a whip-round and gave him a big tip (well, it is a long way from Sugar Reef to Plumstead).

Speaking of whip-rounds, when we were making *Hell To Pay* I happened to mention to someone that I wouldn't mind a fetish party scene in the film. 'No problem,' he said, 'I'll organise one next Sunday'. So we ended up in a big photographic studio in South London with thirty-odd people from the fetish scene. And they were what you might call 'hardcore'. They all looked as filthy as fuck but were all really, really nice. When the fellas talked to you it was all, 'Hello old chap, bloody good party what? Anyone for polo?' I tell you, all the respectable pillars of our society are bang into the old fetish scene. Yep, you've definitely got to watch out for those upstanding members. I don't know what the world's coming to. I don't care as long as it hurries up and comes.

At these sorts of parties you do see the kind of sights that would make your granny cough her teeth across the room. A bloke sat down next to me wearing a full adult-size baby's romper suit and sucking on a feeding bottle filled with Stella! And that was just the cloakroom attendant. Opposite us was a geezer wearing just cowboy chaps and a smile (and it reminded us to turn the heating up); next to him was a cracking looking bird in a rubber skirt and a veil stood next to a mature blonde bird in antique riding gear, a big fella (I think) wearing a red rubber gimp outfit with wobbly spines all over the head-mask, two birds dressed as Christmas tree fairies, a bloke in a Zorro mask and a geezer dressed like Spartacus carrying a bullwhip. Just a normal day at the office for them but it always tickles me to see it.

The theme of the evening was cops and robbers, which made it even funnier. I can't tell you the pleasure I get out of bullwhipping someone who's dressed as a police officer. I thought about the mates I'd got who were banged up inside and I laid into the old whipping lark a bit harder just for them. Take that, 'copper'! And the harder you do it, the more they like it – just like the real ones. Talk about bobbies on the beat. (The *Sunday Sport* ran a story on me when '*Stop the Ride* . . .' came out with the headline 'I've Seen Cops at Fetish Parties'. Mind you, I'm not suggesting that next time you see a copper you go up and smack him on the arse. At least ask first. The worst thing they could say is 'yes'!)

So, after we'd done the filming, and got enough in the can for the scene (listen to me, fucking hell, 'in the can'!), I thought what a shame to send home two dozen scantily dressed women who like being spanked . . . so, we didn't. We carried on into the night. Onwards and upwards – and that was just the dildos. The police truncheon was so in demand it came back with all the varnish rubbed off! And it's always a special moment at a party when you hear that first *spank* of the night, don't you think? Ask your Dad. Pretty soon there were whips and paddles cracking female arse all over the shop – it was like happy hour at an Arse Drummers' Convention.

All the submissive slaves were getting whipped and slapped into shape and even the geezer wrapped head-to-foot in Cellophane was having a good time. I must admit he did look as fresh as a daisy when they unwrapped him. A big blonde bird wearing a strap-on absolutely shit the life out of me, though, and I didn't even know if it was loaded! A sight like that would scare the crap out of any man. The best bit was when she squeezed this strap-on and the tip lit up! Fucking hell, I thought, that certainly tops ET's finger.

One thing about these fetish crowds, they're very 'creative' when it comes to everyday objects. For instance, the pistol with the silencer was a favourite with the female masturbation crowd. Not that a pistol with a silencer is an everyday object . . . you usually wouldn't have the silencer. But I've never seen people have so much fun with a spatula . . . not since my Jen bent over in the kitchen when I was flipping pancakes.

I spent the night learning how to use Spartacus' twelve-foot bullwhip. That is a proper tool, mate. In the right hands you could fillet somebody with that. In the wrong hands you'd just have your own eye out or, like in the Indiana Jones film, it'd just get you shot! Later, I was having a drink with my mates Piers, Paul and Bish when this bird asked me if I wanted to go with her for a minute. The short skirt, stockings and suspenders and whip swayed it for me. She asked me about the stocks and I told her that I didn't dabble in the shares market. But she pointed to the wooden stocks and asked me if I fancied a spank. I said, 'Don't mind if I do, darling . . .' and was preparing to tan her arse when she hit ME. And I nearly hit the roof! Piers pissed himself laughing, and I had to borrow her whip and take it out on a geezer down on all fours dressed as a copper pretending to be a coffee table.

See, once they'd all realised that I was game for a laugh and wasn't gonna kill anybody, the party had really took off and a good time was spanked by all. Every single person there was a really nice woman or fella, as they tend to be on the old fetish scene, and you quickly find that out – once you've got over the shock of what they're wearing and how far a police truncheon goes up their arse.

Not everyone is Dave-Courtney-friendly though, and I don't just mean the police. Jenny had got loads of calls from Trisha, the chat show lady, to do a show about sticking up for your man; and she said, 'And if you feel more comfortable bring Dave . . .' Knowing full well that I'd go.

Now the word on Trisha is that she will only have guests on the show that she thinks are below her abilities so she will always look superior in a battle of wits. But in doing that you will only stay stagnant and never meet anyone to learn from, which is what happened. She's a very influential lady and whether she's doing a silly little chat show or not, people listen to her. Jen always liked her and decided to go on, and I wanted to be there with my Jen as well.

On the day, on the way to the show, we realised we'd forgotten Jen's blue contact lenses so we rang the studio and got them to go out for a couple of pairs. When we got there we had Ricardo the cameraman with us, Brendan, Andy and Francesco from Italy. First off they refused to let us all in 'cos they said there was too many, and then they saw the camera and panicked about that. Ricardo said he wanted to film me coming into the studio but they said no cameras.

Something didn't seem right to me when we got there. For a start off there were loads of doormen. One of them said hello and then apologised for all the security being there. Now I didn't know how much security they usually had on the *Trisha* show, so until he said that I didn't know they were over-manned. That was because the show's people had planned on trying to rile me by bringing a real informant on to the show, and turn the audience against me so they brought in extra muscle in case I kicked off! But half the boys brought in for security were big fans of mine, so they all came up to say hello and just said you do what the fuck you want in that room Dave. Touch. We were one up already.

An example of how everyone on the show had been primed to guarantee a bad reaction was the fact that the make-up lady wouldn't have the dressing room door closed. She asked for the door to be left open as if we'd pounce on her and suck her bones dry! It was fucking mental. They were all genuinely frightened, because they knew I was there to be set up. Then after the staff had gone they locked me and Jen in the dressing room. Brendan and the others went to go sit in the audience but they were stopped and told to go. Then Bren heard that they were planning on bringing some informant on stage at the same time as us to try and rile me. So Brendan said that if they did that I would kick the living daylights out of him and anyone who tried to intervene. In order to get them to let him stay Brendan said he was the only one who could control me so he better stay in case it kicks off.

And this was all before the show had even begun. Fucking hell. It was a proper sneak attack.

As soon as Jen walked out on stage Trisha started attacking her and me. But my Jen is very, very used to defending Jennifer Courtney and Dave Courtney because, since I wrote the book, I've had to do nothing more than parry attacks on Dave and Jen. And Jen was superb. Jen was more than an equal in a battle of wits and so old Trisha got frustrated, and then when I came on and started making the audience laugh that just put the cherry on it for her. At one point she turned to the audience, and went, 'What are you all laughing at? What's the matter with you!'

I said, 'Slow down, Trisha, we'll both have our say and the audience will make up their own minds, but you're trying to turn them – that's not fair.' She said, 'You're obviously both well-oiled little machines, aren't you?' I said, 'Yeah, an awful lot better than you, babe!' She's used to being sarcastic to people with half a brain that don't answer back so she needed sharpening up, while on the other hand I've sharpened my wits with ten grand a day lawyers in the Old Bailey.

Trisha went, 'You love the attention don't you?!' I said, 'I absolutely get a hard-on over it: I've had a hard-on for the last three months.' She said she found that offensive and I said I thought it was wicked, although it made walking a bit awkward. The audience were loving it. Then this woman came out on Trisha's side and jumped up and went, 'My husband was *murdered!*' I went, 'Hold it, love. Did I murder your husband? No. Thank you. I've got enough numbers on my plate thanks, without you adding one to the pot!'

She said, 'And you was *guilty?!*' I said, 'Yes.' She went, 'Well if I was on the jury I'd have found you guilty!' I said, 'Well I'm bloody glad you weren't then.'

Then she went, 'Well you're not popular among your friends.' (which don't even make sense). I said, 'I am popular among my friends but not among people who don't like me!' Everybody was having a riot now and we were just slinging stuff right back. Trisha made sure she sought out people with the microphone that were gonna slag us off. Brendan put his hand up every time to say something but she swerved him like she was a professional rugby player.

The best one was when this old lady stood up and asked me if I was earning well. I said I wasn't doing too badly but not as well as when I was being naughty, so to speak. She said she knew I had a Rolls Royce. I pointed out that weren't strictly true – actually I had two. Then, get this, she went, 'Well, what would you do if someone *scratched* your car?' Like that's the worse thing she could imagine. I told her that a fella I knew had already crashed it and nearly written off my Rolls Royce. She said, 'What did you do?'

I said, 'I ain't caught him yet. But if I did catch him I was only gonna cut off *one* arm!' She went, 'Ooh, look at your eyes. You're evil.' I put my hands up and went, '*Woooaahhh!!*' This woman asked Jenny why she was with me if I'd killed people. I said, 'You can't help who you fall in love with,' and Jen went, 'He's a good shag!' *Ha*. That's my baby. I explained that if any of them were in the same position as me of being shot at – and also they'd just seen the fella stood next to them get shot – and they still didn't shoot back then I'd show them an idiot. And, I said, if Trisha had lost half a million pounds to someone and she had my number she'd ring me to get it back.

Someone said to Jen that if I was keeping her in the way that she'd become accustomed – y'know, Chinese take-aways every night, shopping at Tescos, that kinda thing – then that meant if I had to kill to get money it meant I was killing for her, for Jen. (You can hardly follow the logic of that one.) I said I ain't ever killed for money, only in self-defence. Jen went, 'No, he hasn't killed for me . . . but he would.' Fucking hell, that put a hand grenade amongst the pigeons.

It was chaos by the end of the show 'cos most of the audience liked us and were laughing along, Trisha was busy bounding about between the ones who were sympathetic to her view and at the same time making sure to dodge Brendan, the security guys were watching on and laughing, and I was thinking there's no way they're ever going to show this – and I was right, they didn't.

At the end of filming Trisha shot off like a cat with its tail on fire. She weren't going to stick around any longer than she had to! The best bit was that loads of the show's staff came up to us and said that even though we'd been set up we'd done really well. I signed loads of books and posters, and gave one to one of the staff to give to Trish. It said: '*To the lady herself – Nice try, Trish!*'

Afterwards I decided to send a letter to old Trisha saying how I could see how it was a genuine backhanded attempt to humiliate me and my wife, but one that hadn't worked. I said I completely understood the way things were run, and we are continually punished for past crimes, but there was no need whatsoever to punish my missus for being with the man she fell in love with: 'cos she has no control over that as much as she had no control over what I'd done for a living. I also said that I was sure after she'd read the letter and then watched her own performance she would not allow the show to go out.

And that's exactly what happened. She wrote back to say they were rescheduling the show. I thought, yeah, probably to three o'clock in the morning on New Year's Day. I knew even if they edited it right down to the bare minimum we still ripped them to pieces. There wasn't one minute when people weren't laughing.

That *Trisha* show just never appeared. Wonder why. Then one day it popped up on telly but only as part of a *Trisha Unseen* programme where they show bits off all different shows. I'd been more right than I knew. They obviously couldn't salvage enough footage to show us in a bad light to even make a full show!

Some people are more genuine, though. There's this geezer Gyles Brandreth. He writes books and does radio and telly and was even a Conservative MP at one point. His dress sense is perfectly suited to radio and he's a proper posh fella but he's a really nice geezer as well, and you can't but laugh at the way he says things. I first met him when he made a documentary on leadership and what made a leader of men. He interviewed really different people – from politicians to *me*.

Anyway, old Gyles, bless him, invited me onto his radio show. And this is a Sunday night religious programme on the BBC! What the fuck was he on. He came to see me in the studio before the show; 'Well, David, this programme is called *Stairway To Heaven* and I'm going to ask you twenty questions concerning your after life in heaven.' I said, 'I'm pretty touched that you're convinced I'm going *up*, Gyles. Cheers.' Actually, he gave me one of the best intros I've ever had; he said: 'Well, now, I've had *best* selling authors in the studio *and* mayoral candidates but never a man who's been *both*!' Brendan was in the studio creasing himself.

First question was, *Who is the first person you would like to meet when you get to heaven?* I said, 'Winston Churchill.' He went, '*Oh* what a great answer. Why's that?' I said, 'Cos he'd be the only one up there with any cigars.' Then I was asked which four people from history I'd go to dinner with and to which show. The last guest picked something like Elvis, Buddy Holly, Marilyn Monroe and Jesus to watch *Busby's Babes* play. I said I'd go with Adolf Hitler, and Reggie, Ronnie and Charlie Kray to see Madonna. Gyles went, 'But she's not dead!' I said, 'It's my heaven, innit?'

Tell you another funny one. He said, 'Now, David, you're in a *big* waiting room for God and there's a cinema there and you can watch a film before you go to heaven; dear boy, *what* is your choice of film?' I said, '*The Exorcist*.' You could just see his face thinking this is the last time he was going to be allowed to do the show.

It was a wicked one that show 'cos we'd been out all Saturday night – *No!* Oh yes – and this show was on Sunday evening so we were still proper off it. We thought it was being broadcast live, but thank fuck for him it was being recorded.

It's funny the people that end up knowing you without you knowing they do. If you get what I mean. I knew '*Stop the Ride . . .*' had come out in Japan, and that was piss-funny considering my famous run-in in the past with Oriental waiters, and I'd even been featured in the Japanese *GQ* magazine. Still can't quite get my head round millions of little Japanese geezers reading about me, but there you go. Lately I was getting requests from European countries as well. Bring 'em on. If they've got lap-dancing clubs, bars and nightclubs *we'll be there*.

From Italy I got an invite to go out to Milan by the people who were organising a conference on crime and the media. I think it's only in England that it's acceptable for people who've had shady pasts to go on and earn from it. They find it fascinating. So they sent a crew over to England to film a few of us talking about our lives to make a showreel. I think I wore one camera out. They caught me in one of my rare chatty moods: yeah, my last one lasted from 1959 to 1983, and then I had a sore throat for half a week and then I started up again to the present day.

Anyway, the organisers looked at all the films and chose me, Bruce Reynolds and the filmmaker Mark Munden (the fella who filmed me in *Bermondsey Boy*). So we went out to this conference in Milan and there was an awful lot of interest in the way we can flamboyantly talk about what we've done. What they can't get their head around is that naughty geezers in Britain don't have to say sorry and beg for forgiveness. Italy is a very religious country and you can be forgiven if you *ask* to be forgiven . . . but we don't fucking ask! That's the difference. That's the get-out clause if you're religious – you can go and shoot some cunt but as long as you go to confession and say you didn't mean it (y'know, you only meant to *wound* him!) you get absolved. But for us lot to go 'No' and deny the opportunity to get cleansed . . . *that* freaks them out.

And the more I could see that's how they were out there . . . well you *know* what I was like! Did I play up to it? Oh *stop* it. *Shut* up! Like I didn't. They couldn't get their heads round me turning up to court in a jester's outfit! They asked if it was easy to retire. I said I'd tell them when I got round to trying it. Funny though, sat there with these little headphone and microphone sets on, knowing that what you were saying was being translated into a dozen other languages for the other nations. Fuck knows what the translator made of 'lairy', 'geezer' and 'tasty cunt'.

It turned out that the Italian people that came over to Britain and filmed us for the showreel then put the film out on their TV. They did it without me knowing, or so they thought – as if I wouldn't find out! The tentacles reach far and wide. See I've got a friend in Italy called Francesco who wants to make the Dave Courtney life story. He came over here for a week to live with me, to learn how I speak so he could do the script. We got on really well and he saw me make my own film, and he came out to Cannes with me as well so he's now helping promote the film in Italy. (And both *Stop the Ride . . .* and *The Firm* took off in Italy.)

So then that documentary came out on Italian telly and Francesco thought he was doing the right thing checking with me to see if I signed any authorisation for it to come out, which I hadn't, and then saying we should get into a court battle for loads of compensation. The trouble was, though, that when I saw the documentary they'd put together it was what I would consider the best documentary I've ever done! Because it had been put together from the showreel film. In it I'm telling God's honest truth about what I feel, what I intend to do, what barriers I had to cross, and how I'm handling everything; and it would *never* have been passed like that to be shown in this country. As much as we can pretty much talk and write about a lot of what we like, TV in this country is still much more controlled than people realise. So that Italian documentary would've been cut to ribbons for British telly. In Italy, though, it was shown in its entirety, and gained me a new audience.

So I rang up Francesco and told him to contact the documentary fella, Paolo, and apologise for any misunderstanding and tell him I was blown away by his film. And the last time I was impressed by an Italian was when I got a take-away from Pizza Express.

The film thing's started kicking off big time. I got a part in Nick Moran's new film, *Baby Juice Express*, with Joe Bugner and Denise Van Outen. I play a seaside hard nut – I was going to play a stick of rock but I didn't want to have Margate tattooed right through me. Nick asked me if I'd mind playing a complete and utter silly cunt. I didn't know whether to stick one on him, or play deaf. So I stuck a deaf one on him, just to be safe. Better than being sorry.

I've just made a cover version of the old Clash number 'I Fought The Law and The Law Won' with a new band called Mute. I did make some lyric changes of my own, I wonder if you think really hard if you can guess what the changes were? Answers on a postcard to the Commissioner of the Metropolitan Police, Scotland Yard, London.

Because of all the interviews I'd been doing it gave me a real taste for doing a bit of my own on the old radio. Then I got an invite to do a live web-cam radio broadcast at CN Soho Live. Perfect. That morning I woke up with one of them early-morning hard-ons where you don't know whether it's piss or concrete. Jen got the benefit and then it was off to pick up by motorbike from Pete at Rochester. I'd had the tank resprayed red and portraits of me airbrushed around it. Not that I've got an ego or anything. And as an anti-theft device it's more effective than any alarm I know.

Then straight down to CN Soho Live Total Dance Radio for my live web-cam broadcast – as made famous by the one and only Daniella

Montana. They've got more than fifty DJs playing house, garage, techno, trance, drum'n'bass, hip-hop and r'n'b over the net 24/7. I tried to sneak in some penny whistle music but they weren't having it. Wyclef, Robbie Williams, Bryan Adams, Atomic Kitten, Howard Marks, Brian Harvey and Nigel Benn have already been guests on the show. And with it all being linked to the web through computer, and through a camera as well, you get millions of worldwide viewers and listeners. It's the bollocks. You can reach the world from one room – and act like a silly cunt to millions of people!

They didn't know what to do when I put the gas mask on. Half of Europe thought Britain was under attack so I had to explain that I'd accidentally overdone it with the aftershave this morning and the fumes were getting to me. My own fault for still wearing *Hai Karate*. I did some DJing, mixed a few tunes, got everyone into the swing of things and chatted about any old thing. Quite a useful way as well of highlighting some of the police problems we have over here. Remember that the dance crowd people were the first to suffer from laws being made to stop you actually *having a party*! What the fuck's that about? So dancey people are aware of certain misuse of powers. They're also aware of misuse of other things . . . but that's a different matter.

(By the way, that reminds me, when they call it 'misuse of drugs' what the fuck are they on about? If someone takes some coke and shoves it up their nose that ain't misuse – that's what you're *supposed* to do with it. It's called 'use'; there ain't no 'mis' about it.)

After a minute or two of stunned silence hundreds and hundreds of e-mails started firing in from all over the world – America, Australia, Italy, Sweden, Germany, Ibiza – asking me loads of questions; everything from how many people I'd shot to what I was doing next Tuesday evening. And a gay geezer from Amsterdam asking me to breathe heavily into the gas mask! I think he must have had some kind of asthmatic fetish – anybody's for a wheeze.

I was instantly addicted to this web radio idea 'cos the response is just immediate, instant feedback. I want my own show now and I'd have my son Beau spinning the discs and a list as long as a supermodel's legs of interesting guests. One at the top of the list would be Jeffery Archer when he gets out.

What was that judge on anyway – the one in the Jeffrey Archer case? He gave him *four years* just for telling a lie. That's the same as the bent copper in my case got for fitting up people with drugs. Massively different crime but same fucking sentence. Don't make sense. One got too much, the other got too little. I'm afraid poor old Jeff is going to find out like I did – the hard way – what exactly the powers in charge can be like when they decide to target you and start getting you in their crosshairs. I sent him a letter of support actually. No, straight up. We both ran for Lord Mayor of London and were both shafted in case we won. We both have very strong women behind us, we're both best-selling authors and we're both seen as threats to the establishment and both been up at the Old Bailey. And we both feel the best Teletubby is La-La. We've also both done time in Belmarsh and both had the honour of meeting Mr Ronnie Biggs.

The similarities end there, though 'cos Jeffrey didn't watch his back. Also, one of his friends actually grassed him up whereas mine stick by me. That must be the biggest bastard of all for him, knowing that he was bubbled by his old mate. Fucking hell, what a cunt. With 'friends' like those . . .

Yeah, what about that, Warnes only getting four years. No one could still believe it. Even the Old Bill did a good job of pretending to be surprised. Read on.

28. KISS KISS BANG BANG

The law on guns, the law on the law and the law on me. Plus — my mum's right hand, my left foot, and the Queen's cheek!

The law regarding guns is this — shoot first and fuck the lot of 'em. That's my law anyway! If the thing holds six and you are shooting at someone then at least empty the thing. Don't save them for a rainy day 'cos it usual rains at funerals. Have you noticed that? No wonder they soon started moving cremations indoors.

If you get caught with a firearm it's ten years for possession, mandatory: more if it's loaded. I think you can get about three or four years for just having some grub – some ammunition. The thinking goes that you wouldn't have ammo unless you had a gun somewhere or was intending to get one.

I've actually got a lifetime's firearms ban because I've been to prison. The only time I get caught with anything on me these days is with blocked firearms that I've been using in photo shoots. Jenny's now got a business called 'Proper Job', hiring out props for films. There's guns, swords, grenades, suits of armour, kung fu stars, bayonets, daggers, spears, throwing knives – and that's just in her handbag. You name it, she could kill you with it! And because my persona is on the gangster trip what am I supposed to have my photo taken with – a bow and arrow?

It's funny 'cos I've gone from risking doing time in the past for carrying the real thing to now, when I can carry one with a plug in its throat 'cos I make films and do photos. Fucking crazy. I think I'm the only person in the country with a licence to carry a knuckleduster. Well, 'unofficial' licence, but they've nicked me so many times for it and lost because I proved it was part of my public image that they don't bother any more.

I was actually stopped once driving away from a club that Jenny had been singing at and doing her gangsta rap, and when I stepped out of the car they searched it and turned up an Uzi. They rang up for reinforcements and they came down double quick. I told them that all this fuss was stupid 'cos the gun wasn't active and they'd had it off me ten times already and returned it. Now there's no way in the world they could tell if it was a genuine replica, but they didn't nick me 'cos with all the money they were spending listening in to me they didn't want to nick me for something they knew I'd beat. Just like when BT didn't cut off my phone even though I'd not paid a bill for two years. They didn't do it as a favour to me but as a favour to you-know-who. Someone wanted to keep listening to me. That's the 'let them run' tactic: see where they go – then nick 'em.

So that night they just took the gun off me and said they'd check it out! But to all intents and purposes it could have been real. That's mental. They've become that used to me.

They're still very much on my case. I still think the house, phone and car are bugged. I know they came out to Cannes with me and I took an awful lot of pride in knowing that I cost them a lot of money just to watch me on holiday in Tenerife. Mind you, some lucky fucking plods get the long straw when they draw surveillance duty on me – half of them get a fucking foreign holiday out of it. Least they could do is give me their Air Miles.

If they're looking for something sinister for long enough they'll find something they think they can use. (Like on Tenerife when four or five geezers went missing when we were there – but that's holiday food for you!) If they tape you for two years they'll only use maybe three conversations out of those two years to make you look guilty, and fuck the rest of the ten thousand conversations you had that show you're innocent – they will *not* allow the rest of the unused surveillance to be used to prove your innocence. I believe that's what they call loaded dice. You ask for the other thousands of hours of tape to show a different context and they just say no. A big fat 'no'.

Like if someone's stabbed outside a nightclub, for instance, and they question 100 people: 90 say the attacker was white, 10 say he was black. They can decide to only call on the 10! As a defendant you used to be able to ask to look at unused evidence, but that was fucking up too many police cases so they changed it and now you can't look at it. And 10 out of 10 saying 'black' looks good to a jury, that's 100 per cent. But really it's only 10 out of 100, which is only 10 per cent! – you wouldn't convict on that, would you? No fucking way. It's the same with them piecing together conversations taken from over maybe two or three years, they don't let you or the jury hear the bits that made the conversation make sense.

You can angle anything if you try. But the trouble with something being at an angle is you can't see it straight . . .

What's black and white and red all over? A vicar with a spear in his head. And what kind of women do vicars like to shag? Nun. Come to think of it, the last time I saw a vicar was at a fetish party. Difference was, his dog collar was a proper one with metal studs and a name disc – 'Prince', I think he was called, but he answered to a good whistle – and he was being led around on a chain lead by a black dominatrix in a wheelchair. You could tell she was into dishing out pain 'cos the wheelchair had snow tyres. Oh, them spikes do hurt. So the scene weren't really that different from down at many a local, late-night church hall gathering – apart from the banging techno hard house. And the go-go dancing goats.

(Which reminds me. See that in the news about the geezer who got sent down for having it off with a young goat? There must have been at least *ONE* woman in that town that was a better option than that, surely. Just one. Old Mother Hubbard. With her teeth out. And he was caught fucking it up the arse. I suppose, like they say, buggers can't be choosers. I heard that sales of local goats' cheese took a dive. He'll be in for a rough time in prison, though, when they hear he's been messing with a Kid. I want to know where he gets his Es from because that must've been one proper pure fuck-off MDMA buzz he was on: 'Yeah, babe, yer beautiful, no I even love your whiskers, go *on* – swish yer tail . . .' He only got nicked 'cos the goat reported him when she found out he'd also fucked her sister. Tart. And now the goat's pregnant. That child won't be pretty but it'll be fucking good at headbutts.)

Anyway, I got a call offering me a part as a demonic vicar in a new film called, funnily enough, *Demonic*. I thought, hang on a minute, just hang on, what will this entail? Dressing up flash, carrying a gun, doing what I want, having a laugh, being filmed, hanging around with nice-looking birds, and loads of people looking at me. Well, I don't know about that; that don't sound like my kind of gig at all, does it? But anyway, I thought I'd give it a good go. It took me several tenths of a second to say I'd do it.

I was due to play a a pretty fucked-up vicar – my mouth was preaching God Is Love, but my eyes were saying 'I'll drink your blood!' That kind of thing – bit like the characters in *The Omen* and *The Exorcist*, with a bit of Tony Montana from *Scarface* thrown in for good luck. (And if you combined those last two films you'd get *Scarfist* – the story of a gangster with a swivelling head. Well, *I'd* go see it. In fact I think I'm gonna make it!)

I'll tell you what though, walking into a newsagent's dressed as a vicar and asking for twenty Castella cigars, a pack of large Rizlas and a copy of *Asian Babes Anal Special* don't half cause a stir. Especially on a Sunday morning. *Ha*. Anyway, he'd sold out of *Asian Babes* so I had to go for *Big Whoppers!* I left singing, 'Ding-dong the bells are gonna chime, so get me to the church on time!' But that was only the start of it.

Burning up the road at half six one Sunday morning going to the film shoot I saw the familiar sight of one of the Metropolitan Police Force's mobile liquorice allsorts in my rear-view mirror. Fucking hell, I thought, they're starting early. For Deptford. Mind you, at seven o'clock Sunday morning I suppose they've got nothing better to do than stop the only car on the road with all tyres balder than me, and being driven by a tooled-up vicar with a diamond earring. Last day of filming as well, fucking typical.

They both looked pretty shocked when they saw me decked out in the full God Squad clobber, but they said it weren't a nickable offence like impersonating a police officer. And I was so worried. They said they'd pulled me over to have a word about my driving tactics. I said didn't they know that God moves in mysterious ways. Especially when he's a passenger of mine. One of the coppers was okay and he started chatting about when he'd met me on holiday in Tenerife. I said I didn't even *remember* ordering a rent boy from room service! That got a laugh, which is halfway to getting off with it. The other copper was very, very young – he looked about five – and I suppose just being very observant (the way you are when you're only a toddler and everything's new to you) when he pointed out the machine guns in the back. Oh those. Yeah. Things went a bit . . . sort of . . . *downhilly* from then on. Things definitely took a downhill kind of turn.

It all kind of slipped into turbo then: armed response units, helicopters, vans and cars. I was wetting myself though 'cos I knew it was all bollocks. I said for them to ring my Jen and get her to come down with the deactivation certificates for the guns so I could get off 'cos the whole film crew were waiting for me. They were at a woman called Amy's house in Swiss Cottage where we were shooting. It was one of those places where you know how to fucking get there when you're driving but you can't explain it. Which didn't go down too well with the Old Bill and they said they didn't believe me. I was offended.

I weren't alone, by the way. No. God is my co-pilot. But I do wish he'd stop calling out for his son every time I run a red light. 'Jesus!' this, 'Jesus!' that. I said fucking hell, leave the kid alone. Isn't it enough that he got nailed to two bits of wood for you? The poor photographer who was actually with me thought I was talking to an imaginary friend! I said I didn't believe in imaginary friends . . . at least not since the last one nicked my watch. You've got to look out for those invisible cunts, they're slippery *bastards*.

This photographer with me, Max Hardy, was working on the film as a cameraman and just happened to have the previous day's can of film in his bag. I don't know why but he suddenly got a bad case of the nervous giggles. Smoking my puff for the last ten miles probably hadn't helped. Nor did overhearing the copper on his radio letting his imagination and mouth run away with him: 'Urgent assistance needed in Deptford High Street. Two males with numerous firearms. One male, Dave Courtney . . .' Before you could say 'Jesus, Joseph, Mary Mother of God' the whole street was blocked off with orange stripy cars. Welcome to my world . . .

When they were searching me and putting the cuffs on they found my diamond duster; and the photographer stopped smiling when they said they were going to search him as well. He looked at me, and everyone in the world could see he had something on him. They found a lump of puff in his pocket. That pissed me off no end 'cos he'd said he had none and the cheeky cunt had been smoking mine all morning! And he'd had about half an hour to get rid of it. So, things could only get better couldn't they? I mean apart from get worse. But not much. The copper just did a check and found out the car was stolen. I genuinely didn't know it was nicked, but how many times has a copper heard that?

I got the motor, an old Renault, from a scrapyard who gave it to me to blow up in my film. In the end we blew up another couple of cars instead: a Jag and a Rolls Royce. Well you know what it's like when you're spoilt for choice. I explained in no uncertain terms how I couldn't have known it was nicked 'cos I had used it in my film and it'd been parked in my drive for nearly a year, with the other hidden camera mob over the road filming it! And face it, if you were gonna have a ringer you'd get something new and half decent like a Jag or a Discovery, wouldn't you, not some poxy ten-year-old Renault, for fuck's sake.

When I was younger I used to nick old Rovers but my days of paying for bent Austins were over, so to speak. I am now an author and actor! Or, to be more accurate, I was now an author and actor being arrested, cautioned and handcuffed in the middle of Deptford, on a Sunday morning, whilst dressed as a vicar as local churchgoers passed by. You know, sometimes, my mum just *bursts* with pride!

So they did actually nick me. Cheeky monkeys. Not that I'd given them 27 reasons to do it – 'cos I hadn't. It was 26. Apparently it's not illegal to wear a trilby with a vicar's dog collar after all. Wicked. But the gold and diamond knuckleduster clanging to the floor out of my pocket didn't go down too well (and the pavement came off worse). The younger copper tried to do me for wearing a pornographic necklace with a naked geezer on it. I looked down at the cross and said that's *Jesus* you fucking halfwit!

Anyway, down in the cells at the police station (now ain't that a phrase which trips easily off the tongue?) I waited for my mate Craig to come down with my certificates of deactivation for the firearms. There was a bit of a delay 'cos it took Jen about an hour to print them up and let the ink dry. No, they are genuine. So they were handed over, and so was the phone number of Stefan, the film's director. He was pretty pissed off by now, as you can imagine, waiting around on set with Amy, Steve and the rest of the crew doing fuck all. That fucked up the day's shoot. They even sent my personal hairdresser home. She'd run out of polish anyway, so . . .

The photographer got a caution, and they kept his puff, of course. Where *does* that stuff all go anyway, officer? They used to burn it off until a strong wind got hold of the smoke and the next town was completely stoned. The local firemen didn't even answer the alarm; they just went, 'Oh . . . *fuck* it. Soon come, yer'know . . . pass the Ritz Crackers on the left-hand side . . .' Punters got a fucking good deal off the local whores as well 'cos the girls couldn't remember how much they charged – 'That'll be, er . . . one pound fifty for anal twos up, with oral completion, darling.' Bargain.

I, on the other hand, didn't just get a caution. I got banged up all day. To add insult to injury, the copper that had booked me in turned out to be an old classmate from school, Damian Solly! Fucking *stop* it. It was like that website – 'Friends Re-offending'. Anyway, the car happened to be full of posters and life-size cut-outs of little ole me, so that passed a bit of time, signing them for the staff. It should have also proved I didn't know the car was nicked because I'm hardly going to drive around with the boot full of my life story, am I? It was full of Dave Courtney posters, books, DVDs and life-size cut-outs. Bit of a giveaway, dontcha think?

So they were gonna do me for going equipped to a job, in disguise, with offensive weapons, carrying a passenger with drugs, with a knuckleduster in my pocket and in a nicked car. And speeding. I'm only surprised they didn't try and blame me for England not winning the World Cup since 1966 as well, for good measure.

I said I do not believe for one minute you are silly enough to stand me up before a jury and say I knew it was stolen. I even drove back to the Old Bailey a couple of times in it during the last case! One of the coppers came out with a line I'd begun to get used to hearing by now. He said he didn't give a toss whether I eventually got off with it, but getting me on bail for it would be a nice little spoiler for my publicity. So they knew I didn't know, but then it was obvious what their real intention was. This was like another version of what I'd just been through at the Bailey – get Courtney in court at all costs, however stupid the charge, and see what damage we can do to him on the way.

And get this – who turns out to be at this nick when I'm taken in but one of Austin Warnes' old ex-partners. I thought is this a fucking obvious set up or just a joke or what? I didn't know what to make of it at first and thought they were setting me up for fuck knows what. Anyway, he started chatting about the whole thing, saying how they never liked or trusted the geezer.

So to pass the time I signed posters and cut-outs, and even drew a target on the head to make it easier for them. (Funny how even after they nick me for something they always ask for a bloody signed book!) I'd already sent some of these life-size cut-outs through the post to Scotland Yard, Tony Blair, the Queen, the Queen Mum and George Bush. Honestly, I did, and I only got two sent back and one was from CID. Not amused, obviously, they didn't even put enough postage on it.

It all started one day when I got 100 life-size cardboard cut-outs of me delivered. I think they were supposed to be for the firing range at Scotland Yard and got sent to me by mistake, but I kept them. At one point they were all lined up outside and some geezer drove past, stuck his head out the window and shouted, 'You're *all* cunts! The lot of yer!' Worse of all, I don't think he was joking.

On every holiday I go on I send back cards to the Metropolitan Police, CIB3, Sir Paul Condon (still), the Queen, Tony Blair, Ken Livingstone and Jeffery Archer. I've started sending the cut-outs as well. I sent one to CIB3 with a note saying, 'seeing as you're never gonna get me in a prison cell ever again, in case I've deflated your morale I've sent you this life-size cut-out to put in a cell so you can all walk past and look in and pretend you've got me. Love, Dave'. They sent it back – only the second one to do that after CID – with their own note stuck on saying 'We do not intend to get involved in your childish banter.' Ha, I just fucking wet myself!

I also sent one to George Bush with a note saying 'Hi, George, I know you're having a little bit of aggro at the moment but my boys are up and ready and have been doing some sand training down at Camber beach, and we're all ready to go'. And I included a couple of prints of that best-ever picture of me and the boys all stood on that bridge in Tenerife (see *Raving Lunacy*). Never got a reply though.

I also managed to buy an OBE medal. Wearing that for a laugh brought out a good one; someone went oh wow, and then said to me they'd thought that when I put 'OBE' after my name I was only joking. You don't say.

Any road, meanwhile, still back at the police station in my vicar's outfit, they kept me there for fourteen hours. And with no dinner. No way to treat a budding vicar. Seems like they've given up now on trying to get me on anything big – especially after that last fiasco in court – so they're planning on adding up a lot of little ones instead. Like doing me for the car and whatever else they can throw on top. I could become a fucking Hari Krishna and they'd probably nick me for wearing orange before sundown. Anyway, thank fuck I wasn't playing a Roman gladiator because I'd have looked well silly being arrested and cuffed at the side of the road wearing sandals and a leather skirt. Mind you, it looked pretty fucking daft with me dressed as a vicar. It was like *Carry On Clergy*.

The best bit of the day was when they cautioned me and read me my rights. When the copper asked if there was anything I'd like to say I said, 'Yes, there is. Bless you, my son, you are forgiven', which I knew had to be written down as the first thing I said after being cautioned. Almost worth it going to court just to treat the jury to that one. Anyway, it got a laugh from the photographer but no one else. So they kept his film as evidence. I told him, it's cheaper than taking it to be processed at Boots.

When I did get out they couldn't give me all my stuff they'd taken off me that was my property, and they kept the car, obviously. So there's loads of stuff that was still there and when I went back for it some of *that* was missing. More paperwork. Just like happened before. They don't give a fuck; it's so blatant. So I've reported that in a letter. Like I said, paperwork can kill you. That's how they tried to kill me, so that's also how I fight them now. Now I understand that the pen *is* mightier than the sword.

I wanted to get a copy of the interview tapes 'cos my tapes were superb. I sent them a letter about the things they'd taken off me and not given back; I said look, no matter what this case is about, seeing as you stopped me from bringing up that first tape in the Old Bailey trial with me talking about what a pleasure it was to use all those bent coppers that I used – seeing as you lot stopped that, if this comes to court I will take every chance to talk about those things, no matter what questions you ask me.

And I said all that during the interview they were taping. Since then they've said that they're now reviewing the case to see if it should go before the CPS. *Ha*.

One case that would definitely have got passed by the CPS is the following case of assault and battery. My mum was mugged. Some geezer tried to snatch her bag and she wouldn't let go. The violence that followed was terrible. The poor bastard was lucky she only caught him with two or three punches. I'm not joking. When the police called me I thought, oh I wonder how badly she hurt him. My mum's like a really lovely, pretty lady but who just happens to have trained with Mike Tyson. Believe me.

When the police got to my mum's house they thought they were just dealing with another street robbery until they saw pictures of me all round the house and copies of all my books. Then it sort of clicked, oh right, Mrs *Courtney*. Then they panicked and started saying how they didn't want any vigilante justice on the streets and could she have a word with me to calm me down.

I shot round to Mum's straight away and the Old Bill were still there waiting to put a fire blanket on whatever they thought was brewing, which would've been me using the little cunt as a baseball if I got hold of him. But only if my mum didn't get there first. Mum started giving me a blow-by-blow description, telling me how she whacked him; telling me this as if I hadn't known her for forty years and been on the receiving end of her solid right hand for the first fifteen.

Anyway, luckily they didn't catch the bastard so he didn't have to get off his stool for Round Two.

We all have our crosses to bear and just as things were starting to get back to as normal as my life gets, God dropped a big old wooden thing onto my shoulders. If I weren't someone that can, as time goes on, understand things from the Bible and see how people get strength from it then I might curse old Holy Hands upstairs. But ours is not to question why, as they say.

Down to an old war wound, the bullet hole in my shin, I ended up having to go to hospital. What happens after you get shot is this – you go 'Arrgghh!' and fall over bleeding. And then what happens after *that* is that over the years bits of debris like bone fragments and tiny bullet bits sink down through your bones and muscle. Like when wine ferments and the sediment sinks to the bottom. So over the years it's gone down into my ankle, and all this grit has been getting between the bone joints and wearing it away.

Amazing what a bit of grit can do given enough time. I once saw this documentary that showed this Jumbo jet that had crashed into a mountainside. The wreckage went on for miles. On the black box the last thing the pilot said was, 'I wonder what *that* switch does?' No, they traced the cause of it down to some really tiny bits of debris that had got in one of the engines about fifteen years before during a service, and it had taken all that time to wear away at the engine and bring that big Jumbo fucker and three hundred people down to earth. (Sorry, hope you're not flying tomorrow or buying this in the airport, but if you are, good luck.)

So my landing gear was getting a bit of the same treatment. Caused a real problem, it did, and I didn't know what it was. I thought it was arthritis and it was sort of diagnosed as arthritis. That turned out to be wrong. Like the geezer who kept going back to the doctor's, so they give him a complete check up and the doctor says, 'I'm afraid you're going to have to stop wanking.' He says, 'Why's that?' He says, 'The other people in the waiting room don't like it.'

It was giving me proper grief, though, my foot. When it got too bad I had to go in for an operation at the Queen Elizabeth Hospital in Woolwich; and they had to do all these tests on me first. I went in and saw this Dr Tipplewell and he is an absolute genius, mate, a complete genius. At one point even he said, 'We've all got our cross to bear.' I had loads of tests for four days. On the fifth day I was going down for my CAT scan. I thought, I know the NHS is bad but don't tell me they let animals work here! Fucking hell.

I had to go in for three operations there, and during one visit a really strange thing happened. I was laid out on the trolley and this Pakistani gentleman had just given me the little hand scratch injection to prepare me for the anaesthetist. I'm counting back from ten getting ready for lights out – ten, nine, eight – when he leaned over me and went, 'You don't remember me do you?' I thought . . . no – seven, six: he said, 'Back at school you chased me round the playground and call me Fat Cunt!' Oh, right; five, four . . . He went, 'Don't worry. I look after you!' and I was drifting off thinking oh *fuuuuccck*! I had the worse nightmares while I was under. I could just see this geezer going, 'I'm terribly sorry, Mrs Courtney, he died under the anaesthetic.'

I went in again later but before I got a chance to have the third operation they announced that the Queen was due to visit to open a new wing of the hospital, next door to the army barracks.

Now they must figure that if someone was going to assassinate the Queen – and, by the way, have you noticed how so-called important people are 'assassinated' and every other poor fucker is just 'killed'? – yeah, if someone was going to kill the Queen they'd sneak in there beforehand and find somewhere to plot up on the inside, 'cos on the day security is gonna be tighter than a duck's arse.

So they must have had security guys buzzing around the hospital checking it out: using sniffer dogs to ID any dodgy bedpans that might contain explosive, a crutch that might turn into a machine gun, a wheelchair with razor-lined wheels or some fake doctor with kung fu stars up his sleeve. I don't fucking know, it just looked like a ward of sick people to me and everyone else. Which reminds me, a Palestinian woman out shopping says to her mate, 'Does this dress make my bomb look big?'

But the security geezers did notice – 'cos they couldn't help but notice – the gang of fellas that came in to see me. All these dirty great big muscly cunts with shaved heads, tattoos and welding seams on their necks. People like Mickey Goldtooth and Wish, and my old biker mate Outcast Phil in his leathers and top hat. They were walking past rooms and setting heart monitors off like pinball machines. I think we had two heart attacks, three strokes, fifteen serious relapses and twelve sudden cases of diarrhoea. And that was just the doctors. (Diarrhoea isn't hereditary, by the way, but it can run in the family.)

The security geezers went who the hell's that? They said they're here to see Dave Courtney. I got this told me by a good friend of mine, Frank, who was one of the porters in there that I know, among others. Yeah, I was properly laid up and out in the hospital bed; couldn't walk. And when some of the fellas saw me like that they slept in the fucking hospital with me. It was mental. And a bit embarrassing when I shagged a nurse! No, course I didn't, but they were all lovely. Even the one with the 'tache. I did get a shag in there, but more of that later.

Ronnie Biggs was also in there after he'd just come back from Brazil, and in none too good shape as it happens. Mickey Biggs, his son, was with him, and Mickey was fighting his own court case 'cos they were trying to throw him out the country. How compassionate is that? When I could get up and hobble about I popped in to see Ronnie.

Anyway, I was settling down to the day – looking forward to a bedside visit from Her Royal Madge and maybe being insulted by Prince Philip, and inviting them to the barbecue we were having at my gaff the week after – when these security officers suddenly decided that I'd got to leave. They said it was too big a security risk having me in the hospital at the same time as the Queen was visiting! What was I going to do, flick her to death with my bandage? So someone was going to have to come up and give me the news that they were discharging me but no one really fancied the job, and in the end it was one of the catering staff that told me – this girl that did every ward and that was also serving the CID officers. See, there's always a leak.

Apparently, me and Ronnie Biggs were both in the hospital at the same time and it was judged to be too big a security risk during a Royal visit! Oh *shut* up. Fucking idiots. Ronnie was too ill to blow the froth off a frothy coffee, bless him, and I was laid out like Hopalong Cassidy on ice. Zero security risk. In fact, she could've probably had the both of us!

I had to sign out, lose my bed and my appointment, go home, and then go back and sign in as an outpatient and wait in casualty with geezers with axes in their heads or half their chopped-off fingertips in a bag or some kid with a plug jammed up his nose. So I was pretty chuffed, as you can imagine. But I'm so looking forward to the Golden Jubilee now. We're going to have a street party serving spit-roast corgis. I'm told they taste just like chicken: little, yappy, dog-flavoured sorts of chickens.

Being in casualty for six hours gave everybody else in there that wasn't bleeding to death enough time to get out their mobiles and ring every relative they had and then pass their phones to me to say hello. That's when you know your book's sold well! They were having me say hello to brothers, and mums and dads, and Uncle bloody Albert, and even recording messages on their answer machines.

I wouldn't mind but there's no one more patriotic than me. I had my white Roller painted with a red cross of St George during Euro '96; I sponsor the British army football team at Woolwich barracks and was guest of honour at their Christmas bash (see later); and I've got a 50-foot flagpole flying the Union Jack outside my gaff: and then they go and put in the papers that I can't be in the same building as the Queen because I'm a threat. So, after that, Buckingham Palace got a letter from me as well, along with a life-size cardboard cut-out.

Even though I'd only been kicked out for one day I'd lost my bed, and I'd waited eighteen months for that fucker to become available. Now I was an outpatient again. I went one more time to the hospital in an emergency, and then I ended up going private. To Blackheath Hospital. What happened was this – I went out to see a specialist in Belgium and he recommended I go see this specialist in Paris. So I went to Paris and the doctor there was the same one I'd had at the Queen Elizabeth Hospital! He said why did you come all the way out here? I can do it privately for you at Blackheath in London! So after travelling halfway around the world to find this geezer that was in London I ended up feeling like a top wanker, but I did bump up my Air Miles.

The private room at Blackheath was like a hotel room; it was wicked. I didn't half hammer the room service until I found out I had to pay for it all.

The private room did have its advantages. Like me and Jen having a session with British porn star Kathy Barry, a new mate of ours. Good medicine and all. I had to lock the door, and the nurse next door thought it was me making all the noises 'cos I was in pain with my foot – as if my foot could actually shout, 'I'm coming!' and 'Harder!' And we found a new use for a stethoscope, a vibrating telephone, and made sure we made the most of the electric bed. Fucking good therapy. My foot felt better but I put my back out!

Doctors know whether or not you're the type to take their advice and rest like they say. I was supposed to rest for twelve to fourteen weeks with my leg higher than my heart. Anyone who knows me knows I can't rest for twelve to fourteen minutes, and if I could get my leg higher than my heart I'd be Jackie Chan. So, they worked a bit of reverse psychology on me and discharged me wearing a bright, fluorescent, lime green pot on my leg! Imagine being kicked out into the world wearing *that*. It was deliberately calculated to keep me indoors – like, let's see him go out in public wearing that baby: he wouldn't *dare*. Even Jenny thought, no, he ain't going nowhere with that on.

You'd think they'd never heard of Halfords.

I got someone to bring me up a can of black spray paint and thirty seconds later I had a shiny black sexy leg-pot on me. And shiny black sexy toes and toenails as well 'cos I forgot to mask the bastards off. I couldn't decide whether it looked like I was wearing one big fuck-off Doc Martin or one of the Elephant Man's wellies. So I went on a DIY buzz and started decorating it with gold braid, bits of gold jewellery and embellished it with a gold pen. I even impressed myself. I thought that is the most glamorous fucking plaster cast I have ever seen. It looked like I'd stuck my foot in a big Fabergé egg; or like my leg was being eaten by Elton John's pedal bin.

And they'd also given me these crutches. Plain wood ones. Well, that just would *not* do. I made them into Versace crutches. I sprayed them gold and black and wrapped them both in gold braid as well. I'm known for my wrapping me, and these crutches had more wrapping than Eminem.

Walking around like that, with my gold crutches and gold decorated cast, it looked like I'd dipped my foot in Superglue and ram-raided Beaverbrooks.

You should've seen the geezer's face at the hospital when I went back to have the cast cut off. He *knew* it hadn't gone out looking like that. He said it was a shame to damage it. Fucking difficult to damage it as well 'cos it was like it was armoured!

I think they stuck it back together later and used it in the foyer as a vase.

So, there I was sitting in the car wash one day and all the Army's down there from the local barracks so all the Army boys came up to say hello. *Stop the Ride* . . . is a bit of a forces favourite apparently. Their sergeant major didn't have the slightest idea who I was – 'You some kind of celebrity, then? Writing books about virgins or something?' He said that Bepe from *EastEnders* had been lined up to do the regiment's Christmas do but that had fallen through at the last minute and he wondered if I'd do it? Fucking hell, *would* I!

I rung home and got Jennifer to get ready and she rang her mate Angie and we goes back up to the Army base and had it with all these soldiers. And soldiers proper drink, mate. I've a real healthy respect for the army 'cos that is what organised crime is – a criminal doing it like the army does. That's why men say that every man should have a year in prison or the Army because it is invaluable; and I say all that. A real big-up for the army here 'cos they realise that it's not the best fighter that's the one in charge, it's the man who can put the right peg in the right hole: you are a sniper, you are bomb disposal, etc. And, in the same way the army does, a year in prison helps you learn men. A year in prison helps that. Don't matter if you're a silver spoon Guy Ritchie or someone selling the *Big Issue*, you're on the same kind of mattress and with the same fucking uniform. Prison teaches you men and their disguises.

That's what people mean when they say bring back compulsory time in the army for young men, or what they used to call 'conscription'. And they don't mean young men should go to war, just that they should live for a year without their privileges, have all that taken away and be forced to get on with each other. Prison learns you, like the Army does. But in the army you get out more. You get to travel the world, visit interesting countries, meet interesting people. And kill them.

At the Xmas do I met the squaddies of course and all these majors as well and it was so enlightening the way they were so focused on ' The Army'. Everything else was second: wife, children, their own life. It's . . . The Army.

Anyway, I got to sponsor the British Army Football Team. The BAFT. (Which is better than playing for the Dutch version.) I said I'd sponsor the football team for a grand. One of the majors said that whatever name my company was would go across the middle but below that it must say 'Army'. No arguments about that. I said fair enough. So I said my business is me and I'm called Courtney so let's put 'Courtney's' across the shirt. So now I've got part of the British Forces running around with 'COURTNEY'S ARMY' written on their shirts! How wicked is that?

The boys on the ground know who I am but in the officer's mess they don't watch anything but CNN and war footage so they didn't know who I was till it was too late. And, speaking of which, try never to stand in the officer's mess 'cos it's a cunt to get off your shoes.

Now the reason places like Woolwich barracks has armed guards there on the wall is to keep geezers like me out, but now I'm chief footy sponsor I'm in there aren't I? I got in under the radar; I was like a stealth cunt. And that's one big armaments playground. I was in there checking out the tanks and explosives storeroom (joke, sarge). Unfortunately they wouldn't let me take out an armoured wagon. I wanted one of them little caterpillar track trucks to go park it in a clamping zone.

A lot of the officer's part of the Army is full of little boys really. Straight out of school or university and into uniform and routine. You definitely lack learning how to be streetwise when you're locked up in the Army *but* you do gain something; and when you come out you can always get streetwise then and carry on but it don't work the other way – you can't get what the army gives you if you don't go in.

Individually they are a lot of kids but all together as a unit they are mass murderers. One kid's job is to pick that bomb up and put it in that hole and the other kid's job is to close the lid, and then another kid turns and another one looks at a screen and presses a button. And eighty miles away a town blows up. Warfare's now run like a computer game so these kids look like the young kids that sit in front of the telly all day; except here they're in a tank with no windows and zeroing in on the enemy on a little green screen. For a computerised war you want computer whiz-kids.

A couple of the sergeant majors became mates of mine and came round to my house. I took them out raving. That was funny. One fella was the absolute bollocks, he was just the tops. We went out one night, and try and imagine this in a really strong Welsh accent when he said: 'I'm not afraid;

I'm not afraid to come here on my own! I don't care how many black people are 'ere. Or 'ow many *drugs* are taken! If I'm not afraid of an Argy with a bayonet then I'm not afraid of a man with a joint! – Whatever colour 'e is!' And people were coming up and putting their arms around him and saying hello and he was like, 'Take your 'ands away from *me* or I'll break you in half you *bastard*'. It was so funny; it was really, really funny. He did calm down and get into it though, and no one was thrown in the stockade.

He was saying to me how he thought England was trying to please everyone and pleasing no one. He said he's seen the army change so much and right now they were debating whether women should be allowed to wear make-up or not. He said as a sergeant major he wasn't even allowed to shout at anyone individually, only as a pack. I mean what the fuck is *that* about!? So there's no more of that parade ground screaming like *You 'orrible little man – I'm gonna tear off your head and shit down your fucking neck!* because you'd be accused of hurting the guy's feelings.

And the army fully understands the power of propaganda and how the media is a weapon for them and for the authorities. He said they develop situations in the press that are happening abroad, like Bosnia, 'cos they know when one conflict ends, like Northern Ireland where they're all gonna pull out, then they have to have another one to keep them busy and justify the billions spent on defence and weapons and keeping everyone in work. They've always got to find a war; there's always got to be a war.

This fella told me that the actual squaddies were so proud of having my name on their shirts that they used to hoist it in the air and cheer themselves on. He said there's no bigger compliment than that, to give our boys morale. I had another go at him to let me lend of an armoured tank so I could pull up outside a police station in it when I went to claim back my stuff they confiscated – but he stood firm on that one and Welsh sergeant majors will not be moved, boyo!

They said yes to me writing a piece for *Front* magazine about me going out on manoeuvres with them. They were perfectly happy for that to happen until they found out who Dave Courtney is or someone in blue rang them up and had a word and suddenly it wasn't alright anymore. It weren't no surprise to me really because that's been happening to me a lot lately, and especially over the time since the last court case when they've really been giving it to me. You might be surprised by what they can do . . . but then if you've been reading this book so far you wouldn't be surprised at all.

29. GET COURTNEY

Buggings, banks, break-ins, sneak attacks and Tupac! It all kicks off large.

I never knew making movies and music could be so bad for your health.

Of all the people I know that were in my film loads of them have been picked up by the police and everyone that helped out financially is now under investigation from the Inland Revenue and the tax people. It's more than coincidence and if you do my old Scales Theory and place things for and against you'll find there's too many instances for it not to be deliberate. It happened six, seven years ago when I did Ronnie Kray's funeral and then suffered police attention afterwards. They closed down my cab firm, my pub and stopped me working legitimately all over.

My forte is putting myself in the other person's position and seeing why they do what they do, and they cannot be in any rush to have big pictures of Dave Courtney everywhere on the back of a successful film like *Hell To Pay*. They were even trying to say that I was not in Cannes. Any other actor that had been in three films there at the same time – I was playing a judge in *Daddy Fox*, playing a villain in *Hell To Pay* and even in my own porn film *The Freakshow* in the adult films part of the festival – and the press would've been wanking themselves over it. Especially if it was an English geezer doing it big at a foreign film festival. Funnily enough some of the bit of coverage I did get was in the *Sunday Times*: *'Here comes someone with an offer you'd be unwise to refuse. Dave Courtney, the former East End gangster, rode in yesterday on a Harley-Davidson motorbike ahead of 60 "business associates". He is here to promote his Tarantino-esque first movie,* Hell To Pay, *shown last night as part of the festival . . . Courtney is a lone voice for the British cinema.'*

Sometimes the conspiracy of silence trick can con you into thinking you ever even made a film, y'know, like did I dream it? Can't have done, 'cos I'm even more out of pocket now because of it and hundreds of people are ringing me up asking when it's coming out! It weren't a dream it was just a dream come true. Then a book came out called *Your Face Here – British Cult Movies* by Ali Catterall and Simon Wells. It is, surprise, surprise, about the best British cult films like *Quadrophenia, Clockwork Orange, Trainspotting, Lock, Stock . . .* and *Get Carter* and . . . *Hell To Pay*. We get a bloody good write up from them as well. The last chapter starts with them interviewing me on the set of the film – meaning my front room! – and reviewing the film:

> *Hell To Pay* is guerrilla film-making at its best – the logical extension of *Get Carter* and *Lock, Stock*. But this sort of thing blows those films out of the water. All the movie's many 'chaps' are played by the genuine

articles, like Roy Shaw and Joey Pyle. 'And I play a really fucking good Dave Courtney,' says Dave. '*Lock, Stock* . . . opened the door for what I want to do,' adds Dave, 'but Guy Ritchie couldn't tell me how to hold a fucking gun properly.'

And the last word in the book was very kindly given to me:

Back at Camelot Castle, a few hitches. Mark Morrison was supposed to turn up at the *Hell to Pay* set, but has been stuck at the dentist. Courtney decides he'll play a rifle-toting bodyguard. Meanwhile, it begins to rain. The performers start protesting, particularly as Dave wants to do me takes. 'But this is great!' says Dave. 'The Americans love rain! They can't get it over there, so this'll look real great, really *British*!'

So all that was much appreciated because it's so frustrating to not be listened to.

But, like I say, cutting off the supply routes is a warlike tactic and that's what they are doing to me by stopping publicity. So many people that have helped me out are suddenly under investigation. Gary Bushell was sacked from the *Sun* for supporting me because they thought he was going to be a voice piece for me. A woman called Ashley who works in the city and helped get financial backers for the film was sacked after they broke into her computer because they'd seen e-mails coming out of the Stock Exchange with Dave Courtney on them. They said they thought she was money laundering for me! With what I've got in the bank you could launder it in a bucket.

In fact I did try to open a bank account to go legit but they wouldn't let me. I couldn't get my head around it. I was going, 'But I want to put some money *IN*. It's not like those other times with the holdall and the car waiting outside!' I've spent my whole life with nothing on paper so it's now impossible for me to open a bank account. Every time I walk into a bank they put their hands up. It's a cunt when you have to explain that you're not actually wearing a stocking on your head. Or you walk in wearing a balaclava and they go, 'Awright, Dave?'

They said, 'Have you got some ID?' I said, 'Yes. Book, CD or DVD?' That went down like a dead nun.

Another mate of mine is the DJ Caesar The Geezer. Caesar is the prisoner's favourite DJ; the one that always sends out shouts and messages for everyone inside. He's been on Capital Radio, Virgin Radio and now Millennium Radio, or Fusion FM as it's called. That's when all the local radio stations around the country link up at 9 o'clock so then there's only one and it's him.

He appeared in *Hell To Pay* with me in a massive scene at the end where everything's blown up and me and Caesar are stood on top of this tank when the police come screeching round the corner and ask who's in charge. I say, 'I think *I* am, Sarge!' Unfortunately it had to be cut out the film, which was a real painful decision. Or it would've been if I'd had to make it, but 'cos I knew I'd want to leave everybody in it I had to hand the editing over to someone else totally. It was the only way to get the film down from the five-hour epic I would've had.

I had my own radio show with him on Wednesday nights and it went down a storm. I absolutely loved it. I brought in loads of people I knew from films and music and real life. I brought in Joey Pyle, and a man called Dave Ford who is a geezer with real heart: he's been suing the police for wrongful arrest and theft. The money that he gets from that he's pledged to use to help Winnie Bennett find the remains of her son Keith, who was killed by the Moors Murderers.

So I used the show to interview people like that and, of course, I plugged my books and films. All of a sudden the radio station got some police attention and I was asked not to do the show any more. That's another one gone, another outlet being plugged.

See, cut off the ways that you reach people and what can you do? – stand on an orange box in Hyde Park shouting. It's like someone gaffa-taping your mouth. They don't give a fuck that it's not fair – they just want you to shut up. And no one knows it goes on till it happens to you, or till someone like me tells you about it. Even that's not the same thing, though, is it? You know I can only put so much of it across. At least I still have the books to do that.

We've all got the books. Two of the best are by Freddie (Foreman) and Tony (Lambrianou) and then they got together and did a double act in another book. That came out before the trial got going and before I'd had a fair crack, but credit to both of them, they did see through the character of someone who was spreading lies about that time. Freddie says an interesting thing, 'A lie uncontradicted becomes an accepted truth', which is true, and just goes to prove you can't always rely on other people dismissing lies out of hand. Sometimes you have to help them see.

I did an advert with both Tony and Freddie for Pink Shirts. The Thomas Pink company had rung me to see if I was interested and if I had any ideas for other gents I might contact. I put up Fred and Tony and that was that. Well, after I'd rung them and explained that it wasn't actually *pink* shirts they'd have to wear. The actual ads looked wicked. But then when a big spread in the *Sunday Times* was written about the adverts I wasn't even mentioned. Which would've been down to someone like a writer or editor getting a telltale nudge there, I think.

The law and order mob are a fucking powerful team of horses when they get up to speed. They can't silence everyone though, and it's easier to get things out if you're working with someone else. Especially if they're ballsy people that won't be threatened into not doing what they want to. Like I did a recording with the Scottish band Mute. We did an updated version of the Clash's song 'I Fought the Law and The Law Won' but in our version they didn't win, we did. Then Steve Whale's punk band the Business – who are the absolute nuts by the way – recorded the soundtrack and title track for *Hell To Pay*. And I had a fucking top day at the annual punk festival that's held in Tufnell Park. I went on stage with the Business, and me being ever so slightly anti-establishment went down a storm with that crowd. I'd like to have seen the police try to shut that lot up.

The worse one that happened with all this persecution shit was what happened to my mate Ish. Itse Ayonmike is his full name but we call him Ish. Ish is the British middleweight kickboxing champion, a doorman and an actor as well. He's been over here from Nigeria for nine years and married for five, he's never claimed social security or nothing like that, always worked, and he's British champion of his sport. I've sponsored him over the years. Suddenly though, after he's in *Hell To Pay* and in the newspapers because of it, the police decide he should be deported! Just like that. He went into the local police station to sign on like he does every month because of his status as a political refugee. His dad's a high-ranking MP in Nigeria and they sent his family to England as political refugees because their lives were in danger. So Ish walks in and the Old Bill ran round the counter, nicked him and told him he was going back home the next day.

Now that might not be bad news for you or me, y'know, if we were being deported back here to Leeds or Glasgow or Peckham . . . well, maybe not the best examples those three but you get my drift: English places ain't exactly Southside Los Angeles or Bosnia are they? But they were deporting Ish back to Nigeria in the middle of a war he's escaped from – a tribal thing. In the Nigerian airport there were nearly two hundred bodies and no one was taking them away. So they're rotting there and that's where they wanted to send him. He would've been killed in the airport. Not assassinated – fucking *killed*, mate.

Ish was in fear of his life so when they got him to Heathrow airport he kicked off, literally. He's got championship belts for doing it! You can imagine what a handful he was. The plane took off without him so they said they were going to sedate him and take him back next morning. They put him in the holding centre at Heathrow and that's where he rang me from. He was in bits, as you can imagine. He said he didn't know what to do but he couldn't get on that plane tomorrow.

He had about twelve hours to live.

Now he knows, 'cos I've told him, that the power lies in the book. The power lies in those who have most names and numbers in their little black book. And I've got a big black book. So I hit it for all it was worth.

I rang Martin Brunt from Sky TV, Meridian TV, Ian Edmondson and Gary Bushell at their new paper the *Sunday People*, I rang DJs that I knew at radio stations, local press, *South London Press* connections, Ann Widdecombe – she got involved.

In my head I knew that if I didn't help him he dies. That would've been on my conscience if I hadn't done anything because he can't stop it himself, and if I couldn't stop it then he flies and if he flies . . . He kept saying how he couldn't understand why it was happening or what had changed. I thought, I know. He wasn't the first to be chastised for associating himself so publicly with me. But I thought if there's any stick about it all tomorrow in the press they would have to reconsider, because they wouldn't want to be proved wrong when news came back through that he *had* been killed. That would have looked too bad.

And that's exactly what happened. The news broke in the press and they pulled the plug on sending him back. Sweet. So we won. I did an interview on Meridian TV and they went to the holding centre and interviewed Ish, and showed clips of me collecting the belt for him in the ring.

They kept him in there for three weeks while the solicitors tried to find a reason for sending him back and they couldn't find a single one.

Of all the people to go and choose to send back to get mutilated and killed they chose the British champion! Fucking hell, how little pride have they got, cunts. The only difference between before and after was that in-between he'd aligned himself with me and made a high profile film with me. Even Ann Widdecombe backed out when they pointed out to her that the campaign was started by me, and if she continued it looked like she was trying to free one of 'Dave Courtney's boys'. Before that I was just Mr Courtney to her, she didn't know who I was.

Wish from the film was also nicked and put in prison, and Jeremy Bailey, the British No Holds Barred champion; and Johnny Jacket was targeted but he managed to make it back to Base Camp One and he's now living with me.

The Royal National Lifeboats Institute said I could go out with them, no problem, and write all about it for *Front* magazine. Until they were told it was me and then suddenly it wasn't okay any more. Get this – I even lost the gig writing my page at *Front* magazine itself! After all this time.

The documentary I was due to make for Carlton in Ibiza was also mysteriously cancelled, *and* a Sky documentary on gangs and a documentary for Bravo about men behaving badly in Marbella. These producers are all really keen, they're the ones that get in touch with me, remember, and we can even be only days away from doing something when suddenly they cancel it and get all cagey. Weird eh? I feel like I'm being stalked by someone who has a lot of fingers in a lot of pies.

The police now harass my friends and pull everybody over. Journalists are warned to stay away, all builders that leave the house have their bags searched, cab drivers are interrogated when they leave, even our babysitters are warned not to work for us! Even the mothers of my daughters' school friends get little visits. They went into my dry cleaners and asked if there was ever any number or anything left in my pockets! Fellas that want to put on shows with me get the knock and the words in the ear. The worse one was when they sent social workers in as pretend supply teachers into my kids' school; the last week of the last term. Then asking my kids if Daddy had a gun in the house, or lots of cash, and did daddy use large Rizlas – shit like that. (The answer is, of course, that daddy is such a good roller he uses two, three or sometimes even four normal Rizlas.)

One of the women teachers in the school told me all that and warned me about what they were doing. She told me and warned me. She ended up coming to one of the book launches. She weren't easily scared off like a lot of people are.

Just like all those years ago in the Old Bailey before when I had to attend court with an armed escort around me – that made me look like Most Wanted No. 1 to the jury and did me no favours; which was the idea. And the armed guards came after some 'anonymous' phone call saying I was gonna escape. Yeah, right. It got the guns around me though, and that was the plan.

Y'know, after so many 'coincidences' I feel my Scales Theory coming on . . . Never underestimate the power of a group like the Freemasons. There are policeman, judges, politicians, and barristers. Secret service people who are all part of the moody handshake mob.

I found a bugging device in my house and sent it to my solicitor Ralph Haeems:

> Hello Ralph,
>
> This is what I've found in my house. What can I do about it? The CIB are still refusing to answer any of my letters or calls concerning the return of the videos, cassettes and photos that were taken from my home. The videos and tapes are very damaging to them, and I am sure they are stalling, purely in an attempt to say they have lost them along with the letters they claim to have lost.
>
> All my visitors are still being harassed and questioned, and this bug is further proof that they're not going to let go.
>
> Talk to you soon
>
> Dave Courtney OBE

And we sent a letter to CIB3 asking if the bug was theirs – who else's? – and if they'd like it back, or could we keep it 'cos they're worth a bit. They just refused to acknowledge it; and the reason they can do that is by saying you are still under investigation and it may compromise inquiries, blah, blah, blah.

I tell you who I'd love to sit down and have a drink and a chat with, Mohamed Al Fayed, Mr Harrods. If only he knew, me and him would be such good allies. He'd know exactly what I'm saying is true 'cos he's been on the receiving end of those tactics himself. The spies, the cameras, the warning people off, the long-term thinking. He's been through a similar thing to me but his was over getting a passport. And he's got financial backing. He must be fucking scary. He's smart, though.

Mind you, I wouldn't let him book me a cab home, you know what I mean?

Another big, big thing that happened was when I met Tupac's lawyers and legal team in America and had this fascinating conversation. Things are going really well for me now over in the States. I'd first met these guys in a Spearmint Rhino lap-dancing club over there, and I was telling them what I was going to be doing in America and how different it was to my situation back in Britain. Then they came over here and we met up again in the first club Spearmint Rhino's opened over here, on the Tottenham Court Road. I think of it as my local. Well, it's only twelve miles down the road.

The more I painted a picture of my situation the more this geezer saw parallels between what happened to Tupac. He said to me, tell me this Mr Courtney, do you understand that if something unusual happened to me I would probably see it happening before you did, especially if it's happened before? He went on to say that Tupac weren't only just naughty, he was *popular* and naughty, and that's a bad old combination in the authorities' eyes. He was earning so much money doing songs about anti-establishment things that he wouldn't have to do anything genuinely criminal ever again, and if he don't put a foot wrong they can't put him in prison again. He was so publicly anti-establishment, bringing up court cases and people's names who had been brutalised and abused. Because once something's been to court and been mentioned in front of the public gallery you can use the names in songs. And Tupac ended up really giving it to them.

He said to me that they only realised what was happening to him after it was too late. At one stage he was so popular he could have run for public office, something like mayor, and he would have won. Clint Eastwood once ran for mayor of the place he lived and he won it easy, which he would do 'cos he's Clint Eastwood! Too many fans not to win. America voted in an old cowboy actor as their president with Ronald Reagan. Rap music is now the most listened to music in America, and the world. And if you win a public vote then that's that, they can't take that away. You can't fuck around with that really, or it's very difficult in a democracy to alter the vote. That's a democratic thing and they would've had to give it to him. Or kill him. Or just kill him first.

Then the press started manipulating the supposed feud between the East Coast and West Coast, and he said they always wondered why they did that so strongly when it wasn't helping. It confused everyone why they were fuelling the fire. Then you got the silly bastards who actually believed it and started to act on it. Which enabled the police to do whatever they wanted:

shoot a black guy they wanted and put it down to East Coast/West Coast. In the end a geezer comes along behind blacked out glass and shoots Tupac. After the build up that's happened it's immediately put down as gangland – hardly anyone thinks of anything else. He actually said to me, 'The police did it . . .'

This lawyer knew more about me than I would've thought 'cos he'd been hanging out with British rap and dance music people as well. He weren't the least bit surprised when I filled him in on my adventures to try to be London mayor and this latest last case where they tried to paint me as a grass. He said he'd be wrong not to point it out to me if I hadn't obviously seen it already, but the parallels are there: he said the likeable rogue thing combined with someone who can manipulate the press is always thought of as a bigger threat than even the people themselves realise. Meaning even Tupac didn't know what he was letting himself in for, really. Or how seriously they would take him as an influence.

And if you're thinking long-term, like governments and agencies do, then they don't think about mending the problem, they think about averting it. Making it not happen *in the first place* so they don't have anything to mend.

See, music actually brings people together rather than pushes them apart. The old gang war thing ain't as strong as the bonds people form through music. I saw all that in the 80s in the rave scene – see *Raving Lunacy* – and back then when house music came out it destroyed the north/south London thing, 'cos it all became a music thing. It didn't matter that Ministry of Sound was in south London – everyone went there. So any tactics that prevents that power of people getting together and threatening authority will be used. We had it over here with the Criminal Justice Bill banning raves and parties for fuck's sake.

He said that every time a policeman saw a poster of Tupac it was like rubbing salt in the wound: the bad man made good. And he said now that he'd heard all about this case where I was portrayed as being an informant it made it easier for someone to shoot me and get away with it. They'd just put it down to an underworld killing, and they could get away with it 'cos they've laid the foundations and suspicions already. I ain't comparing the way I'm known in any way as the way Tupac was but, then again, in another way, if you think about it Britain is hundreds of times smaller than America so it's actually easier to make an even bigger impact here. And I travel not only this country but also around the world, doing 'Audience With Dave Courtney' concerts.

This geezer said to me that he would give me any help he could that didn't involve putting his hand in his pocket. Now that it is one very handy geezer to know, y'know what I mean? Him and his team. That's how I got to get in touch with Snoop Dog and Dr Dre. It helped that I'd already worked with Tricky 'cos he's rated in America by the dance and rap brigades. That's how we all got together to do a video with ILC, which is the company I work with, who are known for doing all the music videos. Me and Joey Pyle had a laugh playing prisoners in Oxford jail for Brian Harvey and Wyclef's latest video. There's actually a special music version of the Cannes Film festival and I've been there with ILC for the last two years.

And anyway you can never know enough good lawyers.

His warning reminded me of what Lord Longford had said to me not long ago. I'd arranged the wedding reception after Charlie Bronson's marriage and everyone was there – except Charlie of course, he was celebrating on the roof – and Lord Longford was one of the guests. At one point when he was sat down with us he turned to me and said, 'Young man, you do know that fear of your popularity goes to the very top.'

Anyway, as a measure of how I'm going over in the States the thing that happened next was a good example. The American rapper Jay-Z brought out his new album and then I started getting phone calls from people left right and centre asking me if I'd seen it. Yeah, I'm always down Virgin picking up the latest S Club 7 single. So I went down for a look and there was a whole wall full of CDs with a photo of a black *ME* on the cover! Fucking hell, I didn't realise having a black missus had rubbed off on me so much. I'd done a reverse Michael Jackson and got darker! Which is a good move if you can pull it off, 'cos your dick gets bigger, but you do get stopped by the police an awful lot more.

When you looked closer at the CD what it actually was was an exact copy of a picture of me from Jocelyn Bain Hogg's book *The Firm*, but with Jay Z replacing me in the pose. In the original I was at the Oxford Union to give a speech and Jocelyn took this photo from a balcony above and behind me, showing the duster next to me on the table. Wicked picture it is, and that's in a book that is absolutely chocker with wicked pictures.

Now if *Lock, Stock and Two Smoking Barrels* can take what they did from me for stories in a whole film then one geezer copying a photo of me ain't something I'm gonna worry about. In fact, I took it as a big compliment. I e-mailed Jay Z to say that I was honoured that he'd liked the picture that much. Next thing I know, though, is that Jocelyn is taking the record company to court over it. Now I ain't saying he ain't entitled to do that – 'cos I weren't losing anything by them doing it but Jocelyn was, I know that – *but* here I was trying to get on with these people and then that went and reared its ugly head; which I found a bit embarrassing 'cos they probably put it down to me. So they whipped all the CDs and records off the shelves! I had to step in there sharpish to stop that and pretty soon after I did an out of court settlement and everyone lived happily ever after. And the shelves got stocked again. Never let it be said that old DC gets in the way of a new CD.

Something else that was due to be back out on the shelves soon was Austin Warnes himself, believe it or not. He would've been up for parole in the summer of 2002 because of the suspiciously light sentence that he'd been given. No fucker could believe that when it happened. Can't have been 'cos he'd made some kind of deal with the Old Bill by any chance could it? I was at the head of the group making a stink about that and I don't mind saying so. Some people have said you shouldn't want to see anyone go down at all, but I think he was lucky to get off so fucking lightly as to be still breathing, even if it is inside a ten by eight cell.

Not only that but he actually appealed to the High Court to get his conviction quashed! So we all gave a cheer when the judge turned round and actually *increased* his sentence by a year. Oh, dear. Own goal. The *South London Press*, who had stuck it to me a bit during the trial, finally came to their senses and reported it straight: 'Former gangland boss Dave Courtney raised a glass in honour of British justice after a bent cop – who tried to frame him – had an extra year added to his jail sentence . . . Dave added: "It just goes to show that crime doesn't pay".'

That's so cheeky, I know, but I couldn't help it. But after suffering months of snide fucking accusations before the trial, and then full-blown accusations in the middle of it, I thought I was more than entitled to have a celebration wank over a judge getting it right for once. Which brings up another point, can you think of one other case where eight months before the case came to trial the police named their supposed 'informant' like they did with me? Bet you fucking can't 'cos I can't. The police just don't *do* that with real informants, obviously, they *protect* them. Any fucking idiot can see that. But with me, for some strange reason they decided to tell the world. Almost like they thought something might happen to me . . . or am I just being a teensy bit cynical? What do you think? Answers on a postcard to all the graveyards that contain all the people who have been killed or died in police custody, thank you.

Contrary to what some of my peers believe, that you shouldn't even want to see a policeman go to jail, there have to be some exceptions; and that would be paedophiles and other sex offenders because they are the enemy to all. But if you are in the position where someone has tried to get you murdered by what he decided to do I'd say that jail is a small price to pay. Plus, you have to think in the long-term. If that geezer had bat and bowled for so long then how many people had he already put in prison that didn't deserve to go there? That man must have done that to hundreds.

Okay, I've got another question for you. How do you buy the cheapest flight ticket and end up with the best seats in first class? No, using a shotgun counts as cheating. So does shagging the pilot. You do it by having a good mate called Brian who is a commercial airplane weight distributor. No I didn't know what the fuck it was either. Weight distributors are the blokes who have to computer-check that there's a safe and even distribution of weight on the airplane before it takes off. He can order passengers to be moved. He has the very last word before the plane goes. No ifs, no buts.

And when we're on a flight he says that the couple in F11 and F12 should be moved up front to first class. *Touch*. Move the big bald geezer with the sexy black chick. Thanks very much Mr B. He's done that for us all the time.

Well, last time he did that they refused to move us. Which just never happens. But this time the other staff just flatly refused to move me and Jen to another two seats. Brian couldn't believe it either and eventually they were forced to tell him why 'cos he weren't gonna let it take off. They said they'd had prior notice of who was going to be sat in those two seats and the police had been in and *bugged the headrests*. And that info came straight from the weight distributor's mouth. Just another example of how intensely they want me. I always keep my mobile on anyway, wherever we are, so we take calls where other people might not: like on airplanes from geezers called Brian.

Me and Jen went for a shag in the toilet so they missed that, and then we spent the next four hours talking the biggest load of old bollocks you can possibly imagine. I love the thought that somewhere there's a report saying that I am planning on visiting Ronnie Biggs in hospital, dressing him up as a nurse and smuggling him out; that I'm going to change my name to Dave I'll-never-be Courtney; that I'd read a report that said because police numbers were so low the Met were now accepting applications from people with criminal records (which is absolutely true) so I was definitely going to apply; that I was surprised the police hadn't realised yet that the twelve-year-old we pass off as our son Genson is really a short 32-year-old geezer who is actually my right-hand man; and that the next big drug to hit the streets would be a pill containing Valium and vitamin D, they're called VDs; that the Kray twins were really two very butch women; that my mum is a crack shot; I've got three nipples; Jennifer is Jewish; my cat's gay; God is Sagittarius; and my MOT's run out.

So that covered the first half hour of the flight. Then we really got stuck into it. By the time we landed we'd both confessed to being transsexual Mormons originally from Wales with a secret stash of reactivated M16s buried in bags in the back garden (I thought it might get the lot freshly dug over for summer).

I did feel so much better for getting it off my chest. My three-nippled chest!

30. BRIGHT LIGHTS, BIG TITTIES

Get married, get happy, get lucky, get laid . . . Hollywood or bust. And always bet on black.

These days I'm doing more films than Boots the chemist. But before that, we got back from abroad to find that the house had been broken into. Funny though, these burglars didn't take anything but paperwork and stuff from my computer, discs and files. Odd that, innit? What kind of 'burglar' is that then. Either a stupid one or a very clever one. We rang it in and reported it, more out of curiosity to see what would happen than anything else. It took them nearly four hours to send someone out to a 999 call.

Brendan got home at the same time to find his gaff had been done as well. Same thing was missing: paperwork and computer stuff, with a little bit more taken as well, but only enough to try to make it look like a cover act. It's a shame that before we flew out I couldn't have got odds from a bookie on the chances of two mates' houses being broken into when they're on holiday and similar stuff taken from both. A tenner on that would retire you early.

In Brendan's case, even after he'd reported it the police didn't come *at all*. He got his solicitor to complain and they said they'd come out but they couldn't find his house! That's Woolwich police saying they can't find a certain Woolwich street. How likely is that? Now if they'd got a report saying that Dave Courtney had been seen going in that address with an underage nun, a donkey in suspenders and carrying a shotgun, an egg whisk and a tub of jelly, I'm pretty fucking sure the police would've found the house that night! See, it's so blatant sometimes that it's worrying for that reason alone. By that I mean that if someone's being a real slippy cunt about trying to get at you then you know that even *they* must think it looks bad, which is why they do it behind the scenes, so as not to look like the bad guy. *But* if they start doing it openly it means they don't give a fuck what it looks like, they don't give a fuck about looking like the bad guy, and the reason they don't give a fuck is probably because they're too powerful to touch.

Anyway, the Courtney Roadshow rumbles on. The Talking Tour gets longer and longer. The convoy gets bigger and bigger, leaving more pleased, amused and entertained people behind. Even though I do say so myself. And I'm the only one of us guys left out there doing it. Well, Howard's still there, Howard Marks (and he's fucking wicked), but our shows are different; and even the police have relaxed their attitude to dope, so dope stories don't really freak them any more. With what I've got to say about them, though, they still seem to rate me as a Class A. Which is a backhanded compliment I suppose.

I recently did an 'Audience With . . .' show on the Isle of Wight. That was a massive success. Talk about having a captive audience. A few hundred thousand people clinging to a rock. I went on local radio and this prison officer phoned in to have a go at me. He was proper lagging so it weren't difficult to just rip the piss out of him. The gig was arranged by this geezer called Chewy, who also runs the doors over there. Absolute diamond geezer, as they say, and made the stay a pleasure. Wilf Pine (you'll remember Wilf from the other books) also helped make it a very memorable stay.

I got a call from Nick Moran, who played Eddie in *Lock, Stock . . .*, asking me to play a major part in his new film *Baby Juice Express*. So I got hold of a mate of mine, boxer Joe Bugner, and whose son, young Joe, runs doors in the West End, to be in the film as well. I can always bring a lot more to a film than just me. I should open my own casting agency, come to think of it. Guy Ritchie cast *Lock, Stock . . .* from my mates in my back garden. So in *Baby Juice* we had me, Joe Snr and Joe Jnr, Nick Moran, David Seaman, Samantha Janus, Seymour, and Cleo Roccos who was Miss Whiplash from the Kenny Everett shows. She's wicked, is Cleo.

Baby Juice Express is a comedy gangster film. I play Mr Bognor Regis: the Mister Big of Bognor! Bognor ain't even big enough for a Mister Medium but then that's all part of the gag. (Speaking of mediums, remind me of that a bit later on will you? Cheers.) The film's about this Mafia boss who goes into prison and he realises that if he dies in there the police get the whole of his estate unless he has an heir. So he wanks into a jar and they smuggle his spunk out so they can inseminate his wife, but someone kidnaps the spunk and holds it to ransom. There's only two hours before it dies. But it gets dropped and smashed so someone else wanks into a jar and it's a black geezer. I arrange the meet, she gets pregnant and the baby's born black, obviously. She takes it up to the prison to meet the boss and he drops down dead of a heart attack.

Mental story, innit? And it's really funny. The director is Mick Hurst and we'll be at Cannes with it this year. That's if the British police don't try to persuade France to close down the Cannes Film Festival because I'm there. They would if they could, but they can't. *The Big Breakfast* though invited all the cast members of *Baby Juice Express* onto the show, but said they couldn't help out with publicity if I was part of it. That was another blocker taking me out of the game. So the whole cast did the show but me.

Blockers are players in American football games and their job is to just knock over the other players and take them out of the action. That's how I felt, like a team of blockers were on my case. But even though that's an American expression from an American game I ain't got no blockers in America.

The American dream is really big for me now: and more alive than my British one really. Whenever we hit the tarmac in LA airport I thought that it felt more like the place for me every time I went. The best of it is that America lets you reinvent yourself, or at least they don't hold your past against you. Like I said, an old cowboy actor can become president. And an old dope smoker like Bill Clinton can as well. They don't half hold a grudge against the odd blowjob though, don't they, the Yanks? As Clinton found out.

On this last trip out I decided to combine business and pleasure. First I was going out to Joey Pyle's wedding in Las Vegas and I decided to make it a double and marry Jen out there as well. But I didn't tell her that, I just said we'd go for Joey's do. Jen packed her bags and got her best mate Angel to come along with me and Brendan.

Before that, though, we flew into Los Angeles to meet up with Guy Agardia and Scott from Sin City Films, the adult film company I'm working with. I told you all about my first exploits out their in *Raving Lunacy*, well things only got better. I'd been supplying British porn actresses out there with my partners Miles Parker and Ian. The auditioning I'd done back home in London was bloody good fun. The casting couch was alive and well, and the casting carpet and the casting stairs and the casting shower . . .

Being in LA and Hollywood is good enough in itself, but being out there in the sun making porn films is a proper spontaneous look-no-hands orgasm time. It don't get any better. LA's version of medium-sized tits is the same as our 'huge', and their big-titted birds look like they're smuggling basketballs. The town is big titty heaven. The cars don't have airbags 'cos the people do. And whether it be with the right or wrong kind of films I was at least out in Hollywood where it all happens. The reason I was going the porn route was that I've learned to expect walls to be put up before me in the ordinary industry, but in the porn industry that don't happen: that community is frowned upon anyway and came from the wrong side of the law to begin with. So if someone tries to warn them off from using Dave Courtney the porn people are just going to say, 'He used to do what? *So* what? There's a girl next door being anally fisted by a bisexual ginger dwarf. Top that!' See it's not the kind of community to get worried by the so-called morals of a policeman.

Now I've actually made a full-length, mainstream gangster movie of my own, *Hell To Pay*, I've already done the hardest thing first. And done it with fuck all budget. Anything after that experience has got to be easier. I can make another film whenever I want, or a porn film, or combine both. That ain't been done before. I'll find a way to identify my films visually like Tarantino's. When you issue the films on DVD you can do a main version and a sex scene version, like a mainstream film but with five or six proper sex scenes. A gangster film with sex scenes.

I'm into all this do it yourself in a big way 'cos I know I can always rely on *me*. So I've got my own publishing company, magazine, and now my own films. It's the only way to go if they're determined to not let you speak.

Me and Miles Parker finalised a deal that I star in eight adult movies. Miles has these two Russian twin sister dancer/porn actresses on the go making movies, so I think we'll squeeze them in somewhere. The first movie is going to be *Lock, Cock and Two Smoking Bimbos*. Yeah, it's based on that other well-known film – *ET*. Actually, as I've already mentioned, I think there is a porn film called *ET – The Extra Testicle*.

I've already filmed three of them in Barcelona, Beverly Hills and London. In the Spanish film with me there was Bev Cox, Posh Sarah, Bubbly Sam and the Russian twins. Just getting in and out of Spain was an event. On the way in I did the usual thing of putting my dusters and deactivated guns in one bag, knowing I'm going to have to explain it all to Customs. That's when my posters, books and DVDs come in handy to show they're just 'props' for the stage show. And it always works. But on the way back out when we were due to fly home the bag was searched by this Spanish Customs officer. Now I know what the look of love, or lust, looks like so when I saw how he looked at the gold knuckleduster he pulled out of the bag I knew that was that. He said, 'I can't let you take it out. Get on plane!' I said how they'd let me bring it in, what's the difference in it going out!

He weren't having it, though. The geezer was practically fondling the duster he'd fallen for it so much. So we had to leave 'cos the plane was getting ready to go. I just hope the Spanish cunt and my duster are very happy together, and at least now he's got a choice of four holes to put his dick in. And it's like when I flew to Glasgow I had a suitcase full of newspapers and clippings and posters and hundreds of bits of paperwork. That was too much for Customs to resist when they saw it – and my bags are always, *always* searched – the chance to go through Dave Courtney's files. They actually held up the plane while they photocopied the lot. I could tell it had all come out 'cos they made a big fucking mess of trying to put it all back in.

The porn film we did in London was at Mick Colby's mansion and the twin Russian girls insisted on being in it, so I gave in and said yes. And because I'm very lucky and my wife is as twisted as me – in a nice way – I can actually pick my fantasy, do it, film it, and then when it's sold you get paid for it! Is that dying and going to Heaven or what?

The British porn star Kathy Barry (I first saw her perform at my mate Alan Weaver's swingers club, Xanadu, in Manchester) also became part of my film company in this country. Very saucy lady she is and managed by her husband Phil. Good job if you can get it.

I ran into the *Playboy* people again after first seeing them in Cannes. Playboy TV seemed to find me interesting enough to interview and talk to, and they've done a documentary on me for their channel. I think I can live with some *Playboy* centrefolds knowing who I am. The Madonna connection to Guy Ritchie gets his films seen in America, then they like them 'cos they're fucking good films, and that gets Brad Pitt in there as well, and then they hear the stories of who Big Chris was based on and see some English press cutting – next thing you know, or *I* know, David Letterman the chat show big banana was asking to be sent over bits and pieces about me for his late night show. Then there's the Snoop, Dr Dre thing going on through me meeting the lawyers and being in Wyclef Jean's latest video with Brian Harvey.

See I can do all that over there but over here they won't even give me a licence for a bloody pub! Un-fucking-believable. Some of them over here wouldn't give me the time of day with an arm full of wrist watches.

So after we'd done some deals in LA me, Jen, Brendan and Angel caught a flight out into the desert to Las Vegas for Joey Pyle's wedding to his lady Julie. Just as we were leaving to get on the plane Guy shouted out 'Black 29! Play Black 29!' Meaning we should bet that at roulette. Everyone has their favourite numbers don't they, but someone else's lucky number probably ain't gonna be yours so we sort of forgot about it.

In-flight security now on American flights is shit hot since those Muslim geezers parked two planes in the Twin Towers. Jen even had to take off the miniature gold knuckleduster and sawn-off shotgun charms she has round her neck.

Flying into Vegas at night has got to be one of the best things I've ever seen. The desert is completely, totally pitch fucking black all around; totally dark 'cos there's no city lights or anything; below you there's only desert and the skeletons of people who wished they'd joined the RAC. And then gradually this glowing city of lights starts growing below you. It's amazing. Right out in the middle of there like that. It's like finding buried treasure. I was amazed that with all those light bulbs below him our pilot managed to spot the runway. I half hoped he'd get it wrong and land us right down the middle of the main strip. Then we'd just hop out onto a car roof, jump down and walk into a casino. How cool an entrance would that have been? Beat that James Bond. I know I'd pay to see it.

When we got into Vegas for Joey's wedding I asked Jennifer to marry me. She hadn't guessed that I was going to so it was a genuine surprise. But I could tell she thought I meant let's do it some time in the near future. I said, 'No, babe, I mean now. I mean *here*, tomorrow.' It was all guns blazing then to get things ready for the big day. We checked into our hotel the Treasure Island.

Vegas is the home of mental hotels. In fact, if anyone submits plans to build an ordinary hotel they reject it on the grounds that it's too normal. They've got the Luxor, which is a massive black glass pyramid with a laser shooting out the top; New York, New York, which has a half size copy of the New York skykline with the Statue of Liberty; Excalibur, which was right up my street 'cos it was like Camelot Castle – home from home! And Treasure Island hotel, which has a full-scale pirate ship on a lake right outside the main doors! It ain't exactly a Travelodge is it?

America is a wicked place for how easy they make it to do things that take forever anywhere else. Like shoot people. No, I mean like in Las Vegas they had Drive-Through Wedding chapels! Fuck me, how little time have those people got? Better than that was the Drive-Through Divorce! Check *that* out. That would put a new twist on the old Man and Wife Arguing In Car routine wouldn't it? He gets pissed off at her nagging him to pull over and ask directions so he suddenly swerves into the Drive-Through Divorce lane and hey presto – thirty seconds later they pronounce you ex-man and ex-wife and a geezer comes out with a chainsaw and cuts the car *right* down the middle. There – you've both got a motorbike each . . . now *fuck* off.

We went for the more difficult route of walking casually up to hotel reception and booking the full-blown wedding, just like that. You could have the $1,000, the $2,000 or the full monty $3,000. We went for the top dollar 'cos what's the point of not doing. You're *in* Vegas, you're in love, so so fucking what if you're out of pocket. That night, which was the night before we were going to get married, I had a stretch limo pull up outside the hotel to take us to the sheriff's office for the formal ceremony and to get the marriage certificate. On the way we passed the Drive-Through Wedding chapels where you could get married by Elvis for $50. The bloke that we got the certificate from also told us about the Drive-Through Divorce. He said, 'It costs $180 but they don't have two cabs 'cos one of yer's walkin' back, y'know?' *Ha*.

That night we had a good old gamble in the casino. Jen thought she might be like that person you read about who wins the million-dollar jackpot on the massive fruit machine, but after going through a big bucket of coins she realised it weren't gonna happen! Angel wanted to carry on playing but no one else wanted to – everyone else was either shagged or wanted to get shagged – so she dragged Brendan back down to the casino to have a final go. They were banging chips down on the roulette table and at the end of one spin the croupier pushed this massive stack of chips towards Bren. He said how much is there and the croupier went, 'One thousand eight hundred dollars, sir.' And yes, you've guessed it – the win came from a bet on Black 29! They couldn't hardly believe it, and I took some convincing as well. Especially when they woke me up at three in the bloody morning to tell me.

So that win took care of the mini bar bill.

Next morning we went out on a shopping spree to get Jen a wedding outfit. We had to be back at the hotel by twelve so Jen just stood naked in the cubicle and me and Brendan threw clothes over the curtain to her. There ended up more of the shop behind that curtain than there was out front. Part of the whole wedding package is that you spend the morning in the hotel before the ceremony just being totally pampered; massage, sauna, manicure, make-up, head shave, toe wax, tongue brush, nipple polish, nose wipe – that kind of thing. You come out shining like a new coin and smelling sweeter than an angel's fart. When I was down in the sauna there were these two Russian geezers in there with me – hard-looking fuckers that were in security – and I invited them up to the wedding.

I'd been a witness at Joey Pyle's wedding the day before. Not a very good witness because on pure instinct I blurted out, 'I didn't see a thing, guv.' Roy Shaw had been best man there. So next day all the same people attended our wedding Joe, Roy, Brendan, Angel, Orry, Chinese Jack, Dave, Rob, Dave Thurstron, Mitch, Mark Morisson, Brian Harvey, Tricky and Wycliffe Jean (who was in town playing at the Atlantic). Joey Pyle gave Jen away and Brendan was my best man. Roy Shaw was a witness and he didn't see anything either, Sarge.

The hotel actually has its own wedding chapel inside and to be honest, before we walked into it, I thought with it being Las Vegas it's going to be a bit, y'know, tacky. I had visions of a big neon cross flashing over a painting of Jesus singing karaoke with Elvis, with God on drums, and a geezer looking like Liberace's bastard lovechild playing the Wedding March on a Yamaha organ in the corner. I couldn't have been more wrong; it was this really, really beautiful church, absolutely stunning. I've never seen a church like it. I was wearing a leather Stetson hat I'd bought. Nothing else, just a leather Stetson. Jen was wearing white shorts, a white top, white slut boots and a white bowler hat and she looked like the horniest, sexiest virgin bride you've ever seen. I weren't the only one that thought that either – and ain't it distracting when the vicar gets a hard-on?

I hung my hat on it.

He must've taken one of those Viagras I'd given him earlier. I wondered if I'd get to kiss the bride before he did! I turned to Jen and said, 'Baby, you've got eyes like spanners.' She said why's that then. I said, 'Because every time you look at me my nuts tighten.'

When we'd gone into the chapel there earlier I'd put one of my flyers on the altar between Jesus' hands and the whole service was conducted with it there. The vicar wasn't so much a vicar, actually, he was more of a priest. In fact, he was more of a Pope! He did the vows, the whole bit:

'In sickness and in health, for richer and for poorer –'

'Excuse me,' I said, 'Hang on – sorry, mate, but we don't do poorer.'

'Oh, okay . . . for richer and . . . *richer!*'

Then at the end he said, 'You may both now kiss . . .' So together me and Jen leaned forward and kissed him on the cheeks. He went, 'No, no . . . kiss *each other*. Kiss the bride on the lips.' So I bent down and kissed her on the fanny. I did the whole of the ceremony with my hand on Jen's arse because I didn't have a ring. So that's one hell of a wedding video we've got – chaps, naughty geezers, prize-fighters, Russian bodyguards, singers, superstars, cowboy bridegroom, sexy bride, wicked chapel and a champagne reception all in Las Vegas. It'll be out on video and DVD soon: as soon as we've edited in the sex scenes and chosen the soundtrack.

We had the champagne wedding reception at a club inside one of the hotel casinos with Imagination and the Stylistics playing there. That's when Dave Thurston decided to show the Stylistics how to do one-armed press ups with a pint of beer on his head. Not that we were pissed or anything. The Stylistics looked impressed but I couldn't see them adding Dave's trick to their show as an encore. Then we all went to the Excalibur hotel to watch a jousting match. They've got a proper full-on medieval battle staged in the hotel! Like I say, that was home from home for us. It was just like a bigger version of our gaff in Plumstead, but without the undercover police plotted up outside.

Talking of sex scenes, which we weren't but we are now, we went from Camelot to 'come a lot' because as a surprise for Jen we had a hotel room visit from our own British porn star Kathy Barry. So we rounded off an absolutely fantastic day with our own spot of jousting.

While I was there in Vegas who should I bump into in a sports shop but Mike Tyson himself? He remembered us meeting in London before the Julias Francis fight when I'd done a little interview with him. We'd also met before, when I'd gone to America to watch my mate Ian Freeman fighting in the No Holds Barred Fighting Championship. Tyson was there supporting one of his friends. I said the next time we'd meet would probably be when I came out to watch him fight Lennox Lewis. Funny how you can bump into people. Yeah, it's a small world . . . but I wouldn't want to paint it.

Italy's one of those countries where after you land in the airport the first thing you seem to notice is police in 16-eye army boots walking round with machine guns on their backs. And that's just for cigarette smugglers. Going through Customs the geezer asked me if I had any firearms. I said, 'No, what do I need?' I hate that, when you end up travelling with the wrong weapon.

My Italian fella, Francesco, was as eager as ever to kick off the Dave Courtney thing in his country, and he was doing a fucking good job of it as well. The first documentary they'd made in London had been shown in Italy and they loved it. I remember when I was going to the airport that time to pick up the Italian lady who was doing the documentary and the Rolls Royce died on me on the motorway. So I was sat there on the bonnet waiting for the guy from the AA to come, and this bloke was driving past that was a fan of the book so he pulled over and asked me if he could help. I said it'd be blinding if he worked for Rolls Royce or, if not, if he could lend me his car and wait with the Rolls. Which he did, bless him. The car got fixed and he drove it back to my place, where Jenny knew he'd be hungry so she was waiting with something hot for him. And after that he had something to eat. And *I* got to the airport in time in his car to pick up the lady and we all lived happily ever after.

Tell you what though, that's the first and last time I ever drive an old Mini. I told the Italian woman that the Rolls had broken down but all Rolls Royces have a Mini in the boot for emergencies, like a lifeboat.

Any road, so after their own effort was a hit they showed the two British ones (the Channel 4 and Channel 5 programmes) as well, with subtitles.

We'd already been out to Venice to see Francesco over Christmas. Don't know if you've ever been to Venice, but when we were there some idiot had left the taps on. Fuck me, we had to get a boat everywhere.

What they want to do over there is make an Italian film about the story of a load of Italian gangsters coming over to England to watch football, and when they leave they kill my character's friends. I then get ten geezers and go on a vengeance-is-mine trip over to Italy. The comedy bit is I have two interpreters with me who have to translate everything I say. That's when I'll get to find out what 'silly cunt' is in Italian.

What sold me to them over there, and what hooked Francesco as well, was the fact that they've already read about hundreds of bank robbers and villains, etc., but they'd never heard of some cunt going to court forty-handed – and in a court jester's outfit – and punching a copper out in front of everyone. There's a sort of unwritten rulebook about going to court and I guess I tore it up. But it won't happen again, and as I said it was as much luck as anything that I got away with it. 'Cos it weren't planned, so it was lucky I had so many fellas with me. And that was my thing, what I did that day; that was my sort of ultimate event.

See the normal way a man feels about a policeman is you know if you piss him off or act all cocky he can just do you: he can get out of the car and do you for something stupid like a back light or a bald tyre, or some bullshit thing just to get at you. And you can't do fuck all about it usually. That's on the small end of the scale. At the other end of the scale the really bad, bent ones can stitch you up or kill you. And the police themselves *know* all that, so they know they play on it and they know they always have the upper hand in the mental battle. But they know that don't work with me and that I don't give a fuck 'cos they know I laid one of them out across a courtroom floor. So they know I ain't got that little nervy feeling around them that they usually play on. Oh and I hate it that they're not relaxed around me! I do, I hate that – *ha*.

Anyway, big risk – big reward, and the court jester event really helped create interest and sell me abroad. *Stop the Ride I Want to Get Off* is due out in an Italian version this year and they did an eight-page feature on me in Italian Vogue *Homme*. So now I'm a proper Homme-boy.

Remember how in *Raving Lunacy* I said that when rave music first came out, to people with no religious feelings the music scene became like their religion, clubs were their churches and DJs had their own followings. People did go out clubbing religiously. Well, this latest trip to Italy for me turned into an experience of both those sides.

I went down to Rome for a few days. I stayed with a mafia geezer I'd been put onto and I also, get this, opened the first bingo hall in Rome! The main reason I'd gone there was to appear on stage with Tricky because he was doing a live version of *Products of the Environment*, the album he made with me, Freddie, Joey, Tony, Roy and the other chaps where we talked over music. The gig was an absolute ball! Afterwards we decided to do an Italian version of *Products* using their own villains.

While I was there for a few days I went to the Vatican. Somewhere that couldn't be more different from what I'd been doing the night before at the concert, but the Vatican was just as amazing in a way. I don't think you realise sometimes until later what you pick up from your parents when you're growing up in terms of religion, and you probably wouldn't put me down as a religious person, but being there in the churches did help sort my head out about a few things. Going back to when I was on remand in Belmarsh prison for nearly a year in 1996 one of the best things I got sent was a bible. I've mentioned this in *Stop the Ride* . . . and how everyone thought I was joking. It was an antique bible sent to me by the dad of my good mate Posh John. I actually read it through, which I'd guess most people haven't ever done. There are proper life lessons in there. And then I read it through again. Just in case of an emergency. You never know when you might need a good prayer. And if you can't read the Bible through without it making you think, then there's something wrong with you. For one thing, it reminds you that you can repent.

I do envy people that have got deeper faith than me, though; it must be nice knowing that when your time comes old Holy Hands upstairs is waiting to catch you.

Which reminds me of when I was talking to this American tourist in the Vatican. He was a really rich and smart-looking, very well-dressed geezer, and he told me how pissed off he was when the Pope did a walkabout the week before and instead of stopping to talk to him he shuffled past and went over to this scruffy looking tramp and bent down and had a word. The Yank couldn't believe it; he thought he was going to have a story to impress his mates with. I said the Pope was probably doing what he thought he should do by talking to the most disadvantaged in society. He said that he'd thought the same thing, so afterwards he'd actually bought that tramp's clothes off him. Gave him fuck knows how much and the tramp was over the fucking moon.

Next day, he said, he was stood there in the shit clothes looking like this tramp. His pal was stood ready with the camcorder just in case. The Pope came out and did his little shuffle-about, shaking hands and giving blessings, and he came right over to the American and took his hand. He thought, fucking hell, it's worked. Then, he said, the Pope leaned over and said softly in his ear, 'I thought I told you to fuck off.'

31. EXTRA MEDIUM

'The fags were a nice touch . . .'

When I was a lot younger me and my mates did a Ouija board session one night. All the lights off, candles on, letters chalked around a table, and all our hands on this glass in the middle. We said, 'Is there anybody there?' and there was just silence, then a little gust of wind, then the glass shook a bit, and then it started moving slowly and it spelt out . . . 'No'.

So that was the end of that and we all went home. What a fucking disappointment. It was our own fault really – we shouldn't have tried to reverse the charges. Then another time we stayed up all night playing poker with tarot cards. I got a full house and three people died.

If you're out clothes shopping with your missus and bored out of your box just amuse yourself by freaking with the shop assistants. When they ask you if they can help you, say, 'Have you got anything I'd like?' Then when they ask you what size you are, say, 'Extra medium.' Then keep a straight face and watch theirs.

I don't really believe in all that speaking to the dead bollocks. Sometimes it's hard enough just getting through to the living, for fuck's sake. Or someone who works in McDonald's. I did see a medium, though, who was at a gig I was doing, and he cracked on like he was speaking to people I'd known. But he'd just read my book! I could tell it was that. He'd just done *Stop the Ride* . . . in advance to get genned up. So I wrote down on a piece a piece of paper 'I know you've got my book' and folded it. There was loads of people there 'cos I was doing a signing, and he came over to me. I said, 'Listen mate I've got all three of my books here, do you want copies?' He said, 'No I'll have those two there.' Gotcha! That's when I handed him the bit of paper and watched him open it.

Next time something like that happened was when I met another geezer at one of my 'Audience With . . .' gigs called Ian who said he was a medium. He looked more like a large to me, but there you go. He said he was from Scunthorpe, I said that ain't your fault, and he said he wanted to do a show up there with me but first wanted to visit me in London so he could 'tune in'. He said he'd already had a message for me from Ronnie Kray.

So, he came down one day and we went out driving around. Now you know me, I'm more tolerant than most people when it comes to nutters if I think there's some value to be had there. I've got a very high nutter threshold, as it happens. Otherwise I'd have no friends. *Ha.* I said to him that I knew it was difficult for him 'cos most things that he might say I could just think he'd got from the books. Because all that information you get from a book you wouldn't usually have on someone. But when you've read someone's autobiography – *Stop the Ride I Want to Get Off*, Virgin,

£6.99, paperback, all good bookshops (and a few shit ones) – then it is doubly difficult to pull one out the hat. So I weren't expecting much, to be honest.

Then he went, 'Ronnie says, "The fags were a nice touch but the phone was a bit much".' I tried not to mount the pavement and run over a bus queue. I told him he could stop right there, I believed him, and he didn't have to show me any more.

What happened was this: back when Ronnie was lying in state at English & Sons undertakers, me and my boys guarded the place day and night. I thought it would be a nice touch to put a pack of his favourite smokes, Benson & Hedges, in his inside jacket pocket. For the journey. I'd thought, well, if he goes *down* he'll be all right for getting a light and if he goes *up* I'll be fucking astonished. When I went to slip the pack into his jacket I found one already there. Someone had had the same idea. So I took out my mobile phone and tucked it in his other pocket instead. And you know what, afterwards, when the coffin had been sealed, I couldn't for the life of me remember whether I'd switched the fucker off! I was absolutely shitting myself that on the big day, just as he was being lowered into the grave, the phone would go off in the coffin and start throwing out the James Bond Theme ring-tone that I had on it.

Now if I'd ever got a call from that phone *after* the funeral that would've fucking freaked me out big-time. You *know* that. And I did sometimes think of that – what if I just missed getting to the phone one day when it was ringing and then I did a 1471 number trace and my old mobile number came up. Well they say a heart attack can be a quick way to go. But death by diarrhoea I wouldn't fancy.

The reason only very, very few people knew about what I'd done was that during that time that Ronnie was in state the papers ran an untrue story that loads of mental things were going on inside the funeral parlour: people sniffing coke off the coffin or having séances and shit like that. It weren't true, of course, but some people wanted to believe it was. So, even though me giving Ronnie something for the journey was meant to be a nice gesture I knew it would be misinterpreted after what had already been written. So I kept schtum. I think only Jenny knew.

He also said that Ron was upset with me for deserting him. I genuinely didn't know what he meant by that so I asked. He said that he was talking about the night after the picture was stolen from his grave, when I went back there to guard it through the night. I did do that, but not long after the newspaper photographer had taken the picture of me by the headstone I shot off home. It was fucking freezing, mate. I could've caught *my death*. Only a select few knew about that one as well. Then Ian said that Ron weren't alone, he was with Charlie and Reg. I thought, I wouldn't fancy sharing that fucking cloud.

'The fags were a nice touch but the phone was a bit much . . .'

Fuck me sideways with a French kipper. That was absolutely gob-smacking. What a double whammy of a head fuck. First the trip to the Vatican and now the voices from the other side. All I needed now was to hear God's voice in my head; probably saying 'you do wank an awful lot don't you, David?' He sees everything though, don't he? When I thought of that it put me right off. For at least an hour.

Ian said he'd much rather not get messages from these people than get them, because all the other fake mediums always seem to get in touch with well-known dead people. I suppose they've still got box office draw even when they're stiff. He said it had never happened to him before, so now that it had people were more likely to go oh yeah? The Kray twins? *Shut* up. Bit like when I thought that doing Ronnie Kray's funeral would be the best advertisement for me and it turned into a burden.

The people that were with me at the time when Medium Ian said what he said were Don Crosby and the comedian Al Benson. He also gave a message to Jenny from her brother John who died in an accident a couple of years ago. It was also a very personal message that only he and she would know.

Stuff like that rocks you. But it's bloody reassuring as well, y'know what I mean. Just knowing that if you die before you've said everything you wanted to say you could come back through someone else and say, 'Tell so-and-so he's a cunt!' Wouldn't that be really, really funny, to speak from the other side and go, 'I still think you're a prick. And so does everybody else here. Please don't die 'cos we don't want to fucking see you!'

Anyway, I did go up north to Scunthorpe to do an 'Audience With . . .' gig with Medium Ian, which was organised by Jamie. I also sponsor Jamie's football team and they've got www.davecourtney-notfuckingguilty.com on their shirts. I wanted to advertise it as 'The Show That Put the Cunt in Scunthorpe' but the local radio station didn't go for it for some reason. Cunts. And they'll still be cunts when I'm dead. And I'll tell 'em.

He also got messages from my dear old nan, bless her. Although I did say to Ian that him getting messages from my nan did start wobbling my faith a bit. He asked me why. I said, 'I'm just finding it hard to believe that my little old nan and Ronnie Kray went to the same place!' That alone made it hard to believe. Either he did a lot more work for charity than we thought or my nan was a secret mass murderer. Or maybe they all just meet in the lift.

The message from my nan was, 'Remember all those old sayings I told you should be your commandments, and never more than now.' Those were the things she used to tell me as a kid, all those clichés that don't mean anything till you get old enough to see the truth in them. Another thing he said she said was, 'Jealousy never raises its head as itself.' That hit home, and it's so true. Jealousy always does come dressed as something else; it's always in disguise. Think about this: have you *ever* heard *anyone* ever say anything like, 'Yeah, I'm really jealous of him and it fucks me off watching him earn loads of money and the fact that he can buy better clothes and cars than me really pisses me off and I just hate watching him get on!'? Never have I heard anyone say anything remotely close to admitting they are jealous. I mean, jealousy mustn't really exist 'cos you never ever hear anyone admit to it. And if you did accuse someone of it they'd freak out, 'You what! *Me*? Jealous of *him*. That *prick*!' Even though it's very visible to everyone else in the world. It's harder to admit you're jealous than it is you've killed someone.

Bang on again there, Nan – jealousy never raises its head as itself, and that's never more true than now. I didn't ever naively believe that everyone would be happy for me to get on, I know human nature too well to think that, but even I was surprised how some people reacted. From the top right down to the bottom. From friends right down to the police. The court case proved that without a doubt.

But for every big test you go through you get back something from it that you would never have got if you hadn't ever had the test. It's like your little stint in the army, or in prison. Some plants thrive in the heat and some die. That's how I look at it. You find out what you can do yourself and, also, you see the strengths and weaknesses of those around you. Fire fucks up wood but it forges *metal*.

The best side of it – and I always knew this would be true, even before it happened – is being in the position *to take people with me*. Do you know what I mean by that? Okay, one thing I cannot for the life of me understand is when someone makes it successful at something and then leaves their old friends behind. Half of the whole point of it, to me, is to be able to *take them with you*. Like when I used to be the one who'd pay himself in to the cinema and then sneak down to the firedoor and kick it open to let everyone else in. Same thing. No one can ever really retire from crime because your head won't let you do a crappy job for one tenth of the money you've made from what you did before, *unless* someone comes along and offers you the same money for doing something straight. That's why I enjoy throwing out lifelines, ladders and bridges to people.

The more book deals, film parts, TV work, music contracts, advertising gigs, backstage passes, party invites, premiere tickets, holidays, money, sex and chocolate I can get for other people the happier I am. I'm having a ball doing what I'm doing for me but also doing it for me and mine. Me and my people. And you don't even have to have met me to be one of mine. Just the right kind.

We shall go to the chosen land, and the chosen land is Hollywood. Fuck me, that trip to the Vatican and those messages from the dead have spun me off on a proper old biblical/religious trip ain't they? Jesus Christ.

No, just call me 'Dave'.

So I'm still standing, even with a shot ankle! Take more than that to stop me dancing, matey. Hollywood here we come. And Hollywood is a good place to come. Watch this space.

See you out there.

THANKS

The First Lady – my Jen

The Courtney Clan – Beau, Levi, Chelsea, Courtney, Genson, Drew, Patrick, Sue, Mum

The Unusual Suspects – Seymour Young, Brendan McGirr, Terry Turbo, Ray Bridges, Marcus Redwood, Johnny Jacket for absolutely everything, Matt, Christian, Wolfie, Dave Legano, Warwick, Eammon O'Keefe, Lou, Adam, Wilf Pine, Johnny McGee, Joey Pyle Snr, Joe Pyle Jnr, Freddie Foreman, Tony Lambrianou, Bruce Reynolds, Nick Reynolds, Roy Shaw, Ronnie Biggs, Mickey Biggs, Albert Chapman, Amon Ash, Mick Colby, Charles Bronson and Sarah, Tucker, Mad Pete, Wish, Ian 'The Machine' Freeman, the Olefontes, Big Barry, Cas Pennant, Carlton Leach, Marc and Tark, Tony, Big Rob, Lee Smith, Frank and Sheila, Gary, Gavin, Kevin, Blakey, Ben, Lindsay, Shaun, Dave Quelch and his lady, Joe Moore and family, Saskia, Kevin and Steve, James A, Wally, Rocky, Ricky, Ronnie, Mark Bates, Big Ron, Warren, Andy Finlater, Steve, 'Tardis' George, Ebo, Al Benson, Don Crosbie, Mark Ives, Eric, Robbie, John, Lloyd, Colin Robinson, Robert Hanson, Russell Carter, Colin Little, Welsh Bernie, 'Agent No. 10', Kevin Jenkins, Dean, Brenda, Brooklyn John, Gilly, Tom Heckman and Vince Santos, Steve Bogart, Funny Glenn, Nutty Neil, Tony, Basil, John Boy, Manny, Gary Davidson and Billy Aird, Billy and Harry Hayward, Big Reg Parker, Billy Dalou, Nigel Benn, Julias Francis, Joe Bugner Snr and Joe Bugner Jnr, Mike Tyson, John Harty, Roberta, Bradley, Flanagan, Howard Marks, Mad Tim, Ricky English, Big Memmy, Northern Billy, Mickey Goldtooth, Mr McGee, Steve McFadden, Tricky, Costas, Lorna, Jackie, Vinoo, Donna Cox, Jaz, Gilly, Billy, 'Fast Car' Ricky, Mark and Gus at Elite Cars, Boris, Eddie the Eagle, The Peacock Gym, Spike, Mickey Taylor, Diamond Dom, Harry Starbuck, Ned Rawlings, Des & Phil and all Outcasts, Dave Ford, Big Chewy, Les and Joe, Charlie Breaker and lady, Old Mill pub chaps, Birmingham John and Stuart, Gilkicker and Tony, Rhea, Reemer, Liana and Doug, the beautiful Ashley, Paddy Sullivan, Bal and Sue, Andy Jones, AJ, Steve Raith, Jonathan Evans, Ron, Val, Chas, 'Eight Ball', Steve Low, Pard, Pat Brogan, Big Mel, Dean, Short Stories, Danny D, Phil, Des, Kevin Suma, Stormin' Norman, Angela and the Bostock family, 'Leeds' Jimmy, John 'Sir' Edwards, Lord Longford, Ken Livingstone, Gyles Brandreth, Andy Beckwith, Bob and Steve, Dock Gate 20 Harleys, Leon Lee, Gary Ditton, Jimmy at Tills Motors, Craig, Jeremy Bailey, Keith Rose, 'Trisha' security boys, Jason Mariner, Dieter Wittmer, Caeser the Geezer,

Jeffrey Archer, Angel, Orry, Chinese Jack, Dave Thurston, Mitch, Medium Ian, Don Crosby, Al Benson, Scunthorpe Jamie, Mark Fisher, Dave, Nicky James, Jerry & Kate, Bev & Dean Cox, Gavin the gatemaker, Stuart from Relaince Joinery, Phil from Creative Innovation, Scott 'The Tile' Wolstencroft, Miss Karen, Marnie Threapleton, Auntie B, Cherie, Phillipa, Naomi, Trudy, Zoe, Nicole, Mo, Meg, Nancy, Rene, Mollie, Storm, Abigail, Storm, Tracey, Zara, Sarah, Indiana Courtney and Dave Courtney Snr, all doormen and all the boys on the frontline, Jesus Christ himself, God, the inventor of the knuckle-duster, and my cobbler

Pens & Lenses – Marcus Georgio, Ray Mudie, Humphrey Price, all Virgin people, Piers Hernu and Eoin McSorley at Front, Gary Bushell, Tony Thompson, Ian Edmondson, Jocelyn Bain Hogg, Martin Brunt, Tony Jackson, Malcolm, Ricardo, Ali Catterall, Simon Wells, Steve Richards, John Blake, Norman Parker

'Hell To Pay' & Films – Eammon O'Keefe (again), Peter Wells-Thorpe, Ross, Darren, Ursula, Phil, Andy, Rob Gomez, Malcolm Martin, Austin Vernon, Brian Hovmand, Scott Walls, Bill Murray, Joe Guest, Lone Wolf, Big Marcus, Jimmy Kent, John Conteh, Helen Keating, Nick Moran, Max Hardy, Stefan, Kathy Barry, Dave Seaman, Mick Hurst, Anne Foged, Barbara Windsor, Cleo Roccos, Guy Agardia and Scott, Sin City Films, Bev Cox, Posh Sarah, Riccardo, Christine, Martin Hancock, John Altman, Andy Beckwith, Mark Munden, Victor Films, Ray Winstone, Jamie Foreman, Quentin Tarantino, Guy Ritchie

Law – Ralph Haeems, David Haeems, Tokes, Bennett Welch, Mr Litham QC, Austin Warnes (and all bent coppers), Mr Collins QC, DC Tyson, DC Critchley, Dom Sharman, the British justice system

Clubs & Music – The Aquarium, One Nation, Stringfellows, For Your Eyes Only, China Whites, Ministry of Sound, Sugar Reef, Hippodrome, Time & Envy, Linnekers, Dean Lambert, The Belevedere Peckham, Steve Whale and The Business, Mute, Stereophonics, Lulu, Brandon Block, Carl Cox, Terry Ramjam, Heidi, Danielle Montana, Tupac, Puff D, Jay-Z, Mark Morrison, Brian Harvey, Wyclef, Snoop Dog, Eminem, Dr Dre, Death Row

NOTE: And a very, very genuine and massively heartfelt 'sorry' to anyone that is not down here that should be

Dave Courtney OBE

INDEX

Abbot, John 215
Agardia, Guy 266
Agent No 10 130
Al Fayed, Mohamed 258
Alderson, John 181
Altman, John 189
Amy 242, 243
Anderson, Pamela 209
Angel 268, 269, 270
Anti-Corruption Unit, Scotland Yard 55
Archer, Jeffrey 201, 237, 238, 244
'Audience With Dave Courtney' 48, 78, 93, 94, 97, 98, 107, 108, 120–1, 123, 152, 216, 265, 274, 276
Ayonmike, Itse 256, 257

Baby Juice Express 236, 265
Bacon, Francis 91
Bailey, Jeremy 257
Barran, Paul 26, 29
Barry, Kathy 249, 267, 271
Barry, Phil 267
Beckwith, Andy 189, 213
Belmarsh 25–31, 37, 51, 59, 87, 92, 128, 238
Bennett, Keith 255
Bennett, Winnie 255
Benson, Al 276
Big Brother 189
Big Chris 33, 46, 268
Big John 48
Big Marcus 31, 122, 189
Big Mark 122
Big Mel 130
Biggs, Mickey 189, 248
Biggs, Ronnie 124, 130, 189, 215, 216, 238, 248, 263
Birmingham John 130
Birmingham Six 180
Blackwell, Chris 94
Blair, Tony 176, 201, 244
Bobby's Bar, Tenerife 97, 98, 105
Bodingson, Doug 199
Brandreth, Gyles 234
Bravo 257
Breaker, Charlie 198, 229
Brendan 42–3, 45, 59, 64, 81, 84, 97, 130, 149, 154, 187, 195, 200, 202, 203, 204, 205, 206, 207, 208, 210, 211, 214, 227, 229, 231, 232, 233, 234, 264, 266, 268, 269, 270
Bridges, Ray 6
British Army Football Team 251
Brogan, Pat 131

Bronson, Charles 27, 123–4, 130, 224, 263
Brooklyn John 88
Brown, Lee 149
Bruno, Frank 228
Brunt, Martin 256
Bubbly Sam 267
Bugner, Joe 236, 265
Bulldog 95, 97
Bush, George 244
Bushell, Gary 130, 189, 254

Cannes Film Festival 187, 188, 195, 196–205, 210, 212, 236, 240, 253, 265, 267
Carlton 257
Channel 4 124, 155, 164, 167, 272
Channel 5 124, 155, 164, 165, 166, 167, 168, 172–3, 196, 272
Chapman, Albert 130
Chewy 265
Chinese Jack 270
CIB/CIB3 35–6, 37, 38, 41, 43, 51, 73, 74, 75, 84–5, 127, 140, 141, 159, 161, 162, 174, 176, 177, 183, 195, 201, 244, 258
Clinton, Bill 266
CN Soho Live 236–7
Cohen, James 124, 155, 164
Colby, Mick 267
Combat 186
Condon, Sir Paul 74, 244
Conteh, John 189, 213
Cook Report 32
Cook, James 34, 52, 129, 134, 136, 137, 153, 154, 155, 158, 159, 164
Cook, Roger 32
Courtney, Beau 97, 98, 105, 130, 237
Courtney, Chelsea 130
Courtney, Drew 97, 98, 105, 130
Courtney, Genson 85, 97, 98, 105, 130, 263
Courtney, Jennifer 15, 27, 28, 31, 42, 43, 45, 47, 48, 49, 65, 81, 82, 85, 86, 95, 97, 98, 99, 100, 101, 102, 105, 107, 110, 116, 121, 122, 125, 128, 130, 139, 144, 147, 148, 149–50, 154, 155, 169, 173, 187, 203, 205, 212, 231–4, 236, 239, 242, 243, 249, 250, 261, 263, 266, 268, 269, 270, 271, 275, 276
Courtney, Kevin 130
Courtney, Levi 130
Cowboy 130
Cox, Bev 267
Crime Through Time Museum 91, 130
Crimewatch 33, 46, 144, 146, 197, 225
Criminal Justice Bill 260
Crocodile 228

Crosby, Don 276
Crowe, Russell 200
Crown Prosecution Service (CPS) 37, 161, 162, 176, 201, 222, 245

Daddy Fox 201, 202, 203, 253
Daily Express 162, 215
Daily Mail 215
Daily Sport 27, 126
Daily Telegraph 215
Dando, Jill 179
Dave Courtney's Underworld 165, 166, 168
Dave the Builder 130
Depp, Johnny 115
Dholakia & Cummings-John 57
Ditton, Gary 226
DJ Caesar The Geezer 254
Dockgate 20 198
Dougie 40–1
Dr Dre 260, 268

Eamon 156, 159
EastEnders 80, 189, 250
Eastwood, Clint 259
Ebo 47, 48–9, 61
Edmondson, Ian 256
Edwards, John 167
Everett, Kenny 265

Firm, The (Hogg) 212, 261
Ford, Dave 255
Foreman, Freddie 255, 273
Francesco 231, 235, 236, 271, 272
Francis, Julius 228, 271
Freakshow, The 253
Freeman, Ian 'The Machine' 90, 213, 271
Front 31, 33, 46, 47, 51, 61, 80, 90, 112, 139, 146, 167, 214, 227, 252, 257

Gangland Britain (Thompson) 4
Gardener, Andy 97
Get Carter 253
Gomez, Rob 188
GQ 167, 235
Granada 188
Guest, Jo 189
Guy 112, 130

Haeems, David 129
Haeems, Ralph 129, 258
Hardy, Max 242
Harvey, Brian 80, 261, 268, 270
Hayman, Andy 75
Hefner, Hugh 197, 207
Hell To Pay! 1, 176, 187, 189, 195, 198, 201, 204, 205, 210, 213, 214, 226, 228, 229, 253, 254–7, 256, 266
Hernu, Piers 31, 33, 81, 88, 144, 167, 231

Hogg, Jocelyn Bain 130, 212
Home Office 162
Hurst, Mick 265
Huxford 122

ILC 260–1
Imagination and the Stylistics 271
Inland Revenue 196, 253
IRA 5, 122, 164, 179
Isaacs 48

Jacket, Johnny 257
Jackie 97, 98, 102, 105, 154
Jackson, Tony 124, 155, 164, 168
James, Daniel 34
James, Kim 34, 35, 37, 70, 71, 73, 137, 147, 151, 161, 162, 163
James, Simon 34, 35, 52, 77, 129, 134, 136, 137, 154, 158, 160, 162, 164
Janus, Samantha 265
Jay-Z 261
Jenkins, Kevin 78–9, 91
Jerry Sadowitz Versus The People 50
Jones, Andy 91, 130
Jones, Vinnie 33, 114–15, 168

Kathleen 110, 111
Keating, Helen 189
Kevin 31, 121, 123, 130
Kinky House 13–16
Kray, Charlie 1, 87, 90, 103, 112, 170, 180, 197, 234, 275
Kray, Reggie 1, 32, 87, 88, 89, 90, 91, 92, 103, 131, 197, 212, 213, 234, 263, 275
Kray, Ronnie 1, 32, 46, 75, 88, 90, 91, 103, 167, 197, 234, 253, 263, 274, 275, 276
Kray, Violet 88

Lambrianou, Tony 255, 273
Latham, DI 35, 38, 45
Laverick, DS 52–5, 70, 71
Law & Commercial 70, 73
Lawrence, DC 52, 55
Lawrence, Stephen 121
Leeson, Nick 181
Legano, Dave 189
Letterman, David 268
Lewis, Lennox 271
Lock, Cock and Two Smoking Bimbos 267
Lock, Stock and Two Smoking Barrels 33, 46, 114–15, 168, 215, 253, 254, 261, 265
London Metropolitan Police Force 3, 26, 35–6, 37, 43, 60, 73–4, 117, 141–2, 155, 160, 161, 174, 183, 184, 194, 215, 221, 236, 241
Lone Wolf 122, 130
Longford, Lord 261
Los Angeles 113–16
Low, Steve 131

LWT 178

Mad Aussie 198
Mad Pete 14, 81, 88, 121, 122, 155, 172, 190, 207
Madonna 115, 234, 267
Manhattan café, Woolwich 131–2
Manson, Charles 197
Marcus 6, 81, 130, 154, 165
Marks, Howard 80, 96, 95, 96–7, 130, 264
Matt 81, 137–8, 154, 155
McFadden, Steve 131
McGee, Johnny 193
McGirr, Brendan 149
McSorely, Eoin 47
Men & Motors 226
Meridian TV 256, 257
MI5 181
Mickey Goldtooth 85, 96–7, 105, 212, 247
Miss Whiplash 265
Montana, Danielle 236–37
Moorcroft, Nick 167
Moran, Nick 236, 265
Morrison, Mark 80, 228, 254, 270
Mudie, Ray 167
Munden, Mark 235
Murray, Bill 176, 189
Mute 236, 256

Naseem, Prince 228, 229
National Criminal Intelligence Service 215
National Identity Card 222
News Of The World 178–9
Nicholson, DCI 161
Nickel, Rachael 179
No Holds Barred Fighting Championship 257, 271
Noye, Kenneth 178–80

O'Nasty, Jackie 208, 209
Observer 162–4
Oakenfold, Paul 115
Okonola, Tokumba 57
Operation Nectarine 84
Orry 270
Outcast Phil 130, 247–50
Outen, Denise Van 236

Palmer, John 97, 103, 104
Parker, Miles 266, 267
Paul, Chris 115
Paul, Zoe 115
Pedder, Keith 75
Pine, Wilf 88, 130, 265
Pitt, Brad 267
Playboy 1, 207, 267
Police National Computer (PNC) 70
Posh John 130, 273

Posh Sarah 267
Powers, Ed 116
Products Of The Environment 167, 273
Profits Of Crime Act 26
Pyle, Joey 1, 212, 228, 253, 255, 261, 266, 268, 270, 273

Queens Reservoir Club 205

Raving Lunacy 49–50, 50, 75, 109, 115, 123, 124, 168, 170, 201, 212, 261, 266, 272
Reagan, Ronald 259
Rees, Jonathan 34, 35, 52, 58, 70, 77, 122, 129, 134, 136, 137, 154, 158, 160, 162, 163
Reynolds, Bruce 124, 213, 235
Reynolds, Nick 124
Ricardo 231
Ritchie, Guy 115, 250, 254, 265, 267
Roccos, Cleo 265
Ross, Nick 146, 189
Royal National Lifeboats Institute 257
Rules of Arrest, The 55

Sarski 32
Scene, The 27, 131
Scotland Yard 55, 92
Seaman, David 265
Seamus O'Dell's 154, 172
Seymour 81, 88, 95, 97, 98–9, 100, 102–5, 130, 137–8, 154, 174, 202, 212, 213, 265
Shaw, Roy 149, 253, 270
Shayler, David 125
Short Stories 90, 135
Sin City Films 112, 266
Sky 124, 186, 188, 256, 257
Smith, Lee 149
Snatch 213
Snoop Dog 260, 268
Solly, Damian 243
South London Press 149, 195, 257, 262
Spearmint Rhino 259
Special Branch 181
Stefan 243
Stereophonics 80
Stevens, Sir John 75
Stoneyford Lodge 107–8, 109
Stop the Ride I Want to Get Off 1, 15, 25, 27, 40–1, 46, 47, 48, 49, 59, 64, 75, 83, 93, 95, 105, 107, 115, 134, 158, 166, 199, 205, 210, 224, 230, 235, 250, 272, 274
Stormin' Norman 6
Straw, Jack 176, 181, 195
Stringfellows 29
Suma, Kevin 149
Sun 254
Sunday Express 215, 216
Sunday People 256
Sunday Sport 230

Sunday Times 253, 255

Tarantino, Quentin 93, 94, 98, 115, 186, 188, 194, 215, 253, 266
Tardis Studios 46, 124
Tenerife 95–106
Terry Turbo 27, 131
Thomas Pink 255
Thurstron, Dave 270
Tills Motors 225–6
Times, The 215
Tricky 93, 94, 167, 270, 273
Trisha 231–4
Trotter, Andrew 174
Tucker, Ian 6, 33, 122, 144, 145, 146, 147, 148, 149, 164, 212
Tyson, DC 55, 57, 59, 61, 64, 68, 69, 118, 246
Tyson, Mike 228, 229, 271

Vinoo 107, 109, 110, 131
Viper Rooms 115
Virgin 47, 75, 83, 118, 167, 274–5
Vogue Homme 272

W English & Son 89, 167, 275
Walls, Scot 189
Walsh, DS 55, 57, 59, 61, 62–3, 65, 66–7, 68, 69
Warnes, DC Austin 3, 4–8, 12, 13–14, 15, 16, 17, 18, 19, 22, 24, 25–9, 31, 33–6, 37–41, 42–5, 46, 51, 52–5, 58, 59, 61–3, 65, 66, 67–8, 70, 71, 72, 73–4, 75–7, 78, 79, 81–3, 85, 94, 94, 108, 117, 119, 125, 129, 131, 134, 144–5, 146, 147, 149, 151, 160, 161, 162, 164, 170, 195, 218, 238, 244, 261
Warrior 121
Warwick 130
Waterstones 47–8, 59
Weaver, Alan 267
Welsh Bernie 212
Whale, Steve 256
Widdecombe, Ann 257
Williams, Robbie 80, 189
Wimshunt, Paul 167
Wish 121, 122, 213, 247
Wolfie 6, 109, 149, 154, 155
Wyclef 261, 268

Your Face Here (Catterall and Wells) 253